Contents

Sair Linux and GNU Certification®
Level I: Installation and Configuration

Second Edition

Tobin Maginnis

Wiley Computer Publishing

John Wiley & Sons, Inc.

NEW YORK · CHICHESTER · WEINHEIM · BRISBANE · SINGAPORE · TORONTO

Managing Editor: Marnie Wielage
Text Design & Composition: Benchmark Productions, Inc.

Designations used by companies to distinguish their products are often claimed as trademarks. In all instances where John Wiley & Sons, Inc., is aware of a claim, the product names appear in initial capital or all capital letters. Readers, however, should contact the appropriate companies for more complete information regarding trademarks and registration.

This book is printed on acid-free paper. ∞

This publication is designed to provide accurate and authoritative information in regard to the subject matter covered. It is sold with the understanding that the publisher is not engaged in professional services. If professional advice or other expert assistance is required, the services of a competent professional person should be sought.

Library of Congress Cataloging-in-Publication Data:

Maginnis, Tobin.
   Sair Linux and GNU certification level I: installation and configuration/Tobin
   Maginnis. -- 2nd ed.
       p. cm.
    "Wiley computer publishing"
   Includes index.
   ISBN 0-471-41797-1 (pbk. : alk. paper)
     1. Electronic data processing personnel--Certification. 2. Operating systems
   (Computers)--Certification. 3. Linux. I. Title.

   QA76.3 .M32337 2001
   005.4'32--dc21   2001017646

Printed in the United States of America.

10 9 8 7 6 5 4 3 2 1

Preface

At first glance, this might appear to be a regular book; instead, it is a different kind of computer text that has evolved over the last few years called a *study guide*. In the same way that *Cliff Notes* help students study for a test, study guides prepare computer professionals to take a test. Once they have passed a certain number of tests, these candidates earn a certificate, which assists them with job placement, promotions, and pay increases.

Compared with many other study guides, this book is unique. Other study guides focus on one computer vendor, whereas this book covers many distributions of Linux. Other study guides usually focus on one product, but this study guide covers free-to-use, open source software packages. Finally, other study guides usually cover point-by-point user interaction with a vendor's product, but this one presents the common elements that describe all Linux distributions and the key differences among the more popular distributions.

Is this too much broad information for a candidate to absorb? Our experience says no. People do not want to be told by a vendor that its particular Linux distribution is the best. They want to see the "big picture," and how each Linux distribution fits into the open source software landscape. They see the benefits of free, open source software, and they want to maximize its use in their companies.

Therefore, this study guide contains a compendium of theories, principles, and facts that relate to the system administration of Linux and GNU software on the PC platform. The information is organized around a "knowledge array" that contains only the essential concepts and facts for installation and configuration. Information is presented in a no-frills fashion, concept by concept. In Part One, Chapters 1–6 review the first row of the Sair Linux and GNU knowledge array. Part Two provides laboratory exercises that review the concepts presented in Part One. Part Three provides sample questions as a review of the Part One material, a self-assessment guide, and a step-by-step presentation of the installation process. Finally, a glossary of key terms and phrases reviews concepts described in the text.

Acknowledgments

I am a microscopic part of this great experiment in shared intellectual propriety referred to as Linux. Therefore, it is a great honor for me to assist with the establishment of criteria for professional competency in free, open source software through these study guides and tests. Although responsibility for any mistakes rests on my shoulders, I would like to thank the following people for their support in our endeavor: advisory board members Bill Patton, Richard Stallman, Tim Ney, Bruce Perens, Eric Raymond, and Jon "Maddog" Hall. I also want to thank industry representatives Graeme Newey (EXCOM), Evan Blomquist (Viking Systems), The Linux International Technical Board, and Stuart Trusty (Linux Labs).

Continuing the process of shaping mountains of trivia into some semblance of organization and working with the information so that it can be communicated quickly and effectively is the task of the Sair team, and I continue to be deeply indebted to them for all their efforts. These are the people who assisted with the production of the security material:

Managers: Les Driggers, Trish W. Kemerly, Andrew Neel, Carlos Pruitt, Lenny Sawyer, Paul Tate, Omar Uddin, and Tammy Zegledi.

Technical contributors: Stephen Agar, David Austin, Tim Bauer, Tammy Betts, Elizabeth Bonney, Jeff Britt, Steve DeVries, Stephen Goertzen, David Hendrickson, Michael Hipp, Patrick Hood, Jerald Jones, Rex Landreth, Michael McGuire, Jimmy Palmer, Albert Phillips, Tyler Simon, Richard Swinney, Robert Thompson, Sunder Upadhyay, William Vaughan, Sudharshan Vazhkudai, Omar Wilson, and Dennis Wong.

Technical editors: Beau Bourgeous, Michael Broadwater, Brett Brown, Joann Chong, Neil Crampton, Wesley Duffee-Braun, John Furr, Kent Jackson, Dave Nolan, Ben Pharr, and Dana Wilson.

Editors: Melanie Collins, Annie Current, Summer Hill, Randy Jasmine, Jamie Murphey, Ashly Ray, Samantha Rayburn, Suanne Strider, and Vonda Stringfellow.

Web and database: Shafi Al-meher, Nileshwar Dosooye, Arlene Pereira, and Julie Seay.

Systems: Ross Reed and William Taylor.

Productions: Leigh Jennings, Alex Lundy, and Scott Rains.

Administration and marketing: Bob Buntyn and Hollis Green.

Quality Assurance: Chun Huang.

Special thanks go to Stephen Agar, David Austin, Steve DeVries, Patrick Hood, Omar Uddin, and Sunder Upadhyay for their contributions on this study guide and our previous books.

Again, thanks to John Wiley & Sons Computer Publishing, especially Cary Sullivan, for their foresight, effort, and belief in the future of free, open source software.

I thank the thousands of individuals who have helped to create a free and open software system. Special thanks must go to key system architects Ken Thompson and Dennis Ritchie, who co-developed many of the basic ideas now called Linux; to Robert Scheifler and James Gettys, who co-developed the X Window system; to Richard Stallman, who invented the GNU general public license; to Linus Trovalds, who forged an Internet community to build the kernel; and to the Linux developers, who designed and implemented the concept of packages to distribute the software system called Linux.

Finally, thanks to my family (Lindsay, Meredith, Jordan, and Anneal) for continuing to endure an absentee husband and father while we develop the Sair Linux and GNU Certified Administrator program.

Introduction

Welcome to the first of four Level I Sair Linux and GNU study guides. This is the second edition of the *Installation and Configuration* study guide for Sair Linux and GNU Certification Test 3X0-101. This study guide is the first step of the four-step road map to the Sair Linux and GNU Certified Administrator (LCA) certificate. The other three study guides are System Administration (Test 3X0-102), Networking (Test 3X0-103), and Security (Test 3X0-104). The four tests may be taken in any order, but the study guide material is organized under the assumption that the Installation and Configuration test is taken first, followed by the System Administration test, then the Networking test, and finally, the Security test.

Testing is done through Prometric at any one of its 2400 testing sites. To take a test, simply call the Prometric registration line at 1-888-895-6717. Ask the customer service representatives about the 3X0 series of exams, and they will answer any questions related to the test, describe available local testing centers, and, if requested, schedule an exam. It is also possible to register online at www.prometric.com.

Preparing for test content is paramount in criteria-based certification tests, and Sair takes pride in the coordination of test topics from the Knowledge Matrix, objectives, competencies, study guides, and exams. These topics specify exact criteria that the candidate must meet. The tests directly measure these topics, and results are reported with a detailed summary for each of these six areas: theory of operation, base system, shells and commands, system utilities, applications, and troubleshooting. Test results are absolute.

Each exam consists of 50 questions that can be answered, reviewed, and changed for up to 60 minutes. Typical test takers use about 45 minutes to complete the exam. Successful completion of each test requires 74-percent correct, or 37 correct answers. Unlike tests that assign a rank to a test taker relative to all other test takers, Sair emphasizes mastery of material. Results of the test directly inform the examinee of the mastery level in each area, allowing each examinee to focus future studies in areas of relative weakness. Prospective employers can also use the detailed summary to evaluate job applicants' or employees' areas of strength. Sair is unique in this regard. Some other certification examinations only supply the test taker with a relative score of some type, without a raw score, percentage correct, or other criterion measure for evaluating his or her performance. The effect of this practice is to leave the test taker who fails with no guidance as to how to prepare for re-examination.

Passing either the 3X0-101 or the 3X0-102 exams earns the test taker the Sair Linux and GNU Certified Professional (LCP) certificate. Completion of all four exams (3X0-101, 3X0-102, 3X0-103, and 3X0-104) earns the Sair Linux and GNU Certified Administrator (LCA) certificate.

The LCA attests to a certificate holder's knowledge and capability to administer a Linux and GNU system. Two more certificates, the LCE and MLCE, confirm knowledge and skills in increasingly difficult Linux and GNU topic areas.

Minimum Candidate Requirements

The Sair Linux and GNU tests were not designed for the novice computer user. It is assumed that the candidate has approximately two years of computer experience, and has experience in the configuration of one or more operating systems. For example, the candidate should be familiar with basic hardware concepts, such as CPU, cache, memory, interface adapters, hard disks, and network. The candidate should also be familiar with basic operating system concepts, such as booting, file access, and device drivers. Finally, the candidate should know basic commands and the use of a Unix-type editor such as Joe, Pico, Vi, or Emacs.

Knowledge Matrix

The test is based on the first row of the first array in the Knowledge Matrix shown at www.linuxcertification.com. Examination topics are listed here. Note that while the major topics listed in the Knowledge Matrix will not change, some subtopics may be added as needed to update the material. Please check the Sair Web site for any additions to this list.

Installation and Configuration and Theory of Operation

1.1.10   History of Open Source and Free Software
       1. Two historical trends
       2. Advantages and disadvantages of free software

1.1.20   The GNU General Public License (GPL)
       1. A brief history of the GNU GPL
       2. The use of copyright of enforce copyleft

1.1.30   Microsoft Analysis of Open Source Software
       1. The Microsoft memoranda

1.1.40   Living with Free Software
       1. The nature of free software development
       2. The business of selling free software
       3. Using software without warranty

1.1.50   Linux System Concepts
       1. Modular structure of Linux
          a. Kernel
          b. Network

Installation and Configuration and Base Systems

Installation and Configuration and Shells and Commands

Installation and Configuration and System Utilities

Installation and Configuration and Applications

Installation and Configuration and Troubleshooting

Knowledge Matrix

Theory of Operation

Objectives

- State the historical trends, advantages, and disadvantages of free software.
- Compare proprietary versus open source software licenses.
- List the GNU General Public License (GPL) principles.
- Describe how to sell free software.
- Describe the structural components of Linux.
- Contrast multi-user multitasking and single-sequential user multitasking.
- Contrast command-line interpreters and graphical user interfaces, and list possible trade-offs.
- List PC system architecture configuration issues.
- Describe hard disk partitioning strategies.
- Contrast video adapters and monitor capabilities.
- List the network configuration parameters.

History of Open Source and Free Software

Over the years, computer architecture has gone through three stages of evolution: mainframe, minicomputer, and microcomputer. Each of these stages has brought many types of computer architecture to the market. In many instances, software written for one architecture could not be used on another. Consequently, to ease the transition between architectures, manufacturers encouraged the sharing of free source code software through manufacturer-sponsored user groups.

In the late 1970s, AT&T was not allowed to enter the computer industry due to a Federal Communications Commission (FCC) ruling. Hence, AT&T decided to distribute an unknown operating system (OS), Version 6 Unix, for study in colleges and universities. The release of Version 6 Unix launched many significant events. Among the most notable is that it taught a generation of computer scientists practical OS concepts that would have otherwise remained only theory for years to come. Version 6 Unix was also the starting point for other Unix variants, including BSD Unix.

AT&T retained a license for Unix, allowing them to control and market Unix in the future, which made the software not truly free. Nevertheless, the seminal concepts within and the apparent open source nature of Version 6 Unix further encouraged software development and the sharing of source code that had begun years earlier in the manufacturer-sponsored user groups.

Advantages and Disadvantages of Free Software

In spite of the licenses of AT&T and other software companies, the idea of sharing source code to Unix utilities continued, and Unix (and Linux) system administrators carry on this tradition today by developing their personal archive of favorite system programs downloaded from the Internet. This personal archive grows with time and is carried by the administrator from job to job, much in the same way any skilled tradesperson would bring his or her set of tools to the job site.

One of the advantages of open source and free software is that the time invested yields rich productivity benefits, allowing the system administrator to get much more done than with traditional closed software products. Disadvantages of open source and free software include the requirement of expert knowledge to maintain and administer such systems (i.e., knowledge about how to uncompress, de-archive, compile, configure, and maintain large and complex subsystems called packages).

The GNU General Public License

The GNU General Public License (GPL), developed in 1984, was the brainchild of Richard Stallman. He came up with the GPL as a means for ensuring that free software would remain free, not be taken over by large companies and restricted from public use. For this reason, Stallman is referred to as the father of free software. He wanted everyone to have the opportunity to participate in the atmosphere of cooperation that

V6 Unix permitted. Stallman hoped that the GPL would contribute to the continued growth of communities of software developers, and thus contribute to a more productive software environment that encouraged the free sharing of ideas.

The GNU GPL essentially says that one is free to use the software any way one sees fit. Moreover, one may include the software in products and services being sold, as long as two fundamental restrictions are observed:

- Only verbatim copies of software can be redistributed, which also means that all source code must be provided with the software.

- If new software is added to the existing software, it must be prominently documented and included with the original software.

DISCLAIMER **Please note that this is a general summary of a precise legal document. Any action based on the GNU GPL requires that the license be carefully studied.**

To date, the GPL has been very successful in encouraging the proliferation of software products and ideas within communities of software developers who share with each other. The operating system now called Linux arose from this environment, thanks to Richard Stallman and the GNU GPL.

The Use of Copyright to Enforce Copyleft

The genius of the GNU GPL is that free software is accompanied with a detailed software license that employs a strict copyright. To prevent software from being taken over and kept from free public use, the license states that even though the software cannot be integrated and sold as some other software, it can be given to others. The use of a copyright in this manner runs counter to the traditional use of a copyright; hence, in the case of the GPL, it is referred to as *copyleft*.

Some Vendors Only Pretend to Meet GNU GPL Requirements

As mentioned previously, the GNU GPL has two important provisions for any free software that it covers. Essentially, these are:

- All code, including source, must be included in any redistribution of the software.

- Any new code added to the software must be included in the redistribution.

Despite the intention of these provisions, some software vendors have managed to comply only with the law and not with its true meaning. For example, vendors have provided new source code that defies the spirit of the GNU GPL; they have made the new code intentionally unclear through the use of jumbled formatting, twisted logic, multi-use variables, and dead code.

Documentation Is a Gray Area
in the GNU GPL

Another gray area concerns documentation. How much documentation should the software author provide with the source code? This concern becomes even more pressing when confronted with the possibility of developing and marketing information manuals on the software. Then the question becomes, how much information should the author offer in the form of software documentation, and how much should be reserved for sale?

Although the GNU GPL does not address this issue, current practice favors traditional-style source code commenting combined with the provision of Unix-style manual pages at a minimum.

Some Say the GNU GPL Is Too Restrictive
to Free Software

Some open source software (e.g., parts of the X11 system) has a copyright but no other restrictions. Thus, this software may be integrated and sold as another software product, and each version of the free software competes for business in the open market. The GNU GPL will not work in this particular free software model, because the use of GPL code anywhere in the proprietary product would require releasing other source code that directly uses the GNU GPL code.

Microsoft Analysis of Open Source

A Microsoft memo leaked on the eve of Halloween in 1998. Referred to as the Halloween memo, it provides another perspective on open source and free software in general and on Linux in particular. Even though only one memo leaked on Halloween eve, another was subsequently leaked. Both are lengthy and detailed memos describing Linux and the open source community and comparing them to Microsoft. Both are generally referred to as the "Halloween Memos." The following five Microsoft conclusions from these memos are of interest:

The GNU GPL is unique. Of nine types of software licenses examined, the GNU GPL stood out as unique and the most robust.

The GNU GPL provides long-term software survivability. GNU GPL free software has been able to survive as a long-term product when other forms of free software have failed. The GNU GPL allows software to flourish because, (a) anyone may have access to the software, and (b) the GPL prevents the software from being subdivided into competing camps of developers. (Note that this was not a consideration in the creation of the GPL license.)

GPL open source software possesses superior quality. The GPL software is generally superior to Microsoft software.

GNU software tools and libraries propel development. The GPL software superiority is, in part, a result of the open source community employing a powerful software development engine. It is based on standard GNU software tools and libraries that apply to all aspects of the operating system and applications.

The open source community model leads to superior software. GNU GPL software superiority is also, in part, a result of the open source process. It collects and harnesses the collective IQs of thousands of worldwide software developers by employing peer reviewed code, parallel development, and parallel debugging cycles.

The Nature of Free Software Development

In addition to a deep appreciation for the work of those who have come before us, inherent characteristics of GNU GPL software include:

- It is continually modified, but there is a strong sense of trust among those who use the software.
- People continue to improve the software, even though they do not own it.
- It evolves into an independent software product or package.

According to Richard Stallman, who originated the GNU GPL, these characteristics create communities of programmers who help each other by sharing examples of their craft. By sharing benefits from the synergy of the community, the group becomes more productive than individuals working in isolation.

Making the Free-Software Model Work in the Business World

In the past, users of free software have routinely shared the improvements they made to the free software by distributing the modifications. What about the business community and the millions of new Linux users? Presumably, the business community will see the long-term economic benefit of choosing not to compete and share their efforts with a worldwide community of developers.

The Business of Selling Free Software

One sells free software by changing the focus. Once the focus moved away from software as a product and centered on the idea of providing a service, businesses became very successful at selling free software.

An Example of Refocusing

For example, the Linux vendor Red Hat has a business model that includes offering its software free over the Internet; yet, it still sells hundreds of thousands of CDs filled with the same software for $50 to $80 each. Red Hat has changed its focus from selling the software as a whole to selling a particular type of configuration and service. Through its distribution, Red Hat provides the service of making installation and setup with its CDs much easier than setting up the software via the Internet.

Marketing Free Software—A Small-Scale Example

On a smaller business scale, consider a business that has created a user mail agent that will allow mail to be manipulated in a multi-operating system environment, regardless of which operating system is booted. In other words, if the mail were received and saved under MS-Windows, the user would still be able to view and edit it under Linux.

Furthermore, while continuing along a path that will allow a business to make a profit while continuing to keep the software a free source entity, a business might take the following steps:

1. The software, created with source code comments and the Unix-style manual pages, is GPLed and posted to the Internet for downloads.

2. Various newsgroups invite others to try the software and offer advice on how to improve it.

3. Assuming the software is stable and the company is satisfied with its functionality, a CD is created to make the program easy to manage for the inexperienced user.

4. The company, once satisfied with the software, creates a Web site and offers the CDs for sale.

5. Based on the detailed documentation, tutorials, or user manuals other GPL authors have sold, the company may want to offer more detailed documentation as part of the CD or as a separate book.

Can the GNU GPL Software Be Better than Proprietary Software?

One interesting aspect of this process is that since the business that issued the software does not control it, the open source software is now free to follow the needs of its users. Traditional closed source software must put the economic interests of the company first rather than consumer needs.

The companies producing open source software can meet users' needs by having users reprogram the software and by responding to user requests.

Once released, the software is no longer the responsibility of the issuing company; rather, its maintenance is taken over by the open source community in general.

Using Software without a Warranty

Using Linux may require a shift in the way one views and interacts with software. Unlike traditional closed source software, free software comes without any warranty and without an official vendor to complain to about problems. If this seems a little unnerving, a fast-growing industry of Linux consultants is available to help Linux users.

On the other hand, if the idea of not having the safety of a warranty is acceptable, then one may find Linux to be the operating system of choice. One simply needs to remember to rephrase common vendor-dependency questions, as suggested in Table 1.1.

Table 1.1   Vendor-Dependency Questions

INSTEAD OF...	THE QUESTION BECOMES...
Does Linux support xyz function?	How do we reconfigure Linux for xyz function? Which Linux consultant should we call to reconfigure our system?
Does Linux support xyz peripheral?	Can you perform a quick Web search for an xyz peripheral driver on the Internet?
When is the next service pack released?	Has there been an alert? If so, let's do a search to find the patch for it.

In other words, the use of Linux represents not only the adoption of a unique software product, but a fundamentally different way of viewing both software and the software development process. The company now has two choices, to bring in high-priced consultants or rely on its staff and Internet resources for the software warranty.

Linux System Concepts

Modularity is the idea that software should be written so that it can run independently of other modules and work with other modules to achieve an effect larger than any single module. If one module needs a function contained within another module, then the function is re-used, as opposed to being recreated. Modules begin as small programs or subroutines that are grouped to form larger subsystems that, in turn, are grouped into larger systems, and so on.

There are six major independent systems, or modules, within Linux: (1) kernel, (2) network, (3) init, (4) daemons, (5) login, shells, and utilities, and (6) the X Window system. A short description of each follows.

Kernel

The kernel's job is to hide the hardware details and peripherals from users and programmers, which is accomplished by creating general abstractions that refer to specific hardware. For example, access to the CD-ROM drive is accomplished by reading the directory /cdrom. It is the responsibility of the kernel to know what type of CD-ROM drive exists and to be able to read from the drive.

Other independent subsystems within the kernel are the file manager, data cache, and device drivers. Linux allows device drivers to be installed at run time with the `install module`, or `insmod` command.

Network

The network accepts both incoming network traffic from the environment and outgoing local user requests for service. It combines the two data streams in such a way that the user has the illusion of being directly connected to other computers. Even though the network and kernel coexist in the same place (protected mode memory), they are independent.

Init

To understand the init program, one must first understand that the only way a Unix or Linux program can run is to have another program start it. Init is a program that is started by the kernel at boot time, is responsible for starting Unix or Linux, and it is the ancestor of all the other programs in the system.

The init program plays a silent but critical role in system operation. After the kernel completes its initialization, it runs the init program. The init program checks a key system-wide file called /etc/inittab, which lists other programs to execute before anyone logs in to the system. Init then reads which terminals should be used to allow users to log in and begins the getty program for each terminal listed. Finally, init waits for signals from any of its programs or other system events, such as power failure, and dispatches other programs to handle the event.

Daemons (System Processes)

At boot time, the init program begins a series of programs called daemons. Daemons do not communicate directly with any user, but remain in the background until they are needed to provide a service. A typical Linux configuration employs a minimum of 15 separate daemons and may run as many as 50 or more.

Two examples of typical daemons are:

kflushd (kernel flush daemon). Moves the contents of the data cache to the hard disk(s) to limit file system corruption in the event of a system crash.

httpd (hypertext transfer protocol daemon). The Web server.

Login, Shells, and Utilities

These are system programs that run as user programs (i.e., they run in user mode not in protected mode, as the kernel does). The login utility establishes a user ID. Shells accept and oversee the execution of user commands. Many utilities provide user-level services.

Linux supports many types of command interpreter shells that are compatible with other versions of Unix and for easy use. However, for purposes of simplicity, one shell, the bash shell, will be used.

The X Window System

The X Window system is comprised of a series of modules that provide services for a graphical user interface (GUI). The X Window system provides the foundation for display managers, window managers, desktop environments, graphical utilities, and applications.

Preemptive Multitasking Software

Multitasking operating systems, such as Linux, exploit the fact that most programs spend the majority of their time waiting for events to take place. To prevent the system from stalling, a multitasking OS will release the CPU from these waiting intervals by suspending the waiting program and selecting from a list of other programs.

Examples of waiting programs that can be suspended to allow the CPU to continue execution on a ready program include the following: programs waiting for a user to type a character, programs waiting for the hard disk to read a sector, or programs waiting for a network packet to arrive.

A BRIEF DESCRIPTION OF LINUX PREEMPTIVE MULTITASKING

1. While Linux is running a program, an environmental event may occur, such as a clock tick or an interrupt from another device.

2. This event causes the current program to be suspended and the interrupt service routine (ISR) to be entered for the device in question.

3. The ISR transfers data between the device and the computer.

4. Upon completion of the data transfer, the ISR may either (a) return to the program it was executing before the environmental event took place, or (b) preempt this program in favor of the program associated with the device event.

   If (a) is the chosen action, then the ISR may change the status of the program that was waiting on the device event from a suspended state to a ready-to-run state. The scheduler will eventually select and run the program associated with the device. Meanwhile, the CPU continues to run the original program.

   If (b) is the chosen action, then the ISR may both switch the program to a ready-to-run state and increase the priority of the program. This action guarantees that it will run quickly, thus preempting the first program.

Single-User versus Multiuser Software

As the name suggests, single-user systems only allow one user at a time. They may have special programs that allow two physical users to be connected to the machine at the same time, but as far as the operating system is concerned, there is only one user. Some single-user systems have login accounts, giving the impression that they are multi-user operating systems. However, these systems still support only one user at a time, and are referred to as sequential single-user systems.

As with other Unix-like operating systems, Linux is designed as a multi-user operating system. Access to the machine must be gained by logging in to a user account that has been previously set up. The machine may be accessed by the same account through multiple ports of entry at the same time (i.e., a single user may log in to the same account or a different account multiple times).

The use of the term *port* is intended to convey access to the machine from one or more of the virtual consoles (TTY 1-6), from an X11 terminal window, from serial interfaces (TTYs), from the network (PTYs), or from any combination of these devices.

Users exploit the parallel login feature by switching among these access ports. A long-running job can be initiated on one port, followed by a switch to another port where other jobs may be initiated or where progress on the first job can be viewed.

Finally, any time a file is created, it must be done within the context of a user account. If users switch among access ports and switch user accounts, they may not have access to files created by the other account.

Switching Virtual Terminals and Page Scrolling

The Linux physical console supports a series of virtual console terminals that provide access to multiple login sessions. Users may switch among virtual consoles regardless of the application or application state. Most significantly, however, virtual consoles permit the user to switch from a locked-up session to another screen in order to kill the locked process without having to reboot the operating system.

Terminal switching works because Linux uses preemptive multitasking and because the console keyboard driver waits at the lowest level of the Linux operating system for special keyboard scan codes. One console can be selected by typing CONTROL-ALT-Fx, where CONTROL-ALT-Fx is the depression of the Control key, the Alternate key, and one of the Function keys all at the same time. Thus, the user at the console may quickly save the contents of one login session and switch to another. If desired, the user may even switch from the desktop GUI to a fresh command-line session by using the CONTROL-ALT-Fx keys.

One other convenient, but not so obvious feature associated with the console terminals is the ability to review earlier pages that have scrolled off the screen. To see an earlier page, type SHIFT-PgUp. Type SHIFT-PgDn to go back down. Typing any other key will reset the display and insert the typed character on the command line.

CLI versus GUI System Administration

If a user has worked with MS-DOS in the past, he or she has probably noticed similarities in the appearance and user capabilities to Linux. These similarities are common to all Unix-like operating systems and spark debates among users.

The similarities in appearance and user capabilities result from a command-line interpreter (CLI) instead of a graphical user interface (GUI). As you will see later, the command-line interpreters, or shells, are highly advanced tools that perform many repetitive operations using a few keystrokes. Once these tools are mastered, many Linux users prefer the CLI to a GUI. Many Linux users employ a GUI, but also have a number of windows with CLIs running to dispatch the various jobs that must be done on a day-to-day basis.

Because of the modular and layered nature of the operating system, all programs are implemented with command-line activation as well as GUI activation. This modularity and cross-user-interface compatibility creates a very thin implementation line between the command-line shell and a GUI. The GUI window manager displays a desktop and icons, monitors mouse movements and mouse clicks, and runs selected programs by calling the shell with the appropriate program arguments. In other words, except for interactive graphics, all of Linux functionality can be accessed from a command-line shell.

Unfortunately, the Linux GUI-based system administration programs are not developed well enough to be relied on exclusively. Furthermore, these GUI tools silently perform multiple steps that may break other configurations. For example, configuring a network requires three distinct steps: (1) loading the device driver with the `insmod` command, (2) attaching the network interface with the `ifconfig` command, and (3) putting the network address in the routing table with the `route` command. Consider the scenario in which an inexperienced administrator is using a GUI-based program to perform the steps of the configuration. If one of the steps were to fail, and the GUI-based program did not report the error, then it might be impossible for the inexperienced administrator to recover from the misconfiguration. Therefore, the basic configuration steps that are carried out from the command line must be understood before the GUI tools can support and ease system administration tasks.

Mainboard Configuration Issues

To understand the Linux installation process, one must first understand how the generic personal computer (PC) is constructed. Figure 1.1 shows the overall PC system architecture. The center of the figure shows the central processing units (CPUs). One CPU is what would be contained in a 386 chip; one CPU in addition to the floating-point processing unit (FPP) is contained in a 486 chip. The 586, or Pentium class processor, contains two CPUs, the FPP, and a high-speed cache memory.

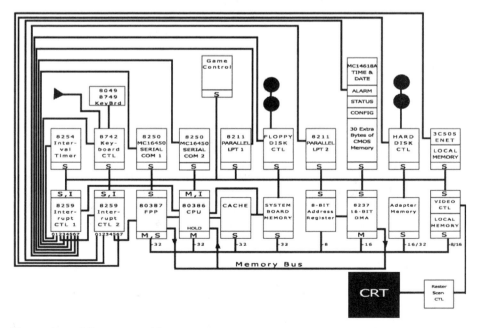

Figure 1.1   PC system architecture.

System Buses

Although there is one physical set of connectors, there are multiple physical and logical buses. The physical buses are PCI, ISA, and memory. Access to each bus requires separate program actions. Access to main memory and shared peripheral memory, such as video memory, is through the memory bus.

The main memory bus runs at 66 or 100 MHz. The main memory bus connectors are the SIMM and DIMM sockets on the motherboard. Access to peripheral controllers is achieved through the I/O bus. Two types of I/O buses are PCI and ISA. The PCI bus protocol allows its connections (adapters) to communicate with the CPU as peers. The ISA bus, on the other hand, employs only slave adapters that must be manually configured at installation time.

Possible Adapter Difficulties

The difficulty with the ISA bus is that each adapter must select values for I/O parameters from a small group of possible values, and no two adapters may use the same values. Furthermore, four parameters must be manually configured:

  I/O address. Although there are many possible addresses, adapter hardware only allows the selection of a few addresses that may or may not conflict with another adapter.

  Interrupt Request (IRQ). There are only about five free IRQ lines, and another adapter may already have allocated the IRQ line being configured.

  Address area of memory shared by adapter and CPU. Adapters generally only offer a few address options, and another adapter may already be using the memory address range.

  Direct Memory Access (DMA) channel. Only seven DMA channels are available, and another adapter may already have allocated the DMA channel the user is trying to configure. Even though there are four possible parameters, only three of them may be in conflict because ISA adapters communicate with the CPU either via shared memory or via DMA.

Other Mainboard Bus Incompatibilities

PCI adapters have changed since they were first introduced, and it is not uncommon for an older PCI adapter to fail in a newer mainboard PCI slot. Also, if the PCI adapter employs the same ISA interrupt values for backward compatibility, then IRQ conflicts may exist among PCI and ISA adapters, not just among the ISA adapters.

Troubleshooting Technique

When these types of reconfiguration problems appear, the best solution is to remove all adapters, except the video card, and perform a test boot. If this action is successful, turn off the power, reinstall one more adapter, and test boot. Failure to boot or failure to detect the adapter indicates a conflict between the adapter just added and an existing adapter. Reconfigure the adapter parameters until the conflict is removed.

RAM Requirements and Configuration Issues

RAM requirements vary depending on the type of installation. The Linux kernel requires about 1 MB of main memory; daemons, applications, and the data cache use the rest of the RAM. Exact memory requirements depend on many factors that revolve around knowing which programs will be running with each other and the amount of memory data each will be processing.

The following general numbers are based on our experience with different applications and configurations. These numbers may not be the same for a particular mix of programs that we have not experienced, and this should be taken into consideration. They are only meant to offer basic guidelines.

Network firewall configurations can run in 4 MB systems. Network servers seem to run well with 16 MB of memory. The GUI and its related graphical programs, however, require more memory, as detailed in Table 1.2.

As for the amount of required swap space, some people prefer to use the rule-of-thumb "twice the size of RAM," but as RAM increases beyond 64 MB, increased swap space has a minimal impact on system performance, making it difficult to justify more than 100 MB of swap space for suspended programs.

Difficulties with Aging Mainboards

Unfortunately, there are two common problems with older mainboards using SIMM memory configurations larger than 64 MB. The first problem is a configuration problem. Linux uses a BIOS service to size memory, and many BIOS-sizing routines do not go above the 64 MB boundary. Therefore, the user must configure the LILO boot-up script to pass a memory size argument to the kernel. The command-line argument is mem=xxxM, where xxx is the amount of memory in megabytes.

The memory size problem has been fixed in the later kernels. If a kernel more recent than version 2.2.1 is used, it will find all available RAM.

Table 1.2 Memory Requirements Based on Application

APPLICATION	MINIMUM	TYPICAL	SWAP SPACE
Network gateway	4 MB	8 MB	None required
Network server	8 MB	16 MB	Usually none required
Network multi-user	16 MB	32 MB	64 MB
X workstation	32 MB	64 MB	100 MB
X with image processing	64 MB	128 MB	100 MB

The second problem is a performance problem. To save on cost, many mainboards do not include all of the tag RAM required for large amounts of main memory. Therefore, as installed memory grows beyond the 64 MB, 128 MB, or 256 MB boundary, the mainboard may no longer be able to cache those memory addresses, thereby causing the system to slow to the access speed of main memory. If there are extra tag sockets on the mainboard, then extra tag RAM will solve the problem. Otherwise, the mainboard will have to be replaced.

New mainboards will solve this performance problem. New mainboards that employ high-speed DIMM PC 100 memory do not use a cache on the mainboard. These 100 MHz memory units have a 10 ns cycle time, making them faster than the 20 ns system cache on older SIMM-based mainboards. There is no need to use the mainboard-based cache in these systems.

Vast Amounts of RAM Change the Computer System

Viewed from another perspective, consider the use of four 512 MB PC 100 DIMMs on a mainboard. System memory would total 2 GB of RAM. There would be no need for swap space, and the complete system working set of all programs would reside in main memory. Thus, requests to the hard disk would be greatly reduced, leaving it to act more as a file server than as a traditional hard disk.

Role of BIOS and Device Detection

All of today's computers employ firmware, or Read Only Memory (ROM), that the CPU executes upon power-up. The firmware performs diagnostics on the CPU, main memory, and installed peripherals. The firmware also allows the user to configure basic system functions, such as the time of day.

In the personal computer (PC) system architecture, the firmware is called the Basic Input Output System (BIOS). In addition to the mainboard BIOS, each adapter contains a ROM-based BIOS diagnostic routine that is used to ensure the adapter is working on system power-up.

The PC BIOS also contains routines to access the hard disk and other peripherals. The Linux loader (LILO) uses the BIOS to boot Linux, or another OS. Unlike MS-DOS or MS-Windows, the Linux kernel does not use BIOS routines to access hard disks or other peripherals except for the time-of-day clock. There are a number of reasons for not using the BIOS, but the essential problem is that the BIOS design does not use interrupts and, therefore, cannot support a preemptive multitasking OS.

Plug and Play

Plug and play is a BIOS enhancement designed to eliminate the need for manual adapter reconfiguration by automatically adjusting the four I/O parameters: I/O address, IRQ, DMA channel, and shared memory address. Plug and play was never able to achieve its goal of full adapter transparency, and the Linux kernel has not used the plug-and-play routines up through the 2.2.0 kernel.

Peripheral Configuration Issues

In addition to the mainboard configuration, there are a number of peripheral configuration issues to be aware of when installing Linux. The most important to consider are hard drive partitions, CD-ROM controllers, video adapters, graphic modes, and diagnostic floppy disks.

Partitions

For at least the last 10 years, hard disk storage advancements have outpaced file system design and firmware design. Thus, when configuring an operating system, one must decide how to best divide huge hard disks into manageable slices for the operating system(s) and the file manager(s).

The lowest-level slice is the partition. Partitions are recognized by the firmware, but not by the operating system. In this way, the firmware allows the user to select which OS to boot up. Once the OS is running from one of the partitions, it can see other partitions as named or mounted volumes.

Volume is an OS relative term meaning the "file system as I see it." Generally, a one-to-one relationship exists between volume and primary partitions except in situations as noted in the following section.

Primary versus Extended Partitions

Since the BIOS contains the routines for system boot-up, it defines the layout of the hard disk, and the layout consists of one to four primary partitions. A partition is usually an OS file system that contains secondary loaders that boot up that particular OS. They are primary because no more than four BIOS partitions exist.

An extended partition occupies one of the four primary positions, which means that if an extended partition is defined, a maximum of three other primary partitions may be defined. Only one extended partition may be defined, and the role of the extended partition is to allow for additional logical partitions contained within the extended partition. Note that these logical partitions also become OS volumes, creating multiple volumes within one extended partition.

Consider the layout of an 18 GB hard disk. Dividing 18 GB by four partitions means that the average size of a partition would be 4.5 GB, which is too large for some file managers. Extended partitions permit dividing the hard disk into even smaller chunks that can be managed both within and across operating systems.

Multiple Operating System Booting

Booting more than one OS from the hard disk allows the user to switch among applications that are unique to each OS. If multiple operating system coexistence is desired, then it is possible to share the disk using multiple partitions. Since the other OS is most often a form of MS-Windows, it is useful to consider the steps that would be required to establish separate partitions for Linux and for MS-Windows. Note that MS-Windows' default action is to format the entire hard disk as one partition, and this scenario assumes that this was done when Windows was installed.

SHARING A HARD DISK BETWEEN MS-WINDOWS AND LINUX

1. Back up the existing OS in the event that one of the following steps fails.
2. Boot MS-DOS and run SCANDISK to find and replace any bad disk blocks.
3. Run DEFRAG to move all files from scattered locations on the hard disk to one end of the hard disk.
4. Run FIPS or another partition manager to search the hard disk for empty space, and to offer placement of the empty space in a new partition. FIPS also allows the changing of the partition type to Linux native or Linux swap so that MS-DOS will ignore the new partitions when it reboots.

Emulation Instead of Coexistence

To prevent having to reboot every time a user wants to switch applications, Linux supports both MS-DOS and MS-Windows emulation. In one form, the DOSEMU utilities access native MS-DOS partitions and directly execute MS-DOS files. There are also emulators for Windows 3.x programs and 32-bit Windows 9x applications.

A second form of available emulation is the proprietary product vmware that emulates the base hardware in the X11 environment. In other words, running MS-Windows 98 inside an X11 window or full screen is possible. These emulators require access to a native MS-DOS partition and a native MS-DOS file system, and can be allocated as a partition (for DOSEMU) or as a large Linux file (for vmware).

Hard Disk Partitioning Strategies

One hotly debated topic in many Linux circles is whether Linux provides too many installation options. One of the debated installation options considered here is hard disk configuration.

Two configuration issues confront the system administrator when installing Linux to the hard disk. One is whether to participate in decisions affecting the partition of the hard disk so that one can customize and fine-tune the workings of disk operations within the OS. The other issue is whether to select a Linux release that will not require any administrator input by automating the partitioning process. This action will not have the benefits of a customized disk setup.

Non-Customized, Automated Partitioning

If, as system administrator, one does not want to be bothered with decisions about the hard disk, then either the Red Hat 6.0 or SuSE 6.1 release of Linux may be appropriate. For example, Red Hat 6.0 offers `server` or `workstation` installation options that erase the entire hard disk and repartition it for Linux.

Customized, Participatory Partitioning

Other Linux releases require the person installing Linux to make a decision on how to divide, or partition, the hard disk. One method is to partition for multiple volume configurations, and another is to partition in order to customize and improve swap space.

Multiple Volume Configurations

Similar to other Unix-like operating systems, Linux generates event logs and accepts mail without user intervention. If for some reason logging or mail gets out of control, then the hard disk could fill up and cause other programs to fail. To eliminate this possibility, many companies create separate partitions for the log and mail files. Thus, as the separate partitions (volumes) fill up, only the programs writing to that volume will be affected. Programs writing to other volumes will continue to execute.

Swap Partition Configuration

More swap space is the other reason for having hard disk partitioning options during the installation process. The purpose of swap space is to provide the system with the ability to run more programs than can fit in the physical memory. This is accomplished by saving suspended programs on the hard disk and creating the illusion that all application programs fit in physical memory (RAM).

Many operating systems swap, or save, the programs in a special file. As with other Unix-like operating systems, Linux saves the programs on a separate disk, or disk partition. The rationale behind the Linux choice is to avoid engaging the file manager. The disk I/O speed is slow enough as it is, without taking on the added delay that processing each swapped page would incur. It is possible for Linux to swap programs to a file with the `swapon` command, although the command is generally used only as a temporary measure.

CD-ROM Controllers

Given the size of a typical Linux software release, installing from a CD-ROM drive is almost always required. An exception to this generality occurs when other computers are located on the same high-speed network, and only then are network-based installations practical. Even though CD-ROM-based installations are frequently mandated, there can be potential difficulties when installing Linux from a CD-ROM.

The CD-ROM is a special type of mass storage. CD-ROM drives attached to sound cards were introduced into the computer market with custom interfaces on each CD-ROM drive model. In these early designs, the manufacturer provided a custom MS-DOS device driver to access the sound card and, in turn, the CD-ROM drive.

Linux has a minimum of 12 types of sound card CD-ROM drivers. Each sound card brand requires its own device driver, such as the Sound Blaster and compatibles (sbcd.o) or the Sony CD (sonycd535.o). Generally, the administrator guesses which type of sound card is present in the machine and then loads and tests the various Linux drivers to see if one works. If so, the CD-ROM drive may be mounted via the device driver entry point (e.g., /dev/sbcd for the sbcd driver). Although Linux operators are aware of a fair number of these sound-card-based CD-ROM drives, there is a chance that none of the drivers will recognize a particular CD-ROM drive.

CD-ROM drives have also been attached to general-purpose SCSI interfaces. Linux device drivers have done quite well with the SCSI-based CD-ROMs. Access to a SCSI CD-ROM drive differs from the process previously described. Instead, the CD-ROM drive is read by a SCSI driver and accessed through the regular SCSI device such as /dev/sdc, or a SCSI disk c.

More recently, another interface was developed for CD-ROM drives so that they could be attached to the common IDE controllers. The new standard is referred to as the ATAPI IDE CD-ROM drive interface. Access to these types of ATAPI interfaces is through the regular IDE drivers. For example, access to an ATAPI IDE CD-ROM drive is through /dev/hdb, or hard disk b.

Early ATAPI Incompatibilities

Generally, Linux does well with all SCSI and ATAPI IDE CD-ROM drives. However, there will probably still be incompatibilities when installing Linux on an older machine that employs an ATAPI CD-ROM drive.

The Video Adapter

Video adapters generate the video signal that ultimately appears as an image on the monitor screen. These adapters are sometimes referred to as video cards, graphic cards, or VGA cards. All video adapters accomplish their function via three major components, which are outlined briefly in the following sections.

The Video Controller (Video Processor)

The video controller chip determines the type of I/O commands required to save, manipulate, and display information on the monitor screen. These chips are complex, many times exceeding the complexity of the CPU chip. Therefore, video adapters are classified more by the type of video controller chip used on the adapter and less by the video adapter manufacturer. Controller chips are classified according to chip manufacturer and chip family. Trident, Tseng, and S3 are examples of well-known chip manufacturers. The Tseng ET6000 series and the S3 ViRGE series are families of video controller chips produced by the manufacturer. The S3 ViRGE/DX and S3 ViRGE/GX are two members of the ViRGE family.

Video Memory (RAM)

Video memory is shared between the CPU and the video controller chip. The CPU places display data in video memory and commands the controller chip to process and display the data. The amount of video memory determines the maximum amount of information that can be displayed. If the video information is shallow, such as a black-and-white drawing, then a large amount of information can be displayed. On the other hand, if the video information is deep, such as a true-color photograph, then a much smaller amount of information can be displayed using the same amount of video memory. The tradeoff between shallow and deep display data is resolved with the use of graphic modes.

The Graphic Mode

A graphic mode specifies the number of picture elements and the amount of information each element may hold. For example, 4 MB of video memory will be able to hold one 2250-by-1750 pixel image with 256 colors per pixel, while the same amount of video memory will only hold one 1280-by-1024 pixel image with 16 million colors per pixel, or two-thirds fewer pixels.

Many times, video controllers use graphic modes that do not use all the available video memory. However, the X Window system exploits this situation by providing multiple virtual desktops that one may switch among, allowing the use of all video memory.

Based on the current graphic mode, the video controller establishes a fixed number of scan lines and a fixed line length. The video controller sends this information with the contents of video memory as a series of bytes to the DAC.

Example Graphic Modes

Table 1.3 lists commonly used graphic modes. The column labeled Resolution shows the number of pixels on the X-axis, the Y-axis, and the number of colors. The Memory column shows the minimum amount of memory required for a given graphic mode. The column labeled Horizontal lists typical row-to-row raster scan sweep rates. The column labeled Vertical provides typical refresh rates for the entire display.

Table 1.3   Graphic Modes

RESOLUTION	MEMORY	HORIZONTAL	VERTICAL
640×480×16	154 KB	31.47 KHz	60 Hz
640×480×256	308 KB	31.47 KHz	60 Hz
800×600×256	480 KB	37.88 KHz	60.31 Hz
1024×768×256	787 KB	78.9 KHz	74 Hz
640×480×32K	615 KB	37.86 KHz	74 Hz
640×480×16M	922 KB	37.86 KHz	72 Hz
800×600×32K	960 KB	57.9 KHz	72 Hz
800×600×16M	1.44 MB	56.5 KHz	70 Hz
1024×768×32K	1.58 MB	81.2 KHz	76 Hz
1024×768×16M	2.36 MB	*	*
1152×864×16M	2.99 MB	*	*
1280×1024×16M	3.94 MB	*	*
1600×1200×16M	5.76 MB	*	*

*Modern monitors dynamically re-adjust for higher frequencies.

Table 1.3 demonstrates several graphic mode features:

- The higher the resolution, the greater the amount of video memory required to hold the information.
- The higher the resolution, the faster the monitor must sweep the display horizontally.
- Vertical sweep rate tends to increase with resolution, but any vertical sweep rate may be used with most resolutions.

The Monitor

A monitor's display is painted as an electron gun, driven by a raster-scan circuit. The gun sweeps from top to bottom, row by row. The total display area is covered a minimum of 60 times per second, or in other words, the total display area is refreshed 60 times per second. If the graphic mode has a low enough resolution, the monitor will have time to refresh the display more often. A refresh rate of 70 or more times per second makes the monitor easier to read; therefore, the temptation is to set the refresh rate as high as possible.

However, if the graphic mode has too high a resolution, it may drive the refresh speed too high, causing the raster-scan circuitry to fail. Even when the monitor is able to process a high-resolution graphic mode, the raster-scan circuitry may fail if the refresh rate is increased beyond the monitor's capabilities.

Monitor Limits

In summary, the limits of a monitor display are:

- The size of the display (15, 17, 19 inches)
- The number of phosphor units per millimeter (.025, .028, .030 mm)
- The maximum raster-scan sweep rate

Note that the graphic mode (image resolution) is independent of the monitor.

Example Monitor Characteristics

Table 1.4 provides example data taken from the user manuals of various monitors. The Units column is the dot pitch, which represents the distance between the phosphor dots in the monitor's Cathode Ray Tube (CRT). Display Area is the total display surface area of the CRT. Addressability is the maximum resolution graphic mode that the monitor can accept. The Horizontal and Vertical columns show the minimum and maximum frequencies that the monitor can accept for each graphic mode. Note that exceeding these frequencies will damage the monitor.

Table 1.4   Property Values of Monitors

MONITOR	UNITS	DISPLAY AREA	ADDRESS-ABILITY	HORIZONTAL	VERTICAL
Seiko 14"	.25mm	240×180 mm	1024×768	31–50 KHz	50–90 Hz
old Magi 17"	.28mm	300×225 mm	1024×768	24–64 KHz	55–90 Hz
new Magi	.28mm	322.8×242 mm	1280×1024	30–69 KHz	50–120 Hz
ViewSonic 17"	.27mm	300×255 mm	1280×1024	30–70 KHz	50–120 Hz
OptiQuest 19"	.26mm	365×275 mm	1600×1200	30–95 KHz	50–150 Hz
Seiko 20"	.31mm	360×270 mm	1280×1024	30–77 KHz	50–90 Hz
Sony 20"	.30mm	350×280 mm	1280×1024	28–85 KHz	50–160 Hz

Examination of Table 1.4 reveals four striking features concerning monitor characteristics:

- Advertised monitor size in inches has little to do with actual display area.
- Monitors accept graphic modes (addressability) approximately 10 percent greater than can be supported by the dot pitch. (In other words, the problem is not with a person's eyes. Those high-resolution images really are fuzzy!)
- Graphic mode and refresh frequency are independent.
- Total display refresh rates can be much higher than is generally used. These higher refresh rates offer improved viewing comfort.

Graphic Modes

Older monitors from the early 1990s like the first two entries in Table 1.4, would only support one or two graphic modes. Newer monitors were designed with the ability to sync up with additional modes. Thus, the term *multisync monitor* came into use; however, since all new monitors are multisync, the term is rarely used.

Changing Graphic Modes

As the video adapter card switches graphic mode frequencies, many monitors will chirp or make clicking sounds. The chirp comes from the change in frequency at which a large capacitor is being charged and discharged. The capacitor is used to adjust the sweep rate of the electron beam as it paints the screen.

The first time a monitor syncs up with a graphic mode refresh frequency, the CRT will have to be adjusted, or fine-tuned, for each frequency. Once tuned, the monitor stores these values for later reference. Most Linux distributions use a different default refresh frequency for the same graphic mode.

Is it Possible to Break Your Monitor?

The short answer to this question is "yes." The author has had the unique experience of observing a student randomly select refresh frequencies and subsequently break the raster-scan circuit of a monitor.

Nevertheless, monitor capabilities have significantly improved over the years, and there should not be a problem with a newer monitor accepting the default refresh rates stated in the Linux configuration files. In fact, these refresh rates can most likely be increased to improve viewing comfort.

Diagnostic and Setup Floppy Disks

Many solutions to configuring the ISA bus parameters for a new peripheral exist. One of the most convenient solutions is to keep an MS-DOS bootable floppy and copies of the various maintenance programs that vendors offer for their adapters. The most convenient, of course, is when the adapter's BIOS announces that you can enter its configuration program by typing a special character at boot time.

For example, consider the task of configuring a network firewall with two Ethernet adapters, such as adapters from the manufacturer SMC. Turn the power off your machine. Install the first adapter into the machine, then turn on the machine and boot the MS-DOS floppy. Then insert the vendor's floppy and run the configuration program, which is `ezstart` in this example. Select the I/O address, IRQ number, and shared memory address range that do not conflict with other existing adapters. Also, be sure to note the values selected. Next, turn off the power and install the second adapter. Repeat the process just described, but configure the second adapter with unique values for the three parameters.

NOTE These vendor configuration programs can usually be found on the vendor's Internet site and downloaded.

Network Configuration

In today's computing environment, the individual computer is not as important as the ability to communicate with other computers. Therefore, an essential part of a Linux installation concerns network access. Four key parameters hold the answer to providing network access: the IP address, the network mask, the gateway, and the name server. Each is considered briefly in the following sections.

IP Address

The IP address is a unique, logical Internet address that identifies the physical location of the computer. This number cannot be guessed because the network administrator must assign it. The format of an IP address is w.x.y.z, where each letter represents a decimal number from 1 to 254, and the dots act as separators between the four decimal numbers.

Network Mask

The mask has the same format as the IP address, except that the least significant bits are zero and represent the size of the subnet to which the host is connected. For example, w.x.0.0 is a subnet with 65,534 possible computers. The pattern w.x.y.0 represents a subnet with 254 possible computers. Finally, the pattern w.x.y.240 represents a subnet with 15 possible computers. Note that host addresses 0 and 255 are not permitted.

Gateway

A gateway (or router, bridge, firewall) is the IP address of a host that accepts messages destined for the Internet.

Domain Name Service

The Domain Name Service (DNS) refers to the IP address of a host that accepts a domain name (an ASCII string) and returns its IP address, or accepts the IP address and returns the domain name, if there is one.

Base Systems

Objectives

- List the different types of installation media and give the trade-offs.
- Explain the Linux device driver lag and give examples.
- List the installation steps common to all distributions.
- Contrast the different high-volume Linux distributions and list trade-offs.
- Install four Linux distributions.
- List the boot-up, login, and shutdown sequences.
- Define package and describe how to use it.
- Describe basic file system principles.
- Explain the use of mounting versus the use of Mtools for removable media.
- List and describe the role of common directories.
- List and describe the use of basic system navigation commands `ps`, `kill`, `w`, etc.
- Describe the use and misuse of the superuser account.
- List the steps in creating a user account.
- Install, configure, and navigate two X11 window managers.

Media Installation

Linux comes as a distribution, meaning that an organization has packaged the software and an installation program with it. These programs are miniature versions of Linux that use shell scripts to perform the installation operations. Each distribution uses its own set of installation programs, which run from various media.

Various media can be used to install a Linux distribution. Each medium has advantages and trade-offs, which are considered in the following sections, and fall into two basic categories: local device installation and network access installation.

Local Device Installation

Local device installations contain three media types: CD-ROM, MS-DOS partition, and floppy.

CD-ROM

CD-ROM is the preferred installation media. Depending on which software release is installed, the 500 MB of archived CD-ROM data decompresses and expands to anywhere from 800 MB to 1 GB on the hard disk. This de-archiving process usually takes an hour or more with older computers. With today's faster CPUs and CD-ROM drives, it may take less than 15 minutes.

MS-DOS Partition

With this method, Linux installation archives are copied to the MS-DOS partition. Although this action may seem odd, it overcomes the older CD-ROM problem previously described. Once the MS-DOS disk archive image is set up, the installation program can be directed to the hard disk.

Floppy

In this case, a minimal system archive is placed on a set of about 50 floppy disks. Each disk contains a fraction of the installation archive. The remainder of the distribution is downloaded from a network server.

Network Access Installation

Network access installations contain three more media types: FTP, NFS, and Samba.

FTP

This method connects to a server that has the archives stored. One problem that continues to occur when downloading a Red Hat Distribution is its non-interactive download process. After specifying the FTP password and directory, Red Hat attempts the connection without feedback. Consequently, an error as simple as forgetting to specify the FTP root directory /pub/ can prevent a successful installation.

NFS

This method is similar to FTP. The archive has been stored on another Unix or Linux box, and the user specifies the NFS server host name or address and the shared directory path. Once set up, NFS works well, but as with FTP, a number of small configuration problems can prevent the user from setting up a Linux install host and an NFS server at the same time.

Samba

As with FTP and NFS, Samba uses the network to share a hard disk with an MS-Windows SMB server. Again, little details, such as using the wrong case for the password, can prevent establishing a connection.

Installations Not Using CD-ROM

It can take as long as three days to set up the correct directory structure, transfer Red Hat 4.2 installation files over the Internet, and confirm that all files are properly located in each subdirectory. Thus, any non-CD-ROM solution requires a time commitment from the installer. A compromise is to mount the CD-ROM on a network server and read the CD-ROM archive via FTP, NFS, or Samba.

Component Compatibility Issues

When purchasing hardware for a new Linux box, it may be tempting to purchase a less expensive PC. Although this strategy sometimes works, the administrator often must deal with incompatible hardware. Incompatibilities arise when device drivers are unavailable for the new components. The administrator's responsibility is to review the PC components to ensure that all the desired peripherals have Linux drivers.

Generally, purchasing an up-scale PC and components can avoid incompatibilities. These machines generally do not use shortcuts that strip out hardware and replace it with MS-Windows drivers.

To be sure about hardware compatibility, the administrator must compare the listed PC components against a compatibility list, such as the one at www.metalab.unc.edu/ LDP/HOWTO/Hardware-HOWTO.html.

Unsupported Devices

Since Linux does not use the BIOS firmware, it is responsible for knowing all hardware details. Generally, this is not a problem with well-established hardware interfaces. However, Linux gets into difficulty when new hardware products appear that have their design details hidden by the manufacturer behind device drivers and when these device drivers are provided only for a particular operating system (OS). Example devices are printers, video cards, and modems.

Printers

On some types of ink or bubble printers, a custom communication protocol is required between the printer and the device driver. Many printers can handle postscript language, but some require a custom graphic mode protocol. Unless a driver for a specific printer is available, it will not be Linux friendly.

Video Adapters

Video adapters can be problematic. Although the XFree86 project supports many types of video adapters, new ones are released every few months, and resellers tend to package the most recent and inexpensive video drivers in the new systems. The result is that the Linux user must check in advance to see whether Linux supports the video adapter hardware before purchasing a new system.

Modems

One innovation in modem design has been modems that do not have controllers, or Winmodems. These devices employ a special protocol between the CPU and adapter.

Since these new designs generally attempt to tap into unused CPU cycles to do the task that the peripheral normally does, it is not clear if Linux drivers should be developed for this type of minimal hardware. The new drives will, by definition, have to slow the system to attend to the less functional adapter.

Installation Procedure

The Linux kernel and each Linux distribution have independent version numbers. The kernel employs three numbers separated by decimal points. For example, the kernel version number 2.4.10 would mean that it is the second major version and the fourth minor version with the tenth patch in place. The middle number, or minor number, has two modes. If the minor number is even, then it is considered to be a stable version of the kernel. If the minor number is odd, then the kernel is said to contain untested or not fully tested experimental code that appears to work; therefore, it is an unstable version.

Linux distribution numbers have two digits separated by a decimal point. From left to right, these are the major and minor version numbers. Distribution version numbers do not refer to the Linux kernel version; instead, they refer to the type and default configuration of all software in the distribution. A distribution tends to change once or twice per year. A large distribution version number gives the suggestion that one distribution is newer than another, even though version numbers have nothing to do with differences among distributions. Nevertheless, expect the more popular distributions such as Red Hat and SuSE to compete with each other using large version numbers.

Nine Linux Distributions

Overviews of nine Linux distributions are provided in the following sections. The distributions considered are Red Hat, SuSE, Caldera OpenLinux, Debian, Storm Linux, TurboLinux, Kondara, Slackware, and Mandrake. Overall, installation programs vary greatly. The X11 environments and default-configured applications vary slightly, and the kernel differences are relatively minor. Sair is presently researching information to compile an accurate and detailed analysis of all distributions. However, we note the differences and let each distribution speak for itself. Each distribution description includes terminology about advanced topics. Although this terminology may be unclear now, the topics will be revisited throughout this course.

Red Hat (www.redhat.com)

Red Hat is a completely open source operating system that supports both KDE (K Desktop) and Gnome (Helix) desktops, and runs on i386 and higher, Alpha, and Sparc architectures. Portability from one architecture to another is optimized, since individual software packages are installable across the three platforms. Red Hat has contributed to open source software by creating the Gnome desktop, the Disk Druid disk partitioning tool, and the Red Hat Package Manager (RPM), which has set the industry standard for package management. Red Hat has partnered with companies, such as IBM and Oracle, to make their software applications available with Red Hat Linux, in addition to the many applications already available on the "Linux Application Library" CD-ROM or through download, using RPM. Applications, such as Star Office, Samba, Apache, Sendmail, Applix, and EST BRU (backup and restore utility), are familiar to the Red Hat user in the list of included applications. In addition to the distribution, Red Hat offers support services at many levels, such as pay-per-incident, customized support contracts, and free support for a fixed number of days following the purchase of CD-ROM software. Red Hat Linux is available from the FTP site http://ftp.redhat.com, local retailers, or from a Red Hat partner that offers certified systems for Red Hat Linux. Red Hat is one of the most popular distributions, having held the largest part of the market since the software's debut in 1994. This is largely due to the advantages of RPM and Gnome (both of which are widely used by other distributions).

SuSE (www.suse.com)

Adhering to international standards, SuSE Linux is available for the Intel, Alpha, and Power PC platforms. In addition to the Linux distribution, SuSE offers technical support, consulting, Partner Programs, and sales support to customers, resellers, and distributors. SuSE's contributions to Linux and to the open source community include kernel development, XFree86, ALSA, KDE, and glibc. The SuSE distribution comes with installation and administration tools, over 1,500 applications, an extensive manual, and 60 days of installation support. Partnerships with such companies as Oracle have resulted in the inclusion of powerful software. An updated distribution is released every four months, allowing SuSE to bring the latest Linux software and technical innovations to the market. A majority of new packages are available from the site's FTP server, http://ftp.suse.com. SuSE is most known for increasing the amount of software available in the box set, which consists of five CD-ROMs and one DVD at the time of this writing. If dedicated to a full install, SuSE would require 6 GB of hard disk space.

Caldera OpenLinux (www.calderasystems.org)

OpenLinux is a 32-bit, Y2K tested and certified OS, including the full Linux source code with matching binaries. OpenLinux integrates with existing systems, such as Novell Netware, LanManager, Sun Microsystems, Unix, IBM, Intel, DOS, and Microsoft Windows NT. It also includes the following applications: Applixware Office Suite; LIZARD (LInux wiZARD), the first point-and-click graphical install of Linux; Partition Magic CE (Caldera Edition), supporting hard drives larger than 8 GB; Star Office; and WordPerfect. In OpenLinux, the COAS System configuration and administration is simplified and integrated into KDE. For programmers who want to assist in development, KDE and GUI KDE development libraries are included, with example code, tutorials, and OpenGL extensions. OpenLinux is best known for its ease of installation via LIZARD and the user-friendly administration interface, COAS. Both of these features make OpenLinux the choice for many novice users.

Debian (www.debian.org)

Debian is one of the oldest distributions available. Ian Murdock began work on the original version of Debian (version 0.01) in August of 1993. Debian underwent a large amount of restructuring in 1994, making it easier for users to contribute to the project. During this time, Debian began to take a solid form and develop specific goals.

Realizing the need for a depackaging tool, Ian Jackson led a group of developers to create dpkg. This soon became one of Debian's many major contributions to the open source community. Used to simplify the installation process, dpkg will install software into its necessary file locations.

Although dpkg worked well with the installation of software, it still neglected to report file dependencies and possible software conflicts. As a result, a new depackaging manager, called dselect, was developed. Dselect acts as an interface for dpkg, and will also report file dependencies and software conflicts for the adding and removing of software.

Not completely satisfied with dselect, the Debian project created apt-get, which functions as an advanced dpkg tool manager. Apt-get is a text-based program that can be used to install, upgrade, and remove software. If configured correctly, apt-get will search the Internet on prespecified mirror sites and download requested software. Like dselect, apt-get will report dependencies and conflicts, but will also automatically configure software.

Debian prides itself on its method of development. Keeping with the spirit of community development, Debian is maintained by an ever-growing group of volunteers from across the globe. Debian also keeps all of its packages and applications free and open sourced.

Storm Linux (www.stormix.com)

Storm Linux was created in 1999, making it one of the younger commercial versions of Linux. However, Storm Linux is based on Debian, which provides it with the same benefits of the more mature Debian. Storm Linux also includes many of the same applications as Debian.

The most noticeable difference between Storm Linux and Debian is the installation process. Debian is known for its difficult installations, whereas Storm Linux offers simple installations. Although Storm Linux maintains Debian's dpkg tool, it also includes a graphical user interface for installation and configuration.

Unlike Debian, Storm Linux contains the Storm Administration System (SAS), which is a set of modules used to perform different system administration jobs. The modules include the System Administration Tool (SAT), a graphical user interface that can modify users and groups. The SAS also includes modules for network setups, NFS, Samba, X display settings, and sound card setup. The SAS offers a choice between a graphical user interface or a text based command line.

Turbolinux (www.turbolinux.com)

Turbolinux, formerly known as Pacific HiTech, has established itself as a major competitor among Linux distributions. Drawing from a large pool of corporate sponsorship, Turbolinux holds a strong position in the Asian market, and at times has outsold Windows in both the Japanese and Chinese markets.

Known for its networking and clustering capabilities, Turbolinux has become a popular choice among Internet service providers. Turbolinux provides clustering software that can integrate both Windows NT and Unix formats.

Turbolinux's basic installation is considered moderately difficult; it offers a graphical user interface for initial installation and package management. Turbolinux also uses `fdisk` and `cfdisk` to partition the hard drive. TurboPkg is the included package manager, and it acts as a graphical user interface for RPM.

Kondara (www.kondara.com)

Kondara Linux was developed for the world market. Known for its multilingual support, Kondara allows users to read and edit documents without changing settings or input devices. Modification can be done to documents written in more than 30 languages, and Kondara is packaged ready for install on any Intel or Alpha machine worldwide. Having multiplatform support and the ability to carry on two-way communication between client and servers, regardless of their default language, makes Kondara a prime candidate for the international market of Linux users. Based on Red Hat Linux, Kondara supports Red Hat applications; however, support focuses on business applications. Digital Factory USA, Kondara's manufacturing company, plans to ship a new language with each new release. Kondara supports the latest kernel version and the most popular desktop environments and window managers. For more information visit http://www.df-usa.com.

Slackware (www.slackware.com)

Slackware is known for its stability, which is drawn from its base in the old BSD style of `init`. This `init` system remains the same as the original Unix `init` system produced by AT&T and Bell Laboratories. Using the BSD `init` system, Slackware is fulfilling its mission "to create the most Unix-like Linux distribution."

Slackware is one of the most popular Linux distributions. Slackware includes support for all of the latest software, including desktop environments, window managers, servers, and networking utilities/applications. Slackware is also available as ZipSlack, a complete, text-based Linux system packaged in, approximately, a 40 megabyte zip archive. ZipSlack boots on machines with four megabytes of RAM and it will fit on a zip disk, so users can carry a personalized Linux system at all times. For more information visit http://slackware.com.

Mandrake (www.mandrake.com)

Mandrake, based on Red Hat Linux, is highly popular in education. It has been reported by educators to be very productive for teaching purposes, because of its ease of use. Mandrake offers both an easy installation program and an online demo and tutorial center. Instead of forcing the user to configure X Window or learn a number of command line tools, Mandrake offers graphic enhancements that place configuration tools within easy reach. Supporting over 90 percent of Red Hat's applications, Mandrake includes reconfigured applications that can be easily understood by novice users. For more information, visit www.linux-mandrake.com/en.

For a more comprehensive list of available Linux distributions, visit www.lwn.net/2000/0217/dists.phtml.

Common Distribution Installation Steps

All distribution installation programs must go through the following steps. The essential difference is whether the installation program describes these steps explicitly or asks for parameters and performs the steps silently.

A. *Miscellaneous.* Select language, keyboard format, etc.

B. *Hard disk allocation planning.*

   1. Choose either a single OS Linux installation or a dual-boot installation.

   2. If the dual boot option is selected, decide whether to share the same hard disk or use separate hard disks. If the same hard disk is to be shared between the OSs, repartition the hard disk with FIPS. If separate hard disks will be used and if DOS or Windows emulation is desired, allocate DOS and Linux partitions on the separate hard disks.

   3. Regardless of the number of OSs and hard disks, decide on the number and size of Linux partitions. A minimum of two is required, one for swap space and one for a root file system. Generally, the swap partition should be twice the size of physical memory.

C. *First, boot from installation media.* Boot the install kernel and install program from the CD-ROM or from boot floppies. If the BIOS cannot boot directly from the CD-ROM, boot floppies must be constructed by employing the DOS-based program Rawrite to copy a minimal Linux kernel image and install program onto the floppy disk. Alternatively, a boot disk could be created from another Unix or Linux box by typing the command:

```
dd if=/kernelimage of=/dev/fd0 count=1024
```

Here, the `device dump` command takes an input file name, an output file name, and a block size argument. The command works without the block size argument, but it takes a while to individually write the small 512-byte default blocks. Most large block size arguments also work, and everyone seems to have a personal favorite value for the `bs` argument.

D. *Creating Linux partitions.* Note that the hard disk is being shared with another OS; the following assumes the hard disk has been prepartitioned with FIPS. Use the fdisk, cfdisk, or Disk Druid program to write native file systems and swap partitions. Sometimes the question of which partition should be first is asked. The ordering of the partitions does have an effect, but the effect is so small that it is not worth the effort.

E. *Format file system and swap partitions.* The installation program will use `mke2fs` and mkswap to lay down the second-level disk format so that it will be able to access these partitions.

F. *Copy files.* De-archive the software and create the default configuration files from the CD-ROM, network, or floppies onto the newly partitioned hard disk, and reboot.

Sometimes this new hard disk is updated with configuration files from a running Linux system. Often, this is done when the administrator wishes to install an updated version of the OS onto the currently running system with a minimum of downtime. Generally, the configuration files of the running system are copied to the new system via an FTP connection. After configuration files of the running system are copied and moved to the new system, this new system should behave like the running system. After testing the new system to make sure that it performs as expected, the administrator can power down the running system, remove the current hard disk, and replace it with the new hard disk. In this way, a running system can be updated with the newest version of Linux while experiencing a downtime of only a few minutes.

G. *Configure a boot-up sequence mechanism.* Many possible configurations and booting possibilities exist. Three general possibilities are:

1. Have the LILO write itself to the primary master hard disk drive MBR. Use the LILO to boot Linux or the other (optional) OS. The LILO can boot either OS as the default.

2. Use a DOS program called System Commander to boot Linux or Windows.

3. Leave the old boot program intact so that it boots the other OS, and use a floppy disk to boot Linux.

H. *Set up network.* If the network was not used as the installation media, configure the network driver, network address, and routing table.

I. *Set up the X Window system.* Select the correct X server for the video adapter, and configure the mouse type, monitor resolution, applicable video RAM, and pixel depth.

Startup and Shutdown Sequence

The startup and shutdown process for Linux machines is executed by LILO and controlled by init, the program that reads the response files and launches other programs. Although Linux distributions interpret the init program differently, the strategies for booting up and shutting down are fundamentally similar. The specific function for each distribution is discussed here for startup and shutdown, as well as procedures for logging in and logging out.

Boot-Up Sequence Steps Common to all Distributions

All distributions begin the boot-up sequence in the same way. After LILO executes, it runs its secondary loader /boot/chain.b, which, in turn, runs the Linux kernel. As the kernel initializes, many messages are displayed on the console screen, including messages about the CPU, its speed, the type of instructions it can execute, the various peripherals it discovered (autoprobed), and the low-level network protocols being activated. These messages can be reviewed with the dmesg command after the system comes up and the user logs in to the system.

The kernel runs the first application (user space) program called init. The init program is the ancestor of all other programs, and its task is to read the various resource control (rc) files, run the background programs, and launch the login programs. Note that messages continue to be displayed on the console screen during the boot-up sequence described next, and the final step in this sequence is the appearance of the login prompt.

Boot-Up Sequence Steps Unique to Distributions

Linux distributions differ in how the init program reads the resource control files and executes the boot-up programs (shell scripts). This difference may seem fundamental among distributions, but, in reality, the strategies are not only similar, but are easy to understand and modify. Note that these are the same resource control files discussed in the following section, *Init and Run Levels*. As noted, the kernel simply runs ancestor init with a run level as a command-line argument. For the various distributions, the subsequent system boot-up sequence is as follows:

1. *Red Hat and OpenLinux.* Both employ a directory called /etc/rc.d/ that contains shell programs and names of shell programs. The programs are contained in a master directory called /etc/rc.d/init.d/. Other directories are named after the run levels, such as /etc/rc.d/rc0.d/ for run level zero. Each of these /etc/rc.d/rcr?.d/ directories, where ? represents a run level, contains a list of program names that are in the master directory /etc/init.d/. A master program called /etc/rc.d/rc accepts a run level argument (0,1,2, etc.) and runs the programs in the specified directory. Finally, the /etc/rc.d/rc program runs another program called /etc/rc.d/rc.local, where programs unique to this computer can be run.

2. *SuSE.* SuSE functions in the same way as Red Hat and OpenLinux, except that the master directory /etc/rc.d/init.d/ links back to the current directory /etc/rc.d/, where all the scripts are held.

3. *Debian.* Debian functions the same as Red Hat, except that it employs a master directory called /etc/init.d that contains all the shell programs. Other directories are named after the run levels, such as /etc/rc0.d for run level zero. Each of these /etc/rc?.d directories, where ? represents a run level, contains a list of program names that are in the master directory /etc/init.d/. A master program called /etc/init.d/rc accepts a run level argument (0,1,2, etc.) and runs the programs in the specified directory. Finally, the last program name in the /etc/rc?.d/ directory is the program called /etc/init.d/rc.local where programs unique to this computer can be run.

4. *Slackware.* Like Red Hat and OpenLinux, Slackware employs the /etc/rc.d/ directory that contains shell programs run directly by ancestor init. Unlike Red Hat and OpenLinux, Slackware does not use the symbolic file linking indirection method of the other distributions. Instead, the files contain directly executed shell scripts.

Init and Run Levels

As noted in the previous section, after the kernel completes its initialization, it runs the first user space program called init. The init program is key to the whole system, since it is responsible for starting all the other user space system programs. A series of resource control files determines which system programs should be run or stopped, and an argument or signal to the init program tells it which resource control file to run.

Thus, the concept of a run level is nothing more than an argument or signal number sent to the init program telling it where to find the list of programs (shell scripts) that must be run to switch from one run level to another. Table 2.1 lists some typical Linux run levels.

As indicated in Table 2.1, the middle levels (3–5) vary in function. One or two of them are unused while the third run level starts the GUI window manager or starts the login sequence (the XDM display manager). For example:

Red Hat 6.0 and OpenLinux 2.2. In both Red Hat and OpenLinux, level 3 is multi-user with networking, level 4 is unused, and level 5 runs an X11 window manager.

Table 2.1 Typical Linux Run Levels

RUN LEVEL	FUNCTION
0—Shut down	Terminate the programs begun at system startup.
1 (or S)—Single-user	Skip the multi-user login step and run a command-line shell on the console terminal. Note that the `s` is allowable because the run level argument is a string passed from the kernel to the `init` program. In the event that signals are sent to the `init` program, then the run level argument is numeric.
2 (or 1)—Multi-user	The normal operating mode (sometimes without network).
3	Varies among distributions (may be multi-user with networking).
4	Varies among distributions.
5	Varies among distributions.
6—Reboot	Go to run level 0, then to multi-user (run level 2 or 3 depending on the distribution).

Debian 2.2. Debian equates run levels 2, 3, and 4 to run the same multi-user plus networking configuration, while level 5 runs a login display manager.

SuSE 6.1. SuSE does not have levels 4 or 5, and level 3 runs the XDM display manager.

Slackware 4.0. Slackware level 3 is multi-user plus networking, level 4 runs the XDM display, and level 5 runs the default X11 window manager.

Logging In and Out

Linux presents the `Login:` message at the virtual consoles and whenever a remote login via network is found. In response, the user enters an account name followed by or ending with the ENTER key. This causes the login program to run and to present the `Password:` message. Next, the user enters a password followed by the ENTER key. For example:

```
Login: jjones<Enter>
Password:<Enter>
```

Successful Logins Result in User Shells

If an existing account name and valid password are entered, the login program will initiate a command-line shell program for the user. The term *shell* comes from the idea of encapsulating layers. In 1975, moving what was then called the monitor out from the kernel and into user space was considered a revolutionary idea. In this sense, the shell encapsulates the kernel much like the shell of an egg surrounds the yolk. Today, the shell is hidden beneath the GUI.

Logging Out

Logging out of the system depends on how the shell has been configured. By default, the shell will accept the end-of-file (EOF) character CTRL as the termination command and return the user to the Login: prompt. Alternatively, some shells may be configured to prompt the user to use the built-in commands logout or exit.

Data Cache and System Shutdown

The goal of a data cache is to reduce long disk I/O delays by saving previously accessed disk blocks in main memory, so that they are quickly accessible when needed (the blocks are flushed to the hard disk when they are no longer needed).

In the event of a power failure or if the computer is turned off, the disk blocks in main memory are lost, and the file system is corrupted and must be reconstructed. Linux will minimize this problem by periodically saving any outstanding modified disk blocks. Therefore, to turn off Linux, one must first terminate the system programs that reset open files and flush the data cache before termination.

Shutting Down Linux

Linux can be turned off with signals or commands given to the ancestor, or parent, of all Linux programs—the init program. Anyone can generate the bottom-up I/O signals sent to init, such as power failure or reboot, but only the superuser can issue commands to the init program. The central program is named shutdown, and it is called from other programs in various ways:

shutdown now	A direct call to the utility with the English argument now.
halt	Effectively the same as issuing shutdown -h now.
reboot	Effectively the same as issuing shutdown -r now; that is, the shutdown program is called with the reboot option indicated via -r switch.
By typing CTRL-ALT-DEL	If there are MS Windows NT users, this option may be removed from the /etc/inittab file to prevent them from shutting down the Linux box inadvertently when using the NT login technique.
Imminent power failure	Some machines provide a signal from UPS, indicating power failure in X minutes. This signal initiates the countdown for system halt in a certain amount of minutes. If power is restored, the UPS will provide another signal that will terminate the countdown and restore Linux to its normal state.

File System Structure

File systems are arranged in a hierarchical structure. This standardization ensures that essential programs are easily located in all Linux distributions.

Global File System Hierarchy

Linux follows the Unix tradition of employing hierarchical file names where the target file is specified by a path. The path contains a starting point, optional directories, and the file name. There are two types of paths: absolute and relative.

Absolute paths take the following form:

```
/var/spool//lpd/lp/lock
```

The first forward slash (/) means the beginning or root directory. Subsequent forward slashes (/) separate directory names and the file name. The double slash (//) was included to show that Linux, like its predecessors, skips extra slashes when looking up file names.

Relative paths take the form:

```
mail/fred/letter5
```

The absence of the first slash means the current directory path should be prepended to the relative path in order to create an absolute path. This situation takes advantage of the fact that the system remembers the position of the current or working directory. The command pwd prints the working directory.

File System Hierarchy Standard

In general, Linux distributions have the root file structure shown in the following program list. Add as few additional directories as possible to the root directory. The file system hierarchical standard is shown in the following *File System* section.

The root directory is recognized at system boot-up time. Other volumes must be mounted onto directories that begin with the root directory. The word *essential* refers to programs that must always be available even though other volumes are not mounted.

/ --	Root directory.
-bin	Essential commands; always mounted binaries.
-boot	Boot loader and kernel images.
-dev	Device driver access points.
-etc	Host-specific system configuration.
-home	User account home directories; large branch.
-lib	Libraries, run-time load libraries, and kernel modules.
-mnt	Mount point of removable media.
-opt	Local add-on application software packages.

`-proc`	Kernel status routines.
`-root`	Home directory for the root user; always mounted.
`-sbin`	Essential system administration command binaries.
`-tmp`	Temporary files; use `/usr/tmp` for applications.
`-usr`	Secondary hierarchy; large branch.
`-var`	Variable data; dynamic logging, spooling, and status information.

Volume Referencing

Since the firmware controls access to hard disk partitions as well as subpartitions (BIOS extended partitions), each partition appears to the OS as a separate and independent volume. Assuming that there are multiple hard disks or hard disk partitions, the OS file manager must have a way to move among these independent volumes. Many have followed a convention where each volume is given a logical name, such as `C:` or `D:`; however, in Unix-like OSs, each physical volume has been hidden within one large, logical directory hierarchy. Consequently, this means that movement among the logical directories results in physical movement among the hard disk volumes.

The mount command may be used to view the physical volumes that make up the logical directory hierarchy. Furthermore, the `mount` command will reveal where in the hierarchy the switch is made between physical volumes. For example:

```
hostname:~$ mount
/dev/sda1   on   /      type   ext2   (rw,errors=remount-ro)
proc        on   /proc  type   proc   (rw)
/dev/sda3   on   /usr   type   ext2   (rw)
```

Here, there are three partitions on SCSI disk a, although the second partition is for the `proc` file system, or a pseudo file system. The first partition, `sda1`, is the root volume. The third partition, `sda3`, provides read-write access to any of the files on its physical volume through the `/usr` directory. As the user negotiates the logical directory `/usr`, he or she is also negotiating the physical volume of `/dev/sda3`.

The File System

In a file system, data is stored in files and directories. In order to access files and directories, a file system must be mounted through the `mount` command.

Mounting Read-Only Devices— CD-ROMs

To place a disk volume into the directory hierarchy, the user must mount the volume with the `mount` command. For example, to mount an ATAPI-type CD-ROM drive, enter a command such as:

```
mount /dev/hdb /var/src
```

The first parameter on this command line is the device name, and the second is the name of the mount point within the logical file system. Now, enter the mount command again but without arguments. This will show the mount table:

```
hostname:~$ mount
/dev/hda2 on /        type  ext2    (rw)
proc      on /proc    type  proc    (rw)
/dev/hdb  on /var/src type  iso9660 (ro,noexec,nosuid,nodev)
```

By examining the mount table data, you can see that entering the directory /var/src switches over to the CD-ROM drive. Also, the Eject button is disabled while the CD-ROM is mounted. Use the unmount command to unmount the CD-ROM and enable the Eject button on the CD-ROM drive. Finally, the CD-ROM is mounted read only, meaning that when a program attempts to write to the CD-ROM, it is refused permission, as opposed to receiving a write error from the device.

Mounting Read/Write Devices—
Floppy, LS120, and Zip Drives

If desired, other disks may be mounted in a similar fashion as the CD-ROM drive. The mount program probes the disk to see if it contains an MS-DOS format or Linux format. It mounts the drive according to its type of file system, which will allow work to be more easily moved between systems. For example, an MS-DOS formatted floppy can be mounted, WordPerfect files can be saved onto the floppy, and the floppy unmounted. The floppy can then be taken to a Windows machine, and the MS-Windows version of WordPerfect can read the files.

Conventional Mount Points

Disk volumes may be mounted on any directory. Sometimes, it is advantageous to mount a volume in a user's home directory; however, most removable media mounts are done in the /mnt directory. Sometimes subdirectories /mnt/floppy and /mnt/cdrom are in the /mnt directory, and other times the /floppy and /cdrom mount points are set up in the root directory. The mount point is used to switch over to the drive that would contain Linux or MS-DOS files.

A Quicker Way to Read/Write
MSDOS Disks

Using Mtools provides an alternative to the mount command. The Mtools program suite may be used to check, read, or write a Linux-based WordPerfect file to or from a floppy with MS-DOS-based WordPerfect files on it. In other words, instead of saving the files on a floppy disk through Linux-based WordPerfect, one would enter the command:

```
mwrite document.wpd a:
```

where the file name document.wpd would be copied to the floppy disk. The file transfer could be confirmed with the command:

```
mdir a:
```

to show the directory of files on the MS-DOS formatted floppy.

File System Abstractions

Unix-like operating systems, such as Linux, are unique in their use of the file manager. Even though the user views a single file manager front-end, there are a number of back-ends. One such back-end is a pseudo file system to report the status of programs, device drivers, and kernel internal events. Access to this pseudo file system, or system abstraction, is accomplished by going to the /proc directory.

In other words, displaying the contents of a file within the /proc directory does not switch hard disk volumes, but switches to a kernel routine that shows system status as a series of directories, files, and file contents. The following are conventional abstractions:

/proc	Provides direct kernel status routines.
/dev/xx0	Provides direct access to device xx0.
/dev/null	Returns End of File when read and ignores all input when written into.
/dev/zeros	Returns any number of characters requested, but they are always the null (zero).

Basic System Navigation

To successfully navigate a Linux system, the user must first understand case sensitivity, the functions of a superuser, and the characteristics of basic programs.

Case Sensitivity

When logging on to a Linux system or another Unix-like operating system, a user notices that most output is displayed in lowercase characters. For example, to view files within a directory, use the ls command.

```
[hostname]$ ls
alpha.txt    edolog    input    mbox
clog         edulog    lc.tz    olog
edclog       flog      llog     wish
[hostname]$
```

The command ls and the file names are in lowercase. If the command LS is typed, the result will be:

```
[hostname]$ LS
bash: LS: command not found
[hostname]$
```

The reason is that the name of the directory program is ls, and typing LS is a request to the bash shell to look for a program named LS. Unlike other operating systems that automatically map uppercase characters to lowercase for file names, Unix-like operating systems use upper and lowercase characters in all file names.

In fact, a user may use most ASCII characters for a file name, including the SPACE character. The security implications of file names made up of spaces will be discussed in a future course. For the present, the user must be aware that all files are case sensitive, and that they may include most characters or sequences of characters.

cd and ls Commands

The two key commands in any operating system provide movement among directories and display of file names. Directory movement is accomplished with the cd command, while file name display is accomplished with the ls command. For example, assume the shell prompt has been configured to show the account name and host name followed by the name of the current directory. In this case, the shell prompt would be:

```
[name@host home]$
```

where name is the user account, host is the network name of the computer, and home is the current directory. Assuming the directory named mail was below the directory named home, issuing the command cd mail would result in the current directory switching from home to mail, as in the following:

```
[name@host home]$ cd mail
[name@host mail]$
```

The ls command displays the owner and access permissions for other user accounts. For example, the command ls -l * gives the long form display for all files in the current directory:

```
[name@host mail]$ ls -l *
-rw---       1 jordan   users      49 Jul 17  1998 clog
-rw-rw-r-    1 jordan   users      46 Jul 29  1998 edclog
-rwxr-xr-x   1 jordan   users      49 Sep 13  1998 edolog
```

These files are owned by the account named jordan, and they belong to the group users. Jordan may not be a member of the group users, but the account name is usually also a member of the group associated with the file.

The owner, group, and all others have separate read (r), write (w), and execute or search (x) permissions for each file in the directory as well as the directory itself. In the preceding example, the clog file has read and write permission for the owner, but no other permissions are provided for the group or others. The middle file edclog is readable and writable for the owner and group, but only readable for others. The last file edolog is readable and executable by all, but only the owner can write changes to the contents of the file.

The execute (x) permission is interpreted as a search permission when the file is a directory. For example, the command `ls -ld` displays the access permissions for the current directory:

```
[name@host mail]$ ls -ld
drwxr-xr-   3 ptm    html    1024 Jun 25 18:09
```

Note that the leftmost character has switched from a dash (-) or regular file in the previous example to a d, meaning directory type file. Now, the meaning of x is changed to mean that the owner and group have search permissions, but not others. The x was replaced with a - for others, and now the `ls` command will not display file names in the directory for others. However, since the x permission only refers to searching, the files in the directory may still be accessed via their file relative permissions, if the file names are already known. In other words, even though others cannot see the files `clog`, `edclog`, and `edolog`, others can still read the files `edclog` and `edolog`.

Finally, the number to the left of the file creation date is the size of the file in bytes. Directories are allocated in logical OS blocks; thus, in Linux their size will always be a multiple of 1024 bytes.

ps—The Process Status Command

As users log in to the system, additional programs are created. The first set of programs is created by the system, and can be viewed by using the `ps` command. By typing `ps` at the shell prompt immediately after login, the following output would be produced on Red Hat Linux:

```
PID    TTY  STAT  TIME  COMMAND
13977  p0   S     0:00  /bin/login -h hostname domain.com -p
13978  p0   S     0:00  -bash
13992  p0   R     0:00  ps
```

Aside from the process identifiers (`PID`s), we can see from the display that the user logged in from the network (`TTY:p0`), that the two system programs (`login` and the `bash` shell) are sleeping (`S`), and that the process status (`ps`) program is running (`R`).

In Red Hat versions, the login program waits in the background. On other versions of Linux, one would see:

```
PID    TTY  STAT  TIME  COMMAND
397    3    S     0:00  -bash
13978  p0   S     0:00  -bash
13992  p0   R     0:00  ps
```

In these versions, the login program terminates before the shell is run. In this display, the same user runs a second shell program from `TTY 3`. (The terms *process* and *program* are being used interchangeably for now. They will be distinguished in a later section.)

The output of the `ps` command shows only the current user, although other users may be logged in to the system. Other forms of the `ps` command show more information, such as `ps-eax`, which shows all system processes.

The kill and renice Commands

As seen earlier, the ps command allows one to see how many other programs have been created and owned by the current user account. Two other basic commands allow one to exercise control over these programs. The kill command terminates a specified process, while the renice command lowers the scheduling priority so that other programs may be selected to run.

The kill command is used in combination with other status commands, such as the ps command. If the ps command has produced the following display:

```
  PID   TTY  STAT  TIME  COMMAND
  397    3     S   0:00  -bash
13978   p0     S   0:00  -bash
13992   p0     R   0:00  ps
```

then the kill command could be used to terminate one of the bash shells. For example, the command:

```
[name@host home]$ kill -KILL 397
```

would send the terminate signal to PID 397 and cause its termination. On the other hand, the nice command could be used to allow other programs to run. For example, the command renice 15 397 would lower the program's scheduling priority from the default of 0 to 15. The lowest GNU priority is 19, and the highest priority is –20. Only the superuser can use the renice command with a negative value to raise the priority of a process.

The who and w Commands

Use the who or w commands to determine if other users are logged in, or if there are other virtual terminals with login sessions.

Example Using who

```
hostname:~$ who
lindsay  tty1     Apr   2 08:58
lindsay  ttyp0    Apr   2 11:01  (host1.yourcompany.com)
lindsay  ttyp1    Apr   3 07:59  (host1.yourcompany.com)
lindsay  ttyp2    Apr   1 13:53  (sales.offsite.com)
```

The user lindsay is logged in four times: once on a virtual system console (tty1), twice over the network from a computer called host1, and once more from a computer called sales.

Example Using w

The w command reports the same information, but includes additional details on system usage. Table 2.2 is an example of the w command's output.

Table 2.2   Example Output of the w Command

USER	TTY	FROM	LOGIN@	IDLE	JCPU	PCPU	WH
carlos	pts/1	:0.0	10:07am	6:00m	0.04s	0.04s	ba
carlos	pts/2	:0.0	01:14pm	2:21m	0.17s	0.15s	ss
carlos	pts/3	:0.0	12:04pm	3:47m	0.16s	0.11s	ss
carlos	pts/4	:0.0	04:06pm	0.00s	0.10s	0.03s	w
carlos	pts/0	:0.0	10:07am	5:59m	0.22s	0.17s	vi

The Superuser

Generally, the shell is configured to provide two types of command-line prompts. The dollar symbol ($) represents nonprivileged (or positive value) UIDs. The pound symbol (#) represents superuser status, and a zero value UID tells the file manager to ignore the file system protection scheme. The superuser is also the only account that can request certain system services such as changing the date and time, adding a new user account, and increasing the priority of a process as described earlier.

The Problem with Doing Routine Tasks as Superuser

The problem with running as superuser to accomplish routine tasks is that the simplest of mistakes can lead to a catastrophe. Consider, for example, what would happen as a result of typing the following commands when running as superuser:

```
rm * .bak
rm -rf / home/fred/tmp
```

In both examples, the inadvertent extra space results in deleting all files in the current directory or in the whole file system, respectively.

Moreover, the problem of accidental file deletion is further complicated by the design of the Linux file system. As with other Unix-like systems, Linux employs a fully indexed file system with direct access to the free-block list. When a file is deleted, its contents form the blocks of the next created file on a first-come, first-served basis. Thus, once a file has been deleted and a new file has been created, the old file blocks have been reused.

Another largely unforeseen consequence of working as a superuser has to do with the files that are created while operating under superuser status. These files will have restricted access permissions associated with them as a result of being created by the superuser. A higher probability of having to run as a superuser in the future to access the files created earlier will most likely be the result.

The Conventional Method for Performing Routine Superuser Tasks

Administrators can quickly switch from user to superuser status with variants on the su command, which changes the current user account effective UID to 0, allowing access to files or services. Another form of the su command is the command su - useraccount. The dash means switch from the superuser account to that user account environment, which is similar to logging in as that user. To return to the superuser account, simply log out of the user's shell, and to return to the original account, log out of the superuser shell.

Starting a Display Manager or Window Manager

The final step in system setup and installation is to launch the graphical user interface (GUI). The X Window GUI has three basic components: a display manager called XDM that provides a GUI login, an X server (the device driver for the monitor), and desktop, or window, managers. Both the x server and the window manager are launched with the startx command.

The console is configured for six virtual terminals, F1 through F6. Starting the display manager with the xdm command or launching the window manager GUI with the startx command may be done from any of the virtual terminals, but the GUI is subsequently displayed on virtual terminal F7.

Once the display manager is launched with the xdm command, it never terminates. Instead, the XDM program waits for someone to log in, and it starts up a desktop (window manager) for the user. Upon session termination, the XDM program automatically restarts the login request screen and waits again for someone to log in. Since the display manager is intended for a multi-user environment, only the superuser can execute the xdm command. To automatically begin the display manager at system startup time, add the xdm command to one of the distribution-specific system boot-up files.

One of the window manager GUIs is launched either from the XDM program or directly from the user's virtual terminal with the startx command. Again, the window manager desktop GUI is displayed on virtual terminal F7, while the other six virtual terminals remain available for use with a command-line shell.

X Window System Initialization Files

The XDM login manager (X server), window manager desktop, and applications each have one or more configuration files with initialization parameters. Furthermore, there are both system-wide initialization files and user-specific initialization files.

1. The user-specific files have precedence over the system-wide files.
2. If the XDM display manager is running, its initialization files have precedence over the startx initialization files.

System-wide initialization files are found in /etc/X11, where:

1.   /etc/X11/xinitrc is read by startx.
2.   /etc/X11/Xsession is read by XDM.

Many times, the xinitrc file name is linked to the Xsession file. In this way, any changes to the xinitrc file go directly into the higher-priority Xsession configuration file.

More recent distributions, OpenLinux 2.2, Red Hat 6.0, and SuSE 6.1, have moved the system-wide configuration files. The new location is /etc/X11/xinit/xinitrc for startx, and in some cases, the Xsession startup file has been renamed to /etc/X11/xinit/Xclients.

The *user-specific initialization files* are in the home directory for each user. These files are:

1.   .xinitrc , which is read by startx
2.   .Xsession , which is read by XDM

Finally, as various GUI applications run, they create and maintain history files in the user's home directory. For example, Netscape creates the .netscape directory that holds, among other things, the last size and position of the Netscape window. In this way, Netscape can position its browser window in the same place as the last time the program was run.

The Virtual Display and Other GUI Tips

The power of the X Window system is that any visual and interactive element can be configured, and as a result, most things are configured in unique ways. Additionally, unlike other OSs, it is difficult to make generalizations about Linux GUIs. A large number of GUIs have been written for the Linux OS, and considerable variety exists among them.

Its particular window manager controls the look of each GUI. Furthermore, Linux GUIs generally have only the most basic features in common. Some common features of Linux GUIs are briefly discussed next.

Access to Pop-up Menus

A right-click, middle-click, or left-click on the desktop will reveal one or more menus that provide access to programs, exit the desktop, configure the desktop, or switch to another area of the virtual display.

The Virtual Display

Unlike other OS GUIs, the X11 window managers can exploit unused video memory by creating a virtual display that is four, six, or more times larger than the screen. The details of navigating the virtual display depend upon which window manager is used. Generally, a pager always remains in the same position on the desktop, which is on top of other visual elements. Clicking on one of the quadrants within the pager switches to that area of the virtual display. However, many window managers provide virtual display navigation via the desktop pop-up menus. On other window managers, such as AfterStep and Enlightenment, movement among virtual display quadrants occurs as the mouse cursor travels to the edge of the display. Also, one window manager (KDE) provides a pop-up menu from the title bar that allows the window, as opposed to the user, to be sent to another virtual display area. The most common window managers are AfterStep, Blackbox, Enlightenment, KDE, FVWM, and Window Maker.

X Window Scrolling

Each window manager employs a widget set that provides common controls within a window, such as scrolling. Most X11 scroll bars function as expected. However, the default X Window scroll-bar widget is found in older X11 applications, and it is unusual compared to other GUIs. Moving the mouse cursor along the scroll bar creates a double-arrow cursor. Regardless of where the cursor is located at the top or the bottom of the scroll bar, clicking on the left mouse button scrolls the window down, and clicking on the right mouse button scrolls the window up. Moving the cursor from the top toward the bottom of the scroll bar results in larger blocks of scrolling either up or down with each mouse click.

X Window Resizing

Generally, windows have a title bar with buttons. The left-hand button(s) on the title bar allow the focus to be switched from window to window. The rightmost title bar button usually contains an X, and clicking it will terminate the window. The two title-bar buttons next to the rightmost button control window size. One will usually contain a dash symbol (-), and clicking it will minimize the window. The other button contains a window symbol, which will maximize the window, although not always enough to fill the screen.

The full-screen effect can be achieved by right-clicking the same button. Sometimes the full-screen operation places the window Resize button under a floating control panel, like a pager or wharf, where the Resize button cannot be reached. The full-sized window now hides both the other windows and the Resize button. If the user needs to reach another window, simply double-click the title bar, and the window will occupy the entire screen. Clicking on and dragging the corner edge may also resize windows.

Be aware that programs like Netscape may pop up a requester or dialog box and wait for user input. If the window title bar has been double-clicked and is on top, the requestor/dialog box will be hidden. The system will appear to be locked. The real problem, however, is that a hidden requestor box generated by the program is waiting for the Ok button to be clicked. Double-clicking the title bar again will allow the other windows to appear.

Copy and Paste

Unlike other OSs, the X Window system does not have a fully evolved clipboard with edit commands such as undo, cut, clear, and select all. There is, however, a minimal copy-and-paste mechanism.

To copy, drag the cursor over the text of interest. Move the focus to the destination window and position the program cursor, not the mouse cursor, to the desired position for insertion. Click the middle mouse button to paste the highlighted text.

Note that this only works between the highlight operation and the next paste mouse click. If the left mouse button is used to highlight other text, even in another window, then the previously highlighted text is forgotten.

If the mouse has only two buttons and three-button emulation has been enabled, then click both mouse buttons at the same time to emulate the third mouse button.

X Terminal Font Sizes

Many times, a high-resolution display in combination with small default fonts makes text difficult to read. To enlarge the font size, position the cursor in the X terminal window, and depress the CTRL key and the right mouse button at the same time. A menu of font sizes will appear. Move the cursor to the desired font size, and then release the CTRL key and mouse button. Some window managers, like KDE, will provide this feature with a right-button mouse click in the X terminal window.

Shells and Commands

Objectives

- Describe shell configuration files.
- Compare and contrast environmental and shell variables.
- Use commands that pass special characters among programs.
- Use commands that allow programs to communicate.
- Manipulate files and directories.
- Use the shell for multitasking.
- Describe common shell editing commands.
- Use the following commands in isolation or in combination: `ls`, `cd`, `more`, `less`, `cp`, `mv`, `mkdir`, `rm`, `rmdir`, `ln`, `head`, `tail`, `file`, `grep`, `du`, `df`, and `zcat`.
- Use the following Vi commands: `i`, `ZZ`, `:w`, `:w!`, `:q!`, `dd`, `x`, `D`, and `J`.

The Shell

A Linux shell is a command-line interpreter that provides the following services:

- Simple command-line editing
- Program execution and flow control in the execution of other programs (batch jobs)

There are many different shells included with Linux distributions, some of which are ash, bash, csh, ksh, tcsh, and zsh. The bash shell will be used in all following examples unless otherwise noted.

Two important shell characteristics are interactivity and script execution. Both are discussed briefly here.

Interactivity

Recent versions of the bash, tcsh, and zsh shells offer command history review and command name completion. Command history is the ability to use the UP and DOWN arrow keys to display and redisplay previous commands, beginning from the most recently typed command. The bash shell maintains this history. By entering the command `history`, one can see a list of all of the commands that have been used, up to the recall limit. By modifying the `$HISTSIZE` shell variable, the number of recalled commands can be changed. The following example:

```
bash$ HISTORY=1000
```

would give the bash shell the ability to recall the most recent 1000 commands.

Command completion is the ability of the shell to complete the directory name, file name, or command name when the TAB key is pressed. If there are several name possibilities, then the shell only completes the name as far as it is unique; it beeps, and waits for the user to type more characters that make the name unique. Pressing the TAB key twice tells the shell to display all possible names so that the user may select the desired name.

For example, if the directory contained the file names `julie`, `angus`, `meredith`, `allison`, and `lenny`, typing a command, such as `bash$ m`, followed by the TAB key will display: `bash$ meredith`.

Script Execution

In addition to running programs, shell commands allow the use of variables, variable testing, and branching based on the value of shell variables. Format of shell variable assignment and testing depends upon which shell is used. sh, bash, ksh, and zsh employ flow control constructs (e.g., while and for loops) that are different from the Berkeley-derived csh and tcsh.

The Bash Shell

Although many users have a preferred shell, the Bourne Again SHell (bash shell) tends to be deployed in Linux as the default shell and, therefore, tends to be the most commonly used shell. Bash is named after the creator of the first programmable shell for Unix, Stephen Bourne, and uses the functions command history and command completion by default.

Environment/Shell Variables

Shell variables provide a means of compiling the command-line information into a shell program, when it is called with parameters and is temporarily storing information within the shell program. Shell variables can also have values assigned to them as follows:

```
bash$ varName=abcdef
```

When value assignments are made, as in the preceding example, a dollar sign ($) should not precede the shell variable. However, in all other uses of the shell variable, a dollar sign must precede the variable name, as in the following example:

```
bash$ echo $varName
```

An environment variable is similar to a shell variable, except that it is a string constant. An environment variable is passed to a child process for program initialization.

Another difference between shell variables and environment variables concerns their visibility both within and outside of the shell program. Environment variables are global variables, since every shell program has access to them. Shell variables, on the other hand, are local variables; their visibility is restricted to the particular shell in which they are located. A shell variable that is established and used inside one shell will not be accessible by another shell, unless it has been exported via the `export` command. Consider the following example:

```
bash$ export varName
```

The variable, `varName`, exported here, will now behave like an environment variable, possessing global visibility.

Naming Conventions

Another difference between shell and environment variables concerns naming conventions. A common practice is to use all uppercase letters for environment variables and mixed case for shell variables. In addition, shell variables can consist of letters, digits, and underscores, but they cannot begin with a digit.

The Path Variable and the Dot Debate

The `PATH` variable is a special shell variable. Type `echo $PATH` to examine the setting of the path variable.

```
bash$ echo $PATH
/usr/local/bin:/usr/bin:/bin:/usr/home/meredith/bin
bash$
```

A list of directory paths appears, and they are separated by a colon (:) character. This is the same directory list in which the shell will search for an executable file when the shell is instructed to run a program.

How the $PATH Variable Facilitates Program Execution

In the home directory, if a user wanted to run a program in /usr/bin, there are two ways this can be accomplished. The first possibility is to explicitly call the program with the full path name:

```
/usr/bin/myProgram
```

The second possibility is to include /usr/bin in the path as shown, and then type myProgram at the command line to have the shell search all the directories contained in the $PATH variable for the executable.

Even if the program resides in the current directory, the full path name must be used or be in the $PATH variable. However, typing ./myProgram is a shortcut, because it directs the shell to search the current directory for the program.

The rationale behind the dot slash (./) requirement originates from a past security problem; consequently, many distributions do not include the current directory (.) in the $PATH variable. The security problem revolves around the routine access of utilities located in the system directories /bin/ and /usr/bin/, such as the directory list (ls) command. If the dot is listed in the $PATH string before the system directory, then a program by the same name in the current directory would be executed instead of the utility in the system directory. In this way, a Trojan horse could be planted in the current directory that has the same name as a common utility, such as the ls command. When the user types ls expecting a directory listing, the Trojan horse would execute and display a message similar to the following in an attempt to gain the user's password:

```
Session error -- terminating program
Login:
Password:
```

In response to this message, the naive user would enter the account name and password. This allows the Trojan horse program to acquire the user's password, and subsequently erase itself. The next time the ls command is entered, everything would work as expected, leaving the user unaware that the password was stolen. Thus, for security reasons, the dot character is not usually included in the $PATH variable. Some distributions do include the dot character in the $PATH string, but it is presented after the system directories.

Passing Special Characters to the Shell

Some characters have special meaning to the shell. A common example of such a character is the asterisk (*), used by the shell as a wild card character. If there was a need to use the * as a literal argument to a command, a user would have to tell the shell not to interpret the asterisk as a wild card character. This can be done by character quoting, also known as escaping the character. There are several methods in the Linux shell for turning off a character's special meaning, which are outlined in the following sections.

Escaping an Individual Character

To escape a single character, place a backslash immediately before the character. For example, if one wanted to list all of the files that had an asterisk (*) in the file name, the following command would be used:

```
ls -a *\**
```

This would cause the shell to interpret only the first and the third *, but not the middle *.

Escaping Multiple Characters

To escape an entire string of characters, use either a pair of double quotation marks ("") or a pair of single quotation marks ("). If double quotation marks are used, the shell will continue to process any shell variables starting with the dollar ($) sign. Alternately, nothing that falls between single quotation marks will be shown to the shell for processing. The single quotation marks can also be used to turn off the meaning of the double quotation marks, and vice versa.

For example, to search all files in the current directory for a string containing special command characters, use:

```
bash$ grep  "I'll find your $name "   *
```

Here, the single quotation marks in the contraction I'll will be ignored by the shell, as will the spaces between words, but the shell variable, $name, will be evaluated to determine its value. This value will be placed into the string just shown, replacing this instance of the shell variable.

Backquoting Strings of Characters

Single back-quote characters (`) can be used in pairs to delimit strings of characters in the shell. By placing an item in back quotes, anything between them will be executed as a separate command and not as part of the arguments to the original command. Here is an example of back quoting:

```
echo The exact date is `date`
```

The output would be similar to the following:

```
The exact date is Wed Apr 14 15:07:33 CDT 1999.
```

The date command was executed, and the output from it was inserted into the string that was subsequently echoed with the echo shell command.

Shell Aliases

Even the experienced Linux user realizes that seemingly easy commands can become harder to remember when switches are added to them. This is where the convenience of command aliases becomes important. Command aliases provide the ability to make up an easy-to-remember name for a more complicated command.

For example, assume that a user wants to see a full (long) directory listing every time the ls command is typed. Using an alias, this can be accomplished as follows:

```
alias ls='ls -l'
```

After this alias is created, each time the ls command is typed, the output will be the same as if the ls -l command had been entered.

To remove this alias, simply type:

```
unalias ls
```

Here are some examples of commonly used aliases:

```
alias ..='cd ..'
alias ...='cd ../..'
alias dir='ls -l'
alias l='ls -alF'
alias la='ls -la'
alias ll='ls -l'
alias ls='ls $LS_OPTIONS'
alias ls-l='ls -l'
alias md='mkdir -p'
alias o='less'
alias rd='rmdir'
```

Unfortunately, aliases are user account specific; a system administrator often finds himself continually switching among user accounts and multiple systems. Therefore, the convenience of aliased commands is overridden by the inconvenience of not having the aliases available as a user moves among systems.

If a command behaves in an unexpected fashion, use the backslash (\) to escape any aliasing. Thus, the command \ls would escape the ls $LS_OPTIONS command and just perform the simpler ls command.

I/O Redirection

In Unix-like systems, input and output are handled via three I/O channels known as standard input (stdin), standard output (stdout), and standard error (stderr). Just as the names imply, input comes from the stdin I/O channel, output goes to the stdout I/O channel, and any error output generated is directed toward the stderr I/O channel.

Normally, the stdin I/O channel is associated with the keyboard, and stdout is associated with the computer's display. However, there are some special characters, > and <, that can be used to redirect the input for stdin or to redirect the output for stdout. Stderr can be redirected as well, should the need arise.

As an example of output redirection, consider the following:

```
bash$ ls > directoryListing.txt
```

If `ls` alone were typed, the output would be sent to stdout, which is usually associated with the terminal screen. However, in this example, a redirection operator has been used to send the output of `ls` to the file named `directoryListing.txt`. This means that the current value (output) of `ls` has been saved in a file so that it can be viewed again or manipulated.

Standard input, or stdin, works very much the same way that standard output does. It allows a program's input to be redirected to come from a source other than the keyboard. If, for example, there was a program called `printNames`, and the input was to come from a text file called `names`, then the `printNames` program would be executed as follows:

```
bash$ printNames < names
```

Table 3.1 lists the redirection characters and their functions.

Program-to-Program I/O Channels or Pipes

Many commands in Unix-like systems read from the standard input and write to the standard output. Pipes are effective in connecting one program or command to the input of another.

When a pipe character (|) is used between commands, the pipe connects the output of the command on the left-hand side of the pipe to the input of the right-hand command. For example, the command:

```
bash$ ls -l | more
```

Table 3.1 List of Operators

REDIRECTION CHARACTER	WHAT IT CAN DO
>	Redirects output to the left-side command to the right-side device or file, overwriting any file if it already exists.
>>	Has the same effect as the > command, but appends to the end of the file if it already exists, rather than overwriting the file.
2>	Redirects the error output of the left-side command to the right-side device or file, overwriting any file if it already exists.
<	Redirects the input of the left-side command to the right-side device or file.

causes the output of the directory listing to become the input of the `more` command. The only limit to the number of commands that can be piped together is the system resources.

Background Program Creation versus Virtual Terminals

One of Linux's most powerful features is its ability to do more than one thing at a time, a process commonly referred to as multitasking. The user can employ multitasking in Linux in different ways, and some of these are discussed in the following sections.

Command Line

When working at the command line, the user does not have to wait for a program to finish before beginning another command. Programs can be made to execute in the background by simply following the command with the ampersand (&) character. For example, the following command runs in the background, searching the entire directory structure for the file named `filename`:

```
bash$ find / -name filename &
```

After starting a command, if the user subsequently realizes that it may take longer to complete than originally thought, the command can be suspended by typing CTRL-Z and pushed to the background with the `bg` command. For example:

```
bash$ find / -name filename -print
<CTRL>Z
bash$ bg
bash$
```

Virtual Terminals

Another way that more than one task can be accomplished at once is by using the Linux virtual terminal feature. Pressing CTRL-ALT and a function key, F1 through F6, may access different virtual terminals. For example, one may log in on F1 and begin a task, and then switch to F2 to do other work while the job on F1 is finishing.

Windowing Environment

In the X Window environment, the user can have more than a single program (window) open at a time, as well as multiple desktops. The multiple desktop feature is dependent on the window manager being used. Most window managers have a default of four desktops that are laid out in a two-dimensional array. However, the Enlightenment window manager allows the user to have 32 desktops on the horizontal and vertical axis, plus an additional 32 desktops on the Z-axis.

Basic Commands

The following section will discuss a number of simple but important commands. These commands allow the user to manipulate files and directories, and to discover what is contained in them.

Redefinition of Special Keys with stty

Many of the commands used at the terminal are single-character commands. For example, the BACKSPACE is a single-character command, and the interrupt signal, CTRL-C, is a single-character command. These commands can be set or redefined using the `stty` command. To display all of the current terminal settings, type:

```
bash$ stty -a
```

To change a `stty` mode that is either true or false, type `stty` followed by the name to turn the mode on, and `stty` with the dash character (-) before the name to turn the mode off. For example:

```
bash$ stty -echo
```

will disable echoing of characters to the terminal, and

```
bash$ stty echo
```

will re-enable echoing of typed characters to the terminal. To change the value of a terminal setting, type `stty name value`. For example, to change the `erase` command to CTRL-V, you would type:

```
bash$ stty erase <CTRL>V
```

ls—Directory Listing

The `ls` command displays descriptive file information. Table 3.2 provides a list of options for the `ls` command.

The `ls` command provides information in varying formats, depending on the switches that are used. For example, the `ls` command in the current directory could provide the following results:

```
luke@xwing:~/test > ls -lF
total 560
-rw-rw-r-  1 luke      users      56780 Aug 21 10:39 file1
-rwxr-xr-  1 luke      users     568832 Aug 21 10:40 prog2*
drwxr-xr-  2 luke      users       1024 Aug 21 10:40 file3/
```

Table 3.2   The ls Command

Command Name	ls
Synopsis	ls [-a -s -F -I -r -R -t -u -1] pathname
Description	Each file has certain attributes associated with it, including name, size, various dates of modification, owner, group, and permissions. The ls command displays this information in a variety of formats depending on the switches used with the command.

Options		
	-a	Includes all files and directories in the listing, including those with a name starting with the character dot.
	-s	Prints the size of the files in blocks.
	-F	Appends a character to each file name to indicate its type. It appends a * for executable regular files, a / for directories, a @ for symbolic links, | for FIFOs, and \ for Unix domain sockets.
	-i	Includes the node number (internal file number) in the display. This option is useful if you want to see whether file names are synonyms. If the node numbers are the same and the files are in the same file system, then they are just different names for the same file.
	-1	Displays a long listing of the file information, including permissions, size, owner, and modification.
	-r	Reverses the order of the sort (default is alphabetic).
	-R	Recursively accesses files in any subdirectory.
	-t	Sorts the listing by last modification date.
	-u	Sorts the listing by last access time.

The output of the ls -1F command has eight basic parts: permissions, links, owner, group, file size, creation date, file name, and symbolic file type. Links refer to the number of directory entries that contain references to the file; they are described in more detail under the ln command. Owner refers to the user account luke, that owns the file, and the group account users that owns the file. It is possible to allow a group with no members to own a file. File size is represented in bytes, and files may be zero bytes in length. Directory files are created with the mkdir command and are a multiple of the logical OS block size, or 1024 bytes. The symbolic file type is displayed after the file name without a space. In the preceding example, the asterisk (*) symbol indicates that prog2 is executable, and the slash (/) symbol indicates that file3 is a subdirectory.

Entering the ls command modified by the -1 (long) option reveals a coded permissions field on the left-hand side. The leftmost column describes the type of file. The dash (-) character for the first and second rows indicates that they are regular data files containing a stream of bytes. The third row has the d character as its leftmost entry; this means that the file is a subdirectory containing pairs of file names associated with index nodes.

The next three permission columns from the left contain a combination of dashes and the characters rwx, where r means read permission, w means write permission, and x means execute permission. The dash character means negation of read, write, or execute permission.

As can be seen from the previous code, there are three sets of the three columns, which are for the user, group, and world permissions. It is important to remember that only one of the three sets is applicable at any given point in time. The first set of permissions refers to the owner of the file, in this case luke, and are only active if the user account, luke, is attempting to access the files. The second set of permissions refers to the group owner or the group users, and this set is only active if a member of the users group is attempting to access the file. The third and final set of permissions refers to others or to any user account that is not the owner or a member of the group that is trying to access the file.

While data files cannot be executed, the execute permission can be set for these files with no effect on the system. If a data file is set executable and an attempt is made to execute the file, then the bash shell evaluates it and the following error message is returned, indicating that it cannot execute binary file. If an ASCII data file has been set executable and the user is trying to run the executable file, then bash shell will attempt to interpret the file contents as a series of shell commands. If a particular interpreter is desired, then the ASCII file may begin with the characters #! and the path to the interpreter. For example, the following line will have the perl interpreter read the file contents:

```
#!/usr/perl
```

Directories are much like any other data files; while they are not to be executable, they have the x permission. Thus, the x permission for directories means that the file name may or may not be viewed by the owner, group, or others. This only refers to viewing; if the read permission is valid for the user account, then the file may be read, even though its name cannot be viewed with the ls command. Also, if the read or write permission is not set for a given directory and owner, then none of the files in the directory may be read or written, respectively.

There are other permission attributes, such as set user ID, set group ID, and set the sticky bit. These are discussed with the chmod command. Another form of the ls command is with the arguments ls -ltr:

```
-rw-r-r-   1 dmw     users     118272 Aug 21 00:02 file
-rw-r-r-   1 jmm     users      53248 Aug 21 00:05 freda
-rw-r-r-   1 dfm     users      20480 Aug 21 02:47 Temp
-rw-r-r-   1 dfm     users      24576 Aug 21 02:47 Temp2
-rw-r-r-   1 jmm     users      45568 Aug 21 07:43 comma
-rw-r-r-   1 cpt     users      28672 Aug 21 12:36 v
-rwxrwxrwx 1 dfm     users         24 Aug 22 01:08 t
-rw-r-r-   1 dfm     users      50688 Aug 22 02:51 commands
```

In this example, the files have been listed based on creation time (-t), and they have been sorted in reverse order (-r). In this way, the file list can be reviewed to determine which ones have been most recently created.

cd—Change Directory

The cd command allows the user to change from the present directory to another specified directory. Table 3.3 provides a list of options for the cd command.

The cd command is not a stand-alone program like most other commands. Instead, it is part of the shell and is called a built-in command. Most people use the cd command in its simplest form. By typing cd <dir>, the user can move to that directory. In the following examples, the bash shell prompt has been set up to show additional information. The prompt shows the account name, john, followed by the host name, sith, followed by the current directory name:

```
john@sith:~ > cd /etc
john@sith:/etc >
```

Here, the ~ sign indicates John's home directory: /home/john/. The cd command means to change working directory. The use of single (.) and double (..) dot symbols allows reference to the present working directory and its parent directory. An example of the use of the (.) is:

```
john@sith:/etc > cd ./opt/gnome
john@sith:/etc/opt/gnome >
```

While the .. moves to the parent directory:

```
john@sith:/etc/opt/gnome > cd ..
john@sith:/etc/opt >
```

There is a special class of files called symbolic links. These files usually contain a path to the real file, but may also contain a path to another directory. If the cd command is used to switch into a symbolically linked directory, the symbolic link is automatically followed. By default, the cd command uses the -L option and shows the symbolically linked name. If the -P switch is used, then the real (hard linked) directory name is displayed.

Typically, a user will change directories temporarily and then return to the home directory. Since the bash shell remembers the previous directory, it is possible to move

Table 3.3   cd Command Description

Command Name	cd	
Synopsis	cd [-P -L] <DIRECTORY>	
Description	Changes from the present working directory to the <DIRECTORY> specified.	
Options	-P	Change to the physical directory and do not follow symbolic links.
	-L	Forces symbolic links to be followed.

between two different directories by using cd -. For example, if the previous directory was the home directory, /home/john, and the current directory is /bin, then the cd - command would have the following effect:

```
john@sith:/bin > cd -
/home/john
john@sith:~ > cd -
/bin
johnos@sith:/bin > cd -
/home/john
```

Associated with the cd command are the shell commands dirs, pushd, and popd. There is a list of currently remembered directories maintained by the bash shell. The dirs command will display this list. The dirs syntax is:

```
dirs [-clpv] [+N] [-N]
```

This list of directories works like a stack. The pushd command pushes a directory onto the list, and the popd command removes a directory from the list. Following is an example of the pushd and dirs commands. This example starts from the home directory (~), and moves throughout several directories within the system:

```
john@sith:~ > dirs
~
john@sith:~ > pushd /etc
/etc ~
john@sith:/etc > pushd /bin
/bin /etc ~
john@sith:/bin > pushd /etc/opt
/etc/opt /bin /etc ~
john@sith:/etc/opt >
john@sith:/etc/opt > dirs
/etc/opt /bin /etc ~
```

There are now four remembered directories. The -l option directs dirs not to use shorthand versions, such as ~, for the home directory:

```
john@sith:/etc/opt > dirs -l
/etc/opt /bin /etc /home/john
```

The -v option will cause dirs to print each directory on its own line with the associated number entry:

```
john@sith:/etc/opt > dirs -v
0   /etc/opt
1   /bin
2   /etc
3   ~
```

The -p option is the same as -v without the associated number entries:

```
john@sith:/etc/opt > dirs -p
/etc/opt
/bin
/etc
~
```

The +N and -N options displays the Nth entry starting with zero. The +N will count from left to right, and the -N will count from right to left, such as:

```
john@sith:/etc/opt > dirs +1
/bin
john@sith:/etc/opt > dirs -1
/etc
john@sith:/etc/opt >
```

Finally, the -c option will clear all elements in the directory stack. pushd and popd allow the user to manipulate the directory stack. The pushd command places a named directory to the top of the directory stack. pushd without any arguments causes the top two directories to be exchanged, just like cd - command. The options available to pushd are:

```
pushd [dir | +N | -N]
```

The dir option will add the directory listed to the top of the directory stack and make it the present working directory.

```
john@sith:~ > pushd ~/download/games/
~/download/games ~
```

The +N and -N options will manipulate the stack such that Nth directory is at the top of the stack and the present working directory. The +N begins counting from the left of the list, and the -N begins counting from the right of the list. For example:

```
john@sith:/home > dirs
/home /bin /etc ~/download/games ~
john@sith:/home > pushd +3
~/download/games ~ /home /bin /etc
john@sith:~/download/games >
```

Popd removes the directories from the directory stack. If no arguments are given, it removes the directory from the top of the stack and changes the user's working directory to the new top directory:

```
popd [+N | -N]
```

The +N and -N options are similar to pushd's +N and -N options, except that it removes the Nth entry from the stack. For example:

```
john@sith:~/download/games > dirs
~/download/games /home /bin /etc
```

```
john@sith:~/download/games > popd +3
~/download/games /home /bin
john@sith:~/download/games > dirs
~/download/games /home /bin
john@sith:~/download/games >
```

more and less—Pagers

There are two commands used to view and navigate ASCII documents: `more` and `less`. `more` is the older command with fewer features; the `less` command is discussed in this section. With the `less` command, the UP and DOWN arrow keys can be used to move one line at a time. The PAGE UP and PAGE DOWN keys move whole pages at once. Table 3.4 describes the `less` command in greater detail.

Table 3.4   less Command

Command Name	`less`
Synopsis	`less [-p pattern] [-N] [-f] [-C] <filename>`
Description	`less` is a program similar to more, but allows both backward and forward movement in a file. Also, less does not have to read the entire input file before starting, so with large input files it starts faster than text editors, such as Vi.
Options	Command- line arguments:
	`-N` Integer value that should be the number of lines of text to proceed forward.
	`-f` Forces non-regular files to be opened.
	`-C` Clears the screen before proceeding with output.
	Commands used after less has been run:
	Space Scrolls a full screen.
	z Scrolls forward a full window if N is not specified.
	? Indicates that the command should be applied to the end of the file first (if relevant or meaningful to do so).
	`-I` Followed by one of the command-line (i) option letters (as described in the remainder of this section) this will change the setting of that option and print a message describing the new setting. If the option letter has a numeric value (such as `--b` or `--h`), or a string value (such as `--P` or `--t`), a new value may be entered after the option letter. If no new value is entered, a message describing the current setting is printed, and nothing is changed.
	`-` Followed by one of the command-line option letters (as described in the remainder of this section), this will print a message describing the current setting of that option. The setting of the option is not changed.

With the less command, a search pattern can be specified with the -p option; less will browse the file and highlight all the hit keywords. To search for a particular pattern, start the less command at the prompt with a search pattern as follows:

```
nilesh@yoda:~ > less -p linux filename
```

This command will search for the word linux in the file called filename and highlight all the hits.

Word occurrences can be searched within the less program environment by typing:

```
<Esc> -/searchkeyword
```

less will search for that new word. The less command can also take several files at the command prompt and permit navigation through them. For example, type:

```
nilesh@yoda:~ > less filename1 filename2 filename3 filename4
```

to load multiple files at the same time. While viewing one file, the user can move to another file, using these two commands:

```
:n  to go to the next file
:p  to go to the previous file
```

While in the less command, the file currently being viewed can be edited. Typing v will invoke the editor specified in the environment variable, VISUAL or EDITOR. If it is not defined, the default is set to Vi. After the file is edited and exited, it comes back to the less command.

Line numbers can be displayed before all lines with the less command, simply by starting the less command with the -N option; each line in the file will have a line number before it. This is helpful when doing a quick search for a line number containing an error. For example:

```
nileshd@yoda:~ > less -N filename
```

cp—Copy

The cp command makes a copy of files or directories. This command will preserve the properties of a file, but will not preserve the ownership of a file. However, the -P option will preserve all the properties of a file. Table 3.5 describes the cp command in greater detail.

In the following example, the passwd file, which was originally owned by root and by the group root, is now owned by the user ajneel and by the group users. Also, there are now two copies of the passwd file on the system:

```
ajneel@maul:~ > ls -l /etc/passwd
-rw-r-r-  1 root    root    1869 Aug 22 18:07 /etc/passwd
ajneel@maul:~ > cp /etc/passwd .
```

Table 3.5   cp Command

Command Name	cp	
Synopsis	`cp [-f -i -p -R -u -v] source_file dest_file_or_directory`	
Description	Copies file or files to new directories or files.	
Options	`-f`	Forces overwriting existing destination files.
	`-i`	Interactively prompts whether to overwrite an existing file.
	`-p`	Preserves the original file characteristics, including owner, permissions, and modify time.
	`-R`	Recursively copies directories as well as regular files.
	`-u`	Overwrites a file only if the file being copied is newer than the destination file.
	`-v`	Verbose mode; prints out the name of each file as it is copied.

```
ajneel@maul:~ > ls -l ./passwd
-rw-r-r-  1 ajneel   users   1869 Aug 23 16:57 ./passwd
ajneel@maul:~ >
```

By default, the cp command does not copy directories. The -R switch can be specified in order to copy a directory. This switch instructs the cp command to recursively copy directory contents as well as regular files. For example, if the command cp /etc/* /etc_backup was issued, then only the files in the top level of this directory would be copied. However, if the same command were issued with the -R option, then all files and directories would be copied. In the following example, the files and directories of /usr are copied to the /tmp:

```
ajneel@maul:/tmp > ls
ajneel@maul:/tmp > cp -R /usr/* .
ajneel@maul:/tmp > ls
IBMdb2      doc               i486-linux-libc6   local
X11         empress           i486-linuxaout     man
X11R6       etc               i486-sysv4         openwin
X386        games             include            sbin
bin         i486-linux        info               share
dict        i486-linux-libc5  lib                spool
ajneel@maul:/tmp >
```

In some cases, a file being copied may already exist at the target. Therefore, cp has some useful options. The first is the -f option, which will force the copying of files without the complaint. The second option is the -i option, which causes the cp command to pause and ask for user intervention when a file being copied already exists. Finally, the -u option overwrites a file only if the file being copied is a newer file.

ln—Link Directory or File Name

The ln command is used to create a link between two files or directories. A link is simply a pointer to another file name or directory name. Table 3.6 provides the options for the ln command.

By default, ln will create a hard link to join two or more file names or directory names. Files having only one name have a directory entry made up of the file name and an associated index node (inode) number, which points to an inode. The inode describes the contents of the file. Hard links are implemented by creating another directory entry with a new name but the same inode number. To track the number of hard links, the inode also contains a link count number. A hard link is a path to another file or directory, such that if the contents of the link are changed, then the original file is changed. For example:

```
ajneel@maul:~/temp > cat original
This is the original file!
ajneel@maul:~/temp > ln original new
ajneel@maul:~/temp > echo This is text added to the file new        >> new
ajneel@maul:~/temp > cat original
This is the original file!
This is text added to the file new
ajneel@maul:~/temp > ls -l
total 2
-rw-r-r-   2 ajneel  users        62 Aug 24 12:57 new
-rw-r-r-   2 ajneel   users       62 Aug 24 12:57 original
ajneel@maul:~/temp >
```

In the preceding example, the appended text to the file, called new, has also changed the file, called original. Notice that the hard link new and the file original are both 62 characters in length. Also notice that the number between the file permissions and the user account (the number 2) is the hard link count number from the inode of the file having the names original and new. The disadvantage of using a hard link is that the link must be within the current mounted disk volume boundary, since inode numbers are only volume relative and not whole file system relative.

Table 3.6 ln Command

Command Name	ln		
Synopsis	ln [-s -v -i] source_file dest_file_or_directory		
Description	Creates a link to directories or files.		
Options	-s	Creates a symbolic link instead of a hard link, which is the default.	
	-v	Verbose mode.	
	-i	Interactive mode.	

However, the `ln` command can also create symbolic links using the `-s` option. A symbolic link is just a pointer to another file, but it can reference a file anywhere in the file system. Symbolic links are similar to hard links except that they are slower to access than hard links. The reason is that once the file manager discovers a symbolic link, it must restart the path lookup process. A second way symbolic links differ from hard links is that the symbolic file size is equal to the length of the file name and not the length of the file. Notice that in the following example, the file `new` has a length of eight bytes, while the file `original` has a length of 62:

```
ajneel@maul:~/temp > ln -s original new
ajneel@maul:~/temp > ls -l
total 1
lrwxrwxrwx  1 ajneel  users   8 Aug 24 13:20 new -> original
-rw-r-r-    1 ajneel  users  62 Aug 24 12:57 original
ajneel@maul:~/temp >
```

mv—Move a File

The `mv` command is used to move a file, group of files, or a whole subdirectory between two higher-level directories. The man pages call this command `rename files`, but it is commonly referred to as `move`. Table 3.7 describes the options for the `mv` command.

The `mv` command has two syntax usages:

```
mv [Option] <source> <destination>
mv [Option] <source> <directory>
```

The first syntactical usage is to rename a file, such as:

```
john@sith:~/test > ls
test
john@sith:~/test > mv test this_is_not_a_test
john@sith:~/test > ls
this_is_not_a_test
```

Table 3.7 mv Command

Command Name	mv	
Synopsis	`mv [-f -i -v] source_file dest_file_or_directory`	
Description	You can use the `mv` command to move a file or effectively change the name of a file.	
Options	`-f`	Forces overwriting of destination files.
	`-i`	Interactive move; `mv` prompts before each move is attempted and waits for a response.
	`-v`	Verbose; prints the name of each file before moving it.

The file test has been renamed `this_is_not_a_test`. Or the file may be moved to a directory as follows:

```
john@sith:~/test > ls
this_is_not_a_test
john@sith:~/test > mv this_is_not_a_test ~/not_a_test/
john@sith:~/test > ls
john@sith:~/test >
john@sith:~/test > cd ~/not_a_test/
john@sith:~/not_a_test > ls
this_is_not_a_test
```

The file `this_is_not_a_test` under the test directory is now moved to the `not_a_test` directory.

mkdir—Make Directory

The Linux file manager does not treat all files equally. Instead, it uses the file type field in the index node, or inode, to determine what to do with the file. If the inode type is `special`, it means that the file contents are really just access pointers to kernel device drivers. If the file type is `directory`, then the file manager knows that the contents of the file are to be used to locate other files. Given this distinction, the `mkdir` command is used to create an instance of the file type `directory`. Table 3.8 describes the `mkdir` command in greater detail.

Table 3.8   mkdir Command

Command Name	`mkdir`	
Synopsis	`mkdir [-p -mmod -parents -mode=mode -help -version] directory`	
Description	`mkdir` creates a directory with each given name; by default, the mode of created directories is 0777 minus the bits set in the mask.	
Options	`-m, --mode=mode`	Set the mode of created directories to mode, which is symbolic as in chmod and uses the default mode as the point of departure.
	`-p, --parents`	Ensure that each given directory exists. Create any missing parent directories for each argument. Parent directories default to the umask modified by the u+wx. Do not consider an argument directory that already exists to be an error.
	`--help`	Print a usage message on standard output and exit successfully.
	`--version`	Print version information on standard output than will exit successfully.

rmdir and rm—Remove a Directory or a File

The commands rm and rmdir remove files and directories, respectively. Table 3.9 provides a list of options for the rmdir command, and Table 3.10 describes the rm command in greater detail.

Although the commands used are rm and rmdir, the kernel service that deletes a file is called unlink, which is more descriptive of how the process is implemented. The rm and rmdir commands disable the directory entries (a directory never shrinks, but it does grow to accommodate more files), and they decrement the link count in the inode. If the link count drops to zero, then the file blocks are returned to the free list of blocks.

There is a special case of the rm command that will also remove directories. The command:

```
fred@xwing:~ >  rm -r junk
```

will remove all the files contained within the directory junk as well as the entire directory. If there are subdirectories within the junk directory, they will also be deleted.

Table 3.9   rmdir Commands

Command Name	rmdir	
Synopsis	rmdir [-p] target_directory	
Description	This command will remove directories.	
Options	-p, --parents	Remove directories and any subdirectories that become empty as a result of the original operation. This is a useful switch for removing entire empty directory trees.

Table 3.10   rm Commands

Command Name	rm	
Synopsis	rm [-r -d -f -i] target_file_or_directory	
Description	This command will remove files or directories.	
Options	-r	Recursively removes files and directories starting at the bottom of the tree.
	-d	Specifies that the target is a directory.
	-i	Activates interactive mode.
	-f	Ignore all errors and never prompt the user.

head and tail—File Previewers

The commands head and tail are helpful for quick viewing of log files or other types of status files. Tables 3.11 and 3.12 provide options for the head and tail commands respectively.

The head command displays the first 10 lines of a file, while the tail command displays the last 10 lines of a file. To view more lines, use the numeric argument. For example, to view the last 50 lines of a log file, enter:

```
fred@xwing: ~> tail -50 /var/log/messages | less
```

In this example, the last 50 lines of the messages file are sent to the pager called less, which displays the file contents one page at a time. As an aside, only the super-user can access the /var/log files.

Table 3.11   head Commands

Command Name	head	
Synopsis	head [#b #k #m −n#] file	
Description	Previews the beginning of a file.	
Options	#b	Displays the first # of bytes.
	#k	Displays the first # of kilobytes.
	#m	Displays the first # of megabytes.
	−n#	Displays the number of lines as indicated by the integer value #.

Table 3.12   tail Commands

Command Name	tail	
Synopsis	tail [#b #k #m −n#] file	
Description	Previews the end of a file.	
Options	#b	Displays the last # of bytes.
	#k	Displays the last # of kilobytes.
	#m	Displays the last # of megabytes.
	−n#	Displays the number of lines as indicated by the integer value #.

file—Determine a File Type

The `file` command can be used to determine the type of information found in a file. Table 3.13 describes the options of the `file` command.

Most non-Unix operating systems employ strongly typed files. Thus, an executable file is named with the `.EXE` file name extension, or a visual basic program is named with the `.VB` extension. Once the files are data typed, other OS utilities can use the data type to carry out their tasks. For example, the printer subsystem may look for the `.DAT` file name extension to assume that the file contains printer commands as well as data.

Since Linux and other Unix-like operating systems do not employ strongly typed files, a user is never certain what type of files are contained in a directory the first time he or she visits the directory. The `file` command is very helpful in discovering what is in the various files. For example, the following display confirms if a file's contents match the suggested data type of the file:

```
fred@xwing:~ > file *
90752535211:       ASCII text
Assets.PDF:        PDF document, version 1.2
BROCHURE.rtf:      Rich Text Format data, version 1, ANSI
Basic-CED.Doc:     data
Comments.txt:      English text
Desktop:           directory
Exam_costs.doc:    WordPerfect document
Mgr_s-Guide.zip:   Zip archive data, at least v1.0 to extract
SysAdm:            English text
allie34:           troff or preprocessor input text
att:               mail text
big_penguin.jpg:   JPEG image data, JFIF standard
bookmark.htm:      exported SGML document text
ch01.doc.2.doc:    Microsoft Word document data
dd.wcm:            WordPerfect document
dns.fig:           FIG image text, version 3.2
fhs-2.0.tar.gz:    gzip compressed data, deflated, last
       modified:   Sun Oct 26 02:36:59 1997,
             os:   Unix
less:              English text
```

Table 3.13 file Commands

Command Name	file	
Synopsis	`file [-f namefile] [-L] file`	
Description	Determines the file's type.	
Options	`-f namefile`	Will use the namefile to examine multiple files. Each line is considered a file name.
	`-L`	Will instruct the program to follow all links.

```
lind.ps:        PostScript document text conforming at
     level 3.0
logo.epsi:      PostScript document text conforming at
     level 2.0 - type EPS
questions.dsk:  HP Printer Job Language data
t.ps:           empty
xw:             MS Windows PE 32-bit Intel 80386
     GUI executable not relocatable
```

grep—Print Lines Matching a Pattern

grep is a program used to search for patterns or strings within a file, multiple files, or standard input. grep will display the line in which the matching pattern appears. Table 3.14 describes the options for the grep command.

If someone is editing several files (letters, invoices, notes, etc.) and wants to return to an idea, the grep command would allow them to search for that information. For example, enter the following command to search for Friday:

```
fred@xwing:~ > grep Friday *
grep: Desktop: Is a directory
MIScontract.doc:\par Re-installation services performed outside of standard operating
hours (8:00 a.m. to 5:00 p.m. Monday through Friday) $500 per location.
clet1:revisions will be completed Friday of this week.
clet2:revisions will be completed Friday of this week.
clet3:revisions will be completed Friday of this week.
jnk:06:00 PM Central Time, Monday through Friday.
jnk2:06:00 PM Central Time, Monday through Friday.
grep: wp: Is a directory
```

Where grep was unable to process a file, it reports: grep. Otherwise, grep reports the file name, and the line in which the string match was found. The grep command

Table 3.14   grep Command

Command Name	grep	
Synopsis	`grep [-f -c -s] pattern file`	
Description	Searches for string variables.	
Options	`-f name_file`	Will use name_file to examine multiple files. Each line is considered a file name.
	`-c`	Suppress normal output; instead, print a count of matching lines for each input file. With the `-v`, `-revert-match` option, grep will count non-matching lines.
	`-s`	Suppress error messages about nonexistent or unreadable files.

also accepts meta-characters as well as literal strings. For example, one can search for all words beginning with a and ending with b using the arguments a[^]*b:

```
fred@xwing:~ > grep ña[^ ]*bî *
note1:  attrib a.out +x
note2:  attrib a.out +x
```

In the preceding command, the SPACE-A and B-SPACE sequences are literal strings, while the [^]* sequence indicates that any character that is not a space occurs zero or more times. These constructions are referred to as regular expressions and will be discussed in more detail in later study guides.

du—Disk Usage

The du command is frequently used to check for disk space used within a directory or directories. Table 3.15 provides a list of options for the du command.

df—Disk Free Space

The df command is used to check space used relative to each disk volume. Table 3.16 provides a list of options for the df command.

Table 3.15   du Command

Command Name	du	
Synopsis	[-c] [-b] [-k] [-m] [-h]	
Description	Will display statistics on the current usage.	
Options	-c	Produce a grand total.
	-b	Displays the disk usage in bytes for each disk volume.
	-k	Displays the disk usage in kilobytes for each disk volume.
	-m	Displays the disk usage in megabytes for each disk volume.
	-h	Human-readable form.

Table 3.16   df Command

Command Name	df	
Synopsis	df [-i] [-b] [-k] [-m] [-h]	
Description	Will display statistics on the current usage.	
Options	-i	Displays the inode usage for each disk volume.
	-b	Displays the disk usage in bytes for each disk volume.
	-k	Displays the disk usage in kilobytes for each disk volume.
	-m	Displays the disk usage in megabytes for each disk volume.
	-h	Human-readable form.

Unfortunately, by default the du command reports in logical OS block size or 1024-byte chunks, while the df command reports in bytes. On the other hand, the GNU versions of these programs allow the human-readable form when the h switch is used. Output from the commands would be similar to the following:

```
fred@xwing:~ > du -h Desktop/
1.8K    Desktop/Trash
3.8K    Desktop/Templates
1.9K    Desktop/Autostart
2.4K    Desktop/Apps
14K     Desktop

fred@xwing:~ > df -h
Filesystem      Size  Used  Avail  Capacity Mounted on
/dev/hda2       5.5G  4.8G  503M    91%    /
```

tar—Tape Archiver

The tar command is the main archive program for Linux. The tar program combines many files into one, compressing the many files if requested. The archiver must also preserve critical system information, such as who owns the files, the permission settings, the directory path, as well as hard and symbolic links. Table 3.17 describes the tar command in greater detail.

Table 3.17   tar Command

Command Name	tar	
Synopsis	tar c|t|x [-vkmx] [f archive] files...	
Description	tar is the main backup utility used in Linux. tar pushes a large amount of files that the user will specify into one large file. It preserves the directory structure of the original file system. Optionally, tar can also call gzip to compress the file. When using tar, the path names of the files are limited to 100 characters.	
Options	-f archive	Name of the file or device that is the archive.
	-k	Does not overwrite newer files.
	-m	Preserves file modification time.
	-v	Verbose; lists file names and more detailed information.
	files	A list of the file names to archive; if a directory is specified, tar descends through that directory tree, archiving the files within those directories.

To create an archive of files in the current directory, enter the following command:

```
tar czf myarchive *
```

To view the archive table of contents, enter the following command:

```
tar tvf myarchive
```

To archive a large amount of disk space and move the files from one part of the file system to another, use the following pair of tar commands:

```
tar cf - . | (cd /newplace; tar xvf -)
```

Here is a great example of multitasking at work from the command line. The first instance of the tar command begins reading the current directory (.), archiving the files, and generating the archive (because of the c, or create switch) to standard out (the combination f - characters). Standard out is then directed to another program through the pipe operator (|). The second program is actually two commands done in sequence, the cd command and the second tar command. The cd command switches from the current directory to the newplace where the files are to be deposited, while the second tar command extracts (the x switch) the archive being read from standard in (the combination of f - characters) and dumps the individual files into the current directory called newplace.

File Compression with gzip

gzip reduces the size of the named files using Lempel-Ziv coding (LZ77). Table 3.18 provides a list of options for the gzip command.

Whenever possible, each file is replaced by one with the extension .gz, while keeping the same ownership modes, access, and modification times. If no files are specified, or if a file name is -, the standard input is compressed to the standard output. gzip will only attempt to compress regular files. In particular, it will ignore symbolic links. If the compressed file name is too long for its file system, gzip truncates it. gzip attempts to truncate only the parts of the file name that are longer than three characters. If the name consists of small parts only, the longest parts are truncated. For example, if file names are limited to 14 characters, gzip.msdos.exe is compressed to gzi.msd.exe.gz. Names are not truncated on systems that do not have a limit on file name length. By default, gzip keeps the original file name and timestamp in the compressed file. These are used when decompressing the file with the -N option. This is useful when the compressed file name was truncated or when the timestamp was not preserved after a file transfer. Compressed files can be restored to their original form using gzip -d or gunzip or zcat. If the original name saved in the compressed file is not suitable for its file system, a new name is constructed from the original one to make it legal. Gunzip takes a list of files on its command line and replaces each file whose name ends with .gz, -gz, .z, -z, _z, or .Z, and which begins with the correct magic number with an uncompressed file without the original extension. Gunzip also recognizes the special extensions .tgz and .taz as shorthand for .tar.gz and

Table 3.18   gzip Command

Command Name	gzip, gunzip, zcat- compress or expand files	
Synopsis	gzip [-acdfh1LnNrtvV19] [-S suffix] [name...] [-acfh1LnNrtvV] [-S suffix] [name...] zcat [-fhLV] [name...]	
Options	-c -stdout - to -stdout	Write output on standard output; keep original files unchanged. If there are several input files, the output consists of a sequence of independently compressed members. To obtain better compression, concatenate all input files before compressing them.
	-d -decompress -uncompress	Decompress.
	-r -recursive	Travel the directory structure recursively. If any of the file names are specified on the command linear directories, gzip will descend into the directory and compress all the files it finds there (or decompress them in the case of unzip).
	-t -test	Test; check the compressed file integrity.
	-v -verbose	Verbose; display the name and percentage reduction for each file compressed or decompressed.
	-# --fast -	Regulate the speed of compression using the specified digit #, where −1 or −fast indicates the fastest compression method (less compression), and −9 or −best indicates the slowest compression method (best compression). The default compression level is −6.

.tar.Z, respectively. When compressing, gzip uses the .tgz extension if necessary instead of truncating a file with a .tar extension. zcat is identical to gunzip -c. (On some systems, zcat may be installed as gzcat to preserve the original link to compress.) zcat decompresses either a list of files on the command line or its standard input, and writes the uncompressed data on standard output. zcat will uncompress files that have the correct magic number whether they have a .gz suffix or not.

The mtools Suite—DOS Utilities

Table 3.19 provides the commands and options for the mtools suite.

Table 3.19 mtools Commands and Utilities

Command Name	mzip, mtype, mtoolstest, mshowfat, mattrib, mbadlocks, mcd, mopy, mdir, mdu, minfo, mmd, mmount, mmove, mpartition, mrd, mread, mren	
Description	A set of tools that can be used to DOS file systems.	
Options	mtype	Displays contents for an MS-DOS file.
	mtoolstest	Tests and displays the configuration.
	mshowfat	Displays the FAT entries for a file.
	mbadlocks	Tests a floppy disk and marks the bad locks in the FAT.
	mcd	Change MS-DOS directory.
	mcopy	Copy MS-DOS files to/from Unix.
	mdir	Display an MS-DOS directory.
	mdu	Display the amount of space occupied by an MS-DOS directory.
	mmd	Make an MS-DOS subdirectory.
	mmount	Mount an MS-DOS disk.
	mmove	Move or rename an existing MS-DOS file or subdirectory.
	mpartition	Create MS-DOS file systems as partitions.
	mrd	Remove an MS-DOS subdirectory.
	mren	Rename or move an existing MS-DOS file or subdirectory.

find—Locate a File

The find and locate commands help by searching the file system for programs and configuration files. Table 3.20 provides a list of options for the find command.

A typical find command takes the form:

```
find / -name fruitsalad
```

Here, / is the starting point of the search, and fruitsalad is the name of the file to be located. The find command will search all directories, but it is slow. Locate is

Table 3.20 find Command

Command Name	find	
Synopsis	find [-p pattern] files	
Options	-p pattern	Starts displaying the file from the first line that contains pattern.

much faster, since it searches a database of files, but the database may not include recent additions to the file system. Use the `updatedb` command to refresh the locate database. A typical `locate` command takes the form:

```
locate fruitsalad
```

The Vi Editor

The `vi` command can be used to search for string matches. Table 3.21 provides a list of options for the `vi` command.

wc—Counter

The `wc` command is used to discover summary information about a text file. Table 3.22 provides a list of options for the `wc` command.

An example of the `wc` command is as follows:

```
ls -l | grep ^d | wc
```

In this example, the `ls` command generates a long listing, and the output is sent to the `grep` program that only shows the lines that begin with the letter `d`, or directories. The output is then sent to the `wc` program, which counts lines and reports the number of directories.

Table 3.21   vi Command

Command Name	`vi`	
Description	Searches for string matches.	
Options	`ESC`	Return from insert mode to command mode.
	`i`	Enter insert mode from the cursor.
	`I`	Insert at the beginning of the line.
	`r`	Replace the character that is on the cursor.
	`R`	Begin overwriting text.
	`o`	Open a line below the current line and enter insert mode.
	`O`	Open a line above the current line and enter insert mode.
	`s`	Substitute a character.
	`S`	Substitute an entire line.
	`/<pattern>`	Search forward for a pattern.
	`?<pattern>`	Search backwards for a pattern.
	`J`	Join two lines.

Table 3.22 wc Command

Command Name	wc
Synopsis	`wc [-clw] [--bytes] [--chars] [--lines]` `[--words] [--help] [--version] [-file`*f*`]`
Description	wc counts the number of bytes, white space separated words, and new lines in each given file, or the standard input if none are given, or when a file named – is given. It prints one line of counts for each file, and if the file was given as an argument, it prints the file name following the counts. If more than one file name is given, wc prints a final line containing the cumulative counts, with the file name total. The counts are printed in the order: lines, words, bytes.
Options	`-c, --bytes, --chars` Print only the byte counts. `-w, --words` Print only the word counts. `-l, --lines` Print only the new line counts. `--help` Print a usage message and exit with a status code indicating success. `--version` Print version information on standard output, then exit.

System Utilities

Objectives

- Describe the general control of X11 desktops.
- List and describe seven tools that provide information on other tools.
- Describe and use LILO.
- Install run-time device drivers.
- Configure a printer capabilities file.
- Configure a printer filter.
- Use lpr, lpq, lprm, and lpc to control file printing.
- List the sections of the X server configuration file.
- Configure the X server video hardware.
- Contrast xf86config, XF86Setup, Xconfigurator, and SaX.
- Describe five components of the X Window system architecture.
- List the trade-offs of AfterStep, KDE, Window Maker, FVWM95, Enlightenment, and Blackbox.

Window Managers

Window managers provide the graphical look to the desktop. Although there are several from which to choose, most users will employ the default window manager.

AfterStep

The AfterStep window manager was originally patterned after the NEXTSTEP GUI. AfterStep employs a wharf, or collection of icons that floats on the desktop and launches programs. Also, the wharf can contain folders of more applications. AfterStep was the first window manager to combine gradient-filled title bars with the NextStep-style `iconize` and `destroy` buttons. The pop-up menus are also gradient-filled and can be configured to accommodate an individual's needs (see Figure 4.1).

To learn more about AfterStep, visit the homepage at www.afterstep.org/.

KDE

KDE, with its Qt widget set foundation, is a highly functional window manager. The Qt widget set provides a library of graphic functions, such as `create a pop up`

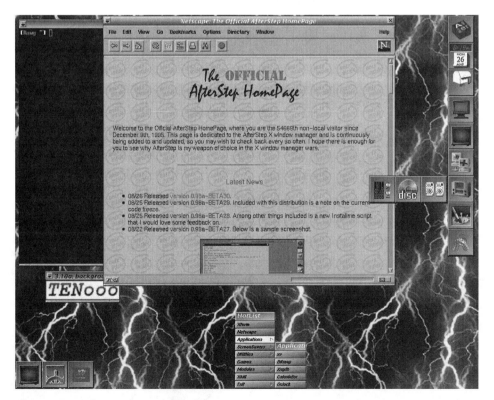

Figure 4.1   AfterStep screenshot.

requestor box, draw a window boarder, and draw a scroll bar. The Qt library was developed by Troll Tech AS (www.troll.no/) and employs a limited free software license controlled by Troll Tech. In other words, Qt is not GPLed.

One key to KDE's success is its default configuration. KDE can be configured to give the look and feel of almost any desktop design, but in its default configuration, KDE looks and feels much like MS-Windows. This initial impression gives new users a sense of continuity and the confidence to try other configurations.

KDE is a true window manager plus support utilities. KDE utilities include a complete file manager that can access local, remote, and Web-based files. KDE has a sophisticated GUI control panel, a task bar with icons, multiple forms of hierarchical pop-up menus, and help manuals; in addition, applications and utilities are still being developed. KDE creates a consistent look and feel for applications by specifying a standard GUI toolkit and support libraries that all KDE applications use, and a Style Guide that KDE application authors are strongly encouraged to follow. Figure 4.2 is a screen shot of the KDE window manager. Visit the KDE Web site at www.kde.org for more information.

In spite of these accomplishments, KDE has critics. In reaction to the Qt license issue, a group called Harmony is developing a complete GPLed widget set that is a free replacement of the Qt widget library (http://harmony.ruhr.de/). Another group, called GNU Network Object Model Environment (Gnome), is also working on a replacement for KDE (www.gnome.org). The Gnome project intends to build a complete, user-friendly desktop based entirely on free software. The desktop will consist of

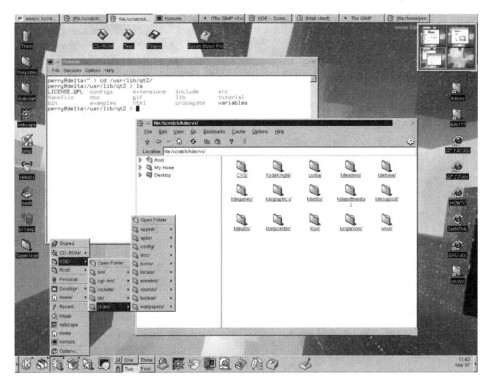

Figure 4.2 The KDE window manager.

small utilities and larger applications that share a consistent look and feel. Gnome uses GTK+ as the GUI toolkit for all Gnome-compliant applications. However, Gnome has not yet developed into a stand-alone window manager.

Window Maker

Window Maker emulates the elegant look and feel of the NEXTSTEP GUI. It is relatively fast (compared to other window managers), easy to configure, and easy to use. Furthermore, Window Maker provides integrated support for GNUstep applications. Figure 4.3 is a screen shot of the Window Maker environment.

To learn more about Window Maker, visit the Window Maker Web site at www .windowmaker.org.

FVWM

FVWM has a long history of development and was designed to have a small memory footprint. FVWM comes in two versions: version 1, which has been finalized, and version 2, which has more functions than version 1. Despite the advantages it offers, FVWM is no longer configured as the default window manager in the distributions, due to a somewhat dated look. Figure 4.4 is a screen shot of the FVWM window manager.

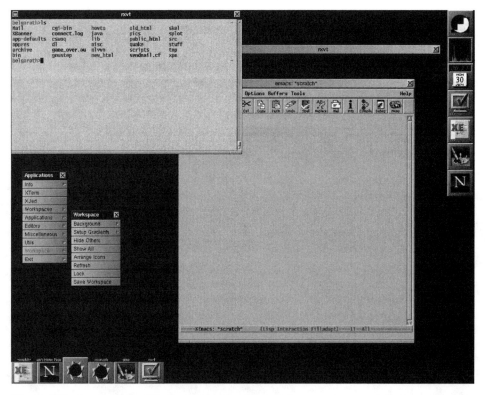

Figure 4.3 Image of the Window Maker environment.

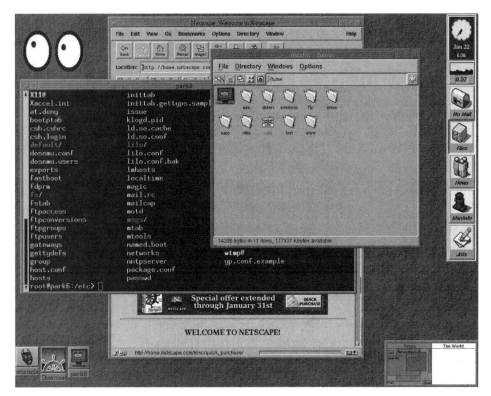

Figure 4.4   FVWM screenshot.

To learn more about FVWM, visit its Web site at www.fvwm.org.

Enlightenment

The Enlightenment window manager is based on the premise that the user should maintain control of the desktop at all times. Enlightenment is designed to embed new low-level features in the window manager by providing an almost infinite number of options, via a highly customizable definition language. The definition language allows control of simple backgrounds as well as multiple window border decoration styles. Unlike other window managers, Enlightenment's design was not based on earlier-generation window manager source code, allowing its designers more freedom in development. As a result, other window managers are unable to offer the flexibility of Enlightenment without a significant loss in performance. Figure 4.5 is a screen shot of the Enlightenment window manager.

To learn more about the Enlightenment window manager, visit the Enlightenment Web site at www.enlightenment.org.

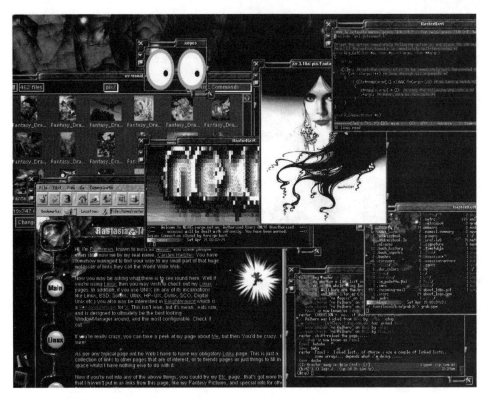

Figure 4.5   The Enlightenment window manager.

Blackbox

The Blackbox design goals are simplicity, speed, and elegance, meaning that it does not support advanced features like multiple image format loading, pixmap decorations, and mouse-less operation. To improve performance, Blackbox images are only rendered when they are needed. Once created, the images are also cached, saving CPU time in Blackbox and the X server. Blackbox runs in user space, in less than 1 MB of memory, and is designed to place only a minimal load on the X server, thus making it ideal for network-based X11 displays. Figure 4.6 is a screen shot of Blackbox.

To learn more about the Blackbox window manager, visit the Web site at http://blackbox.wiw.org.

The Linux Loader—LILO

The Linux loader (LILO) is the program that resides in the master boot record (MBR) of the hard disk. LILO reads a list of internal parameters to decide when and which OS image to load and execute. For example, assume the following setup from the file /etc/lilo.conf:

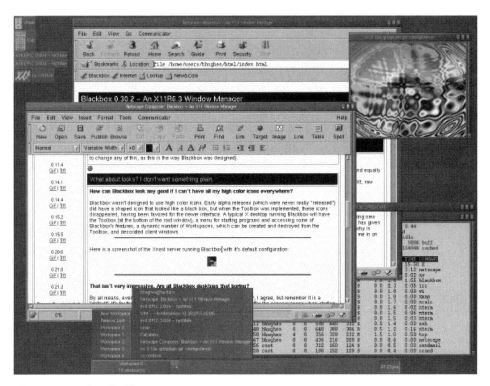

Figure 4.6   The Blackbox.

```
# Tell the kernel we have two Ethernet cards and 128 MB RAM
  append="ether=11,0x280,eth0 ether=5,0x300,eth1 mem=128M"
boot = /dev/hda                     # Which device to boot from
root = /dev/hda2                    # Which partition contains other boot data
prompt                              # Prompt for interaction if key pressed
timeout = 50                        # Wait up to 5 seconds for interaction
image=/boot/vmlinuz                 # 1st boot image on hda2
label=SUSE6.0                       # Name of OS for prompt
root=/dev/hda2                      # Its file system is also on hda2.
                                      read-only


  image=/boot/vmlinuz-2.0.36-3.mandrake  #2nd boot image on hda2
label=Mandrake                      # Name of OS for prompt
root=/dev/hda3                      # But its file system is on hda3


                                      read-only
```

These parameters become fixed in the executable boot image and are placed in the MBR by using the LILO command. In other words, the LILO program is a front-end program that copies its boot code and the preceding parameters (from the file /etc/lilo. conf) into the first sector of the hard disk (the MBR).

In the previous example, the LILO `append` parameter has been used to pass three parameters into the kernel. The first two parameters tell the kernel where to look for Ethernet adapters and their logical names. The third parameter tells the kernel that the system has 128 MB of main memory. The `timeout` parameter tells LILO to wait five seconds (i.e., 50 tenths of a second = five seconds) for the user to press the TAB or SHIFT key. Pressing the TAB key causes LILO to display OS labels SuSE 6.0, Mandrake, and the prompt Boot:. The user then enters the OS name (label) and presses ENTER to begin the boot process.

Note that both boot images are on the `hda2` partition, but the second OS entry (Mandrake) has its file system on `hda3`.

Device Driver Utilities

A key role of any operating system is the masking of physical differences among types of devices in order to present a uniform logical view of all devices to the user. This is accomplished with program modules called device drivers, which can communicate with a physical device and, by encapsulating these details of communication, present a uniform logical view to the rest of the OS.

Kernel Modules-lsmod-insmod-rmmod

Generally, there is one device driver per type of physical device. Traditionally, these drivers are built into the kernel when it is constructed and cannot be changed unless the kernel is recompiled. Linux, however, is unique among operating systems because not only does it have the traditional compiled-in drivers, but the kernel can also load other device drivers at run time. To see the list of currently installed device drivers, type the following command:

```
/sbin/lsmod:
hostname$ /sbin/lsmod
Module      Pages     Used by
serial        8          1
wd            2          1
8390          2   [wd]   0
nfs          12          4
3c509         2          1
rarp          1          0
```

In this example, there are six device drivers loaded that consume 27 pages of memory at 4096 bytes each. (Note that some versions of `lsmod` will list bytes and not pages.) One can also see that the 8390 driver is used by another driver, the wd Ethernet driver. Furthermore, it can also be seen from looking at the `Used by` column that three of the six device drivers have one program using them, while one driver, `nfs`, has four programs using it.

Adding and Removing Drivers

New drivers may be added with the /sbin/insmod command, while other drivers may be removed with the /sbin/rmmod command. The kernel will automatically load these drivers at boot time if they are listed in the file /etc/modules.conf.

Available drivers for a given kernel can be found in the /lib/modules/X.X.X directory, where X.X.X is the version number of the kernel. These modules will only work with that particular version of the kernel.

Linux distributions use generic kernels and the insmod feature to adapt to different environments at boot time; however, once an installation stabilizes, the kernel should be configured for the machine on which it is running. Part of this tuning process includes compiling the drivers into the kernel for better performance.

GUI Utilities: Linuxconf, Lisa/COAS, YaST

The development of all-in-one system configuration utilities is one of the most significant advancements in system setup. These programs are interactive, meaning that the operator is not required to remember the myriad of Linux and GNU configuration commands or their various arguments. Instead, these configuration utilities take the operator through a given configuration process in a step-by-step fashion. The GUI mega-utilities can be invoked from the command line and from the X GUI. Some can even be invoked from the Web. At the time of this writing, Linuxconf is GPLed but can only be found on Red Hat; Lisa is also GPLed and only found on OpenLinux. YaST/YaST2 is copyrighted to the SuSE corporation. Debian and Slackware do not have default all-in-one configuration utilities.

Use Configuration Utilities with Care

Ease of use is a characteristic that makes these tools appealing; yet, since they irrevocably modify the system, they should be used with care. If the operator does not understand the question that the configuration utility is asking, or why it is asking, then the program may silently perform multistep operations that could render the system inoperable. Furthermore, if the operator does not know how to reverse the operations performed, the system will have to be reinstalled.

Another reason these programs are dangerous is that they cannot know the context behind, or the reason for, the attempted change. In other words, they are very conservative in their approach and check for all possible system interactions. As a result, programs like Linuxconf can introduce a short, or a long list, of additional configuration issues. Again, these new issues usually require parameter modifications about which the operator may have no prior knowledge.

Maintenance of User Accounts

User accounts allow multiple users to access a system. Since root should not be used to perform every action on the system, it is important to properly maintain user accounts.

Creating a User Account

The first task to be completed after installing Linux is to create user accounts. Although various programs that can be used to facilitate this process will be reviewed in a subsequent section, it is important to understand the basic operations required to maintain user accounts, since this is the only way one may tweak and troubleshoot automated account creation.

One of the key files in Linux is the user-account passwd file. Each line of the passwd file has seven categories (fields) that are written flush against each other and delimited with colons, as follows:

```
AccountName:EncryptedPassword:UserID:GroupID:UserName:
HomeDirectory:FirstProgram
```

Setting Up New User Accounts

New account creation consists of modifying the passwd file according to these 11 steps:

1. Check to see if the shell prompt begins with a # ; if not, issue the su command to become the superuser.

2. Edit the file /etc/passwd and duplicate the last line, which will look something like this:

```
jordan:0yqyTC1a8iFGw:501:100:Jordan K. Dilnil:/usr/home/jordan:/bin/bash
```

3. Assuming the new account name was meredith, modify the duplicated line to look like this:

```
meredith:0yqyTC1a8iFGw:502:100:Meredith M. Jildil:/usr/home/meredith:/bin/bash
```

Note that the account name field was changed to meredith, the encrypted password was left unchanged, the user ID was incremented to a new value (502) that is unused by other accounts, the group remained unchanged, the user's name was replaced, the new home directory was inserted, and the first program to run was left unchanged as the bash, or Bourne again, shell.

4. Change directory (cd) to /usr/home and create the user's home directory with the commands:

```
cd /usr/home
mkdir meredith
```

5. Change the owner of the directory from root to the account name:

```
chown meredith meredith
```

6. Change the group of the directory from root to the account group:

```
chgrp 100 meredith
```

Note that numbers or names from the file /etc/group work with the chgrp command. There is no requirement that group numbers be consistent from computer to computer. The number 100 was used because it was copied from the previous user in the password file, and the system administrator did not want to look up the group name in the group file. The group number 100 is usually associated with the group users.

7. Give the new user a password with the command:

   ```
   passwd meredith
   ```

   The `passwd` program will prompt for a password for the account. The program will not accept passwords that have too few characters or appear to be too obvious; however, entering the same password again in response to a second prompt will force the program to accept the password.

8. Change the system administrator's identity to the new user (this will automatically switch to the new user's home directory) with the command:

   ```
   su - meredith
   ```

9. Copy the per-user initialization files from the system standard file `/etc/skel` into the new user's home directory with the command:

   ```
   cp /etc/skel/.* .
   ```

   Per-user account initialization files begin with the dot (.) character, which tells the system utility programs to routinely ignore these files. Thus, to copy the files, the dot must be explicitly specified. To further confuse the reader, it must be remembered that the dot character is also the name of the current directory. In this example, the copy command is specifying that `.*`, or all files beginning with the dot character, are to be copied to the `.` or the current directory.

10. Type CTRL-D twice: once to log out of the user's shell and return to the super-user environment, and a second time to log out of the superuser (root) account.

11. At the `Login:` prompt, log in as the first user. From now on, do not log in as `root`. Instead, log in as a user, and use the `su` command to switch to superuser status.

NOTE   The login procedure normally runs a command-line shell, but other programs may be run instead of the shell. For example, it is possible to run an editor that provides access to a text formatter. To do this, place the full path name of the text formatter in the 7th field of the password file for the particular user. In this way, a restricted word processing account can be set up.

adduser

There are a number of programs that assist with the creation and removal of user accounts. Each of these programs assumes that the `/etc/skel/` directory has the proper default initialization files for the new account. Again, remember that only the superuser can add or update user accounts.

The older GNU utility (written by Guy Maor, Ted Hajek, and Ian Murdock) for performing automated account creation is `adduser`. It takes a number of arguments, which may be specified in a control file called /etc/adduser.conf. However, another alternative is to create a small shell script (such as the one in the upcoming example) that will prompt for each account name and then utilize adduser to have the account automatically set up. The shell script can be operated interactively, with the administrator manually entering each account name, or it may have input redirected to come from a file to allow for batch operation.

```
echo -n "Enter Account Name:  "
read name
while [ $name != "done" ]
do
adduser -g users -s /bin/bash -d /home/$name -p $name $name
echo -n "Enter Account name: "
read name
done
```

In this script:

1. The echo command displays a prompt with new line suppressed.

2. The read command accepts an alphanumeric string into the internal shell variable name.

3. The while command evaluates the string and sets up a loop to continue processing the commands in the do-done block until the contents of the internal variable $name equal the literal string done (the sentinel value to be entered either at the command line or as the last line of a batch file). Simply typing CTRL+C may also terminate the program.

4. The adduser command installs a user account by always putting the account in the group titled users, giving the account a bash shell, and labeling the account with the user's name. As can be seen, the adduser program does not create a password. The role of the -p $name argument is to insert the plaintext account name into the encrypted password file, thereby disabling use of the account until a password is assigned with the passwd program.

5. The echo and the read commands are used again, but now they are processing a list of names.

If the name of this shell script was newaccount, then a batch of new accounts could be processed with the command ./newaccount < users, where the last user account name is done.

The adduser program is found in Red Hat 5.2, Debian 2.1, and OpenLinux 1.3. Slackware 3.6 employs the old DEC Ultrix shell script called adduser, which interactively collects the arguments and calls the useradd program (see the next section).

useradd

As discussed in the previous section, adduser is an older program that automates account setup. There are also some newer account maintenance utilities. The useradd program, written by Julianne F. Haugh, takes arguments similar to the adduser program and assumes that the /etc/skel/ directory has the proper default initialization files for the new account. The default arguments to be used with useradd may be specified in a control file called /etc/default/useradd. Like adduser, useradd does not update passwords, and only the superuser has the authority to add or update user accounts.

userdel

The userdel program can disable an account in the same way that the shell script in the previous section did, and can remove the user's files and home directory.

newusers

Unlike adduser and useradd, the newusers program takes a list (batch) of names and plaintext passwords to create or update user accounts. However, the program encourages the operator to keep such a list, which is usually considered an unreasonable security risk. The entire useradd series can be found in Red Hat 5.2, Debian 2.1, and Slackware 3.6.

Adding Accounts with Linuxconf: Lisa/COAS, YaST

The configuration utilities linuxconf, Lisa/COAS, and YaST all employ a hierarchical menu of configuration options as the user interface. Each will be considered in the following sections.

Linuxconf

In linuxconf, to create or update a user account, the following options would be selected:

```
Config -> User accounts -> Normal -> User accounts
```

(Where the arrow (->) means: select from the next level in the menu hierarchy.)

The linuxconf program presents a series of requestor boxes asking for the same account information as described earlier. Eventually, linuxconf will run the adduser program and then the passwd program. Figure 4.7 is a screen shot of Linuxconf.

NOTE Selecting a category from the hierarchy and pressing ENTER will expand the hierarchy by revealing the subordinate categories. Be careful, since pressing ENTER again will hide subordinate category names. Also, be aware that category names tend to repeat at different levels, so it is easy to become disoriented.

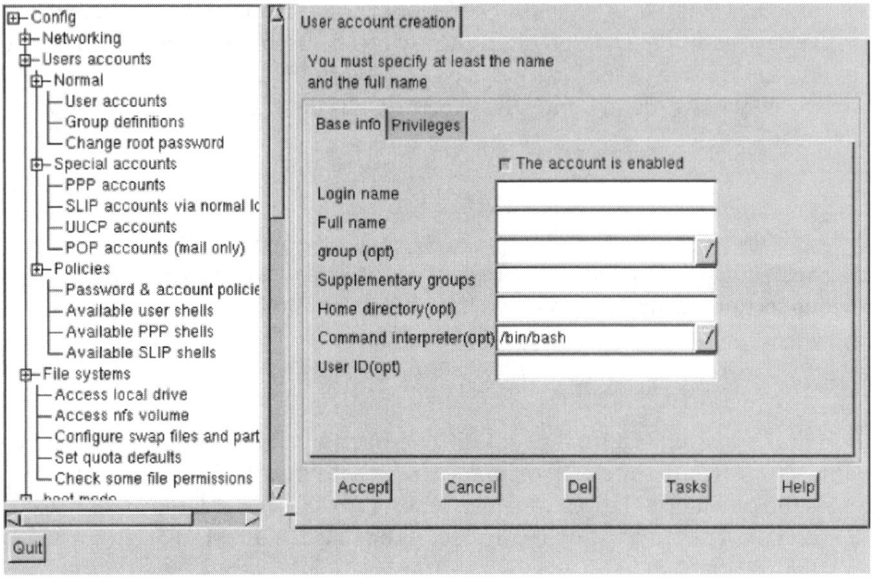

Figure 4.7 Linuxconf screen.

Lisa/COAS

Caldera's OpenLinux 1.3 distribution employs the Lisa system configuration tool, while Caldera's OpenLinux 2.2 distribution employs the COAS system configuration tool. Lisa and COAS are the only utilities offered in OpenLinux to add new user accounts. Focusing on the newer distribution, the following COAS menu items must be selected to add new accounts:

```
System -> Account -> Action -> Create User
```

As with linuxconf, the arrow (->) means select from the next level in the menu hierarchy. The COAS program also presents a series of requestor boxes asking for the same account information as described earlier. The screen shot in Figure 4.8 shows the requestor box that starts the create user account sequence.

```
Config -> User accounts -> Normal -> User accounts
```

It is easy for the user to become confused or disoriented about where he or she is within the menu hierarchy.

YaST

In SuSE, run YaST (it will ask for the superuser password if the user is logged in as a regular user). Then select:

```
System administration -> User administration
```

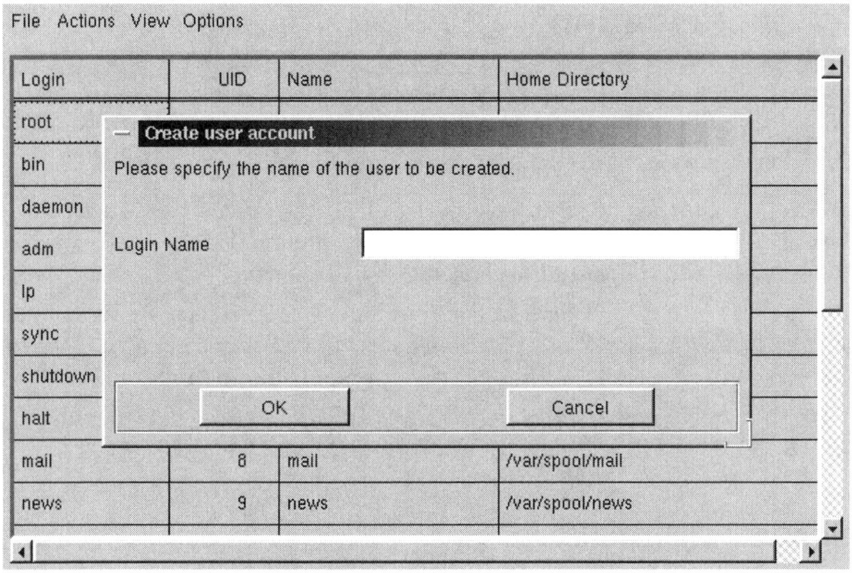

File Actions View Options

Login	UID	Name	Home Directory
root			
bin			
daemon			
adm			
lp			
sync			
shutdown			
halt			
mail	8	mail	/var/spool/mail
news	9	news	/var/spool/news

Create user account

Please specify the name of the user to be created.

Login Name

OK   Cancel

Figure 4.8 Creating an account.

A mask will appear. Enter the user account information into each field of the mask. Figure 4.9 is a screen shot of YaST user account creation.

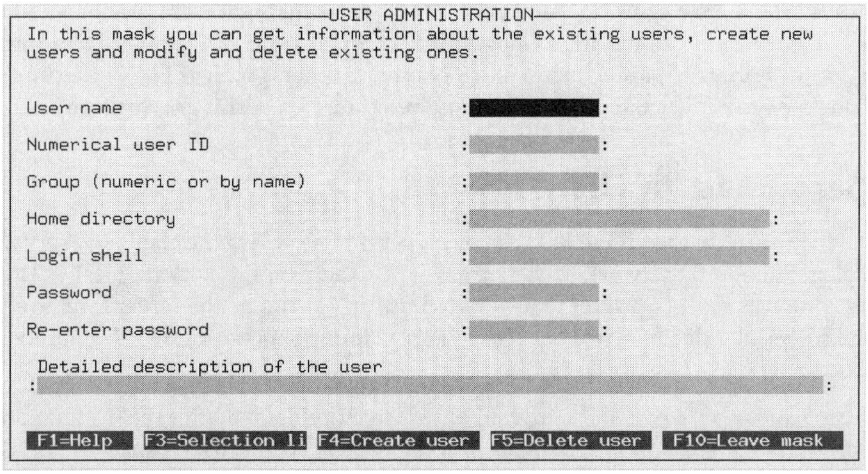

---USER ADMINISTRATION---

In this mask you can get information about the existing users, create new users and modify and delete existing ones.

User name   :   :
Numerical user ID   :   :
Group (numeric or by name)   :   :
Home directory   :   :
Login shell   :   :
Password   :   :
Re-enter password   :   :

 Detailed description of the user
:   :

F1=Help   F3=Selection li F4=Create user F5=Delete user   F10=Leave mask

Figure 4.9 User information.

Printer Configuration

Printers have two basic printing modes, text and graphic. How a printer or program handles these two modes determines what the final printed page looks like. In Linux, the mode is determined using the printcap file and printer filters.

Text mode. In text mode, the printer accepts ASCII characters and prints these characters using an internal font. The internal printer font is usually a fixed-width, Courier typeface that looks old-fashioned.

Graphic mode. When the printer is in graphic mode, it accepts separate commands and data that direct how each picture element (pixel) will be drawn. Today's word processors generally put the printer in graphic mode so that many typefaces can be printed anywhere on the page in many sizes. This strategy also allows graphic images to be included with the text.

Graphic-Mode Commands

Printer graphic-mode commands are generally unique to each printer manufacturer, and are sometimes unique within models from the same manufacturer. For example, one common set of graphic mode commands is Hewlett-Packard's PCL format that is used with its LaserJet family of printers.

The PostScript Printing Language

In an attempt to reduce compatibility problems among hundreds of different printers, each with their own graphic mode commands, Adobe Systems developed a mid-level language that interprets general commands and translates them into PCL or other graphic-mode formats. Most Linux applications generate test format or PostScript format files; therefore, Linux machines tend to be connected to PostScript printers.

However, there are a growing number of applications that will print graphic mode formats. The X Window application Ghostscript accepts various file formats, including PostScript, and prints a graphic mode file to popular printers (such as HP's PCL printers). Corel's WordPerfect and other office suite programs also print graphic formats.

lpd Server and lpr Client

Printing in Linux is based on the BSD client/server model, where the client and server are implemented with network sockets even when the printing is done locally. The client is known as the line-printer request program, or lpr, while the server is referred to as the line printer daemon, or lpd. The general printing process follows this outline:

1. The client lpr program reads the requested file(s) that are to be printed from the user's area and writes them to a spooling directory named after the destination printer, regardless of whether the printer is local to the user's machine or is located on a remote machine.

2. A control file, describing the files to be printed, is also written to the spooling directory by lpr. Then the client lpr program sends a notification message (through a Unix domain socket) to the lpd server and terminates.

3. The lpd server has been scheduled to run after receiving the notification message.

4. The lpd server begins by reading its configuration file and searching for valid printer directories that contain control files associated with the printer.

5. If the printer is local, the lpd server sends the optional header-identification page (specified in the control file) and the data file(s) to the printing device.

6. If the printer is remote, the server establishes a network connection with its peer lpd server on the remote host and sends the control and data files to the peer. The peer lpd server now processes the files in the same way the local lpd server would have.

There are at least two versions of lpd and lpr. Red Hat 5.2 and Slackware 3.6 use the older BSD-version, while Debian 2.1 and OpenLinux 1.3 use a newer LPRng package written by Patrick Powell. LPRng is backwardly compatible with the BSD version.

Configuring the Printer with Printtool and YaST

Red Hat provides a print system manager called printtool. SuSE also provides printer configuration with the YaST program. The printtool program is a GUI utility, while YaST runs as an ASCII-based program with cursor control. The Red Hat printtool program provides a series of pop-up menus that prompt the system administrator for the various printcap parameters. Although the printtool contains an option that suppresses job control headers, the option will not work for remote printer server entries. Both utilities prompt for the type of printer and options required by presenting a requestor box with empty fields, and the administrator must fill in the correct values. Figure 4.10 is a screen shot of Red Hat's printtool program.

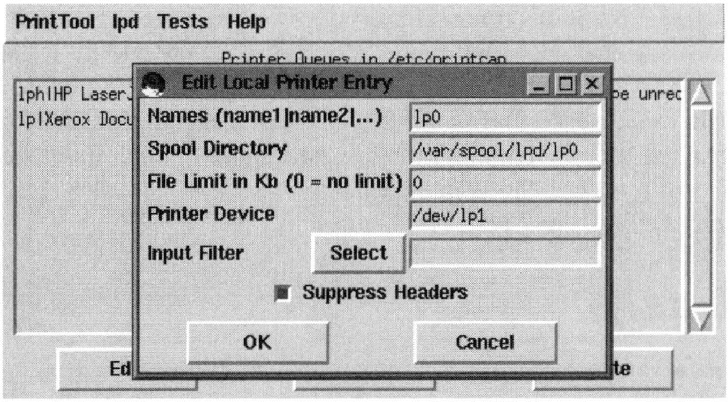

Figure 4.10 Editing printer entries.

The Printcap File

As noted in the previous section, the actions of the client and server provider programs are controlled almost exclusively by the /etc/printcap configuration file. The file is not usually configured in a new distribution, and as a result, system administrators often carry old printcap files to new systems for a template. Here are some typical entries in the /etc/printcap file:

```
lp1|Dot Matrix:\
    sd=/var/spool/lpd/lp1:mx#0:sh:lp=/dev/lp1:tr=\f:\
    if=/usr/lib/lpf:af=/var/spool/lpd/lp0/acct:lf=/var/log /lpd-errors:
lp2|OMNILab (Room 310) Dot Matrix Printer:\
    rm=cy.olemiss.edu:sd=/var/spool/lpd/omni:lf=/var/log/lpd-errors:
lp|lj|lj4|HP LaserJet 4 Plus (PostScript, and Graphic PCL) Printer:\
    rp=text:rm=lj4:sd=/var/spool/lpd/lp:lf=/var/log/lpd-errors:
ljps|HP LaserJet 4 Plus (PostScript) Printer:\
    rp=raw:rm=192.168.1.20:sd=/var/spool/lpd/lj4raw:\
    lf=/var/log/lpd-errors:
```

Reading a Printcap File

The printcap file describes the set of printers that can be reached from the current host. Each line describes a printer capability. The line begins with one or more labels for the printer. For example, the third printer can be called lp, lj, or lj4. Each field is delimited with the colon (:) character, and the backslash (/) character, followed by a new line indicating that the next line is to be joined with the previous line when the printcap file is read by the lpd.

Decoding the First Entry in the Example /etc/printcap File

The first line of the previous code describes lp1 as an ASCII printer. Its spool directory [sd] is /var/spool /lpd/lp1; it has no maximum paper quota: [mx#0]; the job control header page will be suppressed: [sh]; the printer is directly connected to the parallel printer port: [lp=/dev/lp1]; the printer needs a trailer: [tr] string, which is a form-feed character in this case, so that paper can be ripped off the printer. The [if] field says to invoke the input filter program lpf to paginate the output; the accounting filter [af] keeps track of who is printing and how much; and the [lf] directs error messages into the file /var/log/lpd-errors.

Decoding the Second Entry

The second entry describes lp2 as a printer connected to a remote machine with the name cy.olemiss.edu: [rm]. The spool directory is named after the printer as /var/spool/lpd/lp [sd], and error messages are to be placed in the log file /var/log/lpd-errors [lf].

Decoding the Third Entry

The third entry describes lp, lj, or lj4 as a stand-alone printer directly connected to the network, and the name of the remote machine [rm] is lj4 (this could be an IP address). The spool directory is also lj4, and error messages are to be placed in the file /var/ log/lpd-errors [lf]. The name lp is special in that if no printer is named in the lpr command, then the name lp is assumed.

Server Chaining

The remote machine field [rm] on one server may refer to a similar [rm] entry on another machine. In this way, servers may be chained to one another, allowing the print job to be passed from host to host through various gateways.

Decoding the Fourth Entry

The fourth entry is the same as the third, except that it specifies the remote printer [rp] name raw instead of texts. Use of this printer name is a signal to the stand-alone printer that the file contents are to be treated as PostScript and not as ASCII data. The HP LaserJet automatically detects most PostScript files, but some versions of Post-Script require explicit reference to the raw printer before they will print properly.

Some printcap entries, such as the suppress header [sh] command, only work for directly attached printers. If the print daemon is contained within the printer, such as an HP LaserJet, then this option will not work.

Filters in the Printcap File

Printer filters are generic programs that convert from one file format to another. Printer filters may be executed from a command line, from an application program, or from the printer capability file called printcap. A filter reads from the standard input, transforms the input based on an internal algorithm, and places the result on the standard output.

Printers usually require that ASCII or graphic information be converted to a printer-specific format before that print data is accepted. Hence, the role of Linux print filters is to:

- Convert standard OS formats
- Format unformatted text
- Convert OS, industry, or printer formats into a target printer-specific format

Example Print Filters

The **/usr/lib/lpf filter is designed for ASCII text reformatting.** For example, it converts the \n Unix EOL into the two characters \r\n MS-DOS EOL for a printer.

The **/usr/bin/nenscript filter reads ASCII files and converts the information to PostScript (which does not seem like much since most PostScript printers accept ASCII text directly).** However, nenscript will also reformat the ASCII text with a smaller font and with multiple columns that will fit two or more ASCII pages on one PostScript page.

The Ghostscript filter can convert ASCII to PostScript, and it also provides parameters that adapt to printer limitations. For example, if the RAM cannot be increased in the printer, the option −r150 may be added to the invocation of Ghostscript to set the resolution from the default 300dpi to 150dpi.

There are also devices called magic filters that convert format based on file content. One example is automatic detection of DVI format and subsequent conversion to PostScript. Other magic filters can convert DVI, or PostScript, to the printer's native graphic mode instructions, such as HP's PCL format.

The following example shows a printcap entry for the magic filter:

```
lp|lj|hplj4l|HP Laserjet 4L:\
    :lp=/dev/lp0:sd=/var/spool/lpd/hplj4l:\
    :sh:pw#80:pl#66:px#1440:mx#0:\
    :if=/etc/magicfilter/ljet4-filter:\
    :af=/var/log/lp-acct:lf=/var/log/lp-errs:
```

Printer Use and Commands

In Linux, the line printer is used to read all files that are requested for printing. There are several commands and utilities that can be used to augment this spooling mechanism.

lpr—Line Printer Request

To print a file, one would issue the lpr command with several arguments. A typical command is:

```
lpr -P laser -h -s filename.ps
```

In this example, the printer laser receives the lp program, rather than the default printer. The -h switch suppresses the job page, which contains the account and host name. The -s switch allows files larger than 1 MB to pass to the printer; it would create a symbolic link back to the user's copy when the BSD lpr program refuses to copy the large files into the printer spool area. However, in the newer version of the LPRng program, the -s switch is not necessary.

Following is an example script, plj, containing the following line to assist the user:

```
lpr -h -s -P laser $1
```

Now, the command plj filename.ps passes the file name to the lpr program with the correct arguments.

lpq–lprm–lpc

Linux offers several line printer utilities that allow both viewing and control of the spooling mechanism. By default, each of these commands, as well as lpr, assume the printer name lp. The -P switch can change the printer name to be viewed or controlled. Moreover, the lpr, lpq, and lprm programs test the shell variable PRINTER to see if it is defined, and if so, automatically switch to that printer. Be sure to use the following command to pass the shell variable on to new programs:

```
export PRINTER=laser
```

The lpq Command

The lpq command displays the default lp printer queue. For example:

```
Rank      Owner     Job     Files         Total Size
active    lenny     176     calendar       3834 bytes
1st       allison   177     report1       12334 bytes
1st       billy     178     test            38 bytes
```

The lprm Command

The command lprm -P laser removes all the queued print tasks for the current user. The command lprm -P laser 177 would remove the specific print task report1.

The lpc Command

The command /usr/sbin/lpc status laser reveals both the queue size for all users and the printer daemon status. For example:

```
hostname:~$ /usr/sbin/lpc status laser
 laser:
   queuing is enabled
   printing is enabled
   3 entries in spool area
   waiting for 192.168.1.20 to come up
```

The X Window System

The X Window system is made up of a series of modules that reside outside of the kernel and provide layers of increasing functionality that build into a complete GUI. Recently, there have been additions to the Linux kernel called frame buffers, which bring some of the X Window routines into the kernel to provide improved performance. The X Window system is equally accessible through the network as well as the system console. The term *X server* refers to the device driver module that communicates directly with the video adapter; therefore, the X server in a network configuration will be run on the client machine.

Five Components of the X Window GUI Architecture

Setting up the X Window system is the most demanding aspect of Linux configuration. The reason is that each module represents an independent component, and each component has its own configuration parameters.

X Server

The lowest-level component is the X server, which controls the hardware and puts the video adapter into graphics mode (in the same way that a printer is used in graphics mode). It also accepts logical commands from higher-level software, such as move the mouse cursor, and translates the commands into a series of I/O operations on the video adapter.

Display Manager

The second component is the X Window display manager, or xdm. It configures an environment and sets up a graphical login screen. The screen can be plain, show system log messages, have animated graphics, or show system status. Upon successful login, xdm launches the window manager. However, some parameters specified in the xdm initialization file have higher priority than those specified in the window manager initialization files.

Widgets

The third component in the X11 system is the widgets, or desktop environments. These library routines build and form the components within a window, such as scroll bars, menu bars, task bars, pop-up menus, and requestor boxes. Examples include LessTif, GTK+ (GNOME tool kit), and Qt.

Window Manager

The fourth component is the window manager, or desktop, which provides a graphical look and feel. There are 10 or more possible window managers from which to select, but most users will accept the default desktop, or in some cases choose from among a few that are offered in the default installation. The main window managers are After-Step, KDE, Window Maker, FVWM, Enlightenment, and Blackbox.

Themes are the highly visible styles of the newer window managers. *Style* refers to the number of colors supported and the artistic quality of bit-mapped graphics for window frames, title bars, icons, wallpaper, and background.

Applications

The fifth type of component is made up of the applications that run within the desktop environment. Even though they each have their own configuration (initialization) files, most applications can run under any window manager.

Although much effort has gone into the development of window managers, there is always room to improve upon the styles and designs. Added development of cut-and-paste facilities, typefaces, and fonts could help improve window manger performance.

Network Access

The X Window system allows local access and remote access via the network. To permit access by another user to the original user's workstation, allow the connection only from the specified host. Then set the DISPLAY shell variable to the local host address on the remote machine and launch the X11 system on the remote machine with the `startx` command. The X11 system will then connect with the local machine's X server and begin an X Window session on the remote machine.

X servers are also available for MS-Windows machines in the form of X32 servers. These MS-Windows-based servers provide an identical look and feel as being directly attached to an X11 console on the remote machine.

Configuring the X Window System

Since the X Window system consists of several components, it is difficult to configure. Configuration files and utilities can offer the needed assistance for this process.

Location of X11 Configuration Files

Currently, there is not a traditional home directory for the X Window system, and directory contents tend to change from one installation to another. Linux distributions have helped to stabilize file positions, and Linux's effort to create a file system hierarchy standard (FHS) has also helped. With this in mind, the X Window files will be similar to the following:

/etc/X11. The FHS location for X Window configuration programs and symbolic link to the X server (named X).

/etc/X11/XF86Config. The X server configuration file. Alternative locations of this file can be found at:

```
/user/X11R6/etc/X11/ <cmdline>
/etc/X11/<cmdline>
/etc/X11/$XF86CONFIG
```

```
/usr/X11R6/etc/X11/$XF86CONFIG
/etc/X11/XF86Config-4
/etc/XF86Config
/usr/X11R6/etc/X11/XF86Config.<hostname>
/usr/X11R6/etc/X11/XF86Config-4
/usr/X11R6/etc/X11/XF86Config
/usr/X11R6/lib/X11/XF86Config.<hostname>
/usr/X11R6/lib/X11/XF86Config-4
/usr/X11R6/lib/X11/XF86Config
```

where <cmdline> is a relative path specified with the –xf86config command line option, $XF86CONFIG is the relative path specified by that environment variable, and <hostname> is the machine's hostname.

/usr/X11R6/bin. Contains X Window servers, setup utilities, one or more display managers, some window managers, and some common application programs. Here, the X server file, X, is again symbolically linked to one of the X servers having the general name format of XF86_XXX, where XXX is VGA16 or SVGA.

/usr/X11R6/bin/xdm. An X display manager for graphical logins.

/usr/X11R6/bin/fvwm95. An X Window manager.

/usr/X11R6/bin/afterstep. An X desktop manager.

/usr/X11R6/lib. Contains the X Window run-time libraries.

/usr/X11R6/lib/X11. Contains the X Window configuration files for some window managers and older applications.

/usr/local/X11R6/; /var/X11R6/; /opt/X11R6/. These three files contain alternative window managers with configuration files.

To discover where other installation-specific X11-related files are located in the file system, use the command locate X11.

X Server Configuration File Format

The X server configuration file, /etc/X11/XF86Config, provides extra details to the X server on how to configure the video adapter, mouse, and keyboard. Even though the X server can obtain many of the parameters by probing the video adapter at run time, parameters in the configuration file are given precedence, since they may have to override one chip feature in order to obtain a second feature. Variation in system load is another reason for the precedence of the configuration file parameters over run-time discovery. In this way, critical timing values can be fixed for the video adapter in spite of system load variations.

Each section of the XF86Config file is delimited with the key words *Section name* and *EndSection*. The more common XF86Config sections are:

Section Files. Contains file names of color values to be used, and the location of specified fonts.

Section ServerFlags. Enables or disables X server run-time flags generated from the keyboard, such as DontZap (terminate) the X server and DontZoom.

Section Keyboard. Enables or disables X server run-time key binding for non-ASCII key binding, such as LeftAlt mapping and AutoRepeat delay.

Section Pointer. Lists the mouse protocol (PS/2, MouseSystems, etc.), baud of the serial mouse (if any), and a three-button emulation option for two-button mice.

Section Monitor. Lists the monitor's horizontal and vertical frequency ranges and the wave shape for a given dot-clock frequency. These settings require detailed knowledge of the monitor's ability, or one will risk causing the raster-scan circuit to fail. They also control the refresh frequency, which many users prefer to adjust upward.

Section Device. Lists the possible dot-clock frequencies for graphic modes and video adapter specific hardware settings. These settings also require detailed knowledge of the monitor's ability, or one will risk causing serious damage.

Section Screen. Lists possible graphic modes allowed, virtual display size, and initial viewport into the desktop.

Section Xinput. Gives configuration of extended input devices, such as joysticks and graphic tablets.

The X Server Configuration Programs

The X server is responsible for controlling the hardware registers within the video controller chip. Consequently, an X server must be selected for use based on the type of video adapter present in the machine. Technically, X is symbolically linked to the XF86_VGA16 server that will work with any video card, but it is only for the lowest common denominator hardware-compatible graphic mode (640 × 480 pixels with 16 colors). The results of the XF86_VGA16 server are unacceptable when compared to a custom-configured X server that is designed for the video adapter's advanced features.

The name of the X server is X, and it is usually located in /etc/X11/X or /usr/X11R6/bin/X. The first task is to discover which XF86_XXX server needs to be linked to the name X, which can be done with the following steps:

1. Use the /usr/X11R6/bin/SuperProbe utility to identify the correct server for the video adapter, and then link the X file name to that server. Or, manually identify the manufacturer and the video controller chip type.

2. Copy the XF86Config.eg example file to XF86Config and build a custom version of the /usr/X11R6/lib/X11/XF86Config file. Even after the file has been created by one of the utilities listed in the next section, it is not uncommon to re-edit this ASCII file for fine-tuning. Also, the configuration utilities do not support the extended input devices such as joysticks and graphic tablets, and these items must be entered with an editor.

3. Use one of the interactive configuration utilities—xf86config, XF86Setup, Xconfigurator (found in the Red Hat distribution), and SaX (found in the SuSE distribution)—to interactively build the XF86Config file.

The xf86config Utility

The xf86config utility (note the lowercase x and c) is the default ASCII command-line utility for configuring the system. It is interactive, prompting the user for responses with detailed screens full of text to be read. Also, this is typically the only configuration utility that reads the /usr/X11R6/lib/X11/Cards database, where other utilities may perform this function with an internal list. Therefore, xf86config listing of available X servers may be more up to date than the lists displayed in the XF86Setup configuration program.

The xf86config utility also directs the user to read the /usr/X11R6/lib/X11/Monitors database file. Upon discovering the proper entries in the Monitors file, the user is encouraged to copy them into the XF86Config file. Note that these refresh rates are optimized for a particular monitor, and some general classification is provided by the other XF86Setup utility.

The xf86config and XF86Setup utilities cover the same configuration topics, so these topics will be presented using the generally preferred XF86Setup utility. In time, all the configuration utilities will read from the same database to determine the correct adapter and monitor settings.

The XF86Setup Utility

The XF86Setup utility (note the uppercase X and S) employs the XF86_VGA16 X server to create a minimal graphic interface in order to configure a more sophisticated X server. The utility begins with an XFree86 splash panel and a menu bar along the top of the screen containing six options: Mouse, Keyboard, Card, Monitor, Modeselection, and Other. The GUI may be navigated with a mouse or the keyboard. If the mouse has not been properly configured, then press TAB to move the cursor from button to button. After tabbing into a menu, use ARROW to move the highlight among menu items. Pressing ENTER selects the current button or current menu item.

Mouse. Generally, there are two types of mouse protocols: Microsoft two-button protocol and MouseSystems three-button protocol. Furthermore, there are two types of mouse interfaces: the IBM PS/2 interface, or /dev/psaux, and the serial port, /dev/ttyS0. If the Microsoft two-button mouse protocol is selected, the Emulate3Buttons-option should also be selected, since the third (or middle) button is used for paste in the X11 copy-and-paste operation.

Some mice can operate with either protocol. To switch the mouse protocol, flip the mouse over and look for a switch. It will be labeled MS and PC. MS means Microsoft two-button protocol, and PC means MouseSystems three-button protocol. Also, newer Microsoft mice have a third windows scroll button. These mice may have a switch labeled 2 and 3. The 2 refers to the two-button protocol; the 3 refers to the same protocol, but includes a third button. The X server automatically accepts this alternative third button within the two-button protocol, and scroll becomes the third button.

Keyboard. The X Window system has complete control over the keyboard and the bindings of the keys to functions. The default settings are appropriate for most installations.

Card. When an X server supports multiple families (as with the SVGA server), the chipset menu provides a selection from which to choose. It is not uncommon for probe routines to miss more options than they find. Therefore, if other parameters (such as the amount of video memory) are known for the video adapter, select the values as opposed to selecting probe.

Monitor. The monitor menu displays 10 types of monitor categories, each with different frequency capabilities. Select the horizontal and vertical frequencies that are less than or equal to the monitor. Do not select frequencies that exceed the monitor specifications.

Modeselection. The XF86Setup utility presents a column of possible graphic modes ranging from 320×240 up to 1600×1200 pixels. There are also four color depth buttons ranging from one byte per pixel to four bytes per pixel.

For a 17-inch monitor, typical graphic modes selected are 800×600 and 1024×768 at two bytes per pixel. When two or more graphic modes are selected, the XFree86 servers will switch up and down the list of selected graphic modes with CTRL-ALT-NUM + and CTRL-ALT-NUM –. In this way, the user can select the most comfortable viewing image.

Other. This menu allows the enabling of some of the ServerFlags mentioned in the previous section. The two key flags are (1) allowing the X server to be terminated with CTRL-ALT-BACKSPACE, and (2) allowing graphic mode switching with CTRL-ALT-NUM + and CTRL-ALT-NUM –.

To complete the XF86Setup process, activate the `Done` button at the bottom of the screen. This will overwrite the old `XF86Config` file with a new version. Again, please note that extended input devices, such as joysticks and graphic tablets, cannot be configured with these utilities and must be manually entered into the `XF86Config` file. Figure 4.11 is a screen shot of the Xfree86 setup screen.

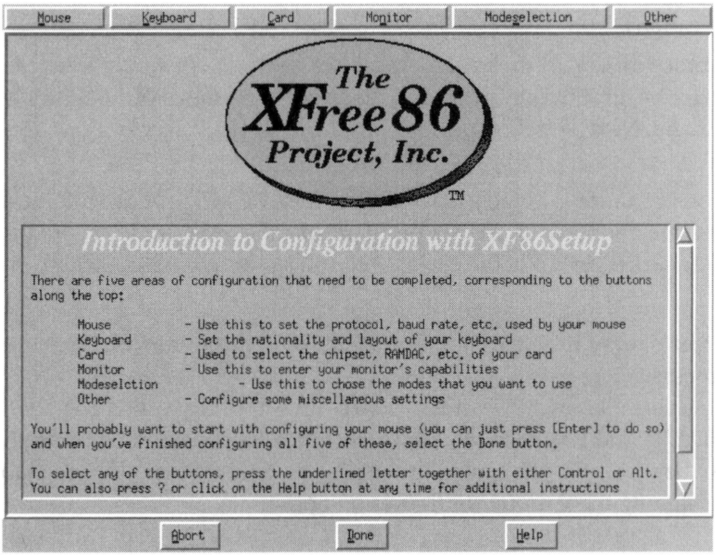

Figure 4.11   Xfree86 setup screen.

The Xconfigurator

Since Red Hat Software developed the Xconfigurator and mouseconfig utilities, they are generally not found in non-Red Hat distributions. Unlike the XFree86 GPL utilities described earlier, the Xconfigurator does not perform mouse configuration. Instead, it assumes that the mouse is already properly configured and uses existing mouse configuration to fill in the Pointer section of the XF86Config file. For this reason, if the mouse is changed, the Xconfigurator utility must be run again to reconfigure the Pointer section.

Remember that Xconfigurator overwrites the XF86Config file without first obtaining user permission. Consequently, if simply experimenting with other possible configurations, keep a backup copy of the XF86Config file.

The Xconfigurator utility employs the typical color-attributed ASCII screens used by many distributions in the install process, and it has the following steps:

1. The Xconfigurator utility begins with a screen announcing that it will edit the XF86Config file, and offers to use the existing file as a starting point. This is a plus if other options have already been configured that are not done by the Xconfigurator program.

2. It lists the /usr/X11R6/lib/X11/Cards database and allows a video adapter to be selected.

3. It lists the /usr/X11R6/lib/X11/Monitors database and allows a monitor to be selected. There are many more types of monitors than are available in the database; consequently, there is a good chance that a particular monitor will not be listed. If so, the custom monitor entry that takes the user to the same screen as the other X11 configuration utilities can be chosen.

4. On the custom monitor screen, the basic frequency capabilities of monitors are listed. Remember, select horizontal and vertical frequencies that are less than or equal to the capabilities of the monitor. Do not select frequencies that exceed the monitor specifications.

   The Xconfigurator will ask to probe the card; once again, it is usually better to select don't probe, and to select the amount of video memory present on the card from the menu. Next, select no clock chip and let the X server figure this out at run time.

5. Finally, select one or more graphic modes to use; then Xconfigurator will automatically overwrite the XF86Config file. If a mistake was made, copy the backup file made earlier on top of the bad XF86Config file and restart the Xconfigurator utility.

Figure 4.12 is a screen shot of the Xconfigurator utility presenting the first screen of the monitor setup process.

Version 6.1 SuSE employs its own X Window configuration utility called SaX. SaX appears to be user friendly and less prone to errors than the other X Window configuration utilities. As can be seen from the screen shot in Figure 4.13, SaX employs the tab metaphor to navigate among the various configuration options.

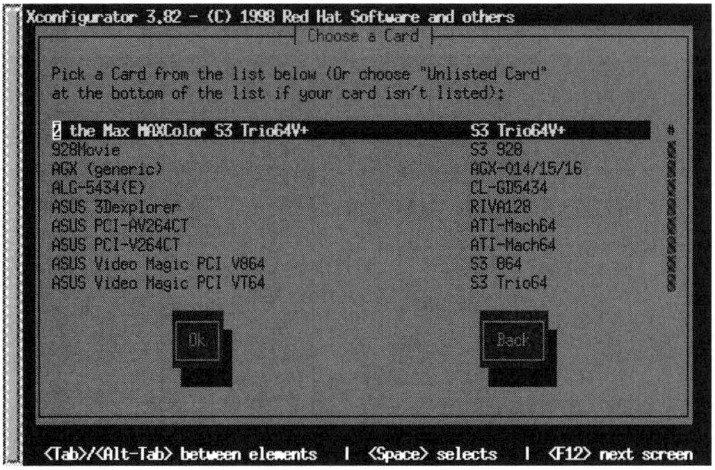

Figure 4.12 The Xconfigurator utility.

After the configuration is completed, SaX provides options to save or readjust settings. If an error occurs during configuration, selecting Reset will return the screen to its previous settings, as though SaX had not been used.

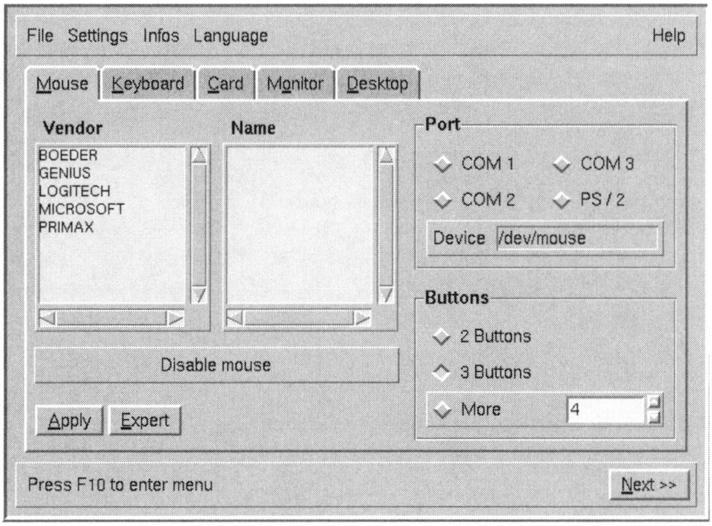

Figure 4.13 SaX configurator.

Applications

Objectives

- Find documentation and use help commands.
- Describe Netscape, FTP, Telnet, and mail functions.
- Contrast WYSIWYG with mark-up word processing.
- Contrast ApplixWare, WordPerfect, and StarOffice.
- Contrast GIMP, xfig, and ImagGathering Information.

Sources of Online Documentation

The Linux and GNU operating system is highly complex; the current distributions are the product of a decade of development by a multitude of contributors worldwide. It is impossible to retain a working knowledge of the vast array of commands, utilities, and applications that compose the systems. Instead, online documentation can assist in using unfamiliar or infrequently used commands. Following is a list of utilities to help the user access information. Each will be discussed separately.

```
-help, -h, or -?
man
```

```
locate
find
info
xman, xinfo, and tkman
```

Command-Line Help Switches

The first step in obtaining information concerning commands, switches, and utilities is to query the program directly using the switches -help, -h, or -?. In response, the program will display a list of required arguments, and optional arguments enclosed in square brackets [ ]. For example, to find out more about the locate utility, type:

```
$ locate
--help Usage:  locate [--d path] [--database=path]
[--version]  [--help]  pattern...
```

The program will list its acceptable arguments following the Usage: banner. Generally, all programs are expected to provide the Usage: banner in response to the -help switch, to wrong arguments, or to incomplete arguments. Also, some commands list more than an entire screen of options, and the output must be directed to a pager, such as less. For example:

```
$ ls -help | less
Usage: ls [OPTION]... [FILE]...
List information about the FILEs (the current directory by default).
Sort entries alphabetically if none of -cftuSUX nor -sort.
 -a, -all do not hide entries starting with . . .
```

Some commands, such as cd, are internal to the shell. Typing cd --help to bash, will result in the shell responding --help is an illegal option (or another complaint, depending on which shell is used).

The --help listings may be too brief for those who have no previous experience with this command; these users may prefer to read the man pages.

man

Although the GNU organization tends to favor the info utility, the man command is the fastest way to get more information on another command or utility. The Linux manual pages are almost identical to the manual pages that appeared in Version 6 Unix, and they narrowly address the characteristics of a given program; however, they do not address the interaction of the program with the rest of the system. Currently, no online documentation exists that provides information related to whole-program interactions. For example, the man pages have sections titled (1) User Commands, (2) System Calls, (3) Subroutines, (4) Devices, (5) File Formats, (6) Games, (7) Misc, (8) System Administration, and (9) New; yet, there is no man switch that shows the table of contents. However, to see the file names of the man pages, go to the /usr/doc/man? directories.

Common Usage of man: Topic Search

When searching for information, enter the man command with the keyword switch -k and the topic entered:

```
$ man -k topic
```

The man command searches each of its sections, comparing the keyword to the title of each man page. However, it does not search the body of each page, and subsequently, the search results are not complete.

Using the man Command More Specifically

One method of seeing program interactions is to examine the format specification of the various initialization and control files. These specifications are found in section (5) File Formats. Much of this information goes unused, since the man -k topic command only checks the title of the file, and users rarely enter the exact file name as a topic. To see how programs interact with each other, use the name of the control file and specify the format section of the manual pages with a command such as:

```
$ man 5 passwd
```

The resulting man page will describe each field of the password file in detail, and list all the programs that use the control file to carry out their various activities.

Two related commands are the apropos command, which is the same as the man -k command, and the whatis command, which displays the title of the manual page.

locate

The locate command does not provide access to documentation; however, it can be used to reveal the file system layout, the types of configuration files employed in the system, and the available programs.

The locate utility is fast, easy to use, and is among the first steps to take when searching for more information about a file, command, or utility. The locate program searches the complete file system and reports any entry (directory name, file name, or device name) that matches the substring specified as an argument to the locate command. For example, to discover more about the X11 system, enter the command:

```
locate X11 | more
```

The more pager is invoked since there will be many directory entries found that have the substring X11. Scanning the output reveals where all the X11 directories are located, as well as the X programs and document files available.

Rapid Searching with locate

The locate command is fast because it searches a database of directory and file names rather than asking the file manager to sequentially step through all the file system inodes looking for the file name. By avoiding the network and the remote file manager, `locate` does not load the NFS.

   `Locate` does have certain drawbacks. For example, if files or directories have been recently added but the database has not been updated, search results using `locate` may be incomplete. To find these recent files, run the `update` utility before using the `locate` program.

find

The `find` utility is similar to `locate`, but it is slower. It also differs from `locate` in that it thoroughly searches out every branch of the directory hierarchy, and provides additional options. Two of the most commonly used options are the searches to find files relative to the creation, access, or modification time of another file, and the searches to run additional commands upon discovery of the search target. Because of this flexibility, `find` requires a number of arguments. For example, the command:

```
$ find / -name "*log*" -print
```

directs the utility to begin searching at the root directory / for any file or directory `-name` containing the `log` string or having the `log` substring embedded within the name. The quotation marks are required to pass the wild card asterisk (*) characters on to the `find` program without shell interpretation. Finally, the `-print` argument directs the `find` program to display the results of its search. Newer versions of `find` do not require the `-print` switch, and display the results by default.

info

The GNU `info` utility provides an ASCII-based hierarchical view of revised man pages. Begin at the root of the hierarchy tree by typing `info`. Programs are arranged by seven usage areas: Development, Miscellaneous, Administration, Console Utilities, Document Preparation, Games, and General Commands. Individual manual pages are accessed by positioning the cursor on top of the program name and pressing ENTER. Subcategories within the command depend upon how the author arranged the material, and they vary depending upon the type of program being described. In general, `info` documents tend to be more helpful than the old man pages; they have a more general approach than the man pages and offer information on the ways in which one program interacts with others. However, the `info` project is incomplete and there are more man pages than `info` pages. Also, new GPLed software tends to contain a man page and not an `info` page.

Xman

There are X versions of both the man and `info` pages. Generally, the X11 versions work in the same way as the ASCII versions. One exception is that the `Xman` utility provides a table of contents for each section and allows the user to select the file name to access the manual page.

Xinfo

The `Xinfo` utility provides additional menu bar buttons at the top of the window, but the positions of the buttons change as the program moves from level to level. Always check the menu bar to see if the desired button has changed position before clicking what might be the wrong button.

tkman

The X11 utility, `tkman`, offers a true GUI front-end to the man pages. Its main improvement is the use of regular expressions in searches; however, `tkman` will not search the body of man pages. The `tkman` utility also offers ease-of-use features, such as custom configuration, history list, and hyperlinks among man pages.

Online Information Access

Online information refers to the many Linux information repositories around the world, including Linux news, and to Internet search engines. A few examples of Linux repositories are listed in the following section, and the course CD has a copy of these repositories for high-speed offline reference.

Linux Repositories

The Linux Documentation Project (LDP) can be found at http://metalab.unc .edu/LDP. The LDP provides links to a wealth of Linux documentation, including:

HOWTOs: http://metalab.unc.edu/mdw/HOWTO/HOWTO-INDEX-3.html.

FAQs: http://metalab.unc.edu/mdw/FAQ/.

Online books: http://metalab.unc.edu/LDP.

The main Linux Web pages http://linux.org and http://linux.com are well-organized sites designed for basic information on Linux, and for users to keep up on news.

There are some Linux sites that only offer information through links to other sites. Two examples of these sites are Linux Links www.linuxlinks.com/ and Gary's Linux Encyclopedia http://members.aa.net/~swear/pedia/.

Linux News

Following are a few of the many Linux news sites and newsgroups:

Linux Today (http://linuxtoday.com/). A listing of news wire reports in the business community concerning Linux events.

Linux Weekly News (www.lwn.net/). Selects and provides a summary of Linux news events for the week.

Slash Dot (http://slashdot.org/). Selects from submissions of Linux-related news stories.

Fresh Meat (http://freshmeat.net/). Accepts submissions of latest software available for Linux.

Linux Games (www.linuxgames.com/). Accepts submissions of the latest games developed for Linux.

Newsgroups are traditionally accessed via a news reader, but the news reader must be configured to read from a news feed. News feeds are high-volume traffic sites that accept over 3 GB of data per day. If properly configured, a news reader can provide access to the Linux newsgroups. Simply select the entry point `comp.os.linux.x`, where x is one of 10 subgroups.

Internet Search Engines

Internet search engines are all helpful in finding Linux-related information. Based on experience, these search engines have the following qualities:

Yahoo! (http://yahoo.com/). Best results with a vague query. Yahoo! provides possible categories to follow and refine the search term(s).

HotBot (http://hotbot.com/). Best results with a set of general unrelated terms. HotBot is generally thought to reference the largest number of pages.

AltaVista (http://altavista.com/). Best results with a specific SQL formatted set of terms. AltaVista does a good job of finding specific pages, but it tends to bring up excess amounts of unrelated material.

Deja (www.deja.com/ [formerly DejaNews]). Provides access to old Usenet postings where a solution to a problem may have been posted. The key to finding this information is to search as if asking a specific question of a co-worker who might know the answer.

Deja will also provide access to the Linux newsgroups. To find the following sample groups, simply enter the newsgroup name as a search string and click the Search button: `comp.os.linux.advocacy`, `comp.os.linux.hardware`, `comp.os.linux.m68k`, `comp.os.linux.misc`, `comp.os.linux.networking`, `comp.os.linux.powerpc`, `comp.os.linux.setup`, or `comp.os.linux.x`.

There is evidence that one search engine can only index about 35 percent of the entire Internet. An exhaustive search, therefore, requires combining the results from at least three search engines, regardless of their characteristics.

Network Applications

Network applications allow users to access and navigate through hypertext documents on local or remote hosts, to transfer files from one location to another, and to remotely login to another computer.

Browser Software

Netscape Communicator is a package of three different communication tools. Each is discussed in the following sections.

Netscape Navigator

The main component of the Netscape Communicator is the Netscape Navigator WWW browser. Netscape has provided a Linux version of this popular browser from the beginning. Netscape's 4.x series browsers are compatible with all of the latest HTML and Java standards, and match up to Microsoft's Internet Explorer.

Netscape Messenger

The next component of the Communicator suite of applications is the e-mail management program. Netscape Messenger, as it is termed, is a solidly built e-mail client. It supports all the latest HTML encapsulated e-mail, as well as POP 3 and IMAP servers. The Messenger's filtering feature is helpful for those who find their mailboxes swamped with messages. Filters find messages based on certain user-specified criteria, and delete, move, or mark them as indicated. This feature can save time when a user receives hundreds of e-mails daily. Along with the Messenger part of Communicator comes the Newsgroup reader. Any Linux enthusiast will quickly learn that knowing how to navigate the newsgroups for troubleshooting information is essential. Messenger uses a tree-structured layout to easily view all of the user's subscribed newsgroups. Figure 5.1 is a screen shot of the Netscape mail application.

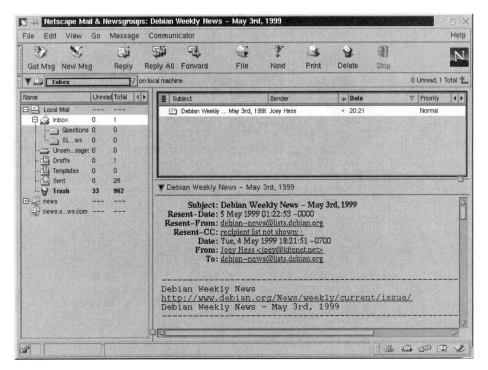

Figure 5.1 Netscape Mail.

Netscape Composer

The final component of the Communicator suite is the new Netscape Composer. Composer is an HTML authoring tool that can compete with other shareware and freeware authoring tools. This tool still leaves many features to be desired, but is a good start for the HTML novice.

FTP Clients

There are many FTP programs for Linux, ranging from the command-line versions, such as ftp, lftp, and ncftp, to full GUI versions, such as gFTP. Many of them support command completion, recursive file retrieval, and simultaneous multiple sessions. As with any of a multitude of X Window programs, the FTP program selected by a user is a matter of personal preference. Figure 5.2 shows an Active FTP screen.

Telnet

The telnet command is used to establish a terminal session with another host using the Telnet protocol.

Mail Clients

There are many e-mail clients for Linux. They range from the command-line type to the X Window GUI-style. Two of the more common command-line mail programs are elm

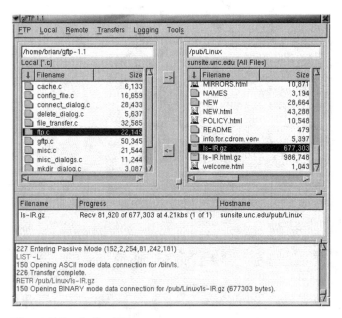

Figure 5.2 Active FTP screen.

and `pine`. Pine, developed at the University of Washington, is more feature-rich than `elm`, and offers many of the features often associated only in GUI-style mail clients. There is a multitude of GUI-style clients available. As with the FTP clients, selection is based on personal preference.

Document Processing Programs

WordPerfect and StarOffice are the two main processing programs that support Linux.

WordPerfect

Corel has supported Linux, beginning with version 7 of its popular word processor, WordPerfect. Most recently, Corel released its version 8 WordPerfect for Linux free of charge. A personal-use copy can be downloaded from http://linux.corel. com. For multi-user versions of the software, or documentation and support, the full, retail version must be purchased. Corel has plans to port its entire office suite to Linux.

The Linux version of Corel's WordPerfect software is shown in Figure 5.3.

StarOffice Suite

StarOffice 5.0 is a fully integrated, Microsoft Office-compatible suite of productivity applications. It provides Web-enabled word processing, spreadsheet, presentation graphics, e-mail, news, charting, and graphics applications. StarOffice runs native on

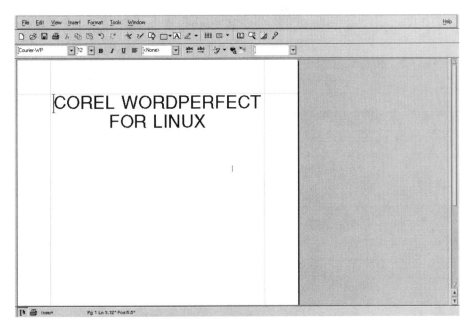

Figure 5.3 Corel's WordPerfect.

the Linux Operating Environment on Intel platforms and is also available for other operating systems. Users can access existing Microsoft Office files and data to create spreadsheets, presentations, and word processing documents. All data may be saved in Microsoft formats or as HTML files to post on the Web or newsgroup servers. StarOffice bridges the gap between Word for Windows and the Linux environment.

Figure 5.4 is an example of the basic StarOffice screen running on a Linux OS.

Text Processing Programs

Text processing includes both spelling correction and text creation.

Ispell

`Ispell` is fashioned after the spell program found on the old Digital DEC System 10 computers (see Figure 5.5). The most common usage is `ispell filename`. In this case, `ispell` will display each word that does not appear in the dictionary at the top of the screen and allow the user to change it. If there are near misses in the dictionary (words that differ by only a single letter, a missing or extra letter, a pair of transposed letters, or a missing space or hyphen), they are also displayed on following lines. `ispell` may also display other guesses at ways to make the word from a known root; each guess is preceded by question marks. Finally, the line containing the word and the previous line are printed at the bottom of the screen. If the terminal can display in reverse video, the word itself is highlighted.

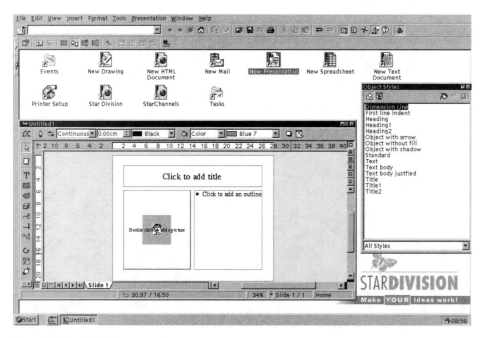

Figure 5.4 StarOffice sample.

Figure 5.5 Ispell.

Two Basic Program Design Philosophies

As part of its Unix heritage, Linux provides a long line of typesetting, or mark-up languages (i.e., nroff, groff, TEX, LATEX, and HTML). In these word processing schemes, text creation and display are two separate processes. During the text creation phase, the user writes the information in a plaintext file and directs how the text is to be displayed by embedding text-based formatting commands to be used by the subsequent display processor. During the text display phase, the display processor interprets the embedded commands in order to lay out the text. However, the typical PC user employs a *What You See Is What You Get* (WYSIWYG) word processor, where the text is displayed as it is entered. To accomplish this, the WYSIWYG word processor must embed nonprinting binary information into the text file.

The Difference in Methods

This distinction reflects a fundamental design issue for Unix (Linux) users, since Unix is predicated on employing all of its utilities (support programs) for processing text files. Embedding binary information into the text file allows only one program, the word processor that created it, to access the text.

A user who moves between the PC and Unix environments must be aware of this distinction and use the various programs accordingly. For example, a user familiar with Microsoft Word or Corel's WordPerfect may continue to work in the same WYSIWYG environment on Linux, but if files are to be used elsewhere in the system, they must be exported as text files.

Mark-up Text Advantages

Both designs achieve the same end, but a mark-up design offers advantages that a WYSIWYG design does not. Mark-up text can be created with any number of editors; text files can be easily processed by other applications; and mark-up actually provides more control over the display than the set of functions provided inside a given WYSIWYG word processor. This process is similar to the transition that experienced users have when they migrate from mouse action to keyboard shortcut keys to quicken their interaction with the machine.

Graphics Tools

GIMP and Xfig are the two main graphics tools used in Linux. Both are freely distributed and easily available.

GIMP

The GNU Image Manipulation Program (GIMP) was inspired by the popular MAC and PC-based program called Photoshop. GIMP is freely distributed software for tasks such as photo retouching, image composition, and image authoring. GIMP can be used as a simple paint program, an expert-quality photo-retouching program, an online batch-processing system, a mass-production image renderer, and an image format converter. Furthermore, GIMP is expandable and extendable, meaning it can be augmented with plug-ins and extensions to perform virtually any task. The advanced scripting interface allows everything from the simplest task to the most complex image manipulation procedures to be easily scripted.

GIMP features include:

- A full suite of painting tools, including Brush, Pencil, Airbrush, and Clone, to name a few.
- Tile-based memory management; image size is limited only by available disk space.
- Subpixel sampling for all paint tools for high-quality anti-aliasing.
- Full alpha channel support of layers and channels.
- A procedural database for calling internal GIMP functions from external programs, as in Script-fu.
- Advanced scripting capabilities.
- Multiple Undo/Redo (limited only by disk space).
- Virtually unlimited number of images open at one time.
- Extremely powerful gradient-editor and blend tool.
- Load and save animations in a convenient frame-as-layer format.
- Transformation tools, including rotate, scale, shear, and flip.

- File formats supported include gif, jpg, png, xpm, tiff, tga, mpeg, ps, pdf, pcx, bmp, and many others.
- Load, display, convert, save to many file formats.
- Selection tools, including rectangle, ellipse, free, fuzzy, bezier and intelligent.
- Plug-ins that allow for the easy addition of new file formats and new effects filters.
- More than 100 plug-ins available.
- Supports custom brushes and patterns.

For a view of GIMP, see Figure 5.6.

Xfig

Xfig is an interactive drawing tool that runs under the X Window system on most Unix-compatible platforms. It is freeware and available via anonymous FTP.

In Xfig, users can draw figures using objects such as circles, boxes, lines, spline curves, and texts. It is also possible to import images in various formats such as gif, jpeg, and epsf (PostScript). Objects can be created, deleted, moved, or modified; attributes, such as colors and line styles, can be selected from various options. For text, various fonts are available.

An example Xfig screen is shown in Figure 5.7.

Xfig saves figures in its native format, Fig format, but they may be converted into various formats, such as PostScript, gif, jpeg, and hp-gl. Xfig has a facility to print figures to a PostScript printer as well.

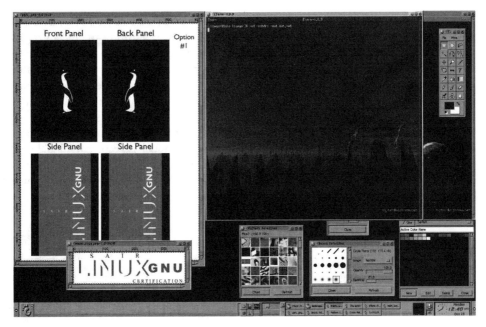

Figure 5.6   GIMP editor.

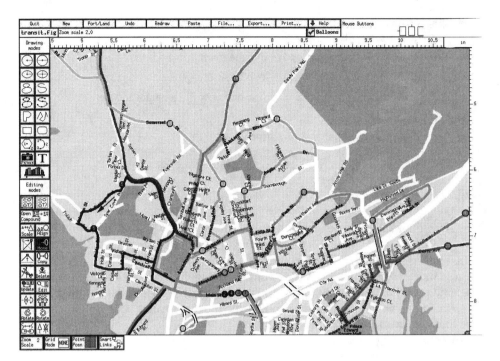

Figure 5.7   Layout of Xfig.

Some applications can produce output in the Fig format. For example, Xfig does not have a facility to create graphs, but tools such as gnuplot or xgraph can create graphs and output them in Fig format. Even if a user's favorite application cannot generate output for Xfig, tools such as pstoedit or hp2xx may allow him or her to read and edit those figures with Xfig. If the user wants to import images into the figure but does not need to edit the image itself, it is also possible to import images in formats such as gif, jpeg, or epsf (PostScript).

Most operations are performed using the mouse, but some operations may be performed using keyboard shortcuts. Use of a three-button mouse is recommended, but it is also possible to use a two-button mouse (if the user has a two-button mouse and the X-server does not emulate a three-button mouse, press the Meta-key and right mouse button together to simulate mouse button 3). Normally, mouse buttons 1, 2, and 3 are assigned to the left, middle, and right buttons, respectively.

# CHAPTER 6

Troubleshooting

Objectives

- Describe the cause of and solution for `read` errors.
- Explain why FTP consistently misses certain files in group transfers.
- Explain the problem and solution when LILO generates `LI`.
- Define a rescue disk and describe three reasons for using it.
- Explain how to circumvent a locked-up program.
- List eight steps to resolve an unresponsive printer.
- Explain why Linux may report the wrong time, and describe how to fix the problem.
- Describe how to reset the console screen, the keyboard repeat rate, and the NUM-LOCK key.
- Describe the role of system logging, and how it is used in troubleshooting.

Troubleshooting

The term *troubleshooting* encompasses an immense landscape of problem analysis that engages several higher-order faculties, including the ability to discriminate between concepts and superficial features, organize concepts in a hierarchical fashion, and systematically test each concept in order to isolate and repair faults.

Although a complete evaluation of these skills will come in subsequent levels, reviewing common troubleshooting scenarios is a constructive activity that is useful for the user.

General Troubleshooting Strategy

Problem solving can be divided into two basic phases: the shortcut phase and the analysis phase. A good troubleshooter understands these phases and will quickly move into the analysis phase after all of the shortcuts have been tried.

Shortcuts

Perhaps the most troublesome aspect of troubleshooting is the fact that, almost unfailingly, the solution with which to solve the problem is very simple and usually just beyond the user's grasp. Most users employ shortcuts to some degree; however, once the local experts have been consulted, and after the Deja search engine does not turn up an answer, the user must employ other methods.

Analysis

Perhaps the best advice available for serious troubleshooting is that the user should not look for the quickest way to solve a specific problem, but rather the most systematic way to solve the problem. Problems are solved systematically by identifying independent components and testing each component for its correct operation. Moreover, these components must be checked in relationship to how the system is constructed. For example, there is little benefit to checking a failed circuit if it has no power; there is similarly little benefit to checking or replacing the power supply if the power cord extension has been unplugged in the next room. More complicated problems can arise when users who possess only a minimal amount of Linux knowledge attempt to troubleshoot major problems. If system components are unknown, then someone must be found who does know the components thoroughly, in order to assist the user in walking through the system checkout procedure.

read or file not found Errors When Installing Linux

Two probable causes of `read` errors or `file not found` errors are poor-quality media and incorrect media format. An example of poor-quality media is the recycling of a free AOL floppy as a boot floppy; an example of incorrect media format is the use of a Macintosh floppy in a PC floppy drive. Other possibilities for media problems are old diskettes, perhaps exposed to heat or moisture, or that are in generally poor physical condition. The solution to all of these problems is either to reformat the media and recopy installation images, or replace the media.

Common tar Errors When Installing Linux

The following error:

```
Tar: read error or gzip: not in gzip format while installing Linux
```

indicates that the media is acceptable, but the archive contents have been corrupted. To correct this problem, download a new copy (in binary mode) from a different site.

device full Error Message When Installing Linux

There is no quick solution to this problem; the user must start over. Generally, this means that the partition or hard drive on which the Linux installation is being attempted does not have enough storage space; therefore, new, larger partitions must be made that will hold the software, or another hard drive must be added.

read interrupt Error Message When Installing Linux

A common read interrupt message is:

```
Read_intr: 0x10 error
```

If this occurs with general hard disk access, the disk drive has bad blocks. Either use the `badblocks` command to search the device for bad blocks, or reinstall Linux, but be sure to check the `scan-for-badblocks` option. On the other hand, if it occurs with `mke2fs` or `mkswap`, then the real partition size is smaller than the stated program argument size.

A user may also want to run the `badblocks` program `standalone` to check the device. If there are a large number of bad blocks on any storage device, it is recommended that the device be replaced.

file not found or permission denied Errors

These error messages are rare, and either mean that there are missing files or that the installation software has bugs that set the wrong permissions. Try a different version of the distribution, or a different Linux distribution altogether.

Problems with Transfers

These problems sometimes occur when transferring files via FTP. Most of the files are received except for the ones with simple file names like README or config. In this case, the problem may be in the way the two FTP commands, mget *.* and mget *, are viewed. Both commands are the same in an MS-DOS environment, but they are different in Linux. In Linux, mget *.* means retrieve only the files that have a dot character embedded within the name. The mget * command means retrieve all of the files.

When LILO Says LI

As LILO executes, it checks the MBR and reads in a secondary (chained) loader that, in turn, reads and uncompresses the Linux kernel image. After the image is loaded, LILO begins executing the kernel. Instead of simply announcing itself with the name LILO, the program displays a letter after each stage of progress has been completed.

The LI problem occurs when LILO attempts to traverse the file system looking for the chained loader image /boot/chain.b and requests a disk block from the BIOS. However, the old BIOS returns the wrong disk block because it was not designed to reach beyond 512 MB.

The solution is to make the first partition small for boot images, and mount the partition as /boot.

Reasons for Making a Linux Boot or Rescue Diskette

At the end of an installation, the install program usually asks if the user would like to create a boot floppy disk; it is highly recommended that every installation have its own boot or rescue diskette. Follow this procedure and keep the floppy in a well-known place for later reference.

This boot floppy will be very important in recovery situations where the system fails to boot or fails to allow anyone access. If such a situation occurs, the user's files become unreachable, and without the boot diskette, a new version of Linux would have to be installed, erasing the root partition in the process. As a last resort, some distributions allow an upgrade or expert path through the install program that may reach the section where a boot disk can be created before they will erase the root partition.

How the Boot Diskette Works

A boot diskette consists of two sections: the compressed kernel image and a RAM disk image called initrd. The boot process reads a compressed file system image from the floppy disk and stores the files in memory (not on the hard disk) through a special device driver that makes main memory appear to be a RAM disk. Next, the kernel is read into main memory and started. The kernel, in turn, mounts the apparent RAM disk as the root partition. Thus, from one floppy, a complete stand-alone version of Linux is booted. Once booted, the hard disk can be mounted, examined, and modified as required.

Ways of Using the Boot Diskette

Following are three common ways to use the boot diskette (creating custom versions of boot disks will be discussed in a later volume).

MBR corruption. If the fdisk program was run improperly, or if the first sector (master boot record) of the hard disk is changed, then the system will not boot. The solution is to refresh the MBR with the LILO program, which can be run from the mounted hard disk.

Password file corruption. Through either a careless or malicious act, the password file can be deleted, thereby preventing any further login. There are two possible solutions to this dilemma. The first depends upon whether a backup copy of the password file exists. If the system does not make one automatically, as Debian 2.0 does, the system administrator may have done so. Following this approach, the solution is to copy the backup of the password file over the original, now-corrupted password file (called `passwd`). However, if the first approach is not feasible, the second approach is to create a new password file for the root account. This technique can also be used to remove the superuser password if it has been forgotten.

Lost dynamic load module library. Newer versions of Linux use dynamic load modules that only have the name of one or more library modules in the executable program, or the ELF binary files. If a required library file is corrupted or lost, the ELF binary needing that library will not execute. In other words, the shell that started the program will continue to run, as will its internal commands (such as `cd`); however, any other external shell command, such as `ls`, will not be able to find its run-time library module. The solution is to mount the hard disk, copy the backup library file on top of the bad library module, and reboot the system.

Boot and Login Errors

Following are some of the possible errors, along with suggested solutions, that may occur once the Linux distribution is up and running.

Error: Drive not bootable—Please insert system disk.

Solution/explanation: The MBR has been zapped. Use a rescue disk for the OS being booted. For example, in MS-DOS, use the command FDISK / MBR.

Error: The wrong OS boots.

Solution/explanation: LILO or another primary boot system is misconstrued, reconfigure and re-install LILO. This is a problem when running a dual-boot system. LILO can be configured to allow users to choose which operating system it boots.

Error: Login incorrect.

Solution/explanation: This is simply a password problem. If all the passwords were forgotten, boot Linux in single-user mode and run the password program as superuser.

Error: Either there is no shell, or the error "Shell-init: permission denied" is displayed.

Solution/explanation: The password file has somehow been erased, or the root permissions are too restrictive. Boot Linux in single-user mode, and copy the backup of the password file over the missing or corrupted password file or chmod the root directory permissions.

Locked-Up Programs

Most Linux distributions include a colorful ASCII-based, GUI-looking program that guides the user through the installation process. Sometimes, however, the GUI gets stuck, and in this scenario, the user will have to restart or reboot the program. It is in situations like these where the benefits of virtual terminals become apparent.

For example, consider a scenario in which the installation GUI is not responding as expected (i.e., it is stuck), and there are a number of virtual terminals available, as is the case with Linux. Different virtual terminals offer various options, and can be accessed by pressing the ALT key and a specified function key. For example, the GUI could be on virtual terminal F1; virtual terminal F2 may provide a superuser shell prompt; virtual terminal F3 might show the batch commands from the install program being executed; and virtual terminal F4 could show all the kernel diagnostic messages as each subprogram runs.

The user can determine where the install process is hanging by using console screens F3 and F4. By switching between these two screens, the user can also determine whether the problem is with the floppy drive, the hard disk drive, the CD-ROM drive, or the network connections. For example, if the kernel cannot read the floppy, time-out errors from the floppy drive will show up on the F4. If the floppy drive does not seem to be the problem, then the user must continue systematically down the list of possibilities until the problem is uncovered and isolated. Only then can a solution be prepared.

Some of the newer and less debugged X servers may fail after several weeks of continuous use and lock up the console. In these cases, the X Window GUI will not respond, and access to the virtual consoles may lock up. However, the user may still log in via a network connection to kill jobs or perform a `reboot` command.

Troubleshooting Unresponsive Printers

The following steps should be applied in order to troubleshoot an unresponsive printer:

1. Check the `/var/spool/lpd/printer/status` file and the `/var/log/lpd-errs` file for error messages. (The path component printer refers both to the name of the printer and its spool directory.)

2. Check for a `/var/spool/lpd/printer/lock` file, and remove if necessary.

3. Check the `/var/spool/lpd/printer/` directory for control and data files. There should be at least one `cf` control file and one `df` data file.

4. Check the `/etc/printcap` entry to ensure that it has not been modified.

5. Test the printer directly with the command: `lptest > /dev/lp1`.

6. Check to ensure that the printer can accept the format that is attempting to print with the command: `cat file > /dev/lp1`.

7. If the printer is a serial printer, check whether UUCP has taken over ownership of the serial port.

8. Finally, verify that the shell environment variables, such as `PRINTER`, are redirecting program output to another logical printer.

The Wrong Time Is Reported

The PC BIOS employs a CMOS clock that Linux reads for the initial date and time. However, CMOS clocks tend to drift. To correct the problem of incorrect time reporting, simply update the BIOS time regularly, or use a timeserver to update the system on the fly. An easy way to do this is with the following command:

```
$ ntpdate clock.isc.org
```

This command queries a time daemon on the isc.org timeserver for the correct time. This is another situation where the user must have a trusted source from which to retrieve the correct time. There are many timeservers available on the Internet.

Adding More Memory Has Made the System Slow

In this case, the amount of main memory has exceeded motherboard cache-tag addresses. To correct the problem, replace the motherboard. The newer PC-100 DIMM motherboards do not have this problem.

Everything Slows When X Is Running

If all processes slow when X is run, it is likely that the main memory is not large enough, and the system is spending more time swapping than computing. Table 6.1 lists some minimum and some typical values for main memory.

Console Screen Has Symbols Instead of Letters

When the console screen is displaying symbols instead of letters, the terminal emulator has been switched into pseudo graphics mode, and it assumes the ASCII characters are commands to display character attributes. Either use the reset command, or switch to another console terminal.

Table 6.1   Values for Main Memory

APPLICATION	MINIMUM	TYPICAL
Network gateway	4 MB	8 MB
Network server	8 MB	16 MB
Network multi-user	16 MB	32 MB
X workstation	32 MB	64 MB
X with GIMP	64 MB	128 MB

Keyboard Repeat Rate Is Too Slow

Some BIOS menus do not offer a keyboard repeat rate adjustment. If this is the case, use the /sbin/kbdrate utility with the arguments -r 30 to get a repeat rate of 30 characters per second.

Num Lock Is Not On by Default

Use the setleds program to turn on the NUM LOCK function. To do this at boot time for all the virtual consoles, insert the following shell script into either /etc/rc.local or one of the /etc/rc.d/* directories.

```
for t in 1 2 3 4 5 6
do
setleds +num < /dev/tty$t >/dev/null
done
```

The script employs a for loop controlled by the shell variable called t. It runs the setleds utility with the +num argument for virtual terminals 1 through 6, /dev/tty[123456], turning on the NUM LOCK key, and redirecting any errors to the bit bucket /dev/null.

X Window System Error: Cannot Open Display: 0.0

The shell variable DISPLAY must be configured. Try the command:

```
DISPLAY=localhost:0.0
```

This sets the DISPLAY environment variable to point to the default X terminal. With this set, the startx command should work properly.

Daemons and System Message Logging

One key to Linux system troubleshooting is to know where to look for run-time error messages. However, many users forget that all background programs (daemons) and many system utilities report general status and error information to a message-logging daemon, called syslog. The syslog daemon usually places information in log files found in the /var/log directory.

Because of the rich amount of system information contained within these files, these are generally accessible only to the superuser. Exact file names depend upon how the /etc/syslog.conf file was set up by the Linux distribution. Typically, there is a file called messages that collects most system status reports. There are also facilities (or types of daemons) that direct specific messages to individual files. For a Debian system, the default /var/log files are:

```
auth.log        daemon.log      debug           faillog
kern.log        lastlog         lp-acct         lp-errs
lpd-errs        lpr.log         mail.err        mail.log
mail.warn       messages        setuid.changes  syslog
```

For a Red Hat system, the default `/var/log` files are:

```
cron        maillog      sendmail.st     wtmp
dmesg       messages     spooler         xdm-error.log
lastlog     secure       uucp            xferlog
```

The number and names of the `/var/log` files are controlled by the file `/etc/syslog.conf`. Its format looks like this:

```
auth,authpriv.*                 /var/log/auth.log
*.*;auth,authpriv.none          /var/log/syslog
#cron.*                         /var/log/cron.log
daemon.*                        /var/log/daemon.log
kern.*                          /var/log/kern.log
lpr.*                           /var/log/lpr.log
mail.*                          /var/log/mail.log
user.*                          /var/log/user.log
uucp.*                          /var/log/uucp.log

*.=info;*.=notice;*.=warn;\
auth,authpriv.none;\
cron,daemon.none;\
mail,news.none                  /var/log/messages
```

This example was extracted from a Debian configuration file. The column on the top left of the code shows the `facilities` (or types of daemons), both with and without message priority levels (where `facility.level` is the format for those `facilities` with a level indicated, such as `news.none` or `user.notice`, and where `facility` is the format of those `facilities` without a level indicated, such as `lpr`). All priority levels are included since the wild card character (`*`) was specified to the right side of the dot. For example, considering the user `facility`, there are messages with priority levels `info`, `notice`, and `warn` so that the format for each of the facilities becomes `user.info`, `user.notice`, and `user.warn`, and all of these user messages are collected in the log file `/var/log/user.log`. The user may also insert messages into the `message log` file with the `logger` command. For example, the command:

```
logger "Hi, What's up"
```

places the string, `"Hi, What's up"` in the `messages` file. If something seems to be missing (such as a `message` or other file), remember to check the most recent additions to the `messages` file with the command:

```
tail -300 /var/log/messages | more
```

Advanced Topics

Objectives

- Explain how to monitor who is using a system.
- Explain various methods of displaying system usage.
- Describe the problems with the backup process.
- Describe the `tar` command.
- Compare and contrast LANs and WANs.
- Explain the difference between hardware and software addresses.
- Explain the difference between an internet and the Internet.
- Describe the organization of IP addresses.
- List the top-level domains.
- Explain the difference between a host name and a domain name.
- Describe how the Domain Name Service (DNS) is configured.
- Explain how to enable mail.
- Describe Apache's configuration files.
- Describe Samba.
- List and describe the components of the Network File System (NFS).
- Explain the `hosts.deny` and `hosts.allow` files.

Monitoring System Status

One of the most important functions that a system administrator performs is monitoring the system. This includes activities such as system security, troubleshooting, and general system maintenance.

The last Command

Who is using the system? On a single-user system, this question has a simple, straightforward answer. However, on a multi-user system or a machine that is connected to a network, this question is not so easy to answer. The ability to track system users will give an administrator a good start in solving both security and troubleshooting software problems. To get part of the answer to the pending question, an administrator can use the last command.

OUTPUT FROM LAST

```
reboot    system boot           Fri Apr 23 16:51
fred      ttyp2 LinuxA.d1.com   Fri Apr 23 10:16 - crash (06:35)
lindsay   ftp   LinuxD.d1.com   Mon Apr 19 21:10 - 21:10 (00:00)
jordan    ttyp0 LinuxB.d1.com   Mon Apr 19 20:06 - 21:09 (01:03)
meredith  ttyp0 LinuxW.d2.org   Mon Apr 19 16:37 - 17:01 (00:24)
allison   ttyp0 192.168.1.45    Mon Apr 19 15:34 - 15:43 (00:08)
kithung   ttyp0 LinuxK.d3.net   Mon Apr 19 14:06 - 15:03 (00:57)
lenny     ttyp1 LinuxK.d3.net   Mon Apr 19 12:22 - 12:23 (00:00)
kithung   ttyp0 LinixC.d1.com   Mon Apr 19 09:43 - 13:16 (03:33)
dfmiller  ttyp1 LinuxF.d1.com   Mon Apr 19 08:35 - 08:35 (00:00)
```

The output from last shows who has logged in, which port (tty) was used, the host from which they came, the date, and how long they were logged in. System crashes are also logged. In the preceding display, we see that fred was logged on for 6 hours and 35 minutes when the system crashed, and the system was rebooted within a minute (10:16 + 6:35 = 16:51).

System Status

At any given time, a Linux system may be running hundreds of different operations, the majority of which usually running in the background. Most users will only run a few programs at the same time and are unaware of the numerous programs and utilities being run by the system. These background utilities are often the cause of system problems. For this reason, a system administrator needs to be able to monitor both foreground and background activities.

The ps Command

To find out how the system is being used, run the process status (ps) command. The ps command was seen earlier, but it also has extended forms; for example, ps eax shows all system processes.

OUTPUT FROM THE PS EAX

```
PID   TTY   STAT  TIME   COMMAND
1     ?     S     0:06   init [2]
2     ?     SW    0:00   (kflushd)
3     ?     SW<   0:00   (kswapd)
12    ?     S     0:01   update
39    ?     SW    0:00   (nfsiod)
64    ?     S     0:00   /home/httpd/httpd
125   ?     S     0:02   /sbin/syslogd
127   ?     S     0:00   /sbin/klogd
134   ?     S     0:00   /sbin/kerneld
144   ?     S     0:00   /usr/sbin/inetd
147   ?     S     0:18   /usr/sbin/named
165   ?     S     0:00   /usr/sbin/atd
5579  ?     S     0:01   in.telnetd: blinky.sairinc.com
                         [vt220]
5580  p0    S     0:01   -bash REMOTEHOST=blinky.sairinc.com
                         TERM=vt220  HZ=100 HOME=/usr/ho
5612  p0    R     0:00   ps eax REMOTEHOST=blinky.sairinc.com
                         HZ=100 HOSTNAME=vis PS1=\h:\w
```

This output shows a list of system processes with only one user logged in from the network. Each program has its process identifier (PID), controlling terminal (TTY), run status (STAT), amount of CPU time consumed (TIME), and the command that initiated the program (COMMAND). The question marks in the TTY column indicate that these system daemons do not have a controlling terminal. Following is the output from another variant of the process status command, ps leax.

OUTPUT FROM PS LEAX

```
FLAGS   UID PID PPID PRI NI  SIZE  RSS  WCHAN       STA TTY TIME  COMMAND
100      0   1   0    0   0  744    60  do_select   S    ?  0:03  init [3]
40       0   2   1    0   0    0     0  bdflush     SW   ?  0:03  (kflushd)
40       0   3   1  -12 -12    0     0  kswapd      SW<  ?  0:12  (kswapd)
140      0  22   1    0   0  720    44  real_msgrcv S    ?  0:00  /sbin
                                                                  /kerneld
140      0 166   1    0   0  780   208  do_select   S    ?  0:25  syslogd
100140   0 175   1    0   0  888    28  syslog      S    ?  0:01  (klogd)
100040   2 186   1    0   0  764   104  nanosleep   S    ?  0:00  /usr/sbin
                                                                  /atd
140      0 197   1    0   0  828   132  nanosleep   S    ?  0:00  crond
```

```
140      0 208  1  0  0 1112 176 do_select   S   ? 0:01  /usr/sbin
                                                           /snmp-ff
140      0 220  1  0  0  756  68 do_select   S   ? 0:01  inetd
100140   0 231  1  0  0 1532 964 do_select   S   ? 3:50  named
100140   0 244  1  0  0  768  20 wait4       S   ? 0:00  lpd
140      0 259  1  0  0 1384 284 do_select   S   ? 0:03  (sendmail)
100140   0 271  1  0  0  728   0 do_select   SW  ? 0:00  (gpm)
```

The ps leax command shows more details on the state of the process. The bit vector, FLAGS, is held in the kernel to describe the state of the process; UID is the user identifier of who initiated the program. PID is the process identifier, and PPID is the parent PID. PRI is the priority of the process where negative numbers are higher priority than positive numbers. SIZE and RSS refer to the virtual and physical sizes of programs; WCHAN is the wake-up channel for which the program waits before continuing execution. The other columns are the same as the output displayed for ps eax.

The top Command

The ps command and its extended forms provide a snapshot of the system state. To see a more dynamic view, use the top command, which is actually a combination of other system commands run every five seconds or when the space bar is pushed. The following code is generated from entering the top command:

```
9:23am up 1 day, 16:35,  1 user,  load average: 0.05, 0.01,0.00
39 processes: 38 sleeping, 1 running, 0 zombie, 0 stopped
CPU states:  4.4% user,  5.5% system,  0.0% nice, 90.1% idle
Mem: 14092K av,12460K used,1632K free, 17612K shrd, 1468K buff
Swap:  40156K av,  32K used, 40124K free 5428K cached
```

The top command displays the general system status, individual system status, and updates the display every five seconds by default. As shown in Table 7.1, it also displays a listing of the most CPU-intensive tasks on the system, and allows process manipulation. It can sort the tasks by CPU usage, memory usage and run time, and can send signals to a process, kill a process, or change its priority. Most features can either be selected by an interactive command or by specifying the feature in the personal or system-wide configuration file.

Table 7.1   The top Command

PID	USER	PRI	NI	SIZE	RSS	SHARE	STAT	LIB	%CPU	%MEM	TIME	COMMAND
5622	ptm	18	0	752	752	572	R	0	8.2	5.3	0:03	top
5579	root	2	0	656	656	504	S	0	1.7	4.6	0:01	in.telnetd
1	root	0	0	352	348	292	S	0	0.0	2.4	0:06	init
2	root	0	0	0	0	0	SW	0	0.0	0.0	0:00	kflushd

netstat

Linux is request driven, and these requests originate from two directions: users and the network. The `ps` command shows the user-driven system state, while the `netstat` command reveals the network-driven system state. For example, Table 7.2 shows the display produced by the `netstat -a` command.

Just as an ignored conversation would not bother a disinterested listener, network activity, per se, would not influence the system unless programs (daemons) have been

Table 7.2 Output of the netstat Command

ACTIVE INTERNET CONNECTIONS (INCLUDING SERVERS)					
PROTO	**RECV-Q**	**SEND-Q**	**LOCAL ADDRESS**	**FOREIGN ADDRESS**	**STATE**
tcp	0	0	vis.sairinc.com: telnet	blinky.sairinc .com:1043	ESTABLISHED
tcp	0	0	*:printer	*:*	LISTEN
tcp	0	0	192.168.1.1: domain	*:*	LISTEN
tcp	0	0	vis.sairinc.com: domain	*:*	LISTEN
tcp	0	0	localhost:domain	*:*	LISTEN
tcp	0	0	*:ftp	*:*	LISTEN
tcp	0	0	*:telnet	*:*	LISTEN
tcp	0	0	*:www	*:*	LISTEN
udp	0	0	192.168.1.1: domain	*:*	
udp	0	0	vis.sairinc.com: domain	*:*	
udp	0	0	localhost:domain	*:*	
udp	0	0	*:daytime	*:*	
ACTIVE UNIX DOMAIN SOCKETS (INCLUDING SERVERS)					
PROTO	**REFCNT**	**FLAGS**	**TYPE**	**STATE**	**I-NODE** PATH
unix	1	[ACC]	STREAM	LISTENING	91048 /dev/printer
unix	2	[]	STREAM		1169 /dev/log
unix	2	[]	STREAM	CONNECTED	1168
unix	1	[ACC]	STREAM	LISTENING	1098 /var/run/gpmctl
unix	1	[]	STREAM		1092

executed to listen for the network activity. You can see the various pending connections of listening daemons. The leftmost protocol column (PROTO) divides the type into three classes: TCP or virtual circuits, UDP or datagrams, and Unix or internal inter-process communication. The TCP connections may be established or waiting.

Backup

Backup is more of a process than a program. It is the idea that if valuable information is placed on redundant media, the information can be copied back to a new instance of the primary medium should the primary medium fail.

Backing Up and the Design Trade-Off

Many times the backup process degenerates into an ideal that is never realized (i.e., everyone assumes there is a valid backup). Some reasons for unrealized backup are: the backup process requires additional equipment that is not critical for day-to-day operations; the backup equipment may have been borrowed to support other day-to-day operations; or the backup device is always used in write mode but never tested in read mode. Another reason for the frequent failure of the backup process is that it requires a consistent commitment to performing the backup operation at the proper intervals, without skipping steps and without overwriting other backup copies in the library.

The Backup Problem

The essence of the backup problem is that without testing the backup copies, there is no way to know whether the backup process is truly providing the desired safety net. Furthermore, if a failure that necessitates use of the backup is suffered and failure of the backup subsequently occurs, the resulting situation is the same as if the user had suffered a catastrophic hardware failure without a backup. Additionally, if the backup data is kept in an encoded format (i.e., archived and compressed), then the decoder cannot be saved with the backup data. How could the user decode the decoder, so that the backup data could itself be decoded? To prevent loss of decoding information, the decoder must be stored independently of the backup process.

Example Backup Suites

The Advanced Maryland Automatic Network Disk Archiver (AMANDA) www.cs .umd.edu/projects/amanda/ is a backup system that allows the administrator of a LAN to set up a single master backup server to back up multiple hosts to a single large-capacity tape drive. AMANDA employs native dump and GNU tar facilities and can back up a large number of workstations running multiple versions of Linux/Unix. Recent versions can also use Samba to back up Microsoft Windows 95/NT hosts. AMANDA is copywritten by The University of Maryland at College Park and offered as free software.

Karsten Balluders wrote the KBackup suite www.phy.hw.ac.uk/~karsten/ KBackup/ that provides a user-friendly, menu-driven interface and command-line interface for inclusion in automated scripts. It features tools such as `afio` and `tar`, automated unattended backups, full or incremental backups, support for tape drives, floppies, or other removable media, remote backup across networks, compression, encryption, and double buffering. Kbackup is built from modular shell scripts, provides extensive documentation, and employs the GNU GPL license.

Sean Vyain wrote the KDat http://sunsite.auc.dk/qweb/kdat/ `tar`-based tape archiver that is designed to work with multiple archives on a single tape. KDat's design goal was to provide a GUI front-end to `tar` that supported the fast selective extraction features of the dds2tar program. KDat provides support for SCSI and floppy tape drives. It manages multiple archives on the same tape. It can selectively back up many files and directories at a time; KDat can also verify and restore selected files within an archive, going directly to each file within the archive rather than reading the entire archive. KDat backup profiles frequently use backups, provide support for GNU incremental backups, and employ the GNU GPL license.

The Backup and Restore Utility BRU2000 www.estinc.com/, is designed for Linux and other Unix-like systems. BRU's primary focus is on data recovery and maximum reliability. The maker of BRU, Enhanced Software Technologies, Inc., states that the commercial backup and rescue system provides the best backup possible under Unix.

Business Critical Backup and Recovery System, CTAR www.unitrends.com/Ctar .html, was designed for stand-alone Unix systems. The maker of CTAR, UniTrends, states that the commercial package has simple yet powerful backup and restore features with integrity checking.

The maker of LONE-TAR, Lone Star Software Corp. www.cactus.com/ lonetar.html, says that their commercial package is a fully menu-driven, data archiving and recovery utility that employs high compression, which guarantees to double the capacity of a user's archive device, as well as offering bit-level verification of archived data against the hard disk. LONE-TAR employs a Master and Incremental strategy to ensure that all your system data is rapidly available in the event of a system failure.

The maker of PerfectBACKUP+, Unisource Systems Inc. www.unisrc.com /Perfect-BACKUP.htm, says that the commercial package is a complete backup and restore program for Unix-based file servers and workstations; it is the fastest, friendliest Unix-based backup management program available today. Its features include NFS support, Unix networked devices, device chaining, history control, backup indexes, progress monitor, preconfigured backups, image and media copy, PC portability, lock during copy, speed, security, multivolume background backups, and support for robotics and autochangers.

Definition of tar and Example tar Backup Commands

`tar` is an acronym for tape archiver, but it is used more as a general file archiver and compressor. The examples of the use of `tar` as both a general-purpose file archiver and a tape archive will be considered, but first, the use of the `tar` command with tape devices will be addressed.

tar and Tape Drives

Tape drives often have certain idiosyncrasies. The following two tape device-drivers, /dev/rft0 and /dev/nrft0, perform quite differently. Accessing the /dev/rft0 tape device-driver causes the tape drive to rewind the tape upon completion of read and write operations. In this way, the user is certain that the tape will be positioned at the beginning as the next command is typed. However, accessing the /dev/nrft0 tape device-driver will not rewind the tape drive upon completion of I/O operations, thus making the user responsible for keeping track of the current tape position. Following are several examples, using the tar command as a general-purpose file archiver and compressor.

Using tar as a File Archiver

Example 1: tar cvzf bu.tz *

This command takes all files in the current directory and any files in subdirectories and copies them, along with their directory names, into an archive file called bu.tz. The tz extension is a shorthand convention to identify a tar and zipped file. The four switches, cvzf, mean:

c   Create an archive.

v   Display each file name as it is added to the archive.

z   Use the GNU zip compressor to compress the archive.

f   Use the file name bu.tz as the name of the archive file.

Example 2: tar tvzf bu.tz

This command displays the table of contents of an archive so that the overall size, number of files, and file placement may be viewed before the files are actually extracted from the archive.

Example 3: tar cvf /dev/nrft0 /etc /home /var/spool/mail

This command creates an archive of three directories, beginning at the current tape position. The tape is not rewound, so additional archives can be written subsequent to the current archive.

Example 4: mt /dev/nrft0 rewind

This command rewinds the tape back to the beginning.

Example 5: mt /dev/nrft0 fsf 2

The fifth command advances the tape by two archive files, positioning the R/W head before the third archive file.

Example 6: tar tvf /dev/nrft0

This command reads the table of contents of the third archive file.

Network Theory

In its most basic definition, a computer network is a collection of computers that can communicate with each other. Networks can further be grouped together to form an internet. In these large groups, individual computers can be identified using IP addresses.

LANs and WANs

A computer network can be divided into two groups: local area networks (LANs) and wide area networks (WANs). The basic differences between the two are the size and speed of the networks. A typical high-speed LAN spans a small area, such as a single building. The slower WANs provide communication over large distances, like a country or continent.

WANs are made from point-to-point (PTP), or serial, connections that require two separate network interface cards (NICs) to pass information from an incoming NIC to an outgoing NIC for another computer in the network. Broadcast LANs (Ethernet), on the other hand, are faster than PTP connections and require only one NIC per host in the local area network.

Internet

In simple terms, an internet is a collection of machines or hosts that can communicate with each other. Since we know that computers are clustered in small networks, an internet is essentially a collection of different networks that can communicate with each other. The Internet, on the other hand, is a collection of networks whose logical addresses are centrally administered. The technology allowing one network to communicate with another network is known as internetworking.

Hardware and Software Addresses

IP addresses, also known as logical addresses, will be discussed in the *IP Addressing* section of this chapter. However, in addition to logical addresses, every computer has a physical address as well. A physical address is one assigned to the hardware in charge of communication, and is usually an integer. For any form of communication to take place, the high-level address (like an IP address) must be translated into the physical address of the destination. Address translation is discussed in more detail in an upcoming section.

Internet Addresses

For any form of communication to take place, the end points of the communication must be uniquely identified. On the Internet, every machine has a unique address known as the IP (Internet Protocol) address. In the IP version 4 protocol, Internet addresses are made up of 32-bit numbers that are divided into four separate bytes. Consider, for example, the following IP address of 192.168.1.3

As mentioned in a previous section, the Internet is actually a collection of many networks, where every host on the Internet is registered to a network. Consequently, the addressing scheme identifies the network and the host within that network. In other words, an IP address is made up of two parts: a network identifier and a host identifier. The idea of embedding the network ID within the address facilitates easy routing of packets within the Internet.

IP Addressing

IP addresses can be divided into three classes: Class A, Class B, and Class C. (Class D and Class E addresses also exist, but they are not relevant to the current discussion.) Every network falls into one of these address classes; the formats of each are shown in Figure 7.1.

As can be seen in Figure 7.1, Class A addresses have 0 as the first bit in their high-order byte. Class B addresses have 10 as their first and second bits in their high-order byte, and so on. By combining this information with what was learned in the previous section, it is clear that an IP address can be divided into three parts: the class, the network ID, and the host ID.

By viewing the information provided in Figure 7.1, it can be determined that Class A addresses use 7 bits to identify a network (allowing 128 networks possible) and 24 bits to identify a host (allowing 16,777,216 possible hosts within each network). Consequently, Class A addresses are used by those networks that need to have more than 65,536 hosts. Class B addresses are used by intermediate-sized networks. The host ID portion of this network is 16 bits, which means that it can accommodate 65,536 hosts. Class C addresses are used for small networks, limited to 256 hosts (since the host ID portion uses 8 bits).

The high-order bits of an address are an important factor in the routing of packets to their destination. The first 1 to 4 bits are used by the gateways to determine the class of the address that needs to be routed. Once the class of the address is determined, the gateway can extract the network ID from the address and route the associated packet using only the network ID. The gateway must know the location of other networks, but not the location of every host on the Internet.

```
CLASS A
+---+------------------+-------------------------+
| 0 |Net ID (7 bits)  |Host ID (24 bits)        |
+-- +------------------+-------------------------+
CLASS B
+----+------------------+------------------------+
|10  |Net ID (14 bits) |Host ID (16 bits)       |
+----+------------------+------------------------+
CLASS C
+-----+------------------+-----------------------+
|100  |Net ID (21 bits) |Host ID (8 bits)       |
+-----+------------------+-----------------------+
CLASS D
+-------+---------------------------------------+
|1110 | Multicast Address (28 bits)       |
+-------+---------------------------------------+
```

Figure 7.1 IP Address class formats.

The Domain Name Service (DNS)

The DNS uses a hierarchical naming scheme made up of domains, which can be nested. Furthermore, the address of a host can be divided into two parts:

```
HostName.DomainName
```

An example of a host name with nested domains is:

```
HostName.Domain1Name.Domain2Name
```

Top-Level Domains

A domain name is written with its local domain first (to the left) and ends with a top-level domain (to the right). Example top-level domains are:

com	Commercial organization.
edu	Educational institution.
gov	Governmental organization.
mil	Military.
net	Major network support center.
org	Nonprofit organization or one not falling into one of the above categories.
[country code]	Identifies a country.

A Linux distribution routinely offers to install five basic network services: Domain Name Service (DNS), mail transfer agent (Sendmail or smail), a Web server (httpd), Microsoft file sharing (Samba), and Sun Microsystems file sharing (NFS). The following discussion assumes that these services were selected for installation.

A user will not usually have to configure a DNS server. Instead, simply point to the current DNS server by placing its name in the `/etc/resolv.conf` file.

To use DNS, two files must be configured: `/etc/named.boot` and `/etc/userdefined`. The format of the `/etc/named.boot` file appears as follows:

```
directory /etc/
; type    Domain                Source        File
cache     .                                   named.root
Server type Domain Name         IP of primary Name of pri-
                                              mary database
;----     -----                 ------        -----
primary   0.0.127.in-addr.arpa  127.0.0.1     localhost.rev
primary   myname.com            192.168.1.111 myname.db
```

The `/etc/named.boot` file lists the domain database files that describe the server's domains.

```
@   IN   SOA   myname.com.   hostmaster@myname.com. (
                        1999072100; Serial number
                        82500     ; Refresh every day
```

```
                          3600       ; Retry every hour
                          1728000   ; Expire every 20 days
                          172800 )  ; Minimum 2 days

myname.com.   IN   NS     ns1.myname.com.
myname.com.   IN   NS     ns2.mayname.com.
              IN   MX     0    mail.myname.com.
localhost     IN   A      127.0.0.1
ns1           IN   A      192.168.1.111
              IN   MX     10   ns1.myname.com.
travel        IN   CNAME  ns1
ns            IN   CNAME  ns1
www           IN   CNAME  ns1
ftp           IN   CNAME  ns1
```

/etc/myname.db describes the name servers and hosts contained within a domain. Two name servers are listed (ns1 and ns2), and the host ns1 is also known as travel.myname.com, www.myname.com, and ftp.myname.com.

To communicate with the name service, use the + command; The command kill -HUP pid directs the server to re-read its configuration files, while the command kill -TERM pid directs the server to close its open files, terminate any child processes, and exit.

Network Services

Network services include electronic mail, Web servers, and file sharing. In Linux, these services can be enabled through the following programs.

Mail

Linux distributions generally preconfigure sendmail as the mail transfer agent. Debian, on the other hand, configures smail as its transfer agent. Most of the user account utilities also add in mail service, but others such as adduser do not install mail service by default.

To enable mail, simply add the user account name to the mail spool directory. Thus, if the account name was lindsay, a file by that name must be created in the /var/spool/mail/ directory. This can be done using the following touch command:

```
touch lindsay
```

Next, the permissions must be changed so that only lindsay and the mail group can read and write the mail. In keeping with the example, the commands to do this are:

```
chown lindsay lindsay
chmod 660 lindsay
chgrp mail lindsay
```

The result of these commands is a file name with the following characteristics:

```
hostname: ls -l lindsay
-rw-rw----   1 lindsay mail 0 Dec 22 10:55 lindsay
```

These files may also be created automatically by the SMTP daemon if mail comes in for a valid user account but the file does not exist.

Finally, the file `lindsay.lock` can be created, which tells the mail daemon not to add mail to the file while the user may be copying or otherwise archiving the file.

Apache Web Server

The location of the Web server configuration files are installation specific in Linux, but often they can be found in `/etc/httpd/conf/`. There are three configuration files: `access.conf`, `httpd.conf`, and `srm.conf`.

access.conf. Controls which directories are valid for Web browsers (each directory can be configured to allow or disable certain services and features).

httpd.conf. The main server configuration file that determines the listening port number, server root directory, number of Web servers, and virtual hosting.

srm.conf. Defines the default directory names that local users can see on the `httpd` server. This file also defines server settings that affect how requests are serviced and how results are formatted.

Each file is well commented and provides detailed parameter descriptions to support modifications to the configuration files. Future versions of Apache will have the ability to consolidate these configuration files into one file.

Samba

Samba allows Linux to participate in the Microsoft file-sharing and printer-sharing server message block (SMB) protocol. SMB is surprisingly complex. It offers the same functionality of much simpler Unix-like protocols, but it also includes literally hundreds of command packets so that the server may take on responsibility for client performance characteristics as well as information exchange.

Samba's main configuration file is `/etc/smb.conf`. Like the Apache Web server, this file and the `smb.conf` file-format man page are well documented. Despite the large number of possible Samba parameters, many installations may be configured using just a few of these parameters. To establish file sharing, three key parameters must be defined:

- IP addresses of client and/or server
- Microsoft network neighborhood host names
- Microsoft passwords, if any

By default in most distributions, files in the home directory and printers listed in the `printcap` file are shared.

Samba is not a single program, but a suite of programs. The SMB service is provided by two daemons: /usr/sbin/nmbd, which provides NetBIOS name server support to clients, and /usr/sbin/smbd, which provides Microsoft LanManager service to Microsoft Windows clients. In addition, there are six other programs that fall within the Samba suite:

Smbclient. Uses the LanManager protocol to act as an FTP-like client and access files on Windows machines.

smbmount and smbumount. Both create and remove a file manager back-end that understands the SMB protocol. Thus, Windows for Workgroups, Windows NT, or LanManager host files appear within the Linux directory hierarchy.

smbtar. A shell script that uses smbclient to back up SMB shared folders directly to the tape drive. In other words, it requires smbmount to perform backups.

smbstatus. List and report status of current Samba connections.

smbpasswd. Allows a user to change his or her encrypted SMB password locally or on a Windows NT server.

make_smbcodepage. Create a code page definition file. An ASCII Samba code page definition file is a description that tells Samba how to map from uppercase to lowercase for characters greater than ASCII 127 in the specified DOS code page.

NFS

The Network File System (NFS) is the Unix solution for direct file access on other hosts. NFS service is provided by one daemon, nfsd, which is activated when a remote file is requested. NFS service is controlled by two files: an export file on the server, and mount files (fstab) on each client. The server file /etc/exports appears as follows:

```
/       master(rw) trusty(rw)
/projects       proj*.local.domain(rw)
/pub  (ro,insecure)
/pub/private   (noaccess)
```

The first line exports the entire file system to hosts master and trusty; the second entry shows example wild card host names; and the third line exports the pub directory to every host in the world. The insecure option in the third entry also allows clients with NFS implementations that do not use a reserved port for NFS. The last line denies all NFS clients access to the private subdirectory.

The client /etc/fstab file appears as follows:

```
/dev/hda1             swap      swap     defaults        0   0
/dev/hda2             /         ext2     defaults        1   1
/dev/hdb              /cdrom    iso9660  ro,noauto,user  0   0
/dev/fd0              /floppy   auto     noauto,user     0   0
proc                  /proc     proc     defaults        0   0
server:/usr/local/pub /pub      nfs      rsize=8192,wsize=8192,
                                         timeo=14,intr
```

The first five lines describe the typical mount parameters for the hard disk partitions, ATAPI CD-ROM, floppy disk, and `proc` pseudo file manager. The sixth line allows the client to mount a local directory called pub from the host called server whose directory is /usr/local/pub.

Network Security

One of the fundamental issues of network administration concerns communication access; that is, to whom should communication access be allowed, and what forms of communication should be included in that access? This issue can be addressed with two files: /etc/hosts.allow and /etc/hosts.deny. Each file is structured so that the network service (server) is listed to the left, followed by a colon, and hosts that may be allowed (or disallowed) the service are listed after the colon delimiter. For example, the /etc/hosts.allow file may have an entry similar to:

```
ALL: 130.74.128.0/255.255.255.0, 130.74.1.0/255.255.255.0, 130.74.96.0/255.255.255.0
```

Here, ALL network services are made available to three class C subnets.
The /etc/hosts.deny file employs the same format but with the opposite effect:

```
ALL: 195.180.128.0/255.255.255.0,
     166.72.235.157
ALL EXCEPT in.smtpd, httpd:  ALL
```

In the first line, ALL network services have been denied to one Class C subnet and one IP address. In the second line, ALL network services except for e-mail and Web service are denied to ALL networks. In the third line, even Web service is denied from one Class C address.

PART

Two

Labs and Exercises

Creating a User Account

Purpose

This lab will familiarize you with three different methods of creating new user accounts: using a GUI tool, a utility (such as `adduser` or `useradd`), or editing the `/etc/passwd` file at the command line.

Theory

The three methods to create new user accounts differ in format, difficulty, and configurability. While the GUI is easy to use, the automation of the process offers the system administrator little opportunity to customize user settings. Text-based utilities such as `adduser` or `useradd` are also automated commands, but they offer a greater degree of control. Creating a new user by editing the `/etc/passwd` file is the most difficult method of the three; however, this method allows a system administrator to edit every aspect of the new account.

GUI-Based Configuration

Most GUI interfaces are not limited to user administration; this allows the system administrator to control most aspects of system configuration. Caldera's administrative tool is the Caldera Open Administration System (COAS); Red Hat distributions include Linux Configure (Linuxconf), and SuSE uses Yet Another Setup Tool (YaST). Not all distributions of Linux offer an administrative GUI. The GUI tools can be accessed either by typing in the command name at the system prompt, or by choosing the appropriate selections from the Gnome desktop.

Utility-Based Configuration

An administrator may prefer to use `adduser` or `useradd` to set up new accounts. These utilities prompt the administrator to fill in all the information necessary to create a new user. The default arguments used with `useradd` or `adduser` may be specified in the control file `/etc/default/useradd`. In some cases, `useradd` may only ask for a new username as everything else is completed automatically. Neither `adduser` nor `useradd` can be used to update passwords.

Command-Line-Based Configuration

Accounts created by editing the `/etc/passwd` file require several additional steps before they are ready for use. Once the user has been created, the administrator must ensure that the new account remains secure. After the new account is created, the administrator must run `pwconv`, encrypting user passwords and moving them to a new location. The password entries previously displayed in `/etc/passwd` file are converted to an x or an *, and encrypted to `/etc/shadow`, which is accessible only by root.

When using Red Hat, `pwconv` must be run before running `passwd`. Also, when using Debian, the command to set shadow passwords is `shadowconfig on`. Once shadow passwords are enabled, the password for the new user should be set by using the `passwd` command.

The final steps in creating new accounts are as follows: make the user's directory, copy all the necessary files for the new user account, and change the ownership of the copied files to the new user.

Lab Exercises

The following exercises involve the creation of a new user account using the previously discussed methods.

GUI-Based Configuration

Use a GUI to create a user account. In this case, Linuxconf was used with Red Hat as the version.

1. Log in as root.
2. Enter `startx` at the root prompt.
3. Choose Gnome main menu.

4. Choose the `system`, then `Linuxconf` menus. (Alternative method: as a user, open an xterm, `su` to root, and run `Linuxconf`.)

5. Select User accounts option by clicking the Normal menu items, then the User accounts submenu.

6. Click the `add` button.

7. Fill in information. Everything but the `username` field is optional.

8. Click the `accept` button.

9. Enter a password.

10. Retype password.

11. Click the `quit` button.

12. Click `Linuxconf Quit` to leave the application.

13. Log in as that user to test the configuration.

Utility-Based Configuration

Use a utility to create a user account. In this case, `useradd` was used.

1. Log in as root.

2. Use the `useradd` command to create the new user account:

```
# useradd newuser
```

3. Use the `passwd` command to change the password of the new account from the default password given to it by the `useradd` program:

```
# passwd newuser
```

4. Log in as that user to test the configuration.

Command-Line-Based Configuration

Use a text editor to modify the `/etc/passwd` file. In this case, Vi editor is used.

1. Log in as root.

2. Use Vi to open the `/etc/passwd` file.

3. Duplicate one of the lower lines with the following format:

```
account name: password: user ID: group ID: comment(gecos): home directory: login
    shell
```

The following is a sample of what you might find:

```
user1:Gre3kO9rqpWjb:501:100:New User:/home/user1:/bin/bash
```

The following four fields must be changed to that of the new user: account name, user ID, gecos, and home directory. user ID is changed to a new value not used by other accounts (e.g., 501 to 502). gecos is miscellaneous information about the user, generally the user's real name. After these changes are made, Vi can be closed.

```
user2:Gre3kO9rqpWjb:502:100:Jane Doe:/home/user2:/bin/bash
```

4. For most versions of Linux, pwconv may be optionally run at this point. However, in Red Hat, pwconv must be run before the password is installed on the system.

5. Use the passwd command to change the password of the new user:

```
# passwd user2
```

6. Use the mkdir command to create the user's home directory. Then use chown and chgrp to change the owner and group from root, to the account name and account group. For a new user named newuser:

```
# mkdir /home/user2
# chown user2 /home/user2
# chgrp 100 /home/user2s
```

Group numbers can vary from one computer to the next, but the number 100 is usually associated with the group users.

7. Use the su command to switch to the new user:

```
# su user2
```

8. Use the cp command to copy the startup files to the home directory of the new user:

```
$ cp -r /etc/skel/.{[A-Z],[a-z]}* .
```

The -r switch will copy directories recursively; [A-Z] represents the uppercase character following the dot (.) symbol; [a-z] represents the first lowercase character following the dot (.) symbol in the /etc/skel directory.

If su is not used to switch users before the files are copied, the files will be owned by root. The command chown -R can correct the problem in the event that the user forgets:

```
# chown -R user2 /home/user2
```

Also, certain commands such as the following might cause problems if used to copy the startup files:

```
$ cp -r /etc/skel/.* .
```

or

```
$ cp -r /etc/skel/.[abc...xyz]* .
```

In the previous example, not only will the hidden files that start with the dot (.) symbol be copied, but an attempt will also be made to copy the parent directory files (..), as they also start with a dot (.) symbol.

Questions

1. Look at the following line from /etc/passwd and explain the meaning of each portion:

   ```
   user1:Gre3kO9rqpWjb:501:100:New User:/home/user1:/bin/bash
   ```

2. What problem might arise if the following command is used when copying startup files from /etc/skel to the new account home directory?

   ```
   $ cp -r /etc/skel/.* .
   ```

Answers

1. user1 is the username. Gre3kO9rqpWjb is an encrypted password. 501 is the userid. 100 is the usergroup. New User is gecos (finger information). /home/user1 is the user's home directory. /bin/bash is the user's default shell.

2. Since the command gives instructions to copy everything after the dot (.) symbol, the parent directory (..) is also copied.

Advanced Questions

1. Why must pwconv be run in Red Hat?
2. Explain the purpose of shadow passwords.

mount and umount

Purpose

This lab will familiarize the system administrator with the function of the `/etc/fstab` file and the `mount` and `umount` commands. The system administrator will edit the `/etc/fstab` file using a text editor to create default settings for mounting a floppy drive. Next, the system administrator will mount the floppy using the `mount` command, and then mount a CD-ROM using the `mount -t` command.

Theory

Before a file system can be accessed, it must be mounted. The `/etc/fstab` file contains the information of devices that are loaded when Linux starts. This information includes the device name (e.g., `/dev/hda0`, `/dev/fd0`, `/dev/hdb`), the mount point of the device (e.g., `/swap`, `/mnt/floppy`, `/mnt/cdrom`), the file system type (e.g., ext2, msdos, iso9660), and the mount options. File contents will vary, but should be similar to the following:

```
/dev/hda5    /swap         swap      defaults
/dev/hda1    /             ext2      defaults
/dev/hdb     /mnt/cdrom    iso9660   noauto,ro
/dev/fd0     /mnt/floppy   ext2      noauto,owner
```

The device name is the default name of the drive or hard drive partition. For example, /dev/fd0 is the default name for the first floppy drive.

The mount point defines the location within the file structure where the device or partition can be accessed. A device can be mounted anywhere on the file system, but it is best to mount it to an empty directory. Otherwise, files in that directory will be hidden from the file system. Common usage suggests creating dedicated directories for each mounted device. The system administrator can decide where to place these directories and what to name them, but often the floppy drive will be mounted in the /floppy or the /mnt/floppy directory, the CD-ROM will be mounted in the /cdrom or the /mnt/cdrom directory, and the swap partition will be mounted in the /swap directory.

The file system type defines the type of files searched for when the device is accessed. Some common file system types are minix, ext, ext2, xiafs, msdos, hpfs, iso9660, nfs, swap, and ignore. For the purposes of this exercise, the user must be familiar with ext2 (the latest version of Linux extensions), iso9660 (the common CD-ROM file system), and MS-DOS.

Many of the options for mounting devices are device specific, such as allowing any user the ability to mount a floppy drive. The system administrator must add the user option to the floppy drive mount options in /etc/fstab.

In the fstab example, both the CD-ROM and the floppy file systems are given the mount option noauto, which specifies that those devices will not be mounted automatically when the system starts. To automatically mount a file system on system startup, change this option to auto.

Finally, it may be necessary for this exercise to unmount a device before beginning an assignment. Typing mount will display information of all currently mounted devices. Unmount the device with the umount command (umount /mnt/floppy, umount /dev/fd0, and umount /mnt/ cdrom). A file system cannot be unmounted if you are in its directory. Change directories before proceeding with the umount command.

Lab Exercises

1. Log in as root, and use the mount command to access the floppy drive.

   a. The standard form of the mount command is:

   ```
   $ mount -t type device directory
   ```

   This command will allow you to use any existing directory as the mount point for a device. Before beginning, make sure the /mnt/floppy (or /floppy) directory exists. If not, create it using the mkdir command. If the Linux kernel is configured to accept the MS-DOS file system, place an MS-DOS floppy in the drive and enter the following command:

   ```
   $ mount -t msdos /dev/fd0 /mnt/floppy
   ```

   This gives access to the floppy drive.

b. Try the same procedure with a Linux floppy, but first umount the MS-DOS floppy. Removable media should never be taken from the drive or switched while mounted, since this can cause complications. To unmount the floppy, enter one of the following commands:

```
$ umount /mnt/floppy or umount /dev/fd0
```

For a Linux floppy, the file system type is ext2. Switch to a Linux floppy and enter the following to access the drive:

```
$ mount -t ext2 /dev/fd0 /mnt/floppy
```

Next, modify the /etc/fstab file to allow users to employ the mount command.

2. Mount a floppy as a user. Adding the user option to the /etc/fstab file allows users other than root to mount a file system.

a. Open the /etc/fstab file using the Vi editor.

b. Locate the line that references the floppy device. If the line does not exist, create it based on the bottom line in the following example:

```
# device        directory      type         options
/dev/hda3       /              ext2         defaults
/dev/ hda1      /boot          ext2         defaults      /dev/cdrom
/mnt/cdrom      iso9660        noauto,ro
/dev/fd0        /mnt/ floppy   auto         noauto
```

device, directory, and type have the same meaning here as with the mount command. The use of auto as a file system type allows the user to mount either msdos or ext2 floppies. In general, it allows mounting to any file system type that is compiled in the kernel.

c. When mounting a file system that has been entered into the /etc/fstab file, give either the device or the mount point:

```
mount /dev/fd0 or mount /mnt/floppy
```

Do not forget to unmount the Linux floppy from the previous exercise. Then mount the floppy file system using one of the preceding commands.

d. Add user to the end of the line under the options column. Use a comma to separate it from the other option. An example of the changes is presented here:

```
/dev/fd0      /mnt/floppy     auto     noauto,user
```

e. Log out root, and then log in as a user. Use one of the following commands to mount the floppy drive:

```
$ mount /dev/fd0 or mount /mnt/floppy
```

You should now have access to the floppy file system under the /mnt/floppy directory.

3. Mount a CD-ROM as a user. The user option must be added to the /etc/fstab file.

   a. Open the file /etc/fstab using the Vi editor.

   b. Locate the line that references the CD-ROM device. If the line does not exist, create it based on the following example:

```
# device      directory       type      options
/dev/hda3     /               ext2      defaults
/dev/hda1     /boot           ext2      defaults
/dev/cdrom    /mnt/cdrom      iso9660   noauto,ro
/dev/fd0      /mnt/floppy     auto      noauto,user
```

iso9660 is the file system type used by most CD-ROMs.

   c. Add the word user to the end of the line under the options column. Use a comma to separate it from the other options. The example should be similar to the following after the changes have been made:

```
/dev/cdrom    /mnt/cdrom      iso9660   noauto,user,ro
```

   d. Log out root and then log in as a user, either the device or the mount point may be specified. The following command uses the mount point:

```
$ mount /mnt/cdrom
```

You should now have access to the CD-ROM file system under the /mnt/cdrom directory. As with floppies, a CD-ROM should not be removed while it is mounted. In this case, the system locks the CD-ROM in place and it cannot be removed until it is unmounted.

Questions

1. What is the mount point?
2. Identify and define the underlined portions of the following line:

     <u>/dev/fd0</u> /floppy   <u>auto</u>   noauto,user

3. Choose the correct command line for mounting a device:

   a. mount -t <u>device type dir</u>

   b. mount <u>device dir type</u>

   c. mount -t <u>device type</u>

   d. mount -t <u>type device dir</u>

Answers

1. A mount point defines the location (directory) where the device or partition can be accessed within the file structure. Although this makes the files on the accessed file system appear as though they reside in the given directory, it is generally an empty directory named /mnt/ floppy or /floppy.

2. <u>/dev/fd0</u>. This column indicates the device being mounted; in this case, the first floppy drive

   <u>auto</u>. This column indicates that the file system type auto allows access to any file system compiled in the kernel.

3. d. mount -t <u>type</u> <u>device</u> <u>dir</u>

Advanced Questions

1. What must be done before a file system can be mounted automatically?

2. Why is an empty directory desirable as a mount point for a file system?

3. If a file system has been entered into the /etc/fstab file, what two equivalent arguments may be used with the mount and umount commands?

Configuration of the lilo.conf File

Purpose

This lab will address the configuration of the `lilo.conf` file, enabling you to modify startup parameters. After completing the lab, you will be familiar with the proper procedure of editing configuration settings, and the consequences of improper configuration.

Theory

LInux LOader (LILO) acts as an interface between the BIOS system and operating system, in addition to coordinating the boot-up process. The following is an example of the `lilo.conf` file:

```
#(Global options)
      boot=/dev/hda
      read-only
      prompt
      timeout=100
      vga=normal

#(Linux Stanza)

      image=/boot/vmlinuz
      root=/dev/hda2
      label=linux
```

In certain versions of Linux, the `lilo.conf` file is structured differently; however, the overall layout is the same. For example:

```
boot=/dev/hda
map=/boot/map
install=/boot/boot.b
prompt
timeout=50
default=linux

image=/boot/vmlinuz
label=linux
root=/dev/hda1
read-only
```

Lab Exercises

You will concentrate on editing the `image`, `label`, and `root` lines shown in the two previous examples. In addition, at the end of the lab, you will save your work and run LILO before rebooting in order for the new settings to take effect.

Configuration

As stated previously, every `lilo.conf` file is organized in essentially the same way, but there are slight differences. You should edit the `lilo.conf` file based on your specific layout.

1. Log in as root.

2. Change from the `/home` directory to the `/etc` directory.

3. Open the `lilo.conf` file using your favorite editor.

4. At the end of the file, enter the following lines:

```
image=/boot/vmlinuz.new
root=/dev/hda2
label=newkernel
```

These lines may or may not already exist in the LILO file. If they do, they will look similar to those listed in the example just shown; if not, simply enter them in addition to the lines given in this step. The result should resemble the following:

```
image=/boot/vmlinuz.new
root=/dev/hda2
label=newkernel

image=/boot/vmlinuz
root=/dev/hda2
label=linux
```

The following describes the function of each added line:

`image=/boot/vmlinuz`	Tells LILO which kernel to boot
`root=/dev/hda2`	Specifies which partition is to be treated as root
`label=linux`	Associates a logical name to the boot image

5. Save the file and exit the editor.

6. Run the LILO program from the command prompt. If you fail to run LILO after saving it and then reboot the system, the new settings will not take effect.

7. Restart the computer.

Recompiling the Kernel

This procedure of editing LILO can be also used to back up a recompiled Linux kernel.

1. Open the new LILO file using your favorite editor.

2. Locate the recent addition to the file:

```
image=/boot/vmlinuz
root=/dev/hda2
label=linux
```

Change the directory in the first line from `/boot` to `/root`. Change the label to reflect its new function. The finished product should resemble the following:

```
image=/root/vmlinuz
root=/dev/hda2
label=backup_boot
```

This saves a copy of the kernel settings to the `/root` directory. If you run LILO before rebooting the system, you will be able to access the system without using a boot disk. Simply log in as root, rerun LILO, and reboot.

Questions

1. What is LILO?
2. Why is it necessary to run LILO before rebooting the system?

Answers

1. LILO is the abbreviation for LInux LOader, a configuration utility that outlines and dictates system settings upon startup.

2. If LILO is not run before the reboot, the new settings will not take effect upon startup.

Advanced Questions

1. Explain the LILO booting process.
2. Explain the importance of the LILO time-out parameter in relation to security.

Loading and Unloading the Device Driver

Purpose

After completing this exercise, you should be comfortable loading and unloading a device driver.

Theory

Since the Linux kernel is modular, the administrator has direct control over what functions are available within the core operating system at any given time. Each device is controlled by its own stand-alone driver or module. By adding or removing modules, either automatically in the startup sequence or manually during the normal operation of the computer, the administrator can configure the system to work optimally for each task being performed. Adding and removing modules enables the administrator to use different devices that would otherwise cause system conflicts if loaded at the same time. Removing unnecessary modules can also improve performance, because less memory is required to store and run the kernel.

In this exercise, you will install a module using the `insmod` command, check the newly installed module using `lsmod`, and remove the module using `rmmod`. Both the `insmod` and `lsmod` commands have options that are explained in the manual pages, but are unnecessary for this lab.

The `lsmod` command displays the currently loaded modules, the number of bytes or pages (one page=4096 bytes) used by each module, and the number of programs that are using each module. This display will vary by machine, but a sample output of `lsmod` follows:

```
Module        Size        Used by
soundcore     2628        0
nfs           28192       2
autofs        9092        1
lockd         30344       1
sunrpc        52132       1
3c59x         18980       1
```

Modules are stored in the `/lib/modules` directory. Because they are written for specific versions of the Linux kernel, a conflict may occur if a module written for one version of Linux is used in a different version. For that reason, modules are stored in directories designated by their kernel version number. For example, if the computer's kernel version is 2.2.14-5.0, the directory in which the modules would be located is `/lib/modules/2.2.14-5.0`. If you are not sure which kernel version is on your machine, the `uname -a` command will display the version number.

The file system driver `ufs.o` will be added in this exercise, and the file system modules are found in the `/lib/modules/2.2.14-5.0/fs` directory. If this file or these directories do not exist on your system, recompile the kernel to include module support for the `ufs` file system.

Lab Exercises

1. Log in as `root`.
2. Use `lsmod` to display the modules currently loaded on your system.
3. Load the `ufs.o` module found in the `/lib/modules/x.x.x/fs` directory (`x.x.x` indicates the version number of the kernel currently running), using the `insmod` command as shown here:

   ```
   # insmod /lib/modules/2.2.14-5.0/fs/ufs.o
   ```

4. Confirm that the module has been successfully loaded through the `lsmod` command.
5. Remove the module using the `rmmod` command. This command removes modules according to their name, unlike `insmod`, which requires the entire file path and name. For example:

   ```
   # rmmod ufs
   ```

   However, the `rmmod` command will not work if the module is being used or if other programs depend upon it to operate.
6. Use the `lsmod` command to confirm that the module has been successfully unloaded.

Questions

1. Why is it important to know which kernel version is loaded when using the `insmod` command?
2. What are the advantages of modularity in the Linux kernel?

Answers

1. Modules from one kernel version may not work with different kernels, and modules are stored in directories according to their kernel version number.
2. It adds flexibility to the operating system, can improve performance, and can optimize memory usage.

Advanced Questions

1. Is it possible to load a module from one kernel version of Linux to a kernel of a different version? If so, how?

V

Installing Software

Purpose

This lab will discuss the use of a package manager and the source code for the installation of software. The exercises in this lab will show you how to install and remove software using both processes.

Theory

When discussing the installation of software, two topics must be considered: package manager installation and source code installation.

Package Manager Installation

Package managers have three main functions: installation of software packages, removal of installed packages, and performing various administrative duties related to software. Package managers provide the most convenient method of installing software.

Most package managers maintain some type of database about installed packages, allowing the user to track dependencies in a number of ways. Dependencies are the software packages and files that are needed by another software package for it to operate properly. Before a package is deleted, the package manager will check all the files belonging to that package. If any of the required files are already installed packages, the manager will not allow those dependencies to be deleted.

When installing a package, the package manager will compare the dependencies to the packages already installed. If any of the dependencies are not present, the user will be warned not to install the new software until the required dependencies are installed. In some cases, the needed files or packages may already be installed, but the package manager does not have this information in its database. The installation can usually be forced; however, this should only be done if you know which files or packages are missing and intend to add them later. To find out which packages and versions are installed on a system, query the database. Most package managers specify which software package a particular file belongs to, and which files are contained in a package.

Items added with the package manager should also be removed with the package manager. In some cases, a command will convince the database that the deleted material is still present. The user can also install packages using FTP by specifying the file with a valid URL. Most package managers also provide the tools necessary to build software packages.

There are a number of package managers available. The Red Hat Package Manager (RPM) is not limited to the Red Hat distribution; Caldera and SuSE also use RPM. The command rpm is used to perform all the functions of the package, depending upon which option is selected. Other package managers operate in a similar manner. The Debian package manager has several tools, including apt and dpkg, that work together to form a package management system. Slackware Package Manager (SPM) is a front-end to a number of tools, including installpkg, removepkg, and rpm2tgz, and can read both rpm and tgz packages.

Software packages designed for the Stampede GNU/Linux package system, or SPM, have the file extension .tgz or .tar.gz. Debian, RPM, and Stampede packages have the extensions .deb, .rpm, and .slp, respectively.

Most versions of Linux have a package converter tool called alien that will convert one package format to another. For a comparison of the major package formats, see www.linuxsolutions.com.

Source Code Installation

While installing from source distribution can be more difficult, it offers greater flexibility. Some software is available only in source code; the latest version of software is generally available in source first. Source files come as compressed archives. The same package can be used as the basis for software running on different types of operating systems. This saves the author of the software time and trouble, but makes installation more difficult for the end user.

Source distributions, or tarballs, usually have .tar.gz or .tgz extensions, meaning they have been archived and compressed using the tar and gzip utilities. After being downloaded, the tarball must be un-archived and uncompressed, which is done with the tar and gzip commands. Both are executed when tar is used with the z option; for example, tar xzvf. The un-archiving process usually stores the files in subdirectories that it creates. bzip2 is a new compression format that provides better compression than gzip. Before un-tarring with this format, run bunzip. Files compressed with the bzip2 program have the .bz2 extension.

The following steps describe installation from source:

1. Run a configure script to determine if the components needed for installation are available on your system. Options may be specified with the configure script, allowing the software to be tailored to your system. It will often create what is called a `Makefile`, although this may already be part of the package.

2. Run `make`, which usually involves simply typing `make`. This will compile the executables and libraries for that particular package as instructed in the `Makefile`.

3. As root, install the new binaries in the proper system directories. Typing `make install` will start this process.

Documentation is very important for all aspects of the installation process and for solving potential problems. When un-archiving or installing, read the documentation files to obtain procedures and information relevant to a particular package or version of Linux. The `README` or `Install` files may instruct the user to edit certain files, or cite the directory from which to install the program.

Lab Exercises

This lab will use the Red Hat Package Manager (RPM). If this is not available, either use `alien` to convert a package to a different format, or install a software package that is compatible with the package manager you have. The RPM package of `pkzip` and the source code for `vim` may be downloaded using anonymous FTP. A good site for RPM packages is http://rpmfind.net, and `vim` can be found at www.vim.org. These packages were chosen because they are not likely to cause compatibility problems. The examples used in this lab were the most recent versions available at the time of this writing. If already installed, choose another version to avoid system complications.

Install and Uninstall a Software Package Using a Package Manager

1. Log in as root.
2. To install, type:

   ```
   $ rpm -i pkzip-2.51-2.i386.rpm
   ```

   The `-i` option instructs `rpm` to install the package. If `rpm` warns that you do not meet your dependencies, add the `--nodeps` option to the install line. The software may not work if this is used, but it will be deleted at the end of the lab.

3. Locate the file `pkzip` using either the `find` or `locate` command.
4. Uninstall the package; the `-e` option instructs `rpm` to erase the package. Type:

   ```
   $ rpm -e pkzip
   ```

5. Demonstrate that the file has been removed. When `pkzip` is run, you should get the message `command not found`.

Install a Software Package from Source Code

1. Log in as root.
2. Change to the directory containing the `vim-5.7-rt.tar.gz` and `vim-5.7-src.tar.gz` files.
3. Use `tar` to un-archive and uncompress the two files.

   For example, this command will extract and uncompress the source code:

   ```
   $ tar xvzf vim-5.7-src.tar.gz
   ```

   The source code and the runtime files will un-archive into the same directory. This should create the directory `vim-5.7`. Remain in this directory for the next few steps.
4. Read the installation notes or README files included with the sources. These will indicate if the files associated with the program need to be edited.
5. Run the `./configure` program; the `./` is used to specify that the local configure should be run.

   ```
   $ ./configure
   ```

6. Run the `make` program:

   ```
   $ make
   ```

7. Run `make install`.

   ```
   $ make install
   ```

   This will copy the files to the appropriate system areas and set the correct permissions.
8. Run `vim`. There should be a splash screen announcing that version 5.7 is running. If not, another program called `vim` was most likely already in existence.

Delete Files

Delete the three files you downloaded, as well as the source directories. Use the `-rf` option with `rm` to delete a directory.

Questions

1. Is it possible to install an `rpm` software package without the RPM? If so, how?
2. When installing from a source distribution, what command is used to start the compile process?
3. What is a dependency?

Answers

1. Yes, by using a package converter, such as `alien`, on a non-RPM package.
2. The `make` command is used.
3. A file that is required for software to work properly.

Advanced Questions

1. For what reason would an RPM query show a file to be in a directory when it had already been deleted?
2. What command is used to both un-archive and uncompress a tarball?
3. Why is `./` included in the `./configure` argument when running the configure script?

Editing a Text File

Purpose

This lab contains a list of the more popular text editors, which range from simple to complex in their capabilities. This lab also demonstrates the use of the echo command to create a file and add text to it.

Theory

Although there are many text editors available, this lab will only cover Vim, Pico, Joe, and Emacs. Each section contains a brief description of the editor, followed by a listing of steps and commands used to perform certain tasks.

Vim

Vim is a powerful and advanced text editor. Therefore, the program is difficult to learn. It is essential to know what mode the editor is in, the basic mode being the command mode. This is the mode in which commands, such as save, exit, and search are entered. By pressing ESC several times until a beep is sounded, the user can be sure that the editor is in command mode. The other important mode is insert mode, in which text can be typed or edited. To change from command mode to insert mode, type i. The commands in the following list should be run in command mode.

To open a file, type the following at the command prompt:

```
$ vim <filename>
```

To save a file, type:

```
:w <filename>
```

To search for a string within the file, type / followed by the string to search for:

```
/ <search string>
```

To copy text, move the cursor to the start of the text to be copied, and type v. Using the Arrow keys, select the text to copy, and press y.

To paste cut or copied text, position the cursor to the place where the text is to be placed, and press the p key.

To exit the program, while in command mode, type :wq to save and exit, or type :q! to exit without saving.

To add text to a file, change to insert mode by pressing i, and insert the text.

Pico

Pico, short for Pine Composer, is a simple text editor that comes with the Pine e-mail program. It can also be used by itself for text editing.

To open a file, type the following at the command prompt:

```
pico <filename>
```

To save a file, type CTRL-O and enter the file name.

To search for a string within the file, type CTRL-W followed by the string to be searched for.

To copy text, position the cursor at the beginning of the text to be copied, and press CTRL-SHIFT-6. Next move the cursor to select all of the text to be copied, and press CTRL-K, followed by CTRL-U. This will cut and paste the text to its original position, leaving the text in memory to be pasted elsewhere.

To paste cut or copied text, position the cursor to where the text is to be placed, and press CTRL-U.

Text can be entered at any time in this program.

To exit the program, press CTRL-X.

Emacs

Emacs is a powerful and versatile text editor from the GNU project. The program has many features, but only the text editor will be discussed here. Like Vim, Emacs is a difficult program to learn, but allows more complex tasks to be performed. There are three parts to the Emacs interface: the text buffer, the mode line, and the command line. Text is entered in the text buffer, and commands are issued at the command line.

To open a file, type the following at the command prompt:

```
emacs <filename>
```

To save a file, type CTRL-X then CTRL-C. Use caution; this will save the file under the name in which it was opened.

The text can be entered at any time, as long as the cursor is in the text buffer.

To search for a string within the file, type CTRL-S followed by the string to search for.

To copy text, position the cursor at the beginning of the text to be copied, and press CTRL-SPACEBAR. Next, move the cursor to select all of the text to be copied and press ALT-W.

To paste cut or copied text, position the cursor to where the text is to be placed, and press CTRL-Y.

To exit the program, press CTRL-X, and then CTRL-C.

Joe

Joe is a simple text editor, similar to Pico. Once the editor is opened, a dialog box can be started that will reside at the top of the screen, which contains the most common commands. To open this box, press CTRL-K-H.

To open a file, type the following at the command prompt:

```
joe <filename>
```

To save a file, type CTRL-K-D and enter the file name.

The text can be entered at any time using this editor.

To search for a string within the file, type CTRL-K-F followed by the string to be searched for.

To copy text, position the cursor at the beginning of the text to be copied, and press CTRL-K-B. Next, move the cursor to select all of the text to be copied, and press CTRL-K-K.

To paste cut or copied text, position the cursor to where the text is to be placed, and press CTRL-K-C.

To exit the program, press CTRL-K-X to save and exit, or press CTRL-C to exit without saving.

Command Line

This section will demonstrate the use of the `echo` command to add text to a file. This can be useful after a faulty instillation, if no text editors were installed and a file must be edited. The following command will create a file named `filename` and add text to this file:

```
$ echo "text to be added to filename" >> filename
```

If repeated, the text, or new text, will be appended to the end of the file. If the file already exists, the text will be appended to the end of the existing file.

Lab Exercises

The following is a series of exercises to familiarize the user with some basic operations of the text editors discussed in this lab.

Command Line

Use the echo command to create a file named themarethose, and add the following lines to it:

```
All them are those
All those are there
Therefore, all them are there
```

Text Editors

The following is a list of tasks to perform using each of the following text editors: Vim, Pico, Emacs, and Joe. Complete the list with one editor, and then repeat it with the next until all the tasks have been performed with each editor.

1. Open the file named themarethose.
2. Open and close the Help menu.
3. Add a line at the end of the file stating which editor is currently being used.
4. Search for the following string are there.
5. Copy the first line of the file and paste it after the last line.
6. Exit the program.

Questions

1. Which text editor(s) would be best for someone who does not know how to use any editor, but needs to quickly edit a text file?
2. In Vim, what happens when a command is entered in insert mode?

Answers

1. Joe or Pico would be best because they are the easiest to use of the editors discussed in this lab.
2. The command will be typed into the document as regular text.

Advanced Questions

1. How can the contents of the file created during this lab be changed without using a text editor, so that only the original lines are left?

PPP Configuration

Purpose

The purpose of this lab is to familiarize the user with the use and configuration of the Point-to-Point Protocol (PPP).

Theory

Users should familiarize themselves with PPP in order to take advantage of the dial-up Internet connection capabilities offered by the Linux operating system. The PPP allows users to connect to the Internet through an ISP with a modem and a telephone line (ISDN line). The user must configure his or her machine to use PPP as its method for connecting to the Internet.

There are a variety of PPP utilities; many Linux distributions come with different PPP tools. However, the wvdial program, which is the PPP utility that will be discussed in this lab, is bundled with most major distributions. Some different PPP tools are listed in Table VII.1.

Table VII.1 Point-to-Point Protocol Tools

UTILITY	DISTRIBUTION	DEFINITION
kppp	All (component of KDE)	Provides a graphical dial-up configuration program and network monitoring front-end for pppd.
diald	All	Will open a connection when there are Internet packets to be sent, and close the connection when it is no longer needed.
rp3	Red Hat 6.2 or later (component of Gnome)	Graphical PPP setup and configuration tool.
wvdial	All	Provides automatic modem detection and dial-up script configuration.
pppd	All	The PPP daemon.
chat	All	Scripting for pppd.

wvdial is one of the easiest PPP utilities to install and configure. To supplement your PPP knowledge, consider familiarizing yourself with the function of the Point-to-Point Protocol Daemon, pppd. The PPP daemon uses three configuration scripts. Two scripts enable and disable PPP; these are usually found in the /usr/local/bin directory with the file names ppp-on and ppp-off. The third script is the ppp-chatfile, which is used to dail up and log in to the ISP. It is commonly located in the /etc/ppp directory. To prevent security breaches, the permissions for the ppp-chatfile should be set so that only the owner has read and write access, since the file will store passwords in plain text; the ppp-chatfile should be owned by root. The ppp-on script checks the ownership and the type of files located in the ppp-chatfile.

Lab Exercises

Confirm that the computer is connected to a modem either internally or externally.

If the modem is external, make sure that the modem is turned on and is getting power. (This may seem trivial, but it is surprising how many times this step is overlooked.) If the modem is internal, make sure it is not a WinModem style modem. While there are some Linux drivers available for Linux, it is not advised to use a WinModem due to lack of viable drivers. Log in as root, and at the command line, type:

```
$ wvdialconf /etc/wvdial.conf
```

This command allows for the creation of the wvdial.conf file if a modem is found. If a modem is not found, check the physical modem connection, then check for a serial driver with the modprobe serial command. Reboot your computer to be safe.

Edit the `Username`, `Password`, and `Phone` fields with the proper values in the `wvdial.conf` file that was just created. This should look similar to the following:

```
[Dialer Defaults]
Username = suse
Modem = /dev/modem
Password = linux
Area Code =
Force Address =
Init1 = ATZ
Init2 = ATQ0 V1 E1 S0=0 &C1 &D2
Compuserve = 0
Dial Command = ATDT
Phone = 000-0000
Baud = 57600
Idle Seconds = 180
ISDN = 0
Stupid Mode = 1
```

Besides the `Username`, `Password`, and `Phone` fields, the user can leave the default values for all the fields. If the number to be dialed is not local, the user may have to edit the `Area Code` field.

Type `wvdial`; this will execute a script that connects your machine to the Internet. The user can check the configuration by running `lynx` and connecting to a Web site. If the Web site loads, then the configuration was a success.

Questions

1. What is PPP?
2. What is required for a PPP connection?

Answers

1. The Point-to-Point Protocol (PPP) is used to connect a computer with a modem to the Internet via a telephone line or ISDN line.

2. To make a PPP connection, the user will need a modem, telephone line (or ISDN line), and an account with an Internet Service Provider (ISP).

Advanced Questions

1. What are some of the disadvantages of using PPP?

Configuring a File Share
Using Samba

Purpose

The purpose of this lab is to introduce the user to the file-sharing capabilities of Linux and Samba, and to learn how to do a simple file share that is accessible by a Windows machine on the same network.

Theory

Samba implements the Server Message Block (SMB) protocol for Unix and other Unix-like systems. It allows a Linux machine to share a drive or a printer with a Windows machine. Samba uses two daemons, a configuration file, and various client programs to accomplish its task. These are described in the following sections.

smbd

smbd is the daemon that provides file and print sharing to clients that access the share on the Linux system.

nmbd

nmbd is the daemon that handles Linux's NetBIOS over IP name service requests produced by clients using the SMB protocol.

smb.conf

smb.conf is the configuration file for the Samba daemons. This is the file that will be edited to create the file share for this lab. The file is generally located in /etc or /etc/samba; the semicolons signify comments. The file will be similar to the following:

```
[global]
   workgroup = SAIR
   security = share
   guest account = nobody
   keep alive = 30
; this share gives all users access to the CD
; mounted under /cdrom
[cdrom]
   comment = CD Drive
   path = /cdrom
   read only = yes
   writeable = no
   browseable = yes
   public = yes
```

smbclient

smbclient is the main client utility used to contact an SMB server. It can be used similarly to an FTP client to contact an SMB share; however, in this lab it will be used to see which shares are present on a host.

Lab Exercises

The exercises in this lab assume that the user has root access to a Linux machine, with Samba installed and running. To download Samba, go to www.samba.org or see the SMB HOWTO at www.linuxdoc.org.

1. Log in as root.
2. Type cd /etc to move to the /etc directory.
3. Open the smb.conf file in any text editor. If smb.conf is not directly in the /etc directory, try a subdirectory of /etc, such as samba.
4. Look for the security entry and make sure that it's set to share. It should be similar to the following:

   ```
   security = share
   ```

5. Using the example for the CD drive, add an entry to the smb.conf file that will share a user's home directory. This will have the same format as the CD-ROM being shared in the example. The following must be added to the smb.conf:

   ```
   [jim]
   comment = Jim's Share
   ```

```
path = /home/jim
read only = yes
writeable = no
browseable = yes
public = yes
```

6. Run the `testparm` utility to check for errors in the configuration file:

   ```
   $ testparm /etc/smb.conf
   ```

   If there are errors, edit the `smb.conf` file and run `testparm` again.

7. On some of the newer versions of Samba, the daemon will not have to be restarted. To be sure, type the following:

   ```
   $ killall -HUP smbd
   $ killall -HUP nmbd
   ```

8. If there is a Windows machine on the network with the Linux box, look for the share you set up by browsing through Network Neighborhood. If there is not a networked Windows machine handy, the share can be found by typing the following on the Linux box:

   ```
   smbclient -L localhost
   ```

   This will show all the shares available on the machine. If the home directory appears, the lab is nearly completed. If it does not, go back and adjust the `smb.conf` file until the share appears.

9. Unless the share is to be left available, remove the entry from the configuration file and restart the daemons again. For more information about Samba, visit their Web site at www.samba.org/.

Questions

1. What does the nmbd daemon do?
2. What type of hardware can Samba be used to share?
3. Why would a system administrator want to use Samba when there is a version of NFS that runs on Windows?

Answers

1. The nmbd daemon resolves the names of computers using the SMB protocol.
2. Samba can share any type of disk drive including hard drives, floppy drives, CD drives, and ZIP drives, as well as printers set up on Linux systems.
3. Most Windows applications will only work with the SMB protocol.

Advanced Questions

1. How would a system administrator configure Samba so that Windows machines on the network could utilize a Linux printer?

2. In what ways can access to Samba shares be made more secure than in the lab example?

ifconfig and route

Purpose

The purpose of this lab is to familiarize the system administrator with installing and configuring an Ethernet card to operate within a network.

Theory

In most cases, the network settings for a Linux system are configured during the installation of the operating system, and are activated as part of the boot sequence. The network settings are not automatically loaded at startup; the system administrator may need to change or add to these settings. In this lab, the system administrator will install a new Ethernet card using the correct device driver, configure the device using the ifconfig command, and establish the network connection using the route command.

The ifconfig command has several options. If given without options, it displays all currently active network interfaces. The following is an example of the output of the ifconfig command:

```
eth0      Link encap:Ethernet  HWaddr 00:50:BA:E8:68:6B
          inet addr:192.168.1.132  Bcast:192.168.1.255 Mask:255.255.255.0
          UP BROADCAST RUNNING  MTU:1500  Metric:1
          RX packets:452237 errors:0 dropped:0 overruns:0 frame:0
          TX packets:644787 errors:0 dropped:0 overruns:0 carrier:0
```

```
                    collisions:0 txqueuelen:100
                    Interrupt:10 Base address:0xa400
lo            Link encap:Local Loopback
              inet addr:127.0.0.1  Mask:255.0.0.0
                 UP LOOPBACK RUNNING  MTU:3924  Metric:1
                 RX packets:11457 errors:0 dropped:0 overruns:0 frame:0
                 TX packets:11457 errors:0 dropped:0 overruns:0 carrier:0
                 collisions:0 txqueuelen:0
```

The device name is at the far left of the first line of each interface. Link encap identifies the type of interface being described. Note that the Ethernet card has an entry, Hwaddr, that the loopback interface does not include. This hardware address is encoded on the card by the manufacturer. In contrast, a loopback is a virtual device whose default address is always 127.0.0.1.

```
Link encap:Ethernet  HWaddr 00:50:BA:E8:68:6B
```

The second line displays the network address, the broadcast address, and the network mask.

```
inet addr:192.168.1.132  Bcast:192.168.1.255  Mask:255.255.255.0
```

The third line displays the status of the interface, which can be up or down and can include a loopback interface and the maximum transfer unit (the largest transferable packet size).

```
UP BROADCAST RUNNING  MTU:1500  Metric:1
```

The next three lines display information on packets sent and received through the interface, and any collisions during transfer.

```
RX packets:452237 errors:0 dropped:0 overruns:0 frame:0
TX packets:644787 errors:0 dropped:0 overruns:0 carrier:0
collisions:0 txqueuelen:100
```

Notice the additional line of information at the end the Ethernet card's output. This line displays the interrupt, or IRQ, and base address of the interface.

```
Interrupt:10 Base address:0xa400
```

When the ifconfig command is entered with the -a option, all interfaces are shown, regardless of whether they are active. If given with the interface option, as in ifconfig eth0, the command displays the information for that device alone. The command ifconfig eth0 up activates eth0, and the command ifconfig eth0 down de-activates it.

The ifconfig command assigns the IP address, the broadcast address, the netmask, and other information for the network interface. For example, in this exercise, the command ifconfig eth0 <IP address> netmask <netmask address> broadcast <broadcast address> will assign the IP, netmask, and broadcast addresses to the first Ethernet card.

The `route` command sets the configurations for the routing table. The routing table contains the essential information that the operating system uses to determine how an outgoing packet is processed. By typing the `route` command, the user can view the routing table. For example:

```
Kernel IP routing table
Destination     Gateway         Genmask         Flags Metric Ref    Use Iface
192.168.1.0     *               255.255.255.0   U     0      0        0 eth0
127.0.0.0       *               255.0.0.0       U     0      0        0 lo
default         gate.domain.com 0.0.0.0         UG    0      0        0 eth0
```

Note that in the last line, the destination is listed as `default`. More than one gateway can be in the routing table, but only one default is permitted. To set the default gateway, issue the `route add default gw <gateway ip address>` command. In the next column, the gateway address is listed as a domain name rather than a numerical address. By using the `route` command with the `-n` option, the numerical address information can be displayed. For example:

```
Kernel IP routing table
Destination     Gateway         Genmask         Flags Metric Ref    Use Iface
192.168.1.0     0.0.0.0         255.255.255.0   U     0      0        0 eth0
127.0.0.0       0.0.0.0         255.0.0.0       U     0      0        0 lo
0.0.0.0         192.168.3.1     0.0.0.0         UG    0      0        0 eth0
```

The `route` command is used in this exercise to activate a device, and it can communicate on the network when added to the `ifconfig` command. Most of the options for the `route` command are beyond the scope of this exercise. Refer to the `route` manual pages for further information.

Lab Exercises

For the purposes of this lab, it is assumed that the Ethernet card is properly installed on the motherboard, and that the appropriate device driver for the Ethernet card is installed. The user must have the IP, netmask, broadcast, and gateway network addresses.

1. Log in as root.
2. Use `ifconfig` to display active network interfaces.
3. Configure the Ethernet card.

   ```
   ifconfig eth0 <IP address> netmask <netmask address> broadcast <broadcast address>
   ```

4. Activate the Ethernet card.

   ```
   ifconfig eth0 up
   ```

5. Check the `ifconfig` display to confirm that the Ethernet card is activated, and that all network settings are correct.

6. Display the routing table by typing route. If the command seems to be taking too long to display the information, cancel the operation with CTRL-Z and use the route command with the -n switch. The delay may be caused by the attempt to locate a domain name (which may or may not exist) associated with the gateway address.

7. Add a default gateway to the network using the route command.

```
route add default gw <gateway address>
```

8. Check your network connection by running Lynx on a popular Web site, such as www.google.com.

Questions

1. Why is the -n option useful when using the route command?
2. What is a possible reason for losing the network configuration when the system is rebooted?

Answers

1. If the system seems to delay while displaying the route command, it may be searching for a gateway domain name that does not exist. The -n switch forces a display of the numerical addresses of the network configuration and bypasses the search.

2. To have the network configuration load on boot, you must create a networking script in the startup file.

Advanced Questions

1. What is the loopback interface, and what does it do?

Using man, find, and locate

Purpose

This lab discusses how to use the man pages, the `find` utility, and the `locate` utility.

Theory

The man pages will help you learn how to use Linux commands. The `find` and `locate` utilities will help you locate files and directories in your Linux system.

man Pages

The man pages are the quickest resource for information pertaining to Linux commands, but they can be intimidating to new users.

Interpreting the man Pages

This section explains how to interpret the output of the man command. Begin by opening a terminal window and typing:

```
man man
```

Find the synopsis in the listing of text:

```
SYNOPSIS
     man [-acdfFhkKtwW]  [-m  system]  [-p  string]  [-C con-
     fig_file] [-M path] [-P pager] [- section_list][section]
     name...
```

Under `Synopsis` is the word `man`, which is the command used to invoke the program. The brackets ([   ]) containing options will vary for each man page. All options inside the brackets are optional, but the options outside the brackets are required. Also, the pipe symbol (|) is the OR command. For example, the command `man  tar` will produce the following synopsis:

```
tar [  -  ]  A --catenate --concatenate | c --create | d
    --diff --compare | r --append | t --list | u --update |x
    -extract --get
```

After the first brackets, there is a list of options separated by the pipe (|) symbol. Since these are not in brackets, at least one of the options, -A, -c, -d, -r, -t, -u, or -x, is required for the program to work.

The program's function is explained in the Description section. The Options section contains a description of the program's optional and mandatory parameters.

Using the man Pages

Use PAGEUP and PAGEDOWN to scroll through the man pages one page at a time. HOME and END will take you to the beginning and the end of the document, respectively.

The search utility is also useful. To use this, type /{string to find}. As an example, type /the in the man pages for man. The word the will be highlighted throughout the document. Use the N and P keys to find the next and previous matches in the search, respectively. The man pages use the Vi editor format, which has many more options that can be found in Vi's man pages.

To exit the man pages, press Q.

Using the find Command

The `find` command can be used to find files and directories with certain names. A user can see the man pages for the `find` utility by typing:

```
man find
```

These pages contain a simple synopsis:

```
SYNOPSIS
     find [path...] [expression]
```

Here, the options are [path...] and [expression]. To make the find utility useful, specify a path to search and an expression to match. For example, search the entire file system (except /root) with the command:

```
find / [expression]
```

Begin the search at /usr/bin with the command:

```
find /usr/bin [expression]
```

Replace [expression] with the string to match. Options for the find command can be found in the man pages. For example, the -iname option does a case-sensitive search. Search for the date program as follows:

```
find / -iname date
```

This directs the computer to start at the lowest-level directory and search for the date program. Similarly, search for all the bin directories as follows:

```
find / -iname bin
```

It is often useful to send the output to a file, which can be done by using the > operator:

```
find / -iname bin > {file we want the output in}
```

To place the output in /home/test, use the following command:

```
find / -iname  bin > /home/test
```

If the output file does not exist, it will be created. However, do not use the name of an existing file, since this will overwrite all the data in the file.

Using the locate Utility

The locate utility is similar to find and will only briefly be discussed. Refer to the man pages for more detailed information. locate, or slocate (Secure Locate), is a secure way to search for files and directories on a system. It will not let users see files to which they do not have access. locate uses a database to search for files instead of searching the directory structure itself. For example, to find the date program, type:

```
locate date > test
```

This starts the slocate utility and outputs the results into the test file. The locate program will return more results than the find utility. If you examine them closely, you will see that they all contain the letters d, a, t, and e. This differs from the find utility, because find only returns exact matches, and locate will return all file/directory names with the expression present. locate has more options, which can be found in the man pages.

Using the Internet for Linux Questions

The Internet provides a rich collection of Linux material, but it can be difficult to find without knowing what resources are available. There are Linux search engines, such as www.google.com/linux, as well as a rich collection of newsgroups, which can be accessed through sites such as www.deja.com. In addition, check sites such as www.redhat.com and www.debian.org.

Lab Exercises

1. Printing man pages can be useful if you have to constantly refer to a particular man page. In most cases, you can pipe the output of the man command to enscript. enscript is a command that is used to convert text files to Post-Script, and then send the PostScript file to the specified printer or file. More can be found on enscript in the man pages. To print the man pages on the man command, type:

   ```
   man man | enscript
   ```

   Now, print the man pages for the find command.

2. The -K option searches for a specified string in all of the man pages. Try this using the tar command.

   ```
   man tar -K
   ```

3. Printing the results of a find search is the same as printing man pages. However, do not print the date command using the following:

   ```
   find / -iname date | enscript
   ```

   This would use most, if not all, of the paper in the printer. To prevent this, send the results to a file before printing:

   ```
   find / -iname date > test | enscript
   ```

Questions

1. Newly installed packages can be found with the find command. Why can they not be found with locate?

2. Why is locate faster than find?

3. What does the pipe symbol (|) mean in man pages?

Answers

1. `locate` searches from a database, and the new program has not been placed in the database. This can be corrected with the `updatedb` command.
2. `locate` is faster than `find` because it searches a database rather than the file system.
3. The pipe symbol (|) means OR. This is important when there are various options in the man pages.

Advanced Questions

1. How can the `find` utility be used to locate files with certain permissions?

Starting and Stopping Processes

Purpose

Linux has two sets of actions that take place during a computer's boot process, which depend on the init system being used. There are presently two types of init systems used by Linux, SystemV and BSD. This lab will differentiate between the two init systems, and detail how to change run-level services initiated at boot time. In addition to starting and stopping processes at startup and shutdown, this lab will introduce ways to start and stop processes from the command line.

Theory

The init program is the sole parent for all system processes, common to all Linux distributions, and responsible for kick-starting all system services. The /etc/ inittab file is first read by init to determine a default run level. After determining a default run level, init calls run level scripts to start servers and daemons. These scripts are usually located in the /etc/.../init.d directory. The /etc/.../init.d directory is not always used in SystemV-based systems. The /etc directory serves as the /etc/.../init.d directory on the system that does not have an init.d directory.

Both BSD and SystemV styles of init are based on the original Unix init system created by AT&T Bell Laboratories. BSD is the oldest and simplest style of init, and is simple because it is based on a few closely dispersed scripts and links. The SystemV init system is based on many widely dispersed links and scripts. Under the BSD style of init, all run-level scripts are located in the /etc/rc.d/ directory. By editing the run-level scripts in the /etc/rc.d/ directory, the booting process of a computer can be customized. The init program runs a script called rc.S or rc.sysinit that is responsible for system initialization and starting all services needed to bring the system to the designated run level. In order to stop a service from being started, on a BSD-based system, file permissions are changed to make a script nonexecutable, which disables the script from starting. If a script starts more than one service, sections are commented out to stop services from starting. The rc.sysinit script commonly starts the following services:

- Plug-and-play devices
- Virtual memory
- File system mounts
- PCMCIA services
- Sets serial ports
- Executes SystemV init scripts
- Network services

Under the BSD version of init, network services are started with respect to init configuration files. To stop a network service from being started at boot time, comment out lines used to execute that service in the configuration file. These files are also located in the /etc/rc.d directory.

The SystemV style of init is slightly different. The /etc/rc.d consists of run-level directories that contain links to the run-level scripts that will be executed by the init program. The name of each link is preceded by a K (kill) or S (start). The init program knows which service to start or stop by evaluating the first letter in the name of each link. Renaming the respective link and changing the proceeding S with a K stops a service from starting at boot time. In a SystemV-based system, the run-level scripts are hardly ever edited to stop a service from starting, only the name of the link. This means that SystemV uses many more scripts and links than a BSD-based system to accomplish the same tasks. Using links to control small standard scripts make the SystemV init system more applicable for use in graphical configuration tools.

In addition to stopping processes at shutdown or reboot, the kill command can be used to immediately stop a process. For example, to immediately stop portmap, the user would first find out the process id of portmap. The ps command should be issued in a fashion similar to the following:

```
$ ps -aux | grep portmap
```

The output should be similar to the following:

```
bin    355  0.0  0.1  1216  220 ?    S   Oct28   0:00 portmap
```

As just shown, the process id of portmap is currently 355. To stop portmap, the kill command should be used as shown here:

```
$ kill -9 355
```

If the ps command is run again, the user will see that portmap is no longer running.

Another way to start or stop processes is to enter the /etc/init.d or / etc/rc.d/init.d directory and run one of the service commands with the start or stop argument. For example:

```
$ cd /etc/init.d
$ ./portmap stop
```

If the ps command is run, the user will see that portmap is no longer running. To restart the daemon, enter the following:

```
$ ./portmap start
```

Lab Exercises

The following procedures will evaluate one's understanding of the BSD and SystemV init systems. Graphical configuration tools should not be used in the following procedures. Each procedure will evaluate the user's ability to manipulate the files and scripts used by each init system to initialize a system during the boot process.

Procedure One

A computer system using the BSD style of init was set to start defaulted in single-user mode for diagnostic purposes. Configure the system so that it starts defaulted in multi-user mode.

Follow these steps to complete this process:

1. Move to the /etc directory:

   ```
   $ cd /etc
   ```

2. Use a text editor to open the inittab file:

   ```
   $ pico inittab
   ```

3. Read the text section at the top of the file to determine the run level for multi-user mode.

4. Locate the following line:

   ```
   id:1:default:
   ```

5. Replace the number 1 with the number of the multi-user run level.

6. Save, and close the file.

Procedure Two

A network server using Sendmail crashes because of a hardware problem. The mail server uses the SystemV style of init and defaults to multi-user mode. Configure the system so that the Sendmail server does not start at boot time.

Follow these steps to complete this process.

1. Change to the default run-level directory, /etc/rc.d/. The default is specified in the inittab file.

2. Delete the Sxxsendmail link or rename it; remember that the link cannot start with an S or K if renamed.

Optional Steps

Find out which run-level script to edit by reading the /etc/inittab file. It contains a text section that describes each run level.

This can be done by using a pager, such as less, to view the /etc/inittab file. Use the following command to view the inittab file with the less pager:

```
$less /etc/inittab
```

Press q to quit the pager.

Questions

1. What is the purpose of running the ps command before a process is stopped using the kill command?

2. What program is responsible for starting all system services?

3. It is safer to configure services to start or stop as a computer initializes a run level on a SystemV-based system than it is on a BSD-based system. (True/False)

Answers

1. The ps command is used to find the process id number, which must be known in order to stop a process with the kill command.

2. The init program is the responsible for starting all system services.

3. True. When configuring a service to start or stop on a SystemV-based system, names of links are changed. On a BSD-based system, file permissions or contents must be changed.

Advanced Questions

1. What problems might arise if a user is not careful when editing the /etc/inittab file?

Group Permissions

Purpose

The purpose of this lab is to explain the use of groups, and the files and programs that manage them. Root access is required to complete the lab exercises.

Theory

Groups allow selected users access to specific files and directories. By making a group the sole owner of a file, users who need access to the file must be members of the group. The file `/etc/group` contains a listing of all the groups that have been created on the system. It is here that a new group can be created. Users must be careful when editing this file, as the file can become corrupted if edited with a normal text editor. To prevent this, the program `vigr` can be used, which opens the file in the Vi text editor with the proper locks so that accidental corruption is avoided. To open the `/etc/group` file, type `vigr` at the command prompt. Each line in the file is divided into four parts, each part separated by a colon, as in the following example:

```
groupname:passwd:GID:user1,user2
```

To ensure that each group is assigned the proper values, the colons must be placed in the line, even if a section is empty. The first field contains the group name, and the second field contains the group password. Most Linux distributions have shadowed passwords, so this field will contain a placeholder, such as an x. If this is the case, the actual password is stored in the etc/gshadow file. The third field contains the Group ID (GID). This is what the system uses to recognize each group, so the number must be unique. The group members are declared in the last field; if multiple users are in a group, the names are separated by a comma.

When changes are made to the /etc/group file, it may be necessary to run the grpconv command. This program will put the changes from the /etc/group file in the etc/gshadow file, ensuring that the system will have the correct settings. It might also be helpful to run the grpunconv command, which does the reverse of the previous command and deletes the etc/gshadow file. If the group needs to have a password, run the gpasswd command and enter the password when prompted. This password is used when a user who is not a member of the group tries to temporarily add him or herself to the group with the newgrp command. If this happens, the user will be prompted to enter the group's password.

Every file and directory has three sets of permissions: one for the file's owner, one for the file's group, and one for world. View the file's permissions using the ls command with the -1 option. The first part of the output of this command is a row of 10 fields. The first field is used to describe the object's type. If it is a directory, the field will contain a d. The next nine fields are split between three sets of permissions. The first set of three contains the permissions for the file's owner, the second set is for the file's group, and the final set is for world. The first field of each set indicates if read permissions have been given, the second field indicates if write permissions have been given, and the third field indicates whether execute permissions have been given.

To change a file's owner and group, use the chown command with the following syntax:

```
$chown newuser.newgroup filename
```

To change the group, use the same syntax, but leave off the username and place the period before the new group's name, as shown in the following:

```
$chown .newgroup filename
```

To change the permissions for a file, use the chmod command. The command is typed, followed by three fields and then by the file name, as in the following:

```
$chmod 123 filename
```

The three fields correspond to the three sets of permissions for the file, the first being for the owner, the second for group, and the third for world. Each of the three fields is calculated by adding the desired permissions to 0. No permission is 0, read-only is 4, write is 2, and execute is 1. Any combination of the values may be used. For example, to give a file read and execute permissions but no write permission, enter a value of 5. The following command will give read and execute permissions to the owner; read, write, and execute permissions to the file's group; and no permission to anyone else.

```
$chmod 570 filename
```

Lab Exercises

In this exercise, a group named `staff` will be created and a user will be added to the new group. A program will then be created and set to run for that group only. Root access is required to complete this exercise.

1. Log in as root.
2. Open the `/etc/group` file using the `vigr` command.
3. Add a group at the end of the file with a GID of 500, or as close to this as possible. Add a user to this group. This is done by adding a line similar to the following at the end of the file:

   ```
   staff:x:500:username
   ```

4. Close the file.
5. Create and save a new file that contains the `ls` command.
6. Give the new file read, write, and execute permissions for only the owner and group. This is done by entering the following at the command line:

   ```
   $chmod 770 filename
   ```

7. Change the file's group to `staff` by entering the following at the command line:

   ```
   $chown .staff filename
   ```

8. Log in as the user and run the file.

Questions

1. How many colons must be in the every line of the `/etc/group` file, and why must every colon be there?
2. How would a user change the group ownership of a file?

Answers

1. Three colons must be in every line of the `/etc/group` file; they must be there to separate the fields so that when the file is read, the proper values will be given to the group.
2. Using the `chown` command followed by the group name preceded with a period. For example:

   ```
   $ chown .groupname filename
   ```

Advanced Questions

1. What command would change the group permissions from read, write, and execute to write and execute only?

Environment Variables

Purpose

This lab discusses environment variables and their uses. You will learn how to create, view, and modify those variables. The exercises will cover various methods of displaying and changing environment variables, both temporarily and permanently.

Theory

Environment variables allow programs to understand the state of current user and system settings. These variables can be global or local, depending on who set them. They are set at system startup, logon, inception of a new shell, or manually at the command prompt. The actual life of the variable is only as long as the shell client is alive, or as long as the system is up, in the case of global variables. However, they can be set automatically at login by means of the resource file.

The default shell will invoke the login, profile, or resource file. These files are located in the home directory and automatically set up local variables. Global variables are set by the system for all users. Some of the more common variables and their uses are listed here:

BROWSER	Default Web browser.
EDITOR	Path name of the default editor.
HISTSIZE	Number of records held in the history.
HOME	Current user's home directory.

HOSTNAME	Current host name.
MAIL	Path name of user's mailbox.
OSTYPE	Operating system type.
PATH	List of directories searched by the shell to find executables.
PS1	Main prompt variable.
PS2	Secondary prompt variable.
RUNLEVEL	System mode, such as multi-user or X11 login.
SHELL	Path name to the default shell (in /etc passwd).
TERM	Current terminal type.

Environment variables are case-sensitive tags assigned to a variable string by a user or the system. These exist to allow the system to call these known tags and retrieve a desired directory, entry, or name that may be changed often. Without these, the system would not have an efficient way to retrieve this data.

Lab Exercises

Environment variables control aspects of the shell, ranging from the structure of the command-line prompt to the PATH where the shell looks to find executable programs. For this reason, you should understand how to analyze, set, and automate the creation of these variables.

Displaying Environment Variables

Environment variables can be viewed in a number of ways.

The env command displays all local system variables. This output stream can be formatted by the more or less command, or it can be streamed to a file:

```
$ env
XAUTHORITY=/mnt/home/bond/.Xauthority
USER=bond
EBIN=/usr/bin
EPID=16858
GDM_LANG=(null)
BASH_ENV=/mnt/home/bond/.bashrc
EROOT=/usr/share/enlightenment
QTDIR=/usr/lib/qt-2.1.0
BOOT_IMAGE=linux
DISPLAY=:0.0
SESSION_MANAGER=local/billabu.sairinc.com:/tmp/.ICE-unix/16825
LANG=en_US
OSTYPE=Linux
WINDOWID=62914574
GDMSESSION=Default
SHLVL=3
```

The printenv command does everything that env does, with one difference. If you use printenv with an environment variable argument, it will return its value:

```
$ printenv HOME
/mnt/nfs/home/bond/
```

The set command, when used with no arguments, will print both local and global variables:

```
$ set
BASH=/bin/bash
BASH_ENV=/mnt/home/bond/.bashrc
BASH_VERSION=1.14.7(1)
BOOT_IMAGE=linux
COLUMNS=80
CONSOLE=/dev/console
DISPLAY=:0.0
EBIN=/usr/bin
ECACHEDIR=/mnt/home/bond/.enlightenment
ECONFDIR=/mnt/home/bond/.enlightenment
EPID=16858
...
```

Some of set's other uses are presented in the next section.

If you know a variable's name, use the echo command to display the variable's settings. For example:

```
$ echo $PATH
/usr/bin:/usr/X11R6/bin:/usr/local/bin:/mnt/home/bond/bin
```

Modifying Your PATH Variable

The shell uses the PATH variable to find which directories to search for executable programs that are run at the command prompt. This variable is important because it is tedious to type in the full path name of every executable that is run. Instead, set this variable to enter the name of the program. First, display the path using printenv:

```
$ printenv PATH
/usr/bin:/usr/X11R6/bin:/usr/local/bin:/mnt/home/bond/bin
```

Suppose you have a program calc in /mnt/home/username/calc/bin and use this program frequently. To find the entire path name, edit the PATH variable as shown:

```
$ PATH=$PATH:/mnt/home/username/calc/bin
$ export PATH
$ printenv PATH
/usr/bin:/usr/X11R6/bin:/usr/local/bin:/mnt/home/bond/bin:
mnt/home/username/calc/bin
```

Notice that the variable references itself by using the $ character. This command reflexively adds the current PATH to a new PATH, followed by the new path name of the calc program. Remember, that the lifetime of this variable is only as long as the life of the shell. The next exercise demonstrates the creation of permanent variables.

Setting up the Resource File

To enable permanent variables, edit .bash_profile, which is located in the home directory. Next, find your PATH directory, which should be similar to the following:

```
PATH=$PATH:$HOME/bin
```

The system uses the reflexive method seen earlier to preserve the previously set global PATH and to add your home binary directory to the PATH. Add a colon followed by the path that you want in your PATH variable and save the file. It should look like this:

```
PATH=$PATH:$HOME/bin:/usr/newpath/bin
```

Other variables found may include BASH_ENV, USERNAME, and HISTSIZE, which can be edited in the same fashion.

Removing Entries and Deleting Variables

To permanently delete a variable, remove its entry from the resource or login file. To remove a variable from the environment for the life of the shell, just set its value to nothing. The set command may be used to unset variables for the life of the program following it:

```
$ env --unset=HISTSIZE calc
```

This will effectively remove the variable HISTSIZE from the environment and run the calc program. The variable will be restored upon the completion of calc.

Questions

1. Describe an easy way to view an environment variable.
2. What is the difference between the variables set from .bash_profile and .bashrc?

Answers

1. Using the `echo` command is the easiest method:

   ```
   $ echo $PATH
   /usr/bin:/usr/X11R6/bin:/usr/local/bin:/mnt/home/bond/bin
   ```

2. The `.bashrc` is invoked every time the user starts a non-login bash shell; `.bash_profile` is loaded when the user logs in.

Advanced Questions

1. Develop a method for finding specific variable values.
2. How can you start with an empty environment without deleting the profile and login files?

Controlling Processes Using ps, kill, nice, renice, and top

Purpose

The ability to control processes increases productive time on a system. This lab will cover some basic commands concerning process control, allowing the user to get information about a process, scheduling priority, altering priority, and stopping a process.

Theory

Linux is a multitasking operating system, which is a type of OS that exploits the time spent by most programs waiting for events to happen. A multitasking OS will suspend waiting programs and choose from a priority list of other programs that are ready to run. Linux uses preemptive multitasking, which means that it may interrupt one process in favor of another. The value of the priority can be set when a process is started with the `nice` command; the value can be changed during a process with the `renice` command. Process priority is set at a `nice` value between –20 and 19; higher `nice` values have lower priority.

The syntax for the `nice` command is as follows:

```
nice [option] [command[arguments]]
```

`option` is -n, and n ranges from –20 to 19. Using the `nice` command without arguments prints the default scheduling priority, which is usually zero; a regular user can only lower the priority from this value. A privileged user can raise the priority of a process by specifying a negative value for the adjustment.

To alter the priority of a process while it is running, it is necessary to use the renice command. The syntax for the renice command is:

```
renice [priority] [options] [target]
```

If no option is specified, the default is to specify one or more process identifiers (PIDs) as the target:

```
renice [priority] [PIDs]
```

Regular users may only alter the priority of processes they own, and can then only decrease the priority within the range 0 to 19, even if they were the ones who decreased the priority in the first place. This is to prevent overriding administrative sanction. A privileged user can set the priority of any process to any value in the range.

To get information about the processes running, use the process status (ps) command. The output of this command will have several fields that give information about the processes listed. The PID column is a constant; other fields vary according to which options are used. The syntax for ps is as follows:

```
ps [options]
```

There are many options for ps. The command:

```
ps aux
```

would show most of the system processes. The elements of the aux argument are as follows: a (all users), u (by effective user ID), and x (processes without the controlling terminal). Use this command to find the priority of a process with the PRI option.

The top command is similar to the ps command. While ps gives a snapshot of the current processes, top gives an ongoing look at processor activity with frequent updates. Among other things, it displays a listing of the most CPU-intensive tasks on the system. The syntax is as follows:

```
top [options]
```

If no interactive commands are given, the default is to sort processes by CPU usage.

To terminate a process, use the kill command with the appropriate PID; normal users can only terminate the processes they own. This command is especially useful when used at a virtual console to stop runaway programs that do not respond to other means. The syntax for the kill command is:

```
kill [options] IDs
```

If no option is specified, the default is to send the terminate signal to the processes specified.

Lab Exercises

The basic procedure in this lab is to run two `yes` commands and vary their priorities. Both processes will be terminated using the `kill` command after comparing the processing times.

1. Log in and run the first `yes` process by typing:

    ```
    yes > /dev/null
    ```

    This ports the output to `/dev/null` and it is basically dumped; type `yes` without porting to print out a string of y's. Move to a virtual console by typing CTRL-ALT-F2. Log in if necessary. Moving to a virtual console is useful if you have a runaway process that you cannot get rid of with CTRL-C or other means.

2. Check the `PID` for the first `yes` process with the `ps` command:

    ```
    ps ux
    ```

    The u option includes username and start time; x includes processes without an associated terminal.

3. Use `nice` to execute the second `yes` process. This time, put the process in the background by adding the ampersand (&) character to the end of the command. This is an alternative to using a virtual console.

    ```
    nice -n 5 yes > /dev/null &
    ```

    This gives it an initial priority adjusted lower than the default by a value of 5. Type `nice` without options to print the default priority.

4. Use `top` to check the order of the two `yes` processes by looking at the `PID` column. The first `yes` process should be using more processing time than the second. Note the `PID` for the second `yes` process.

5. Use the `renice` command to change the priority on the first `yes` process:

    ```
    renice 20 [PID]
    ```

    This sets the first process at an absolute value of 20, which is the minimum priority.

6. Use `top`, and again note the order of the two `yes` processes. The `PID` numbers should be switched from before, now showing the second process using more time on the system.

7. Use `kill` to terminate both processes by typing the following:

    ```
    kill [PID(1)] [PID(2)]
    ```

    Use the `ps` command and check that the two processes are no longer listed.

Questions

1. What command is used to set the priority of a program that is running?
2. What does the `nice` value determine?
3. A normal user can adjust the priorities of which processes?

Answers

1. renice.
2. This value determines scheduling priority for processes on the system.
3. Only the processes owned by the user can be adjusted.

Advanced Questions

1. What is the process priority value range for the `nice` command?
2. Which command is used to print the default scheduling priority?
3. How would a runaway process be terminated on a console that cannot be stopped with regular means, such as CTRL-C?

Setting Up a Dual-Boot System

Purpose

The purpose of this lab is to configure a computer to dual boot to either Windows 9x or Linux using the LILO (LInux LOader) utility.

Theory

It is common to find Linux users who run their computers with a dual-boot configuration. In the simplest terms, this means that they have both Linux and another operating system, usually a Windows system, installed on their computer. The operating system can be selected according to the required tasks and personal preferences at startup.

Although it is possible to create a dual-boot system with Windows NT and Windows 2000, these operating systems require specific procedures, which are beyond the scope of this exercise. It is also possible to create a dual-boot system using a computer with a previously installed version of Windows 9x, using a DOS utility included on your Linux CD, called `fips.exe`. Using `fips.exe` can damage or destroy data, however, so back up the system before attempting that method.

To prepare the drive for dual booting, use the `fdisk` utility to create a Windows FAT32 partition, a Linux swap partition (128 megabytes should suffice), and a Linux partition. Create the partitions in this order for the dual boot setup to function properly.

NOTE These instructions are for the minimum installation of Linux. Check the installation guide for your version of Linux, and evaluate the usage plans of your computer system to determine whether additional Linux partitions are desired or necessary for optimal system performance.

Once the appropriate partitions have been created, the operating systems can be installed, beginning with the Windows OS. If Linux is installed first, Windows will overwrite the MBR (master boot record: the default boot commands read by the system BIOS) and the dual-boot configuration will not work. Next, install Linux, paying particular attention to the disk-partitioning options of the install process. Do not alter the Windows partition.

Next, install LILO into the MBR. This allows the OS to be chosen at startup. Upon prompting, create a boot disk; this will allow you to start the system without using LILO, if LILO is ever overwritten or damaged.

Lab Exercises

In this exercise, the user will take a freshly formatted hard drive, partition it for use by Windows 9x and Linux, and set up LILO so the user can choose which operating system to run when booting the system. You will need a Windows 9x floppy boot disk, a Windows 9x installation CD, a Linux installation CD, and a blank floppy disk that will be used to create a boot disk for LILO.

1. Boot the computer using the Windows 9x boot disk, and format the hard drive from the `a:` prompt.

   ```
   a:format c:
   ```

2. Partition the hard drive using `fdisk`.

   ```
   a:fdisk
   ```

3. Follow the `fdisk` instructions to create the appropriate partitions for system configuration. The Windows 9x operating system must be the first partition, and the swap partition must be the second partition. Label the partitions appropriately to assist in differentiating between them during the OS installation processes.

   Make each OS partition large enough to accommodate the OS, including some additional space. The swap partition does not need to be any larger than 128 MB.

4. Install Windows 9x. Refer to the operating system's installation documentation for assistance and reference.

5. Install your desired version of Linux, referring to the installation documentation for assistance, but ensuring that the FAT32 (Windows) partition is not altered during the installation process.

6. During the installation of Linux, configure LILO to allow operating system selection. Also, create a boot diskette during this step. Refer to your Linux documentation for assistance.

Questions

1. What is a possible reason for LILO not to work on a large-capacity hard drive?
2. Is there any way to install Linux without reformatting the hard drive and losing the files and configuration of a previously installed Windows 9x?

Answers

1. You may be running an older version of the Linux kernel that does not recognize disk sectors above sector 1024 (8 gigabytes). Try installing a newer version of the Linux kernel.
2. Yes. Most Linux distributions include the utility `fips.exe`, which will repartition the hard drive, dividing it between used and free space, allowing you to use the newly created partition for another operating system. `FIPS` can cause damage or loss of data, however, and it is important that you become familiar with the documentation before running `fips.exe`.

Advanced Questions

1. Can files be shared between the Linux and Windows 9x operating systems?

Shortcuts in Bash

Purpose

This lab will cover some of the more useful shortcuts that can be taken at the shell prompt. The lab will focus on the Bash shell, since it is the default shell for most Linux distributions.

Theory

Shells provide a basic interface between the user and the operating system. There are several different choices of shells for the Linux user, all of them providing slightly different features. While some shells may be very basic, providing only the necessities for command execution and file manipulation, other shells attempt to include every possible feature, such as command aliases, redirects, and command history review. The default shell for many distributions of Linux is the Bourne Again Shell (Bash); this lab will guide you through some of the more useful commands available in Bash.

Command-Line Editing

One basic but useful feature of Bash is the ability to edit the command line. At any point, use the left and right Arrow keys to move the cursor back along the command line. The command may be edited by deleting or adding characters, or by using one of the editing shortcuts described in the following sections.

Command-Line Review

The shell will keep a history of previously attempted commands. By pressing the Up and Down Arrow keys, you can scan the history of commands and edit them.

CTRL-T

The CTRL-T command is an interesting shortcut for editing the command line. When pressed, CTRL-T will switch the character under the cursor with the character immediately to the left of the cursor. The cursor will then move one space right. This saves the three keystrokes it would take to delete both characters and retype them in the correct order.

CTRL-W

The CTRL-W command will cut everything from the character immediately to the left of the cursor position until the beginning of the current word. The cut portion of the command line will be saved for future pasting. For example:

```
$ cd /etc
```

The cursor is currently resting on the c in /etc. After CRTL-W is pressed, the command line is:

```
$ cd c
```

Everything between the cursor and the beginning of the current word has been removed.

CTRL-U

The CTRL-U command operates very similarly to the CTRL-W command, except that everything before the cursor location is cut. The portion of the command line that is cut is also stored for later pasting. Using the previous example:

```
$ cd /etc
```

Again, the cursor is resting on the c in /etc. Once CTRL-U is pressed, the command line is as follows:

```
$ c
```

CTRL-Y

CTRL-Y is the pasting command used in conjunction with CTRL-W and CTRL-U. After CTRL-Y is pressed, pasted material will be placed before the current cursor position.

If CTRL-Y is used immediately after a CTRL-W or CTRL-U and the cursor has not moved, the original command will be restored. Using the previous example:

```
$ c
```

CTRL-U has been used to cut the entire command before the c. The cursor still rests on the c. After CTRL-Y is pressed, the command is restored:

```
$ cd /etc
```

The Exclamation Point (!) Operator

Simple command-line review is not the only way to make use of the history list. The exclamation point (!) operator was originally a feature of the C shell, and can be used in conjunction with other operators to recall previous commands from the history list. For example, ! followed by a number will recall that number command from the history list. Using a colon, it is also possible to select specific words from a command in order to use them with other commands. The words themselves are numbered left to right with the first word, usually the command name, being 0.

!!	Recalls the most recent command.
!-5	Recalls the fifth most recent command.
!30	Recalls the thirtieth command from the history list.
!l	Recalls the last command beginning with the letter l.
!:1	Recalls the second word in the last command.

CTRL-O

To use CTRL-O, use the Up Arrow key to scroll up the history list to a previous command. When CTRL-O is pressed, the command currently showing on the command line will be executed; the command line will show the next command in the history list. The command that is executed by CTRL-O will then be added to the end of the history list. For example, at a blank command line, the Up Arrow is pressed to review previous commands:

```
$ ls -a
```

Again the Up Arrow is pressed:

```
$ cd ~
```

And once more:

```
$ cd /etc
```

The prompt now shows the third command from the end of the list. After CTRL-O is pressed, that command is executed and the history list scrolls down one:

```
$ cd ~
```

If CTRL-O is pressed again, the current command is executed and the history list scrolls down once more:

```
$ ls -a
```

Since commands executed by CTRL-O are added to the end of the history list, typing CTRL-O at this point will bring up the first command executed by CTRL-O:

```
$ cd /etc
```

If CTRL-O is continually entered, a loop is created, since commands are added to the end of the history list. Thus, CTRL-O is mainly useful if you wish to repeat a sequence of commands entered on the command line.

cd ~

The cd ~ command is a useful shortcut for traversing your file system. The ~ is used in all commands as an alias for the home directory. Thus, cd ~ will return to the home directory.

cd -

Using cd - is also a shortcut to another directory. In this case, - is used as an alias for the last directory visited before the current one; therefore, cd - will return you to your previous directory.

Lab Exercises

This portion of the lab will guide you through the actual use of the shortcuts just described. Access to a Linux terminal running Bash is required.

CTRL-T

Use CTRL-T to correct a typographical mistake in a command. First, misspell a command:

```
$ mroe /etc/passwd
```

To correct this, move the cursor on top of the o and press CTRL-T. The mistake should now be corrected as follows:

```
$ more /etc/passwd
```

CTRL-T will only switch the positions of two characters. Other mistakes must be fixed by hand.

CTRL-W, CTRL-U, and CTRL-Y

Type a command into the command line as follows:

```
$ ls -l /etc | more
```

Suppose that you do not wish to pipe the command through more. Simply enter CTRL-W twice, once for more and once for the pipe character. The command line will now be as follows:

```
$ ls -l /etc
```

You then change your mind and want to restore the command. Just press CTRL-Y to paste the cut portion of the command back onto the command line.

```
$ ls -l /etc | more
```

CTRL-U works the same way. Press CTRL-U to cut the entire command from the command line. The command line will now be empty:

```
$
```

Press CTRL-Y to restore the entire command.

```
$ ls -l /etc | more
```

The Exclamation Point (!) Operator

The exclamation point (!) operator has the ability to recall specific words from commands. Type the following:

```
$ cd /etc
$ ls mail
```

Now cd to the mail directory, but rather than retyping the word mail, simply enter:

```
$ cd !:1
```

Using the exclamation point (!) followed by a colon and a 1 recalls the second word in the previous command. The first word in the previous command is numbered 0.

Questions

1. What would happen if you continue to press CTRL-O after you scroll upward in the history list?

2. What is the easiest method for recalling the fifteenth command in the history list?

3. Which characters can be substituted for the home directory and the previous directory?

Answers

1. Since commands executed using CTRL-O are added to the end of the history list, you would end up in a loop beginning with the first command executed with CTRL-O through the end of the history list.

2. The easiest way to recall the fifteenth command in the history list is to type `!-15`.

3. The ~ character can be substituted for the path to the home directory, and the − character can be substituted for the path to the previous directory.

Advanced Questions

1. What would the command `!8:2` do?

2. How could you use CTRL-T to turn `dc/et/camli` into `cd/etc/mail`?

3. Suppose your cursor is resting in the middle of a word on the command line. If you press CTRL-W, will the entire word be cut? Why or why not?

Exporting an X Display

Purpose

In this lab exercise, the user will export an X display from a local computer, export an X display from a remote computer to a local computer, and secure X display exportation with SSH.

Theory

Through exporting an X display, programs that are run on one Unix variant can receive the display from an entirely different Unix variant. For example, an X application on a Solaris machine can have its display exported to a Linux machine. Although the program would actually be running on the Solaris machine, the display would appear on the Linux machine as if the program were running locally. A Linux user could export the display of Microsoft Internet Explorer from a Solaris machine, even though there is no version of Internet Explorer for Linux.

The X server is sometimes referred to as a traffic cop between applications and the power of the local system. The server itself sends network messages, intercepts the same from other clients, performs two-dimensional drawing, monitors system resources, and allows multitasking and distributed processing. The X server also allows access to a display by other clients.

Exporting an X display requires at least two steps. First, use the xhost program on the client (the machine that will be importing the display) to allow the host (the machine that will be exporting the display) to send the data. Second, log in (locally or remotely) to the host and run the X application that will export its display. Depending on the situation, the DISPLAY environment variable may have to be changed for the X application to send data to the correct display.

Lab Exercises

This lab exercise is divided into three parts. The first section discusses displaying a program running remotely on the local display. The second section covers displaying a program running locally on a remote display. The third section discusses using SSH instead of Telnet to provide a secure method of exporting an X display.

To perform these exercises, there must be two machines on the network, one machine to export and one to import. Both machines must have an X11 server installed, and the user must have an account on both machines.

Exporting to a Local Display

To export a display from a remote computer to a local machine, first run the xhost command to allow the client to receive data from the remote host. To do this, run xhost with the host name or IP address of the host:

```
xhost +(host's hostname/IP)
```

For example:

```
xhost +grind.lucasdigital.com
```

Next, connect to the host machine (the remote machine in this case) using the Telnet program:

```
telnet grind.lucasdigital.com
```

After connecting to the host, run an X application from the command line. For example:

```
$ xcalc
```

The xcalc program should be displayed as if it were running locally.

Exporting to a Remote Display

To export a display to a remote client, the user must have physical access to the remote machine in order to run xhost.

From the console of the client, run xhost to allow the X display to be exported to it. For example, if the host was sand.lucasdigital.com, run the following:

```
xhost +sand.lucasdigital.com
```

Next, determine what the DISPLAY environment variable is set to on the client using the echo command:

```
$ echo $DISPLAY
:0
```

Usually, the display will be 0, but it may vary. Be sure to note the value revealed by the echo command.

From the local host machine, change the DISPLAY environment variable so that X applications will have their display sent to the remote client. The export command can be used to change the DISPLAY temporarily:

```
export DISPLAY=(client's hostname/IP):(client's display)
```

For example:

```
export DISPLAY=grind.lucasdigital.com:0
```

Now the user can run an X application on the local host and it will appear on the remote client.

Securing an X Export with SSH

The display can also be exported by using ssh as a safe substitution for Telnet.

Run the xhost command to allow the client to receive data from the host. To do this, run xhost with the host name or IP address of the remote host. For example:

```
xhost +grind.lucasdigital.com
```

Next, connect via SSH to the remote host with the -X option, which enables X11 forwarding through ssh. For example:

```
ssh -X grind.lucasdigital.com
```

Now the user can run an X application from the command line and it will be displayed as if it were running locally. However, the transmission between the two computers will now be encrypted.

Questions

1. What is the purpose of the xhost command?
2. What is the purpose of using the -X option with ssh?

Answers

1. The xhost program must be run to allow an X display to be exported to it from a remote computer.
2. The -X option enables X11 forwarding.

Advanced Questions

1. Why was the export command not required to export an X display to the local computer in the first exercise?

Creating a Simple Shell Script

Purpose

This lab will demonstrate the creation and use of a shell script to automate a task. The use of the `mail` program will be shown, as well as the use of several different files and directories. During the lab, a shell script will be created that will mail the contents of the /etc directory to the user at boot-up.

Theory

Shell scripts are programs that contain shell commands that are run in order at specific times. Scripts are useful when a set of commands must be run on a routine basis. A script will automate the process and free the user from entering commands at the shell prompt.

Creating a shell script is a simple process involving two basic steps: create a file with shell commands using a text editor, and make the file executable with the `chmod` command. The name given to the script is important, since it determines when the script runs.

It is important to know the default run level for the computer on which the script will run at boot time. This determines where the file is placed on the local file system. To determine what the default boot level is, open the /etc/ inittab file, which will contain a line similar to the following:

```
id:3:initdefault:
```

This indicates that the default run level is set to 3, which, along with 5, is the most commonly set run level. Once the default run level is known, the location of the file can be established. The file should be placed in the /etc/rc.d/ rc3.d directory if the default run level is 3. If not, replace the 3 with the value of the default run level for the local machine. Files contained in this directory are run at boot time, and are named by the following scheme: the first letter is an S, or K, which determines whether the file is to be started or killed, and the next character(s) in the file name tells the system the order in which to run the file. For this lab, the number 50 will be used. If 50 is taken, use the closest unused number.

NOTE   **The S or K at the beginning of the file name must be uppercase or the program will not run during boot-up.**

The script in this lab will run the mail command, and send the contents of the /etc directory in the body of a message to the current user. Mail is an e-mail program that can read, create, and send e-mail. For the purpose of this lab, the ls command will be piped into the standard input of the mail program by using a command in the script file that is similar to the following:

```
ls /etc -al | mail -s "testing my script" username
```

username should be replaced with the username of the person who is to receive the e-mail at boot time. The -s option directs the mail program to place the next string in the sequence in the subject line of the e-mail. It is not necessary for the script file to contain any other text or commands, unless more are desired.

Once the file has been created, or moved, into the correct directory, and is named properly, the file must be made executable for it to be run as a script file. Although this can be accomplished several ways, the chmod command will be used in this lab. The following is an example of how to change the S50myscript file to an executable:

```
$chmod 776 S50myscript
```

After the file has been made executable, the script is ready to be run. To test the script, reboot the system. Then type mail at the command prompt to verify that the e-mail was sent successfully.

Lab Exercises

Create a shell script that will send the contents of the /etc directory in the body of an e-mail to the current user upon boot-up. Verify that the script worked by opening the e-mail message using the mail program.

Questions

1. Is the name of a script file important if it is to run at boot time?
2. What is the purpose of the `mail` program?
3. How can a text file be converted to a shell script?

Answers

1. Yes, the name determines what the file does and when it runs.
2. The `mail` program allows e-mail to be read, created, and sent.
3. A file is turned into a shell script by making it executable.

Advanced Questions

1. What is the purpose of the pipe (|)?
2. Using the `mail` program, can the contents of a file be piped into the body of an e-mail?
3. What attributes does the `chmod 776` command give to a file?

Using chmod, umask, and chown

Purpose

This lab will familiarize the user with methods for changing a file's permissions using the chmod command, methods for setting the default permissions for newly created files with the umask command, and methods of changing the owner and group files and directories with the chown command.

Theory

In Unix and Unix-like systems, all files belong to a specified user and group. In addition, all files have a set of permissions that control user access. These permissions are divided into three sets, which control the permissions of the file owner, the file group, and others. Permission sets will contain one or more of the permissions shown in Table XIX.1.

Table XIX.1 lists all the possible permissions; however, this lab will only discuss the three most common: read, write, and execute. A file's permissions can be shown by using the ls -la command. For example:

```
$ ls -la test
-rw-rw----    1 dwilson  users      58 Nov 16 16:03 sample1
-rw-rw----    1 dwilson  users      29 Nov 16 16:04 sample2
```

Table XIX.1 Permissions for User Access

PERMISSION	DESCRIPTION
r	Allows the user to read the file.
w	Allows the user to write to the file.
x	Allows the user to execute the file.
s	Grants permission to set user or group ID upon execution.
t	Called the "sticky bit," it saves program text on the swap device.
u	User's current permission.
g	Group's current permission.
o	Others' current permission.

The permissions are shown at the left for each file. The owner is first, followed by the group, and then everyone else. Here, both the owner and the group have read and write permissions, and others have no permissions to access the file.

Here is another example:

```
rwxr-xr-x    1 freddie  users    458 Nov 16 16:23 program1
```

The owner has the ability to read, write, and execute the file; the group and others have read and execute permissions.

chmod

chmod will change the permissions specified for the file(s) or directory specified. The syntax of chmod is in the general form:

```
chmod [OPTION]... MODE[,MODE]... FILE
```

The mode may be in symbolic or octal format. The symbolic format is broken down into the following form:

```
chmod [ugoa][+-=][rwxXstugo] [filename]
```

When chmod is used, the command argument must specify at least one mode for at least one file. For example:

```
$ chmod u+x script
```

This command gives the user the ability to execute the file. This could be used in the case of a file being executable script. Another example:

```
$ chmod u=rwx,g=rx,o=x somefile
```

The permission of the file `somefile` would be changed so that the user has the ability to read, write, and execute the file, the group can read and execute the file, and others can only execute the file. The can be shown by issuing the `ls -la` command:

```
$ ls -la somefile
rwxr-x--x    1 freddie  users      19 Nov 14 16:44 somefile
```

In addition, the mode can be issued in octal form. These same permissions could be set by issuing the following command:

```
$ chmod 751 somefile
```

When specifying the mode with `chmod` in numerical form, the command is always issued in the general form:

```
$ chmod xxx somefile
```

The first number following `chmod` controls the permission for the user, the second number controls the permissions for the group, and the third controls the permissions for everyone else. If the mode 000 was used, no one would have any access to the file. If the mode 777 was used, everyone would have full access the file. When specifying the mode numerically, 1 gives permission to execute, 2 gives permission to write, and 4 gives permission to read. If multiple permissions are given, the numbers are simply added together. For example, to give someone read and write permission, the number 6 would be used, since 2 + 4 = 6. To give someone read and execute permission, the number 5 would be used, since 1 + 4 = 5. As just shown, to give someone execute, write, and read permission, the number 7 is used, since 1 + 2 + 4 = 7.

umask

The `umask` command is used to set or change the default permissions obtained by newly created files. The `umask` is the complement of `chmod`, so the same values are represented in the opposite order. For instance, a `chmod` of 777 would be the same as a `umask` of 000; or, a `chmod` of 744 would equal a `umask` of 033. To set the default permissions using the `umask` command, the command is the general form of `umask xxx`.

If the user wanted to set the default permissions to have full permissions, and the group and everyone else only have read and execute permissions, a `umask` of 022 would be set by issuing the following:

```
$ umask 022
```

It is important to remember that this change will only last as long as the life of the shell. The following exercises show you how to make the change permanent for a user.

chown

The chown command is used to change the owner of a file and/or the group. The syntax of chown is in the general form:

```
chown [OPTION]... OWNER[.[GROUP]] FILE
```

To change the owner of a certain file to the user matt and the group writers, the command could be issued as:

```
$ chown matt.writers somefile
```

These changes could be verified by running ls -la:

```
$ ls -la somefile
rwxrwxrwx   1 matt   writers    29 Nov 16 16:04 somefile
```

Here, the owner and group were changed to matt and writers, respectively. chown supports recursion via the -R flag; use this flag to change the ownership of an entire directory:

```
$ chown -R matt.writers b*
```

If this command were issued, the owner and group would be changed for every file in the current directory that begins with the letter b.

Lab Exercises

The exercises of this lab cover basic usage of the chmod, umask, and chown commands. The first exercise shows the user how create a file and change its permissions. Next, the user will change the default umask by adding a line to the user's .profile. Finally, the user will change the owner and group of an entire directory recursively using the -R flag with chown.

Using chmod

Create a new text file named sample using any text editor; save and exit the file.

Now list the default permissions that the file was given by issuing the ls -la command:

```
$ ls -la sample
rw-r--r--   1 freddie  users     5 Nov 17 17:08 sample
```

Next, change the permissions using chmod, so that the group and owner have read and write access, and others have no permissions:

```
$ chmod 660 sample
```

The number 6 was used for the owner and group to give them read and write access, since 2 + 4 = 6. The number 0 was used for others to give them no permissions.

Finally, issue the `ls -la` command to verify that the changes were made:

```
$ ls -la sample
-rw-rw----    1 freddie  users      5 Nov 17 17:08 sample
```

Setting the Default umask

Edit the `.profile` file; add the following line:

```
umask 027
```

After adding the line, save and exit the file. This grants all permissions to the owner, read-only permission to the group, and no permissions to others.

Test this change by logging out, and then logging back in and creating a new file. After creating a new file, check to make sure the changes were applied:

```
$ ls -la sample
-rw-r-----    1 freddie  users      5 Nov 17 17:08 sample
```

If the `umask` command is issued without any arguments, the current `umask` will be shown:

```
$ umask
027
```

Since the default `umask` was changed in the startup file `.profile`, the change will stay until the file is edited and the change is removed.

Using chown

This exercise assumes that there is a user named `joeuser` and a group named `fakeusers`. Log in as root to perform this exercise. Create a folder called `test`; create three sample files:

```
$ mkdir test
$ cd test
$ pico sample1
$ cp sample1 sample2
$ cp sample2 sample3
```

From the parent directory, issue the following command:

```
$ chown -R joeuser.fakeusers test
```

List the contents of the `test` directory to confirm that the owner and group settings have been changed:

```
$$ ls -la test
drwxrwx---   2 joeuser   fakeusers    4096 Nov 17 17:43 .
drwx------  37 freddie   users        4096 Nov 17 17:46 ..
-rw-r-----   1 joeuser   fakeusers       4 Nov 17 17:52 sample1
-rw-r-----   1 joeuser   fakeusers       4 Nov 17 17:52 sample2
-rw-r-----   1 joeuser   fakeusers       4 Nov 17 17:52 sample3
```

It is important to note that the parent directory (represented by a dot) was not changed.

Questions

1. How are privileges represented differently in the umask and chmod commands?
2. What is the significance of the -R flag when used with chown?

Answers

1. umask is the complement of chmod, so the same values are represented in the opposite order. For instance, a chmod of 740 would be the same as a umask of 037.
2. The -R flag implements recursion under chown. The ownership of a directory and all the files under it can be changed in one command using this flag.

Advanced Questions

1. What problems might arise if a user were able to chown his or her files to some other user?

Using Redirect Symbols

Purpose

The following lab will familiarize the user with the redirect symbols, and the `grep`, `cat`, and `mail` commands.

Theory

Redirect commands perform a number of useful actions when combined with the `grep`, `cat`, and `mail` shell commands. Table XX.1 describes the function of these commands.

The redirect symbol > takes the output of a command and enters it into a file. If the file does not exist, it will be created. For example:

```
$cat file1 > file2
```

This line will output the contents of `file1` into `file2`.
The redirect symbol < will input a file into a command. For example:

```
$cat < file
```

The redirect symbol >> appends the output of a command to the end of a file. For instance, if you were to use > to send the output of a command to `file1`, any information stored in `file1` will be replaced. However, if you use >>, the information will be appended to the end of the existing information.

Table XX.1   Commands and Redirect Symbols

COMMANDS AND REDIRECT SYMBOLS	COMMAND FUNCTION
>	Places the output of a command into a new file.
<	Places a file into a command.
>>	Appends output of a command onto the end of another file.
<<	Begins a stream of continuous input.
grep	Searches for a string variable.
cat	Displays contents of a file.
mail	Composes and sends or reads e-mail messages.

The redirect symbol << initiates a flow of information. The << will hold open an active command and allow a user to input various information before closing the active command. The use of the -n flag in the following command directs ftp not to use auto login. This prevents the ftp session from accepting data faster than the << can enter it:

```
$ftp -n <<endvariable
>open address.com
>user username password
>cd ..
>put samplefile1
>get samplefile2
>bye
>endvariable
```

An end variable must be entered immediately following the redirect symbol <<. This string of text is used to indicate when the command is finished. It is important to use an end variable that will not be used during the session, in order to prevent early termination of the session. After the << and the end variable have been entered, the << symbol will prompt the user for more information with a > symbol. Each time the user enters a new line of information, << will send an ENTER keystroke.

The grep command is used to search for a string variable. For instance:

```
$grep penguin file1
```

This command argument searches for any line in file1 that contains the word penguin, and displays each line that it finds.

The cat command is a simple file reader that generates the contents of a file onto the screen. cat does not make any distinction between long or short files; a long file will scroll past the user before he or she has a chance to read it.

The mail command is used to perform a number of different e-mail functions at the command line. mail allows a user to read mail, compose, and send messages with files as the body of a message. The following command argument will send an e-mail to recipient@emailaddress with file1 as the body of the message:

```
$mail recipient@emailaddress < file1
```

Lab Exercises

1. Open a terminal; create a new directory named test in your home directory using the following command:

   ```
   $mkdir test
   ```

2. Move to the /test directory; use any text editor to create a file named sample1 containing the following list of words:

   ```
   dog
   cat
   house
   door
   kite
   stick
   dorothy
   camping
   honor
   kiss
   ```

3. Use the cat command to list the contents of the sample1 file. This should generate the following output:

   ```
   $cat sample1
   dog
   cat house
   door
   kite
   stick
   dorothy
   camping
   honor
   kiss
   $
   ```

4. Use the grep command to single out any words with the letter combination ca in the sample1 file:

   ```
   $grep ca sample1
   cat
   camping
   ```

5. Using the grep command and the redirect symbol (>), create a new file named sample2 that contains words with the do letter combination from sample1:

```
$grep do sample1 > sample2
```

6. Use the cat command to list the contents of the sample2 file:

```
$cat sample2
dog
door
dorothy
```

7. Using the grep command and the redirect symbol >>, search for all words that have the ca letter combination in the sample1 file and append them to the sample2 file:

```
$grep ca sample1 >> sample2
```

8. Use the cat command to list the contents of the sample2 file:

```
$cat sample2
dog
door
dorothy
cat
camping
```

9. Use the mail command and the redirect symbol < to mail the sample2 file to yourself:

```
$mail < sample2 yourname@youraddress.com
```

10. Using the mail command, send another letter explaining what you just did with explanation as your subject:

```
$mail yourname@youraddress.com
Subject: explanation
bodytext bodytext bodytext bodytext
"control-D" is the escape character
Cc:
```

11. Using the redirect symbol << and ftp, open a remote session, get a file, and close the session with the following argument:

```
$ftp -n <<abcdeffedcba
>open remote.address.com
>user username password
>get fakefile
>bye
>abcdeffedcba
```

12. Check to see if the file was received.

Questions

1. If the following command is given, will `file2` contain its original information?

   ```
   $cat file1 > file2
   ```

2. The `echo` command generates to the standard output. With this information, complete the table with the output of the following command arguments.

COMMAND ARGUMENT	OUTPUT
$echo this is a test >> testfile	
$echo more testing >> testfile	
$at testfile	
$echo last test > testfile	
$cat testfile	

Answers

1. No, any information `file2` previously stored will be replaced by the contents of `file1`. To preserve the information already in `file2`, >> should be used instead of >.

2.

COMMAND ARGUMENT	OUTPUT
$echo this is a test >> testfile	
$echo more testing >> testfile	
$at testfile	this is a test more testing
$echo last test > testfile	
$cat testfile	last test

Advanced Questions

1. How can you prevent the > redirect symbol from overriding existing files? (Hint: The redirects are shell features. Look in the shell help files.)

2. Use the `cut` command and the two redirect symbols (> and <) to take the input of the /etc/passwd file and output all of the UIDs into a single file, called ~/uid. Perform this task in one list.

Run Levels

Purpose

This lab will familiarize the user with run levels, what each run level accomplishes, and how it functions The user will also learn the effects that run levels have on the operating system's functions.

Theory

A run level is a number or letter that specifies the current system state. This means that each run level dictates the action of one or a group of commands with that same number. All run levels are located in the /etc/inittab file. Here is a sample of a typical inittab file:

```
id:3:initdefault:

si:S:sysinit:/etc/rc.d/rc.sysinit

10:0:wait:/etc/rc.d/rc/0
11:1:wait:/etc/rc.d/rc/1
12:2:wait:/etc/rc.d/rc/2
13:3:wait:/etc/rc.d/rc/3
14:4:wait:/etc/rc.d/rc/4
15:5:wait:/etc/rc.d/rc/5
```

```
16:6:wait:/etc/rc.d/rc/6

ca::ctrlaltdel:/sbin/shutdown -t3 -rf now

c1:12345:respawn:/sbin/agetty 38400 tty1
c2:12345:respawn:/sbin/agetty 38400 tty2
c3:45:respawn:/sbin/agetty 38400 tty3
c4:45:respawn:/sbin/agetty 38400 tty4
c5:45:respawn:/sbin/agetty 38400 tty5
c6:45:respawn:/sbin/agetty 38400 tty6
```

In this particular example, the default run level is set to 3 (see the top line). The system startup will execute all entries in the `inittab` file containing that number.

In most versions of Linux, the run-level numbers function the same way. These are:

0   Halt.

1   Single-user mode.

2   Multiple-user mode (without networking).

3   Full multiple-user mode (with networking).

4   This is unused, but it can be set up for networking in a different location.

5   Full multiple-user mode with X Windows system (foundation of GUI).

6   Reboot (the machine switches to this one upon pressing CTRL-ALT-DEL).

There are distributions of Linux in which run levels are differently attributed.

Lab Exercises

In this lab, you will change the system's run level to cause and then fix a problem.

Changing Run Levels

1. Log in as root.
2. Move from `/home` to the `/etc` directory.
3. Open the `/etc/inittab` file using your favorite editor.
4. Locate the line containing the default run level that should be set to multiple-user mode.

    ```
    id:3:initdefault:
    ```

5. Change the default run level to 6.

    ```
    id:6:initdefault:
    ```

6. Save the `inittab` file and exit the editor.
7. Reboot the computer. Since run-level 6 is the reboot command, the computer will keep rebooting itself over and over again.

Solving the Problem

1. During the rebooting process, the system will come to a LILO prompt. During the time-out interval, type `linux 1`; in some distributions of Linux, the command is `linux S`. This will put the system into single-user mode.
2. While in single-user mode, change directories to `/etc` again.
3. Open the `inittab` file with any editor and locate the default run level.
4. Revert the run level to its original setting, or to another run level of your choice.
5. Save the file and exit the editor.
6. Reboot your computer.

Questions

1. What is a run level?
2. Choose the correct function for run level 5:
    A. Single-user mode (no networking)
    B. Full multiple-user mode with X Windows
    C. Full multiple-user mode (with networking)
    D. Single-user mode (with networking)

Answers

1. Run level is a number or letter that specifies the current system state.
2. B. Full multiple-user mode with X Windows.

Advanced Questions

1. What is the function of symbolic links?
2. Give an example of how a run level can be set up for networking in a different location.

Lost Root Password

Purpose

This lab discusses the use of LILO to recover a forgotten root password.

Theory

LILO is the LInux LOader, a program used to start an operating system when a computer is first turned on. LILO is easily configured and can be used to load any operating system. In addition, LILO can be used to gain unauthorized root access. This is beneficial if a user forgets the root password, but this ability can present a security risk. In order to compromise the root password, using LILO, the specified operating system must be used.

Lab Exercises

Forgetting the root password is not a significant problem once you know how to use LILO to gain root access. Following are the steps involved in gaining root access and reconfiguring the password.

linux init=/bin/bash

Press TAB at the LILO prompt to present boot options. Normally, this action is used to see a list of operating systems that can be booted on multiple operating system computers.

To get a shell as a console root, type `linux init=/bin/bash` at the boot prompt. Then remount the file system in read-write mode, using the following:

```
$ mount -n -o remount /dev/hda5
```

Replace the 5 with the specific partition to mount.

Next, open the `/etc/shadow` file in a text editor, and remove the password string between the first and second colons after root. For example:

```
root:xjk23f95ksdk5k35:0:0:root:/root:/bin/bash
```

This line should be changed to:

```
root::0:0:root:/root:/bin/bash
```

Save the file and exit.

The `sync` command is used to force changed blocks to disk and to update the superblock. If `sync` is omitted, the changes will be made incorrectly. Run `sync` as shown here:

```
$ sync
```

Wait a few moments and then reboot. When you log in normally as root, Linux will not ask for a password. At the command prompt, use the `passwd` command to add a new root password.

linux single

An alternate method of recovery is to type `linux single` at LILO.

```
boot: linux single
```

Then enter the `passwd` command and follow the instructions.

linux init=/bin/sh

The final recovery method is to type `linux init=/bin/sh` at the LILO prompt:

```
boot: linux init=/bin/sh
```

Again, enter the `passwd` command and follow the instructions.

Questions

1. On a dual-boot system that has Windows on hda1 and Linux on hda3, what command is used to remount the file system, as shown in the first method?

2. In this lab's exercises, an sh shell is used. How could another shell, such as csh, be used?

3. Assume that the following is part of the /etc/shadow file. Which segment should be removed, and how would the modified line look?

```
root:$1$436.uMfb$ixIoAaOqOfl/gwMrlz.fD/:11267:0:99999:7:::
bin:*:11267:0:99999:7:::
daemon:*:11267:0:99999:7:::
adm:*:11267:0:99999:7:::
lp:*:11267:0:99999:7:::
sync:*:11267:0:99999:7:::
shutdown:*:11267:0:99999:7:::
```

Answers

1. `mount -n -o remount /dev/hda3`
2. The csh shell would be used instead of bash by typing `init=/bin/ csh`. This command can be applied to any shell.
3. Remove the `$1$436.uMfb$ixIoAaOqOfl/gwMrlz.fD/` segment that is between the first and second colons to produce the following line:

   ```
   root::11267:0:99999:7:::
   ```

Advanced Questions

1. How would this procedure change if shadowed passwords were not used?

Passing Arguments to the Kernel

Purpose

In this lab, the user will pass various boot-time parameters to the kernel, and explore the various actions that can be performed using boot-time arguments.

Theory

Certain tasks require the user to pass arguments to the kernel. Parameters that can be passed are divided into two groups: those that aid in performing tasks, such as `single` (single-user mode), `ro` (read-only mode), and `rw` (read/write mode); and those that provide default values to the kernel, thus acting as configuration arguments, such as disk geometry, RAM disk size, available memory, VGA modes, and default root system specifications.

Lab Exercises

The user will perform a file system check on the root partition of the system, boot the single-user mode to restrict logins to root, and mount the root partition in read-only mode.

1. Start the system; enter the kernel name along with the arguments needed to accomplish the features mentioned in this lab. Possible installed kernels can be obtained by pressing TAB at the LILO prompt; the list of kernels installed in the system can be obtained from the /etc/lilo.conf configuration file.

```
bash# linux single ro
```

2. Once the system has booted, verify that the arguments passed to the kernel had the desired effect.

   The run level should be 1, denoting single-user mode. To verify the current run level of the system, run the following:

```
bash# /sbin/runlevel
```

   To check if the root file system is mounted as read only, enter the following command:

```
bash# mount
```

   Use the id command to verify that you have a root shell.

```
bash# id
```

3. Perform a simple file system check on the root partition using the fsck command. Use the following format:

```
bash# fsck <root-partition-name>
```

   The root partition name can be obtained by examining the lilo entry for the kernel in the /etc/lilo.conf file, under the root tag, as shown in the following example:

```
bash# fsck /dev/hda2
```

4. Exit the root shell for the normal boot process to continue.

5. Identify various other boot-time arguments and their associated implications. For example: specify the default RAM disk size for your system, specify a file system as the root partition, and override the default root partition mentioned in the lilo.conf file.

Questions

1. Identify three tasks that the system administrator might wish to perform in the single-user mode.

Answers

1. Change password for superuser, make backups of the entire system, and run file system checks.

Advanced Questions

1. Give an example of a configuration argument to the kernel.

Recompiling the Kernel

Purpose

The purpose of this lab is to download, configure, compile, and install a customized Linux kernel.

Theory

The Linux kernel is the main part of any Linux system; in the strictest sense, the kernel *is* Linux. The remainder of a typical GNU/Linux system is filled out by tools from the GNU Project, as well as various other applications and network daemons. The kernel performs the low-level functions required by programs such as I/O, hardware interaction, TCP/IP stacks, and memory management.

Kernel modules are a relatively new idea; they allow some kernel functions to be used even when they have not been compiled into the kernel. Instead, they are compiled as individual modules and can be used as they are needed. This allows kernel functions that are not used often, such as obscure file systems or sound support, to be compiled as modules and loaded when needed. When compiled directly into the kernel, modules remain loaded at all times.

Lab Exercises

To complete this lab, the user must have root access to a Linux machine with about 200 MB of free disk space, and access to the Internet, so the new kernel source can be downloaded.

Download the Source

Before it is possible to configure and compile the kernel, the source must be on the hard drive of the local Linux machine. It is likely that an older version of the Linux kernel is already on the hard drive; however, it is best to use the newest stable version.

The Linux kernel has a numbering system that allows users to quickly identify the stable versions, which have an even second number, such as 2.2.16 or 2.0.11. Development versions have an odd second number; for example, 2.1.14 or 2.3.3.

Using an FTP client, go to ftp.kernel.org and find the latest stable version; download it and place the file into the /usr/src directory.

Unpack the Kernel

To unpack the source code, move into the /usr/src directory and enter the following:

```
$ tar -zxvf name_of_file.xx.xx.xx.tar.gz
```

This will extract all of the source code into the appropriate subdirectories.

Symbolically Link the Kernel

If the kernel is unpacked into /usr/src/linux, the user need not worry. However, if it is unpacked in a directory such as /usr/src/linux-2.2.16, then it needs to be symbolically linked to /usr/src/linux. For example:

```
ln -s /usr/src/linux-x.x.xx /usr/src/linux
```

Replace x.x.xx with the kernel version being used. Before this step, make sure nothing is in /usr/src/linux.

Configuring the Kernel

Configuring the new kernel requires more knowledge than any of the other steps do. The user must know which parts of the kernel are needed, which are not needed, and remember to add functions to the kernel whenever necessary.

To ensure that kernel configuration begins with the defaults, run the make mrproper command. However, to begin with the options selected during the last compilation, do not run make mrproper.

The configuring of the kernel can be done in three different ways: make config, make menuconfig, and make xconfig. The make config command asks, line by line, which parts of the kernel are needed; if one mistake is made, the user must start over. The make xconfig command uses a graphical interface to allow the user to choose between the options. The make menuconfig command uses menus to make the process easier to go through. A Linux box might not always have X installed, so it is good to be familiar with an alternative.

For the purposes of this lab, make menuconfig will be used. When this command is run, a menu will appear listing the major options that can be configured in the kernel. Under each of these topics are numerous subtopics. For the average user, the defaults of most options will be fine. However, a few options will require modification.

First, configure the CPU type. It can be found listed under Processor type and features. Also, look at the support for Parallel Port, Network devices, Sound, SCSI, and file systems; each one has its own heading.

When the configuration is complete, select exit. You are then asked to save the new kernel configuration; select yes.

Prebuilding Chores

Before building the kernel, a few commands should be run. First, run make clean to ensure that there is nothing remaining in the kernel source directory structure that should not be there. Second, run make dep to ensure that all the files and libraries needed for the kernel to compile are in place.

Building the Kernel and Modules

You will now build the kernel and the modules that assist it, which is a fairly simple process. First, type make bzImage to compile the kernel. This will require a few minutes even on fast machines.

When the kernel is finished compiling, compile the modules. To begin this process, type make modules. Depending on the number of modules being compiled, this process could be as long as the compilation of the kernel. When the modules finish compiling, they must be installed. Type make modules_install to place the modules.

Installing the Kernel

This process consists of two parts: the new kernel must be put in the correct location, and LILO must be configured for the new kernel.

First, the new kernel must be copied to the directory where the kernels are kept. This is generally in the /boot directory. To do this, enter the following:

```
$ cp /usr/src/linux/arch/i386/boot/bzImage /boot/newkernel
```

Any name can be substituted for newkernel.

Once the kernel has been placed in the appropriate directory, it should be referenced in the LILO configuration file, which generally resides in the /etc/ lilo.conf file. An entry must be added to lilo.conf that is similar to the following:

```
image=/boot/vmlinuz-2.2.14-5.0
   label=linux
   read-only
   root=/dev/hda5
```

This entry is a kernel residing at /boot/vmlinuz-2.2.14-5.0. Its root directory is on /dev/hda5, and its name is linux. The read-only line indicates that the file system will initially be mounted as read only. This line should be included for all Unix-like file systems with the exception of UMSDOS.

The user should create a similar entry for the compiled kernel. After the file has been saved, lilo should be run to commit the changes. If this is not done, the new kernel will not be able to boot.

To boot with the new kernel, type the name, or label, of the kernel at the LILO prompt during the boot process. The SHIFT key may have to be held down just after the BIOS check for the LILO prompt to appear.

If the new kernel does not support all that you would prefer, simply return to /usr/src/linux and repeat the configuration.

Questions

1. Strictly speaking, what is Linux?
2. Why are kernel modules used instead of building everything directly into the kernel?
3. Stable kernel versions are differentiated from development version by noticing:

    A. An odd number in the second location of the version number (e.g., 2.3.12).

    B. Linus Torvalds' latest public PGP key in the tar file.

    C. An even number in the second location of the version number (e.g., 2.2.12).

    D. The addition of test after the version number (e.g., 2.4.0-test4).

Answers

1. Linux is simply the kernel of the OS, not the entire OS, which is typically filled out with GNU tools.
2. Certain features of the kernel are not needed very often, but are needed on rare occasions, such as support for an obscure file system. Kernel modules are intended for features such as this.
3. C. An even number in the second location of the version number (e.g., 2.2.12).

Advanced Questions

1. What is the process for patching a kernel, as opposed to downloading the entire new version?
2. How would a system administrator make third-party additions (such as LIDS) to the kernel?

PART

Three

Practice Questions and Answers

Practice Questions

Chapter 1: Theory of Operation

1. A machine has a 2 GB hard drive with 64 MB of memory. It is using the incorrect hard disk geometry (size=258/cycl=125/head=64/sectors=63 because of BIOS limitations). It is running fine on the installed machine, but now you would like to move the hard drive to a new machine. After the hard disk is moved and the machine is rebooted, the LI error message appears. Which of the following techniques best solves the problem? (Background: You cannot install a brand new Linux distribution, and you do not have the original rescue disk.)

   A. Boot the system using another boot disk, recompiling the kernel.

   B. Enter the BIOS setup, type in the geometry (size=258/cycl=125/head=64/sectors=63) in the setup file, and reboot the system.

   C. Use the MS-DOS-based program (system commander) to boot the system.

   D. Remount the hard drive on the original Linux machine (recompile the kernel).

2. It is a common system administration practice to:

   A. Always run as root.

   B. Always run su in single-user mode.

   C. Always run as a user and su.

   D. Always run su in a bash shell environment.

3. In superuser mode, which of the following commands will lead to a system crash?

A. `rm /*.bak`

B. `rm -rf / home/fred/tmp`

C. `rm -r f /tmp`

D. `rm -rf /home/fred/tmp`

4. You have 64 MB of memory and you are running an X11 desktop GUI with applications. Which number is a good size for the swap partition?

A. 16 MB

B. 32 MB

C. 64 MB

D. 100 MB

5. While you are running the X Window system, you can activate a TTY console by pressing one of the Fx keys.

A. True

B. False

6. To switch between virtual consoles when *not* running the X Window system, you can use:

A. ALT-Fn (where n is an integer representing the console number)

B. SHIFT-Fn (where n is an integer representing the console number)

C. CTRL- Fn (where n is an integer representing the console number)

D. TAB

7. Which one of the following statements about the `init` program is *not* correct?

A. `init` starts as the last step of the kernel booting.

B. `init` is the first program that initializes and configures your system for use.

C. `init` works by parsing `/etc/inittab` and running scripts in `/etc/rc.d` according to either a default or desired run level.

D. `init` is not a daemon.

8. Which of the following statements is *not true* about the structure of Linux?

A. Linux tends to come as a set of building-block components that you may or may not choose to use.

B. Even though the kernel and networking code reside in the kernel memory space, they are largely independent modules.

C. Linux supports preemptive multitasking except when doing disk I/O.

D. Preemptive multitasking supports multiple concurrent user accounts.

9. Which statement is *not true* about installing Linux over a network?

A. You should get an IP address from the local system administrator.

B. The network mask tells Linux how many hosts can fit in this subnetwork.

C. You need a gateway IP address to send and receive information over the Internet.

D. Most often, Linux installs just as fast from a local area network or from an Internet-based server.

10. Assume that a vendor distributes a binary-only program free of charge along with an open source program, also free of charge. What is the resultant product?

A. All of the software is open source software.

B. Just free software.

C. A hybrid of free and open source software, with a separate license required.

D. It becomes GPL software.

11. A process is:

A. The state of a program itself.

B. The state of a program as it passes control through itself, libraries, and the kernel.

C. The state of all programs in the system, at any point in time.

D. A series of steps the typical Linux user must take to load the high moby.

12. The format of an IP address is w.x.y.z, where each letter is:

A. A singleton (1 bit)

B. A quad (4 bits)

C. An octet (8 bits)

D. 16 bits

E. 32 bits

F. None of the above

13. The most fundamental aspect of the software system called Linux comes from:

A. Linus Torvalds, who forged an Internet community to build the kernel, beginning in 1991.

B. Richard Stallman, who invented the GNU general public license, beginning around 1984.

C. Jim Gettys, who codeveloped the X Window system, beginning around 1984.

D. Ken Thompson, who developed many of the basic ideas used in Linux, beginning around 1975.

14. Which of the following statements are *true* about GNU GPL? (Select all that apply.)

A. Even though Linux is called free software, most everyone pays some fee, direct or indirect, for the software.

B. The word "free" in "free software" is about freedom to use the software and not about the cost of software.

C. If you improve GPL software, and you do not distribute your improvements, then you are not required to show anyone your improvements.

D. If you do share your improvements in GPL software, you must comment your improvements in the source code and write man-page documentation describing the improvements.

15. Some use fear, uncertainty, and doubt (FUD) tactics to describe Linux; others describe trade-offs of using free software versus proprietary software. Which of the following statements are trade-offs of GPL software?

    A. No product warranty; must have inhouse support or contract support.

    B. No patent protection; anyone can claim a patent on the open software.

    C. No long-term software survivability; all the software may fall into disuse.

    D. Lack of security; everyone sees the source code.

16. A daemon is:

    A. A network sniffer program.

    B. A virus that attaches itself to the master boot record of any disk.

    C. A program that stays resident in memory (or swap space) at all times, waiting for requests for service.

    D. A specialized printer system administration tool for the print system.

Chapter 2: Base Systems

1. You have a 12 GB hard drive system with 64 MB of memory, and want to install both Windows 98 and SuSE Linux 6.1 using LILO loader to load the desired OS. Which of the following steps will achieve the goal?

    A. Create two partitions, install Windows 98 on the first partition, SuSE Linux on the second, and boot from the first partition using LILO.

    B. Create three partitions, install Windows 98 on the first partition, SuSE Linux on the third, a /boot partition on the second, and boot from the second partition using LILO.

    C. Create one FAT32 and two Linux partitions (swap and native), install Windows 98 on the FAT32 partition, SuSE Linux on the native partition, and boot either Windows 98 or Linux from the MBR using LILO.

    D. Create one FAT32 and two Linux partitions (native and swap), install Windows 98 on the FAT32, SuSE Linux on the swap, boot from the floppy disk using LILO, and swap in either OS.

2. The company wants to attach its intranet to the Internet through a Linux box. To ensure that the kernel detects the two required Ethernet adapters, which of the following commands is added to which of the following files:

    A. `append="ether=11,0x280,eth0 ether=5,0x300,eth1" /etc/lilo.conf`

    B. `append="ether=11,0x280,eth0 ether=5,0x300,eth1 mem=128M",lilo.conf`

    C. `append="eth0:1=11,0x280,SMC eth0:2=5,0x300,3COM" /etc/lilo.conf`

    D. `append="eth0:1=11,0x280,SMC eth0:2=5,0x300,3COM mem=128M"lilo.conf`

3. The first Ethernet adapter has an address of IRQ=5, I/O=0x280. Now you want to add a second interface adapter in a Linux box, and the Linux kernel can recognize only the first Ethernet adapter. Which LILO argument will solve the problem? (Background: IRQ=10, I/O=0x300 for the second adapter.)

A. append="ether=10,0x280,eth0 ether=5,0x300,eth1"

B. append="ether=5,0x280,eth0 ether=10,0x300,eth1"

C. append="eth0:1=5,0x280,ether eth1:1=10,0x300,ether"

D. append="eth0:1=10,0x300,ether eth1:1=5,0x280,ether"

4. Which command-line argument serves the purpose of mounting a CD-ROM to a mount point /mnt/cdrom? (Background: the CD-ROM drive is an ATAPI type, and the CD-ROM drive is installed as a slave.)

A. attach /dev/cdrom /mnt/cdrom

B. mount /dev/cud535 /cdrom

C. mount /dev/hda /mnt/cdrom

D. mount /dev/hdb /mnt/cdrom

5. You want to transfer a WordPerfect file (document.wpd) from a Linux box to a Windows 98 machine, but the network has not been set up. Which command line allows you to copy the file to a floppy disk?

A. copy document.wpd a:

B. mv document.wpd a:

C. cp document.wpd a:

D. mcopy document.wpd a:

6. John is running two X-term windows in an X Window environment. He is using an emulated three-button mouse. What are the copy and paste operations to move a string from one virtual terminal to another?

A. CTRL-C to copy, and CTRL-V to paste.

B. CTRL-C to copy, and CTRL-P to paste.

C. Highlight the string with the cursor on the first console, and click the middle button with the cursor on the second console.

D. Highlight the string with the cursor on the first console, and click the left and right mouse buttons with the cursor on the second console.

7. If the computer BIOS cannot boot directly from the CD-ROM and there is not an MS-DOS machine around to create a boot floppy, which of the following command(s) can create the install boot disk from another Linux machine?

A. rawrite vmlinuz a:

B. FIPS vmlinuz a:

C. dd if=vmlinuz of=/dev/fd0 bs=1k count=1024

D. mcopy vmlinuz a:

8. An inexperienced user installed Red Hat 5.1 Linux on a machine and forgot to create and mount a separate file system for the /usr subdirectory. The following is the fstab file on that machine. How can you help this user solve the problem?

```
# /etc/fstab: static file system information.
    # <file system>    <mount point>    <type>    <options>    <dump>    <pass>
    /dev/hda1          /ext2            defaults  1            0
    /dev/hda2          none             swap      sw           0         0
    proc              /proc            proc      defaults     0         0
```

A. Boot from the original CD-ROM and upgrade the system.

B. Run `mke2fs` to create a file system, and add an entry into the `fstab` file.

C. Run `mke2fs` to create a file system, and add an entry into the `lilo.conf`.

D. Run `fdisk` and `mke2fs` to create the volume on another drive, and add the entry into the `fstab` file.

9. Assuming you are not the superuser, which of the following commands would you use to safely turn off a Linux machine?

A. Type CTRL-ALT-DEL

B. `halt`

C. `shutdown -h now`

D. `reboot`

10. You cannot remember a file that was recently created, so you sort file names by creation time, but you also reverse the order of the sort so that the most recently created files will appear at the bottom of the screen. Which of the following commands is the correct one to do this?

A. `ls -lt *`

B. `ls -lats`

C. `ls -ltr`

D. `ls -olt`

11. Which of the following commands will let you see who is logged in and from where?

A. `w`

B. `ps`

C. `top`

D. `proc`

12. Which of the following commands will start the X server?

A. `X11start`

B. `startx`

C. `winstart`

D. `displayrun`

13. To avoid the LI hang-up problem, which of the following approaches is considered to be a reasonable prevention step during installation of Linux?

A. Make the first hard disk partition a `/boot` partition for storing kernel image(s).

B. Create several logical extended partitions.

C. Use the MS-DOS-based program System Commander as the OS loader.

D. Use the latest BIOS.

14. Describe the role of the Linux `/etc/rc.d` and `/etc/init.d` initialization scripts. (Select all that apply.)

A. Some distributions refer to the `rc.d` directory, which holds the scripts for all run levels.

B. Some distributions refer to the `init.d` directory, which holds lists of indirect scripts.

C. Some distributions refer to the `resource.d` directory, which holds lists of indirect scripts for all run levels.

D. Some distributions refer to the `resource.d` directory, which holds lists of scripts for all levels.

15. One reasonable location for the system-wide initialization files for `startx` is:

A. `xinitrc`

B. `/var/X11R6/Xinitrc`

C. `/etc/X11/xinit/xinitrc`

D. `/usr/RX11/bin/xinitrc`

16. There are many compatibility issues that should be considered before installing Linux. Which of the following answers prevents Linux from working with the hardware?

A. Linux does not have device drivers for larger hard disks.

B. Newer video adapters tend not to have X servers available.

C. Linux drivers work with most of the HP DeskJet printers, but not with the PostScript LaserJet printers.

D. All of the above.

17. Which of the following version numbers indicates a stable version of the Linux kernel?

A. 2.3.5

B. 2.3a.5

C. 2.2.5

D. 2.4.5a

18. During installation, the install program will lay down the second-level disk format using which set of the following utilities?

A. `swap, cfdisk`

B. `mk2fs, swap`

C. `makeinode, makeswap`

D. `mkfs, mkswap`

19. In addition to the swap and root partitions, you decide to configure a third partition. You want mail, log, and printer spool files to go into this separate partition. Which mount point is used by convention for storing these files?

A. `/`

B. `/usr`

C. `/var`

D. `/log`

20. One of the network protocols did not activate during the boot-up process. You want to review the boot-up messages to see which device failed. Which of the following commands will allow you to see the messages?

    A. more /usr/log/boot.messages

    B. dmesg

    C. /proc/kmsg

    D. mesg

21. Henry, a new Linux user, is working on a project for his college operating-system class, and he would like to know how many processes are running in order to determine system load. Which of the following command(s) can he use?

    A. pwd

    B. ps

    C. ls

    D. grep

22. Which of the following statement(s) about the file system is *false*?

    A. Swap partitions are included in /etc/fstab.

    B. Swap partitions are not mounted.

    C. The fstab file contains a special entry for the /proc file system.

    D. The mount command may be used only by the superuser.

23. Suppose you have a single IDE hard drive with three primary partitions. The first two are set aside for MS-DOS, and the third is an extended partition that contains two logical partitions, both used by Linux. Which of these devices refers to the first Linux partition?

    A. /dev/hda1

    B. /dev/hda2

    C. /dev/hda3

    D. /dev/hdc1

24. When partitioning the hard disk, you got a warning that cylinder > 1024, or you are unable to boot a partition using cylinder numbers above 1023. Which of the following is *not* a valid reason for this?

    A. The BIOS limits the number of cylinders to 1024, and any partition using cylinders numbered above this will not be accessible from the BIOS.

    B. The limited number of cylinders affects only the booting process, and once the system has booted, you should be able to access any place on the hard disk partition(s).

    C. Your options are either to boot the Linux from a boot floppy, or boot from a partition using cylinders numbered below 1024.

    D. Partitioning can be done after the system is set up.

25. Which of the following statements about swap space is *false*?

    A. You may define multiple swap space partitions.

    B. You need to execute the appropriate mkswap command before using a swap partition or file.

C. You must set the BIOS `swapon` setting to enable swap space before booting the operating system software.

D. The command `swapon` is used to enable swapping to a file as opposed to swapping to a disk partition.

26. Which of the following statements about shutdown and its options are *not true*?

A. `shutdown -k now`—Do not shut down, but send the shutdown announcement to all users.

B. `shutdown -h now`—Halt after shutdown.

C. `shutdown -c now`—Cancel a running shutdown.

D. `shutdown -quick now`—Do a fast reboot.

27. Which of the following are *not* good practices that assist in avoiding system crashes?

A. The superuser should always log in as root, and users should log in using their accounts.

B. Make backup files and keep them physically off the premises.

C. Prepare emergency boot disks.

D. Copy configuration files to a subdirectory for later reference.

28. Which of the following pseudofiles are system abstractions?

A. `/opt/usr/log`

B. `/proc/devices`

C. `/usr`

D. `/tmp/conner2`

29. Based on the GNU utilities, which command can you use if you want to see a list of the currently logged-in users?

A. `id`

B. `w`

C. `users`

D. `uname`

30. Which statement is *false* when describing run levels?

A. Run-level zero is the shutdown level for all distributions.

B. Most distributions agree that run level five will start the KDE GUI.

C. Run levels one or two are the multi-user levels for most distributions.

D. Run level six is the reboot run level for all distributions.

31. If only the root account can use the console and no one else can log in to the system, then it is said that the system is in which of the following states?

A. Remote-file sharing

B. Multiple user

C. Single user

D. User defined

32. You are working in a multitasking state and you want to kill a process, so you try to find the PID of that process. Which of the following commands should you use to find the PID?

    A. top

    B. free

    C. nice

    D. ps

33. A hard disk volume used by Linux:

    A. Is given a logical name in the file system that can vary from mount to mount

    B. Has a transparent or unknown location (to the typical user) within the directory hierarchy

    C. Is always mounted in the same mount point

    D. A and B

34. Directory paths are always resolved:

    A. With reference to /

    B. With reference to the user's home directory

    C. With reference to the present working directory

    D. With reference to the superuser's home directory

35. Assume that the superuser wishes to set up a user account manually. Which of the following reasons is justification for using the chown command?

    A. To change the owner of the account from the previous user.

    B. By default, the superuser is the owner of each new account, so to make the user the owner, the superuser has to use chown.

    C. So that the superuser can still monitor each account after users have started using them.

    D. So that the superuser can turn on shadow passwords for the account.

36. Assume Kevin and Jack are two users on one Linux machine, and they each have the same GID. This means that (select all that apply):

    A. Kevin and Jack have the same access privileges to each other's files regardless of the rwx settings.

    B. Kevin and Jack may share access using the same file by setting GID permissions to rw.

    C. Kevin and Jack could also have the same access privileges to the files of other users who also belong to the same group.

    D. Kevin and Jack must first disable the others permission before being able to share access with the GID permissions.

Chapter 3: Shells and Commands

1. As a system administrator, you want to speed up the daily routines and provide some convenience for the users. Can you create a universal shell alias file for all users?

   A. Yes

   B. No

2. The bash shell has a command completion function. Which of the following keys will active the function?

   A. CTRL

   B. SHIFT-CTRL

   C. TAB or TAB-TAB

   D. TAB-Pg Up

3. Environment variables are the same as shell variables.

   A. True

   B. False

4. Which of the following is an invalid shell variable?

   A. 34shelltest

   B. Shell_Test

   C. SHELLTEST

   D. Test2Shell

5. Assuming the bash shell is being used, which of the following files in the current working directory will be displayed using the command `ls ?t.c*`?

   A. `Test.cpp`

   B. `Tt.cpp`

   C. `Test.c`

   D. `TT.c`

6. Which of the following `mtools` descriptions is/are *false*?

   A. `mdel`—Deletes files from a DOS disk without mounting the disk drive.

   B. `mdir`—Lists the files on a DOS floppy disk.

   C. `mgetty`—Monitors incoming logins to set terminal speed, type, and other parameters.

   D. `mesg` —Is run by the user to control the read access of others to the terminal device associated with the standard error output.

7. Ann, a Linux system user and a high school student, needs to write a 750-word report. She creates the report, but does not want to spend a lot of time counting the number of words. What utility can she use to perform the counting for her?

   A. `wordcount`

   B. `count`

   C. `wc`

   D. There is not a word count utility; she must use the Vi editor to count the words.

8. Emily, a Linux system user, types the command `wc report`. The resultant output is:

```
89      776     5025 report
```

This output means:

A. 89 lines, 776 words, and 5025 characters

B. 89 lines, 776 words, and 5025 bits

C. 89 words, 776 characters, and 5025 bits

D. 89 pages, 776 paragraphs, and 5025 lines

9. Katey, a Linux system user, needs to erase all the temporary files she has created for a software project. She has five files, named `test`, `test2`, `test3`, `test4`, and `test5`. How can she erase these files?

A. `del test?`

B. `del test*`

C. `rm test*`

D. `erase test?`

10. Cary, a Linux system user, has completed her software project and needs to erase all the files in the directory `proj`. How can she do this?

A. `del proj/*`

B. `erase proj`

C. `rm -r proj`

D. `rmdir proj/*`

11. Elizabeth, a Linux system user, needs to create a new directory `newproj` for testing a new software project. Assuming there are no shell aliases, how can she do this?

A. `rm -r proj`

B. `md newproj`

C. `pico -d newproj`

D. `newdir newproj`

12. Lindsay, a Linux system user, needs to copy the `/etc/printcap` file to her directory `/home/ann`. Assuming no shell aliases, and assuming her current working directory is `/home/ann`, how can this be accomplished? (Select all that apply.)

A. `copy /etc/printcap /home/ann/*`

B. `cp /etc/printcap ~/printcap`

C. `cp /etc/printcap`

D. `copy /etc/printcap /home/ann/printcap`

13. Christina, a Linux system user, is currently in the directory `/var/spool/lpd/lpj`, and needs to change to her home directory, which is `/home/clb`. What is the fastest way to do this?

A. `chdir /home/clb`

B. `cd /clb`

C. cd

D. cd ..

14. Julie, a Linux system user, wants to read the contents of file README. Without thinking, she types README at the shell prompt. What would most likely be the output from the bash shell?

A. No output, just another bash shell prompt.

B. The contents of the file README will be displayed.

C. The bash shell will echo the command and output the file README.

D. bash: README: command not found.

15. Marcel, a Linux system user, sometimes has trouble typing the command more, usually typing it as mroe. She complains to Janet, a coworker who also uses Linux, to find out if there is a way to set up her system so that she does not have to go back and correct the spelling all the time. Janet tells her:

A. There is no way to correct this problem.

B. Use the alias command alias mroe=more.

C. Run ispell as the last command on the command line.

D. Create a script that runs ispell for each word on the command line.

16. You want to see the report of the disk usage for the current directory. You are going to redirect the output to a file called status, and place the time and date in front of the disk usage. Which of the following commands should you use?

A. du > status

B. (date; du) > status

C. date; du > status

D. date > status; du >> status;

17. What will be printed by the command echo * ?

A. All files in root directory

B. All files in current directory

C. '*'

D. Empty and waiting for standard input

18. To find out the number of user accounts on the system, which of the following commands would you use?

A. more /etc/passwd

B. less /etc/passwd

C. wc /etc/passwd

D. cat /etc/passwd | more | less | pr

19. Which of the following bash shell meta-characters would instruct a command to run in the background?

A. ;

B. ()

C. &

D. $

20. The commands setenv and umask are the bash shell:

    A. Built-in commands

    B. Shell variables

    C. Environment variables

    D. File system programs

21. You want to append the contents of the newfile.txt file to the end of the contents of the oldfile.txt. Which of the following operators would you use?

    A. .

    B. >

    C. >>

    D. |

22. You typed the command cat /etc/passwd > /dev/null. What happened?

    A. The contents of the file /etc/passwd are stored in the file /dev/null.

    B. The output is redirected to /dev/null and was discarded.

    C. A new empty file is created, named /dev/null.

    D. The contents of the /etc/passwd were nullified.

23. Which of the following statements is *False* of the following output of the command ls -l?

    ```
    " -rw-rw-rw-  1  david  staff    227  Dec 12 19:33  note "
    ```

    A. The owner of file note and any other user accounts cannot execute this file.

    B. The owner's user account name of file note is david.

    C. The file note is first created on Dec 12, 1933.

    D. The size of the file note is 227 bytes.

24. You are going to rename the file test to sample. Which of the following is the correct operation?

    A. cp test sample

    B. mv test sample

    C. ln test sample

    D. rn test sample

25. For the file permission rw----r-x, which of the following numbers is correct from symbolic permissions into numeric?

    A. 605

    B. 655

    C. 755

    D. 022

26. How do the find and locate commands differ? (Select all that apply.)

    A. locate is slower than find because of database fragmentation.

    B. find is slower than locate because of database fragmentation.

   C. `locate` is faster than `find` because it uses a possibly old database of file names.

   D. `find` is faster than `locate` because it does not have database overhead.

27. For the bash shell, which of the following are valid shell variable names?

   A. `temp`

   B. `1xyz`

   C. `abc9`

   D. `efg_1_`

28. Amanda wants to read a few files at the same time, yet she does not want to open and close each file individually. Which of the following commands would allow her to do this, and what would be the command syntax?

   A. `more -n filename1 filename2 filename3`

   B. `less filename1 filename2 filename3`

   C. `more filename1 filename2 filename3`

   D. `B and C`

29. The command `ln test1 test2` will:

   A. Count the number of lines in file `test1` and `test2`.

   B. Count the number of lines in file `test1` and output the results in file `test2`.

   C. Create a new directory entry so that `test1` and `test2` reference the same file.

   D. Nothing; there is no such command as `ln`.

30. A hard link has been created between the files `alpha` and `beta`. This means that:

   A. When the file `alpha` is removed, `beta` will also be removed.

   B. Any changes that occur to file `alpha` will also appear in file `beta`.

   C. Only a superuser can remove files `alpha` and `beta`.

   D. When the file `alpha` is accessed, file `beta` will automatically be appended to it.

31. The result of the command sequence `ps aux | grep "smith"` will:

   A. List all processes on the display.

   B. List all processes whose user ID contains the name `"smith"`.

   C. List all lines of the output containing the substring `"smith"`, including the `ps` command itself.

   D. List all processes and output them to the file `"smith"`.

32. When performing `ls` on your home directory, you notice a file named `jpgs.tar`. Most likely, this file is:

   A. A compressed archive of files.

   B. A compressed archive that automatically decompresses when `jpgs.tar` is typed.

   C. The compressed directory listing that the operating system refers to when performing the `ls` command.

   D. An archive of files.

Chapter 4: System Utilities

1. You have a Red Hat 5.0 machine and want to configure X Window on your system. Which set of the following utilities can be used to set up X Window?

   A. `xf86config, xset, SaX`

   B. `xf86config, Xconfigurator, XF86Setup`

   C. `xfm, SaX, XF86Setup`

   D. `X, xdm, xf86config`

2. There are two Ethernet adapters in a Debian Linux box. The first card is a 3Com card attaching Ethernet interface 0 (eth0), but the second card cannot be recognized by the kernel. You know the second card uses the Western Digital chipset. Which command-line sequence can solve your problem? (Background: Western Digital driver objects are wd.o and 8390.o. Wd.o requires 8390.o to run.)

   A. `append="eth0=wd.o,8390.o"`

   B. `insmod 8390.o; insmod wd.o`

   C. `insmod wd.o; 8390.o`

   D. `loadobj="8390.o, wd.o"`

3. A Linux machine is running kernel version 2.0.30. Unfortunately, one of the network device drivers is suspect; it may have been corrupted. There is no source code to rebuild the driver, but a set of network modules for kernel 2.2.5 are accessible from another machine. *True* or *false*: these modules will work with the kernel 2.0.30.

   A. True

   B. False

4. Windows 98 is installed on the first hard drive with an ATAPI CD-ROM as a slave drive. A second hard drive is installed on the secondary controller with the Linux on it. Which of the following `lilo.conf` stanzas is correct?

   A. `image=/boot/vmlinz`

      `root=/dev/hda1`

      `label=Linux`

      `other=/dev/hdb1`

      `label=Windows98`

   B. `image=/boot/vmlinz`

      `root=/dev/hda1`

      `label=Windows98`

      `other=/dev/hdc1`

      `label=Linux`

   C. `image=/boot/vmlinz`

      `root=/dev/hda2`

```
label=Linux
other=/dev/hdc1
label=Windows98
```

D. ```
   image=/boot/vmlinz
   root=/dev/hda3
   label=Linux
   other=/dev/hdc1
   label=Windows98
   ```

5. You were trying to print an ASCII document to a networked printer. The following error message appeared on the screen: `lpr: cannot create /var/spool/ lpd/lp/.seq`. Which of the following techniques will solve the problem? A segment of the printcap file looks like this:

   ```
   "lp|xerox|Xerox N40 Printer:lp=:rp=raw:rm=192.168.1.21:\
   :sd=/var/spool/lpd/lp:lf=/var/log/lpd-err:ar:bk:mx#0:tr=:cl:sh:
   ```

   A. Add the correct `if` printer filter.
   B. Restart `lpd`.
   C. Use the `-s` switch in the `lpr` program.
   D. Make a new directory `lp` under directory `lpd`.

6. Jason, a Linux user, has a problem while running X11. A program goes into an infinite loop, locking the X server up; therefore, he presses CTRL-ALT-BACK-SPACE. What effect does this key combination achieve?

   A. Kills the X server (assuming the X server is configured to do so).
   B. Restarts the computer.
   C. Restarts the window manager.
   D. Instructs the X Server daemon to reread the configuration files.

7. If the last command in `.xinitrc` is `exec twm`, then killing the `twm` process will:

   A. Delete the X Window server
   B. Exit the X Window server
   C. Disable the X Window server
   D. All of the above

8. When booting LILO from the hard drive, you discover that MS-DOS boots by default instead of Linux. Which of the following statements about this situation are *true*?

   A. If you wish to select Linux as the default booting operating system, you have to edit the `/etc/lilo.conf` file and reinstall LILO.
   B. While the system is booting, hold SHIFT-CTRL and press L to boot Linux.
   C. While the system is booting, hold ALT-F7 to boot Linux.
   D. None of the above.
   ```

9. Which of the following descriptions about the printer and printing service is correct?

   A. The `lpc` command is used by the system administrator to control the operation of the line printer system.

   B. `lpd` is the line printer daemon and is normally invoked at boot time.

   C. The `lpd` program examines a spooling area looking for files to print on the line printer.

   D. The `lpq` program reports the status of the specified jobs or all jobs associated with a user.

   E. All of the above.

10. A program that converts one file format to another for the purpose of printing is called a:

    A. Printer filter

    B. Translator

    C. Printer driver

    D. Printer screen

11. The program to identify installed video hardware is:

    A. XF86config

    B. SuperProbe

    C. X Window

    D. XF86Setup

12. Tom, a Linux system administrator running as the superuser, needs to take printer `lj5` offline so it can be moved. He has checked to see what jobs are waiting to be printed, and now he wants to remove them. How can he do this?

    A. `lpr -Plj5 -`

    B. `lpc -Plj5 -`

    C. `lpq -Plj5 -`

    D. `lprm -Plj5 -`

13. The file that controls the behavior of the client and server provider programs for printing is the _____ file.

    A. `/etc/printcap`

    B. `/printcap`

    C. `/etc/pcontrol`

    D. `/etc/print.conf`

14. Two users are logged in as the superuser and they are both editing the `/etc/passwd` file to add new user accounts. Which of the following statements is *true*?

    A. Linux ensures `/etc/passwd` file integrity and consistency.

    B. The file manager automatically creates a new user's home directory upon completion of editing the `/etc/passwd` file for both instances of the superuser account.

C. There is a problem here; the last superuser to exit the editor will overwrite the account just added by the other superuser account.

D. Linux automatically creates the /etc/shadow file when done creating a new user.

15. Creation of a user account involves which of the following steps?

(i) Edit the /etc/passwd file to add the user.

(ii) Create the home directory and set its ownership.

(iii) Copy the shell startup files to the home directory.

(iv) Create the new group to which the user must belong.

(v) Edit the /etc/login.defs for the user's default settings.

A. i, ii, and v

B. i, ii, iii, and v

C. i, ii, iv, and v

D. i, ii, and iii

Chapter 5: Applications

1. *True* or *false*: the Deja search engine assists with troubleshooting by indexing, searching, and retrieving detailed technical assistance from past Usenet news group postings.

A. True

B. False

2. You can get all kinds of help from Linux documentation. Which of the following sequences of help programs provides information from the briefest amount of information to the most detailed amount of information?

A. Xman, man, --help, Linux Documentation Project, Deja, locate/find, info

B. locate/find, --help, man, man section 5, Xman, info, Deja, Linux Documentation Project.

C. Deja, Xman, --help, Linux Documentation Project, locate/find, man

D. Linux Documentation Project, --help, Xman, Deja, locate/find, info

Chapter 6: Troubleshooting

1. In which of the following situations would a rescue disk be helpful? (Select all that apply.)

A. When the system fails to boot

B. After a hard disk failure (e.g., head crash)

C. After the root file system was deleted accidentally

D. When no one (including root) can log in to the system

E. After the file system has been severely damaged

2. Which of the following generalizations are *true* about Linux troubleshooting?

   A. Much of Linux's complexity comes from module layering and module integration.

   B. Generally, it is more efficient to analyze a problem and solve it step by step, than it is to query a local expert or use a search engine.

   C. Generally, there are only one or two ways you can solve a typical Linux problem and, therefore, the key to successful troubleshooting is to not stop searching until you find that best way to solve the problem.

   D. Many Linux problems can be solved by just knowing configuration concepts and configuration alternatives.

3. A Linux installation has hung up with the error message `Device Full`. Which of the following statements is the reason for the error and the solution to the error?

   A. The floppy disk has filled with temporary data; insert a new floppy and press ENTER.

   B. The RAM disk is full; select from the available RAM addresses and select a new address.

   C. The hard disk partition is too small to hold all the selected software; restart the installation process and select a larger partition size.

   D. The aggregate partitions are too small; the hard disk must be upgraded.

Answers

Chapter 1: Theory of Operation

1. **B.** Enter the BIOS setup, type in the geometry (size=258/cycl=125/head=64/sectors=63) in the setup file, and reboot the system.
2. **C.** Always run as a user and `su`.
3. **B.** `rm -rf / home/fred/tmp`
4. **D.** 100 MB
5. **B.** False
6. **A.** ALT-Fn (where n is an integer representing the console number)
7. **D.** `init` is not a daemon.
8. **C.** Linux supports preemptive multitasking except when doing disk I/O.
9. **D.** Most often, Linux installs just as fast from a local area network or from an Internet-based server.
10. **B.** Just free software.
11. **B.** The state of a program as it passes control through itself, libraries, and the kernel.
12. **C.** An octet (8 bits).
13. **B.** Richard Stallman, who invented the GNU general public license, beginning around 1984.

14. **A.** Even though Linux is called free software, most everyone pays some fee, direct or indirect, for the software.

    B. The word "free" in "free software" is about freedom to use the software and not about the cost of software.

    C. If you improve GPL software, and you do not distribute your improvements, then you are not required to show anyone your improvements.

15. **A.** No product warranty; must have inhouse support or contract support.

16. **C.** A program that stays resident in memory (or swap space) at all times waiting for requests for service.

Chapter 2: Base Systems

1. **C.** Create one FAT32 and two Linux partitions (swap and native), install Windows 98 on the FAT32 partition, SuSE Linux on the native partition, and boot either Windows 98 or Linux from the MBR using LILO.

2. **A.** `append="ether=11,0x280,eth0 ether=5,0x300,eth1" /etc/lilo.conf`

3. **B.** `append="ether=5,0x280,eth0 ether=10,0x300,eth1"`

4. **D.** `mount /dev/hdb /mnt/cdrom`

5. **D.** `mcopy document.wpd a:`

6. **C.** Highlight the string with the cursor on the first console, and click the middle button with the cursor on the second console.

7. **C.** `dd if=vmlinuz of=/dev/fd0 bs=1k count=1024`

8. **D.** Run `fdisk` and `mke2fs` to create the volume on another drive, and add the entry into the `fstab` file.

9. **A.** Type CTRL-ALT-DEL

10. **C.** `ls -ltr`

11. **A.** `w`

12. **B.** `startx`

13. **A.** Make the first hard disk partition a `/boot` partition for storing kernel image(s)

14. **A.** Some distributions refer to the `rc.d` directory, which holds the scripts for all run levels.

    B. Some distributions refer to the `init.d` directory, which holds lists of indirect scripts.

15. **C.** `/etc/X11/xinit/xinitrc`

16. **B.** Newer video adapters tend not to have X servers available.

17. **C.** 2.2.5

18. **D.** `mkfs, mkswap`

19. **C.** `/var`

20. **B.**   dmesg
21. **B.**   ps
22. **A.**   Swap partitions are included in /etc/fstab.
23. **C.**   /dev/hda3
24. **D.**   Partitioning can be done after the system is set up.
25. **C.**   You must set the BIOS swapon setting to enable swap space before booting the operating system software.
26. **A.**   shutdown -k now—Do not shut down, but send the shutdown announcement to all users.
27. **A.**   The superuser should always log in as root, and users should log in using their accounts.
28. **B.**   /proc/devices
29. **B.**   w
30. **B.**   Most distributions agree that run-level five will start the KDE GUI.
31. **C.**   Single user
32. **D.**   ps
33. **D.**   A and B
34. **A.**   With reference to /
35. **B.**   By default, the superuser is the owner of each new account, so to make the user the owner, the superuser has to use chown.
36. **B.**   Kevin and Jack may share access using the same file by setting GID permissions to rw.
    C.   Kevin and Jack could also have the same access privileges to the files of other users who also belong to the same group.

Chapter 3: Shells and Commands

1. **A.**   Yes
2. **C.**   TAB or TAB-TAB
3. **B.**   False
4. **A.**   34shelltest
5. **B.**   Tt.cpp
6. **C.**   mgetty—Monitors incoming logins to set terminal speed, type, and other parameters.
    D.   mesg—Is run by the user to control the read access of others to the terminal device associated with the standard error output.
7. **C.**   wc
8. **A.**   89 lines, 776 words, and 5025 characters
9. **C.**   rm test*

10. **C.** `rm -r proj`

11. **A.** `rm -r proj`

12. **C.** `cp /etc/printcap`

13. **C.** `cd`

14. **D.** `bash: README: command not found.`

15. **B.** Use the alias command alias `mroe=more`.

16. **B.** `(date; du) > status`

    D. `date > status; du >> status;`

17. **C.** `'*'`

18. **C.** `wc /etc/passwd`

19. **C.** `&`

20. **A.** Built-in commands

21. **C.** `>>`

22. **B.** The output is redirected to `/dev/null` and was discarded.

23. **C.** The file note is first created by Dec 12, 1933.

24. **B.** `mv test sample`

25. **B.** 655

26. **A.** `locate` is slower than `find` because of database fragmentation.

    D. `find` is faster than `locate` because it does not have database overhead.

27. **A.** `temp`

    C. `abc9`

    D. `efg_1_`

28. **D.** B and C

29. **C.** Create a new directory entry so that `test1` and `test2` reference the same file.

30. **B.** Any changes that occur to file `alpha` will also appear in file `beta`.

31. **C.** List all lines of the output containing the substring `"smith"`, including the `ps` command itself.

32. **D.** An archive of files

Chapter 4: System Utilities

1. **B.** `xf86config, Xconfigurator, XF86Setup`

2. **B.** `insmod 8390.o; insmod wd.o`

3. **B.** False

4. **B.** `image=/boot/vmlinz`

    `root=/dev/hda1`

    `label=Windows98`

```
other=/dev/hdc1
label=Linux
```

5. **D.** Make a new directory `lp` under directory `lpd`.
6. **A.** Kills the X server (assuming the X server is configured to do so).
7. **B.** Exit the X Window server.
8. **A.** If you wish to select Linux as the default booting operating system, you have to edit the `/etc/lilo.conf` file and reinstall LILO.
9. **E.** All of the above.
10. **A.** Printer filter
11. **B.** SuperProbe
12. **D.** `lprm -Plj5 -`
13. **A.** `/etc/printcap`
14. **C.** There is a problem here; the last superuser to exit the editor will overwrite the account just added by the other superuser account.
15. **D.** i, ii, and iii

Chapter 5: Applications

1. **A.** True
2. **B.** locate/find, --help, man, man section 5, Xman, info, Deja, Linux Documentation Project

Chapter 6: Troubleshooting

1. **A.** When the system fails to boot.
   D. When no one (including root) can log in to the system.
2. **A.** Much of Linux's complexity comes from module layering and module integration.
   D. Many Linux problems can be solved by just knowing configuration concepts and configuration alternatives.
3. **C.** The hard disk partition is too small to hold all the selected software; restart the installation process and select a larger partition size.

Installations

1. Caldera OpenLinux eDesktop Release 2.4

In this appendix, we presume that your computer has:

- No hard drive partition (i.e., Linux is the only OS)
- No upgrade from a previous Linux version (initial install)
- No shared hard disk
- A bootable CD-ROM
- No network connection
- A modem
- No Ethernet card

BEFORE INSTALLATION

System requirements: The minimum system specifications required to successfully run the Caldera OpenLinux distribution.

Hardware and network information: A list of the hardware that you will need to install and run Linux, and a list of information regarding your hardware and network if installing for a network computer.

SYSTEM REQUIREMENTS

- 32-bit Intel-base PC (i.e., 80386… Pentium)
- ISA, EISA, PCI, VL-Bus
- Minimum MB RAM (16 MB preferred)
- Approximately 418 MB free hard disk space
- Supported mouse and video card

HARDWARE AND NETWORK INFORMATION

- Three 3.5" floppy disks
- CD-ROM drive
- Mouse, port used
- Graphics care manufacturer/model or number
- X server for graphics card (see www.caldera.com/products/openlinux/hardware.html for a list of supported hardware)
- Graphics card memory size in MB
- Monitor, max scan rates (vertical/horizontal)
- Modem, manufacturer/model and serial port

OPTIONAL NETWORK INFORMATION

- Host name of computer
- Domain name of network
- IP address assigned to computer
- Network address of LAN
- Netmask address
- Network broadcast address
- Gateway or router address
- DNS name server address
- Additional addresses

Step 1: Getting Started

- Insert the installation CD and turn on the computer.
- Select `Standard Install Mode` and press ENTER.

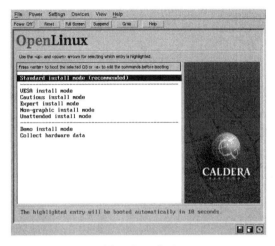

Figure A.1.1   Caldera installation.

Step 2: Language Selection

- Choose the preferred language.

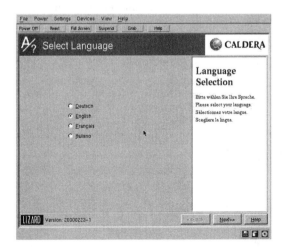

Figure A.1.2   Caldera language selection.

Step 3: Mouse Selection

- The setup program auto-detects the mouse.
- Double-check the chosen items; manually select any corrections.

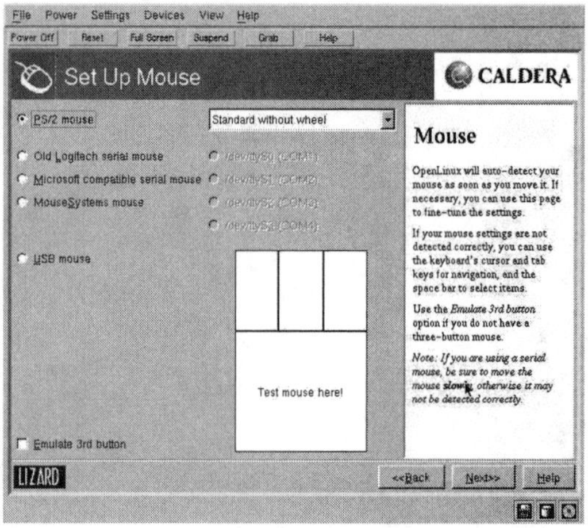

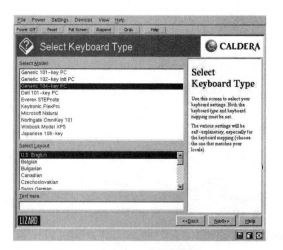

Figure A.1.3 Mouse selection.

Step 4: Keyboard Selection

- Select the keyboard type from the choices given in the first menu box.
- Select the keyboard mapping by choosing your locale in the second menu box.

Figure A.1.4 Keyboard selection.

Step 5: Video Card Selection

- Although OpenLinux should auto-detect your video card, select it from the drop-down menu.
- Click `Probe` to detect the video RAM and clock.

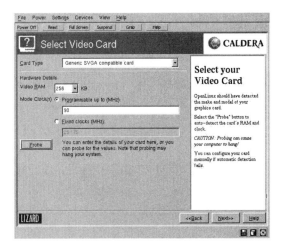

Figure A.1.5   Video card selection.

Step 6: Monitor Selection

- Click the + next to the manufacturer, and select the model.
- If you do not have documentation on your monitor, specs may be found at the manufacturer's Web site.

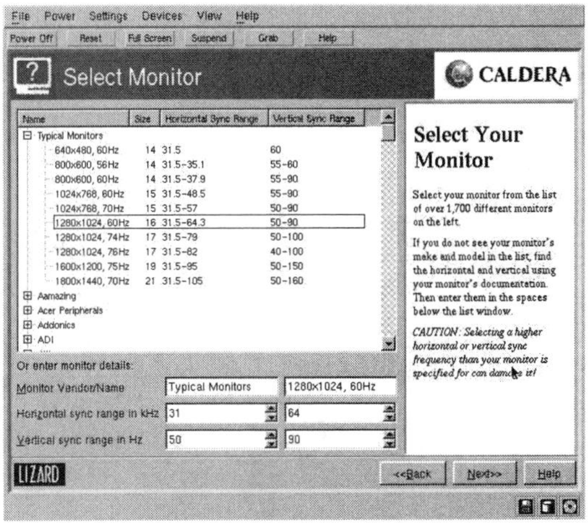

Figure A.1.6   Monitor selection.

Step 7: Video Mode Selection

- Select the video mode based on the horizontal and vertical refresh rates.
- Click Test this mode.
- Click Ok at the startup box to proceed.

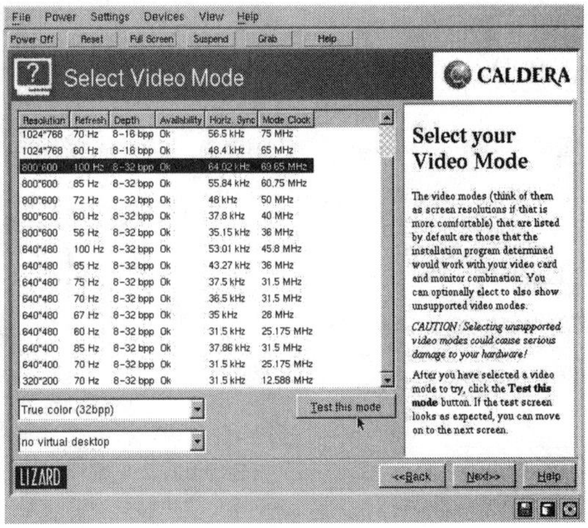

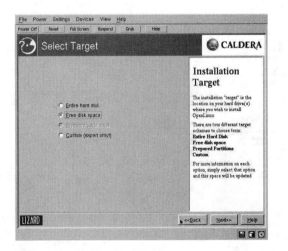

Figure A.1.7   Video mode selection.

Step 8: Target Selection

- This option determines where Linux will be installed.
- You should choose Free disk space or Entire Hard disk, if Linux will be the only OS on your machine.

Figure A.1.8   Target selection.

Step 9: Target Verification

- Confirm the installation target, by selecting Use Free Disk Space for Linux.

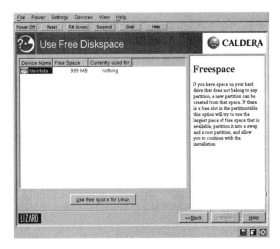

Figure A.1.9 Target verification.

Step 10: Software Selection

- Select the recommended installation, comprising only 750 MB.

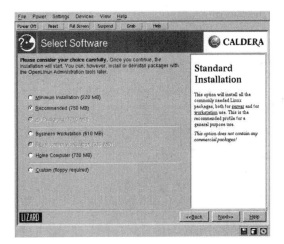

Figure A.1.10 Software selection.

Step 11: Login Selection

- The name of the user, John Q. Doe, was entered, followed by the login name, john.
- John's password was entered and retyped.

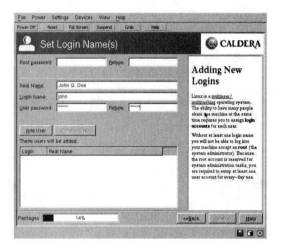

Figure A.1.11   Login selection.

Step 12: Login

- Enter and confirm a root password.
- Repeat step 11 to create multiple user accounts.

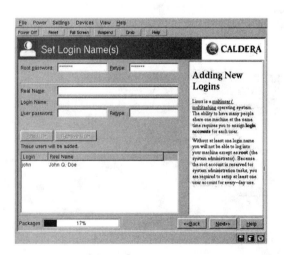

Figure A.1.12   Caldera login.

Step 13: Network Configuration

- For our installation, use of a modem was assumed. Therefore, `No Ethernet` was selected.
- Although no network exists, a host name may be chosen.

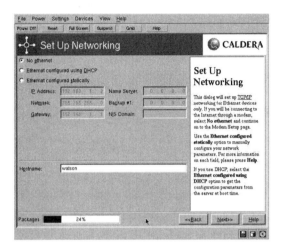

Figure A.1.13   Network configuration.

Step 14: Modem Configuration

- Select the modem model.
- Select `dev/tty//S0` for the modem's port.
- Initstring refers to a modem initialization command.

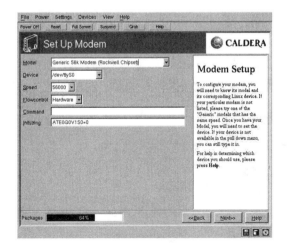

Figure A.1.14   Modem configuration.

Step 15: ISP Configuration

- Use dial-up was chosen for the modem connection.
- The USA/user selection was highlighted.
- Save authentication information is left unchecked for security purposes.

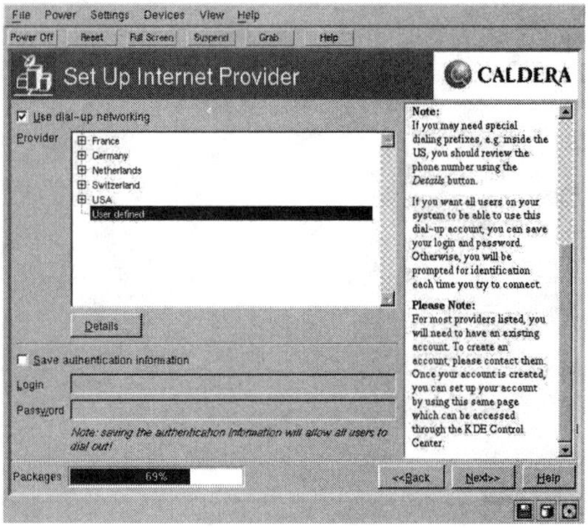

Figure A.1.15 ISP configuration.

Step 16: DNS Server Information

- Select Details to bring up the text box for the ISP name and dial-up number.
- Enter DNS server information here.

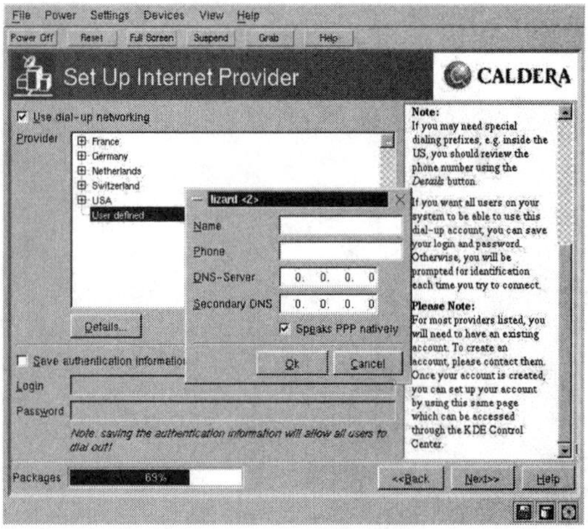

Figure A.1.16 DNS server information.

Step 17: Boot Loader Configuration

- Since Linux is the only OS, select `Write master boot record`.

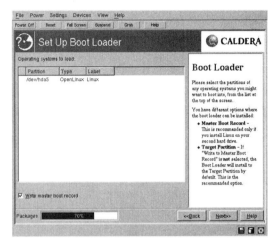

Figure A.1.17   Boot loader configuration.

Step 18: Printer Configuration

- Select printer options from the drop-down menu.
- Select the appropriate port and paper size.
- Select `Test` to print a test page.

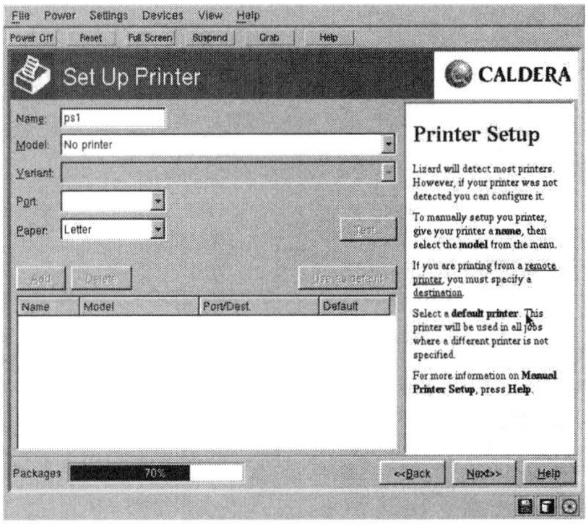

Figure A.1.18   Printer configuration.

Step 19: Time Zone Selection

■ Choose the appropriate time zone.

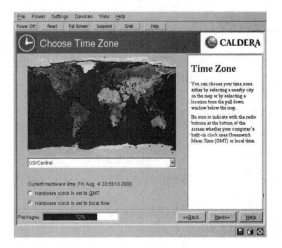

Figure A.1.19 Time zone selection.

Step 20: Play Pac-Man

■ There are several games available while the user is waiting for the installation process to finish.

Figure A.1.20 Games during installation.

Step 21: Creating the Rescue Disk

- When prompted to do so, insert a blank floppy disk and click Write Disk.

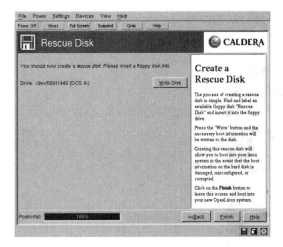

Figure A.1.21   Creating the rescue disk.

Step 22: Wait for Startup

- The setup program has completed installation and is now starting the system.

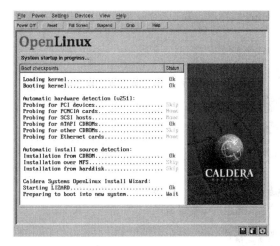

Figure A.1.22   Wait for startup.

Step 23: Login

- At the login prompt, log in by typing the username, or `root` (to log in as administrator).
- Press ENTER after typing the username; type the password, and ENTER again.

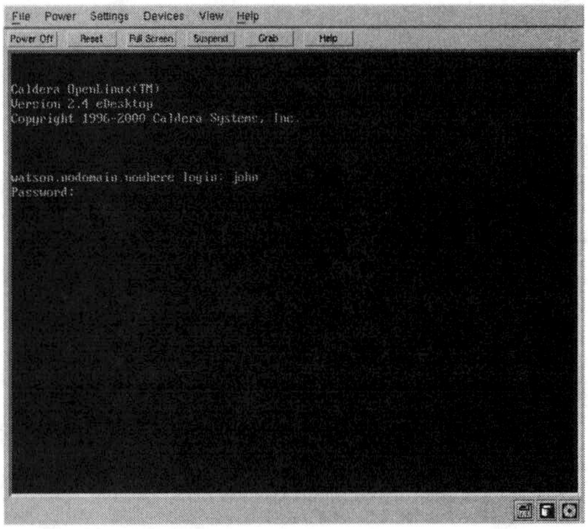

Figure A.1.23   User login.

Step 24: Use Linux

- Any user space tools or Linux commands may be used at the command prompt.

Figure A.1.24   Use Linux.

Step 25: Use X-Win

■ Type `startx` at the command line to run the X Window program.

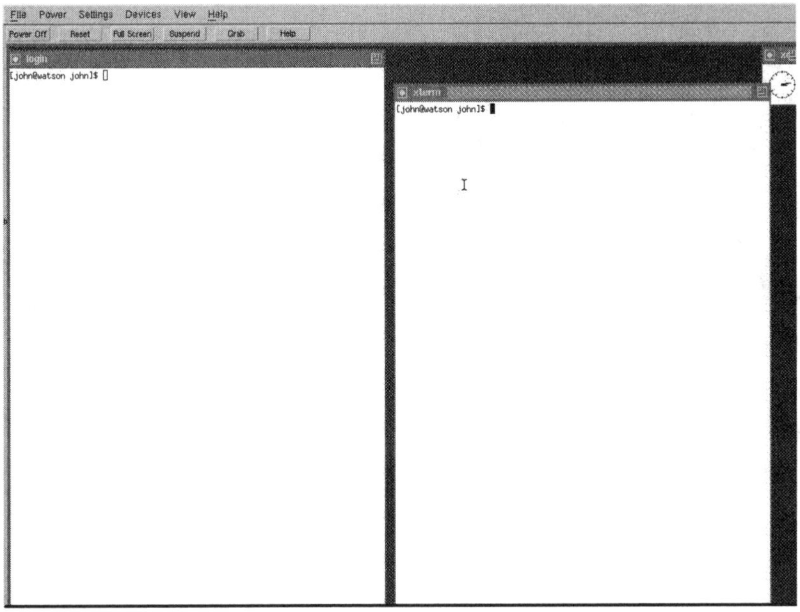

Figure A.1.25 X-Win.

2. Corel Linux 1.1

The installation software, Corel Install Express, detects and configures the hardware on your machine. Therefore, gathering hardware information is helpful in trouble-shooting, but not necessary to install.

MINIMUM SYSTEM REQUIREMENTS

■ Pentium processor.

■ 24 MB RAM (64 MB recommended).

■ 500 MB of hard disk space.

■ CD-ROM drive, 2 MB VGA PCI card and mouse.

■ Supports most hardware designed for Pentium computers. A list of compatible hardware is available at www.corel.com.

Step 1: Wait

- The installation software will load and start Corel Linux from the CD-ROM.
- At this point, hardware is detected and drivers are selected.

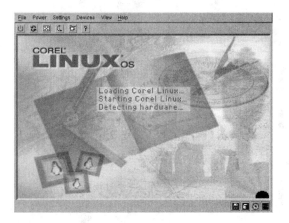

Figure A.2.1   Load Corel installation software.

Step 2: License Agreement

- Read the License Agreement and select Accept to continue.

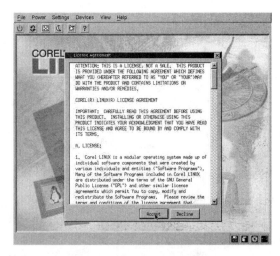

Figure A.2.2   Corel license agreement.

Step 3: User Login

■ Log in to create the username for your account. The username should have lower-case and alphanumeric characters.

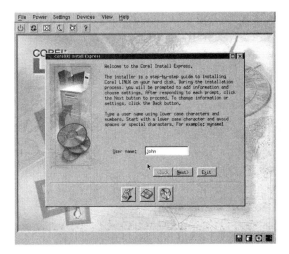

Figure A.2.3   User login.

Step 4: Installation Type

■ The default `Install standard desktop (recommended)` was selected.

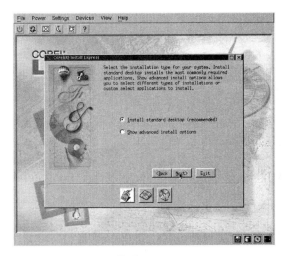

Figure A.2.4   Installation type.

Step 5: Hard Disk Configuration

- Since this distribution will be the only OS on the hard disk and there are no pre-existing partitions, Take over disk was selected.

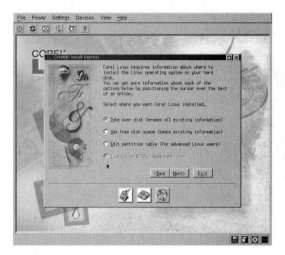

Figure A.2.5   Hard disk configuration.

Step 6: Remove Hard Disk Information

- Select Yes to confirm the decision to remove all information from the hard disk.

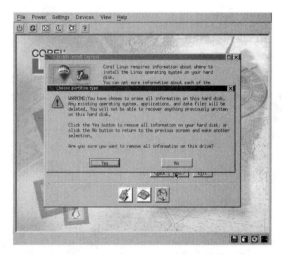

Figure A.2.6   Removing hard disk information.

Step 7: Installation

- Check Scan for bad blocks while formatting.
- Select Install.

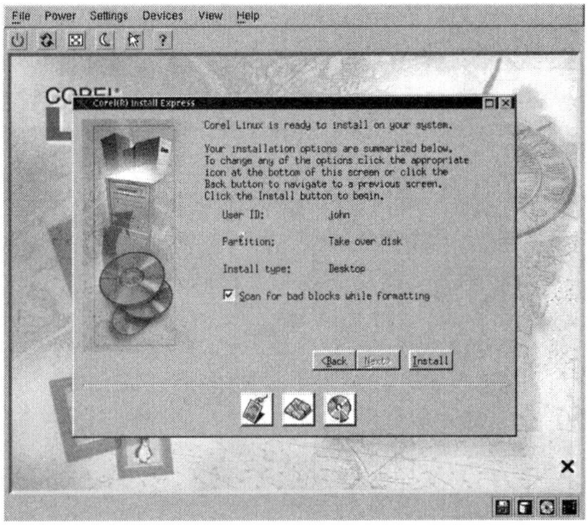

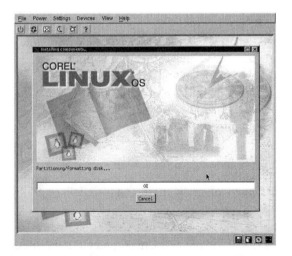

Figure A.2.7   Corel installation.

Step 8: Wait

- Corel Linux will install from the CD-ROM; this will take a few minutes.
- If the installation must be halted, select Cancel.

Figure A.2.8   Wait for completion of installation.

Step 9: Reboot

- Eject the CD-ROM from the CD-ROM drive.
- Select Ok to reboot the system.
- This completes the installation and will bring you to the Corel KDE desktop interface.

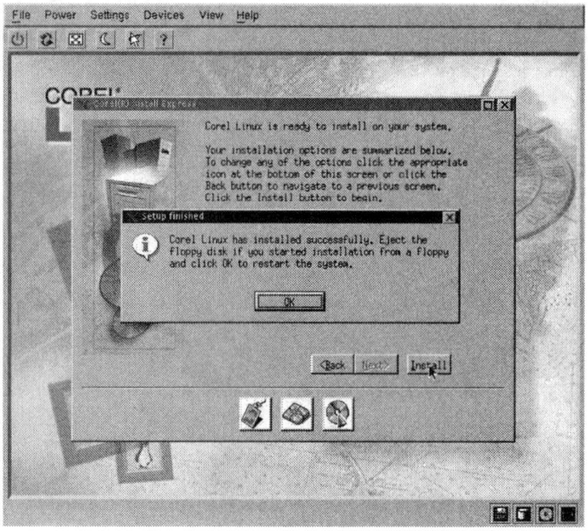

Figure A.2.9   Reboot the system.

3. Debian Linux 2.2

Debian has one of the most interactive installations of any Linux distribution, since it contains over 100 user prompts.

MINIMUM HARDWARE REQUIREMENTS

- **Supported processors:** Cyrix 6x86, AMD K5 and K6, Intel 80386 (X runs slow), 80486, Pentium, Pentium Pro, II, III, (80286 and earlier not supported). Supported hardware can be checked at www.debian.org.
- **Supported motherboards:** ISA, EISA, PCI, and VESA (VLB). Supported hardware can be checked at www.debian.org.
- At least 16 MB RAM (64 MB recommended for X Window).
- At least 250 MB hard disk.

REQUIRED SYSTEM INFORMATION

- **Hard drives:** Number, size, and type of each; master/slave; IDE or SCSI; whether BIOS is set to LBA mode (for IDE drive).
- **RAM:** Amount installed.
- **CD-ROM:** IDE or SCSI, for each non-IDE and non-SCSI, make and model of drive.
- **NIC:** Make and model (no networking is assumed for this installation).

- **Mouse:** Type (serial, PS/2, bus), protocol (Logitech, MouseMan, etc.), number of buttons, serial port for connection (if serial).
- **Video adapter:** Make and model of card, amount of video RAM.

Step 1: Boot Installation

- Insert CD-ROM and turn on the machine to bring up the introductory screen.
- Press ENTER to continue.

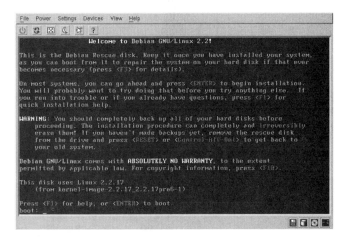

Figure A.3.1   Boot installation.

Step 2: Release Notes

- These are the Release Notes for Debian GNU/Linux 2.2.
- Select Continue.

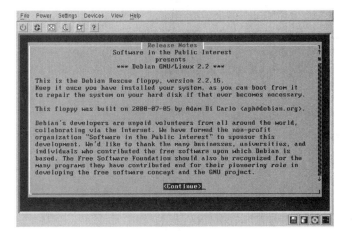

Figure A.3.2   Debian Release Notes.

Step 3: Keyboard Configuration

■ Select Next: Configure Keyboard.

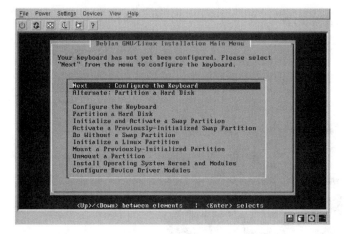

Figure A.3.3a   Keyboard configuration.

■ Select the appropriate keyboard type, and press ENTER.

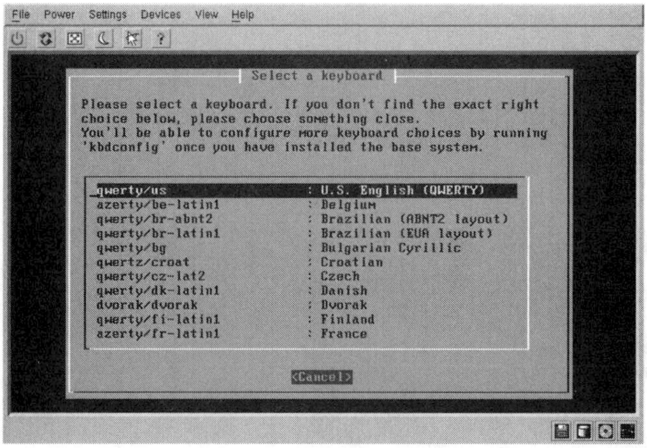

Figure A.3.3b   Keyboard type.

Step 4: Hard Disk Partition

■ Select Next: Partition a Hard Disk.

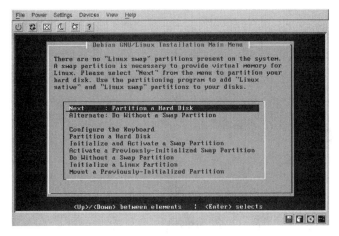

Figure A.3.4a   Hard disk partition.

■ Select /dev/hda.

Figure A.3.4b   Select /dev/hda for hard disk partition.

Step 5: LILO Limitations

- Read the information provided.
- Select Continue.

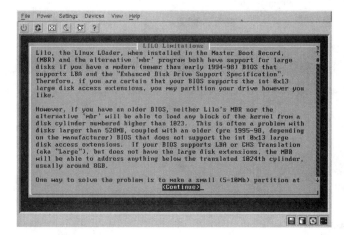

Figure A.3.5 LILO limitations.

Step 6: Partition the Hard Disk

- The next few steps describe the process of partitioning a hard drive using the cfdisk program.
- Select New to partition a new hard disk.

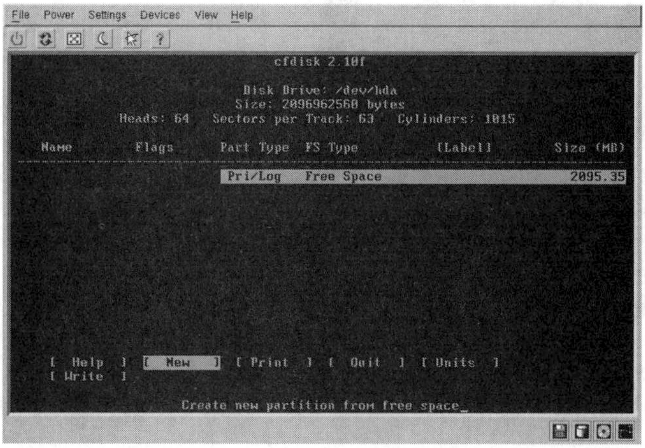

Figure A.3.6a Partitioning a new hard disk.

■ Select Primary, for a primary partition.

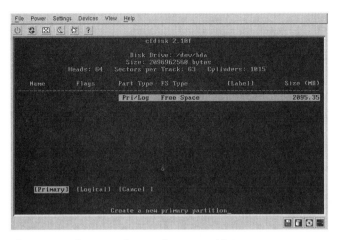

Figure A.3.6b Creating a primary partition.

■ The number displayed in MB is the default size of the partition, which equals the remaining size of the disk.

■ Delete the default value, and enter 64, since this is the swap partition.

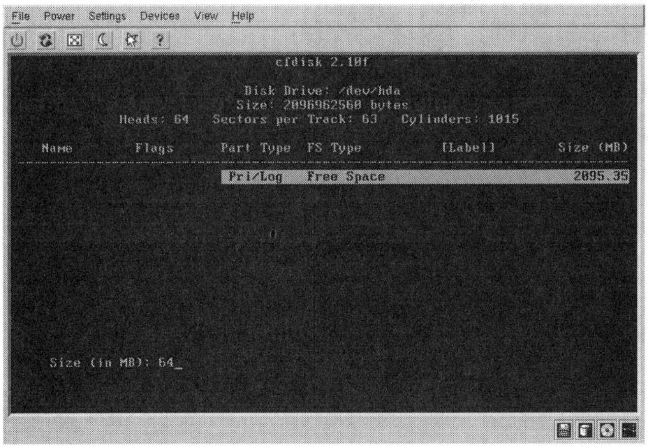

Figure A.3.6c Partition size.

■ Select `Beginning` to mark the beginning of the partition.

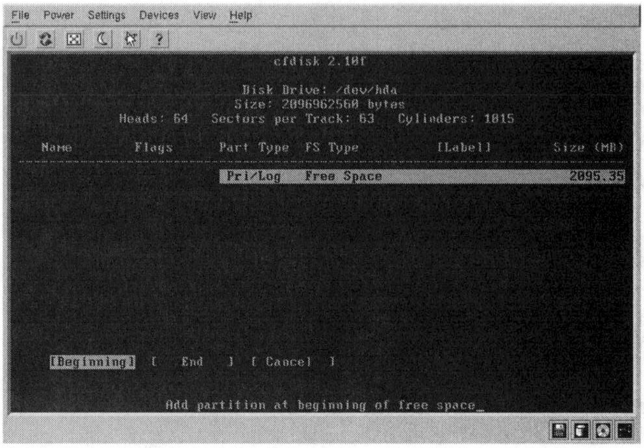

Figure A.3.6d   Mark the beginning of the partition.

■ Select `Type` to change the type of the partition that was just created.

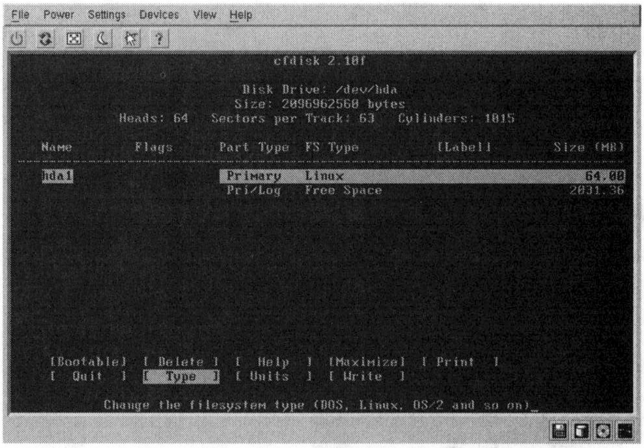

Figure A.3.6e   Change the partition type.

- This brings us to the main menu for partition type. Press any key to display the rest of the menu.

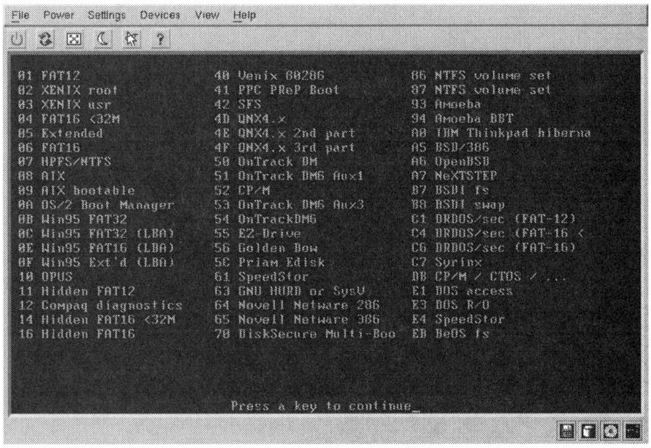

Figure A.3.6f   Partition type menu.

- For the first partition to be a Linux swap partition, enter the number 82.

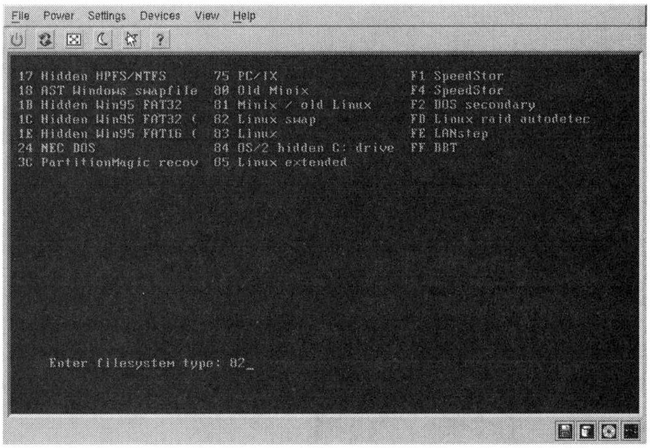

Figure A.3.6g   Create a Linux partition.

- Select `Pri/Log Free Space`. This will be the target partition, onto which Linux will be installed.
- Select `New` for a new partition.

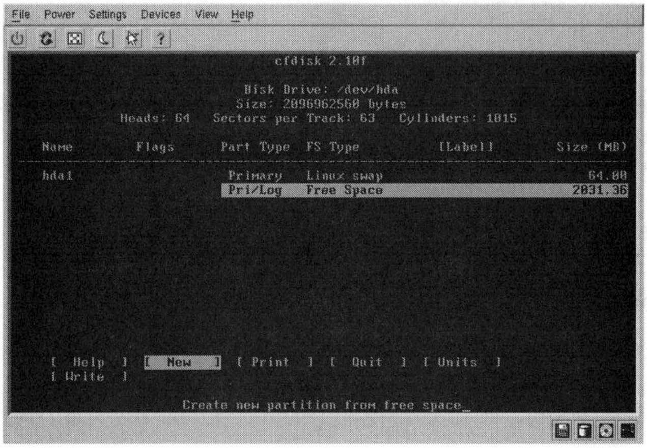

Figure A.3.6h   Select the target partition.

- Select `Primary`, since this is a primary partition.

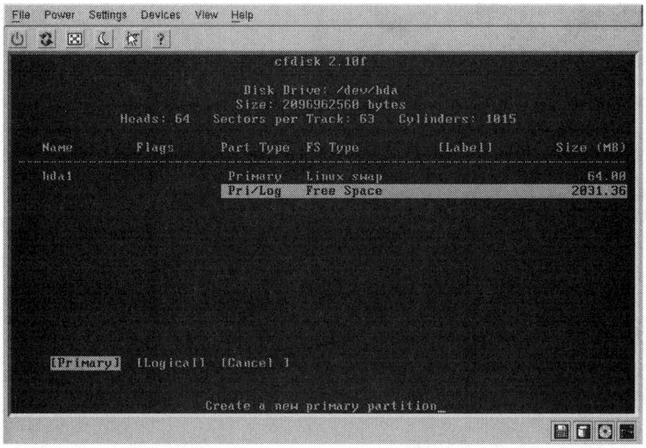

Figure A.3.6i   Select the primary partition.

- Again, the number displayed in MB is the default size of the partition, which equals the remaining size of the disk.
- Press ENTER, since we want the remaining disk to comprise this partition.

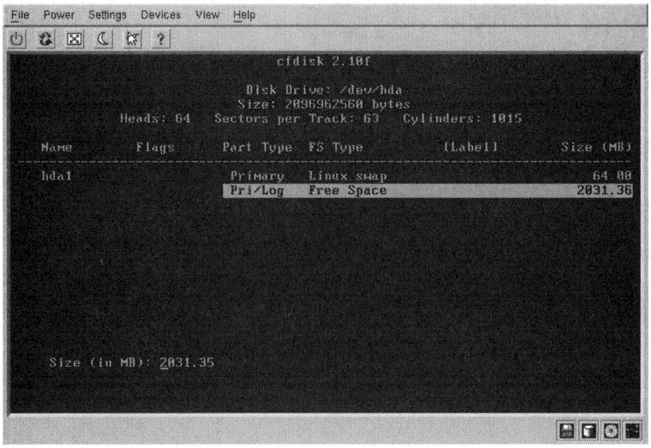

Figure A.3.6j   Select the default partition size.

- Select Bootable, so that LILO will boot the Linux kernel from this hard drive partition.

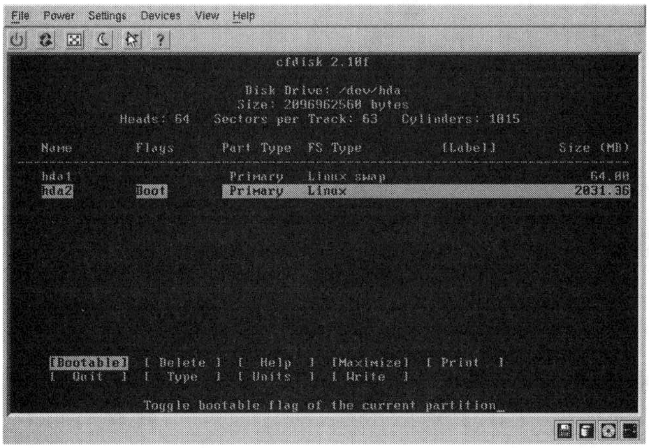

Figure A.3.6k   Make Linux bootable.

■ Select Write to write this partition table to the hard drive.

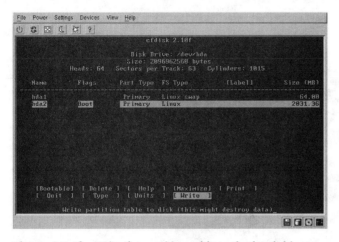

Figure A.3.6l Write the partition table to the hard drive.

■ Type Yes to confirm the writing of this partition table.

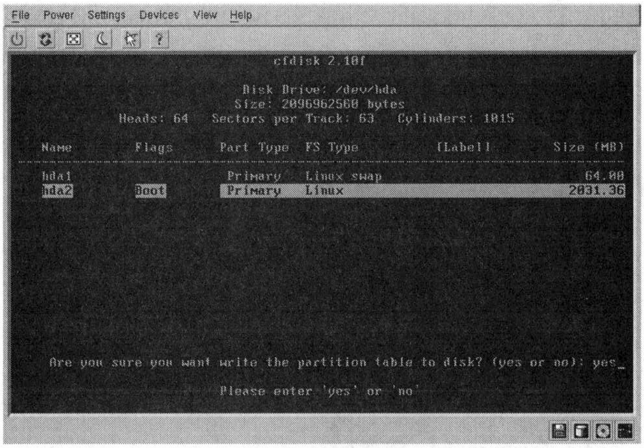

Figure A.3.6m Partition table confirmation.

Step 7: Swap Partition Selection

■ Select /dev/hda1 : Linux swap.

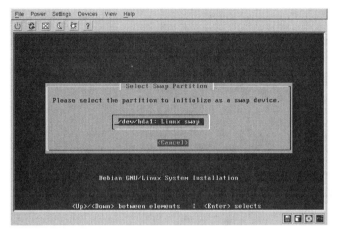

Figure A.3.7   Swap partition selection.

Step 8: Bad Block Check

■ Select No to check the hard drive for bad blocks.

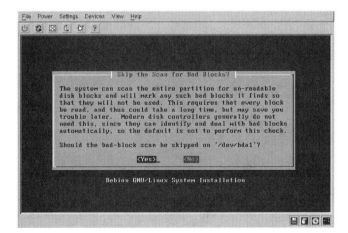

Figure A.3.8   Bad block check.

Step 9: Partition Confirmation

- Select Yes to confirm the creation of this swap partition.

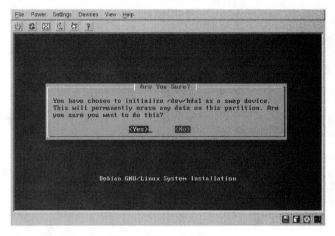

Figure A.3.9   Partition confirmation.

Step 10: Initialize Linux Partition

- Select Next: Initialize a Linux Partition.

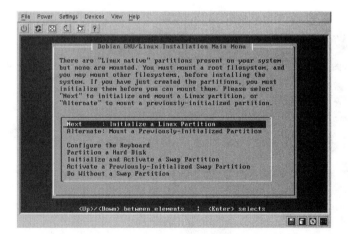

Figure A.3.10   Initialize Linux partition.

Step 11: Linux Partition Selection

- Select /dev/hda2: Linux native.

Figure A.3.11 Linux partition selection.

Step 12: Kernel Compatibility

- Select No if you do not need compatibility with older Linux kernels.

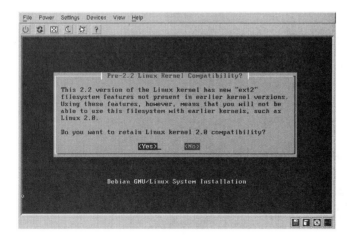

Figure A.3.12 Kernel compatibility.

Step 13: Bad Block Check

■ Select No to scan this partition for bad blocks.

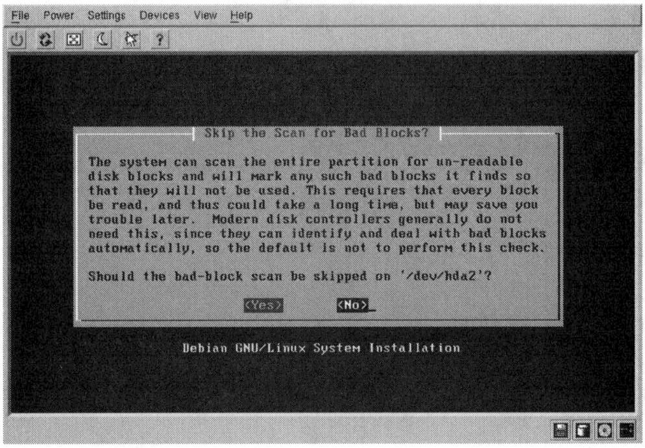

Figure A.3.13 Second bad block check.

Step 14: Partition Confirmation

■ Select Yes to confirm the creation of this Linux native **partition**.

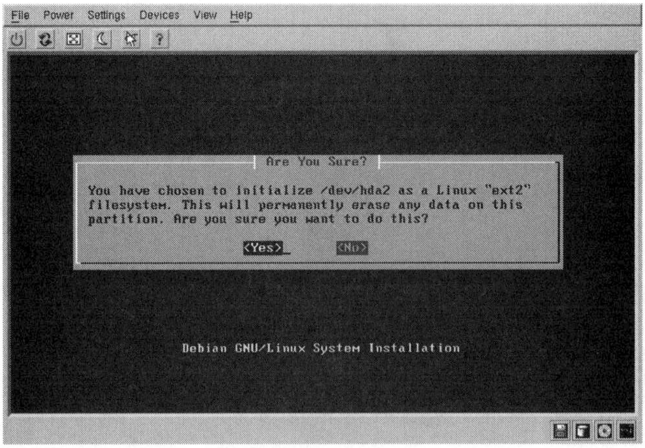

Figure A.3.14 Linux native partition confirmation.

Step 15: Root File System

- Select Yes to mount the primary Linux native partition as the root file system.

Figure A.3.15 Root file system.

Step 16: Begin Installation

- Select Next: Install Operating System Kernel and Modules.

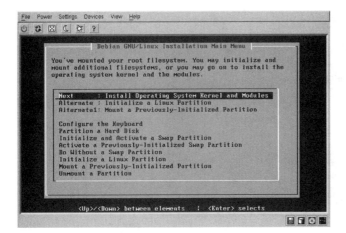

Figure A.3.16 Begin Debian installation.

Step 17: Installation Media

- Select cdrom: CD-ROM drive.

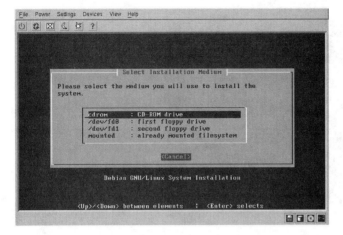

Figure A.3.17 Installation media.

Step 18: Continue

- Select Continue.

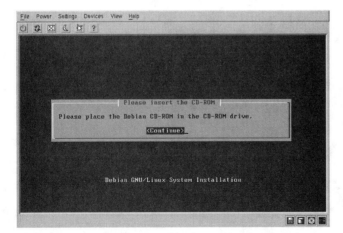

Figure A.3.18 Continue installation of media.

Step 19: Path Selection

- Select the default Debian archive path, within the CD-ROM.

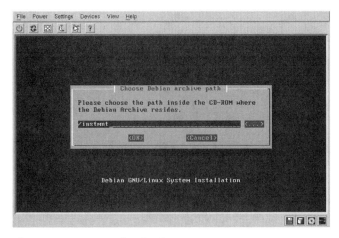

Figure A.3.19a   Path selection.

- Select default: The default stable Archive as the file directory.

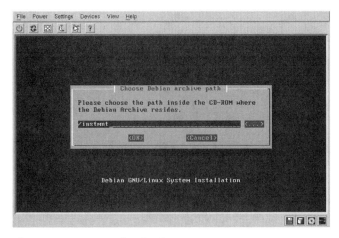

Figure A.3.19b   Set file directory.

Step 20: Driver Configuration

■ Select Next: Configure Device Driver Modules.

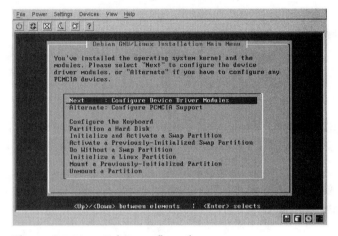

Figure A.3.20a Driver configuration.

■ At this point, precise knowledge of your components will be necessary to choose the correct drivers.

■ Select block Disks and disk-like devices.

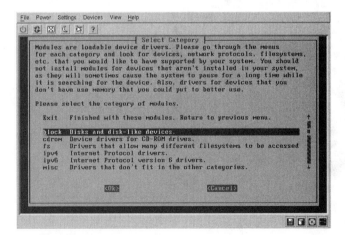

Figure A.3.20b Block disks.

- From this menu, make the correct selection(s) for your disk devices.

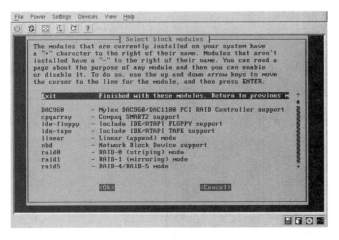

Figure A.3.20c   Disk devices.

Step 21: Base System Installation

- Return to the Installation Main Menu.
- Select Install the Base System, since no network exists to be configured.

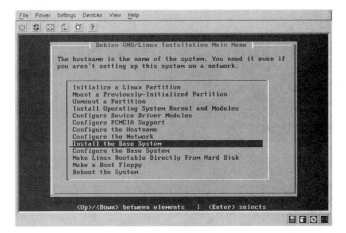

Figure A.3.21   Base system installation.

Step 22: Installation Media

- Select cdrom: CD-ROM drive.

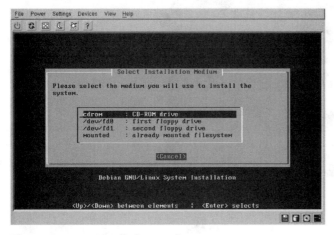

Figure A.3.22 Installation media.

Step 23: Continue

- Insert the Debian CD-ROM.
- Select Continue.

Figure A.3.23 Continue installation media.

Step 24: Path Selection

■ Select the default Debian archive path.

Figure A.3.24a　Default path selection.

■ Again, choose the default path.

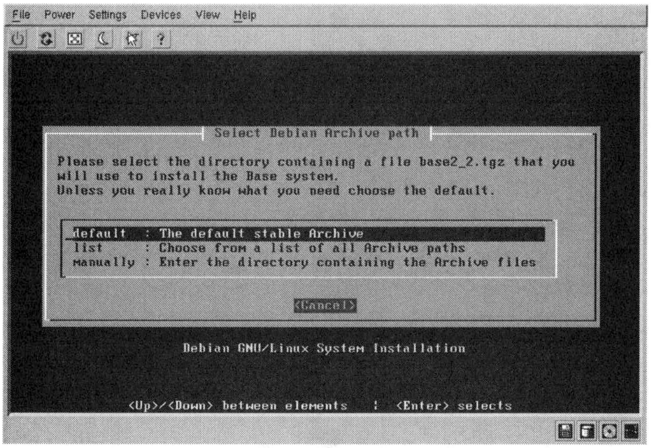

Figure A.3.24b　Second default path selection.

Step 25: Host Name Configuration

■ Select Next: Configure the hostname.

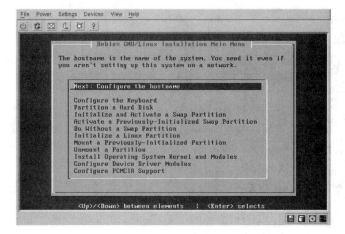

Figure A.3.25a   Host name configuration.

■ Since no network exists, the default host name debian **was kept.**

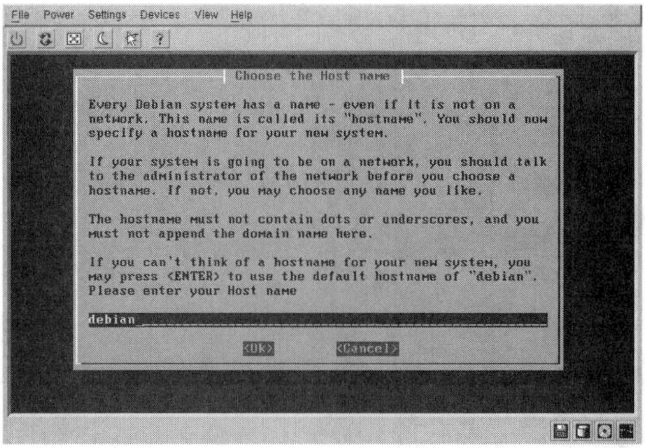

Figure A.3.25b   Default host name.

Step 26: Base System

■ Select Next: Configure the Base System.

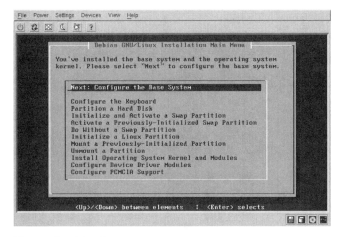

Figure A.3.26   Base system.

Step 27: Time Zone Selection

■ Select the appropriate Time Zone.

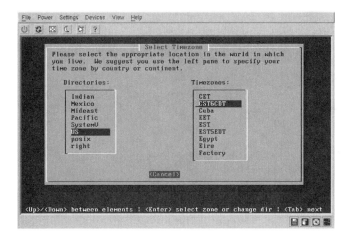

Figure A.3.27   Time zone selection.

Step 28: Time Zone Configuration

■ Select Yes for the default GMT setting.

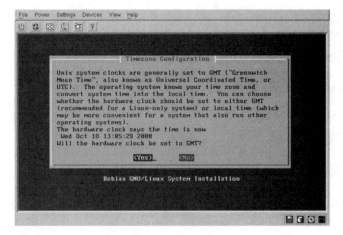

Figure A.3.28   Time zone configuration.

Step 29: Boot Configuration

■ Select Next: Make Linux Bootable Directly From **Hard Disk**.

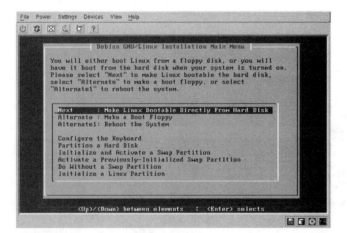

Figure A.3.29   Boot configuration.

Step 30: Location of LILO

- Select /dev/had: Install Lilo in the MBR (master boot record).
- LILO (Linux Loader), usually located in the MBR, is capable of booting more than one OS.
- LILO will boot Linux on /dev/hda2.

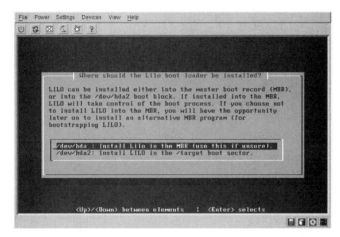

Figure A.3.30   Location of LILO.

Step 31: Boot Disk Creation

- Select Next: Make a Boot Floppy.

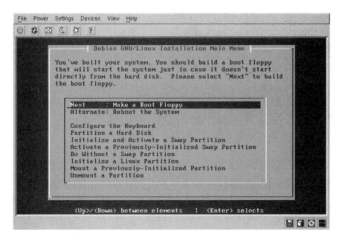

Figure A.3.31a   Boot disk creation.

■ Insert a blank floppy disk, and select Continue.

Figure A.3.31b   Continue boot disk creation.

Step 32: Reboot the System

■ Select Alternate: Reboot the System.

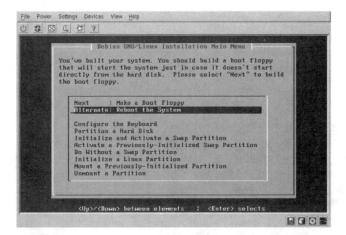

Figure A.3.32a   Reboot the system.

■ Remove the boot disk that was just created, and select Yes to boot directly from the hard drive.

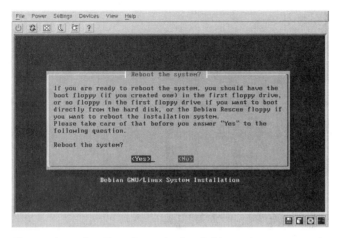

Figure A.3.32b Boot from the hard drive.

Step 33: Md5 Passwords

■ Select No unless Md5 passwords are preferred.

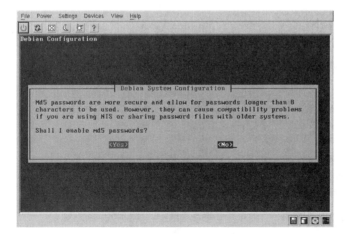

Figure A.3.33 Md5 passwords.

Step 34: Shadow Passwords

- The selection of shadow passwords depends on your **preference**.
- Select Yes if NIS will not be used.

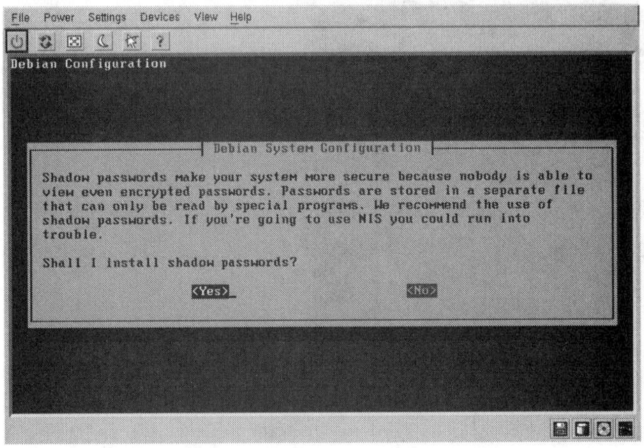

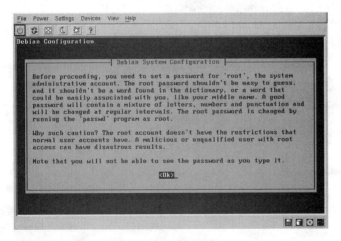

Figure A.3.34 Shadow passwords.

Step 35: Root Password

- Select Ok to proceed with the creation of a root password.
- The root password gives access to the file system on the Linux partition, restricted to administrator usage.

Figure A.3.35a Root password creation.

- Enter a password for root.
- Re-enter the same password for verification.

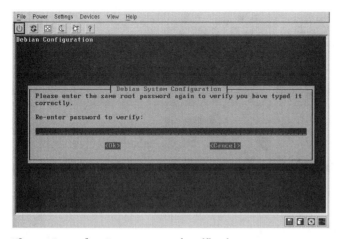

Figure A.3.35b Root password verification.

Step 36: User Account Creation

- Select Yes to create a normal user account.
- Accounts can be created after installation via the useradd command.

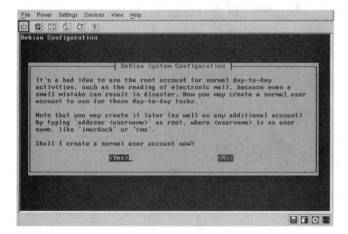

Figure A.3.36a User account creation.

- Enter, in lowercase letters, the username for the account.

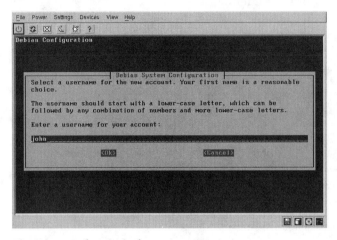

Figure A.3.36b   Enter the username.

- Enter a password for the account user.
- Re-enter the password when prompted to do so.

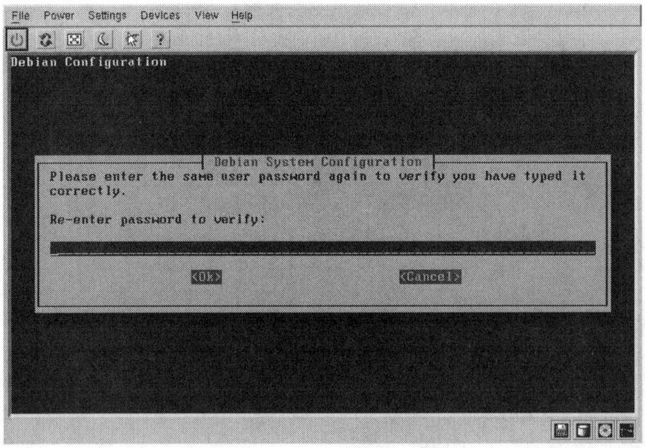

Figure A.3.36c   User password verification.

Step 37: Continue

- Select Yes if PCMCIA packages were installed.

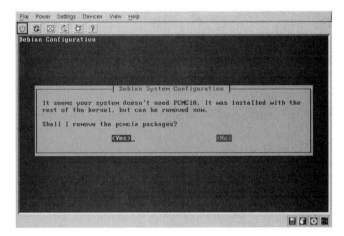

Figure A.3.37   PCMCIA packages.

Step 38: Package Download

- No was selected.
- At this point, an ISP has not been selected.
- Package download can be done after installation.

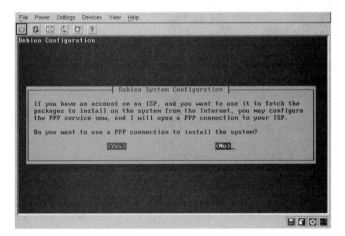

Figure A.3.38   Package download.

Step 39: Continue

■ No was selected at this point, since only one CD-ROM was used in this installation.

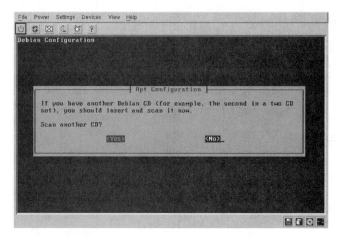

Figure A.3.39   Continue package download.

Step 40: Source Selection

■ Packages were installed via CD-ROM, so No was selected.

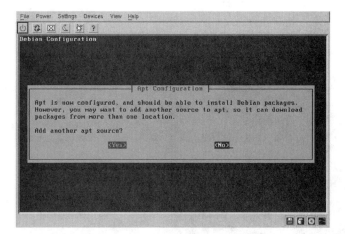

Figure A.3.40   Source selection.

Step 41: Additional Software

■ The default, `simple`, was selected for additional software installation.

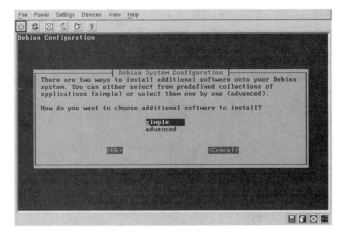

Figure A.3.41 Additional software.

Step 42: Package Installation

■ Press TAB to highlight additional packages to install.
■ Press SPACE to select.

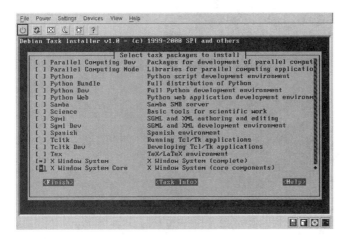

Figure A.3.42 Package installation.

Step 43: Video Card Detection

- Select Yes for video card detection and recommendation.

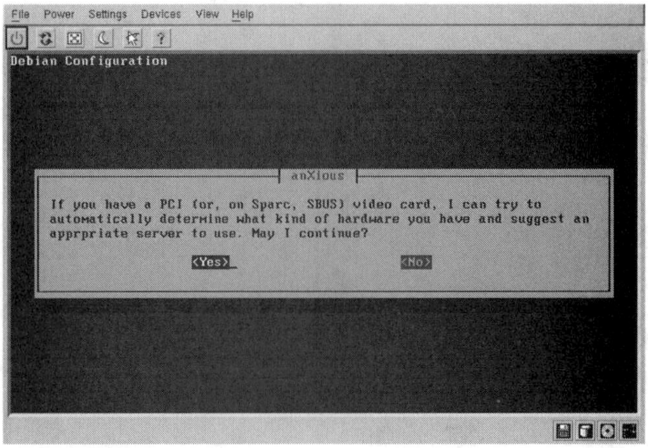

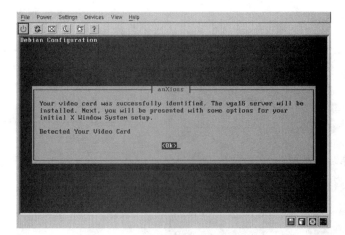

Figure A.3.43a Video card detection.

- This is the identification of the video card.
- Select Ok to continue.

Figure A.3.43b Video card identification.

Step 44: Font Selection

- Select xfonts-100dpi with SPACE .

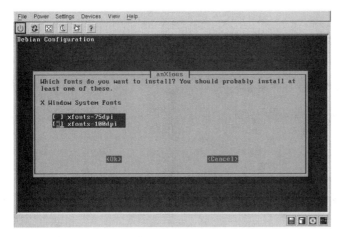

Figure A.3.44   Font selection.

Step 45: Select Terminal Emulator

- Use SPACE to select xterm.

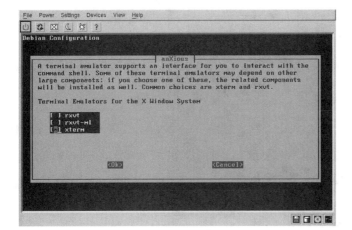

Figure A.3.45   Terminal emulator.

Step 46: Window Manager

■ Press SPACE to select twm.

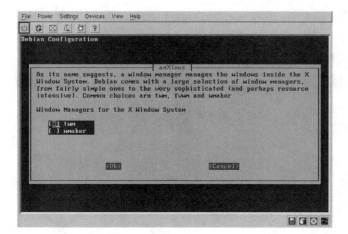

Figure A.3.46 Window manager.

Step 47: xdm Selection

■ Select Yes to install xdm X (display manager), which will provide a graphical login box.

Figure A.3.47 xdm selection.

Step 48: Mouse Selection

■ Press SPACE to select the correct make and model for **your mouse**.

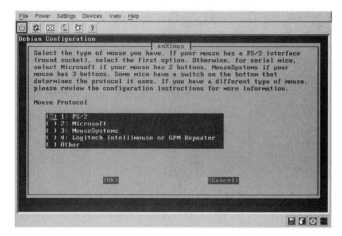

Figure A.3.48a Mouse selection.

■ Since our mouse is already a three-button mouse, No **was selected**.

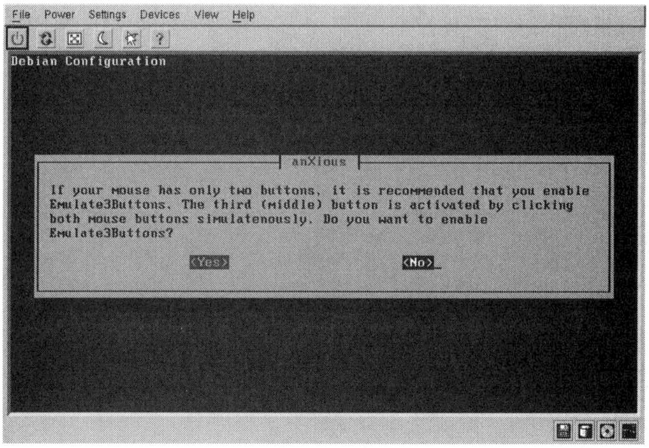

Figure A.3.48b Continue mouse selection.

■ The default /dev/mouse device was chosen.

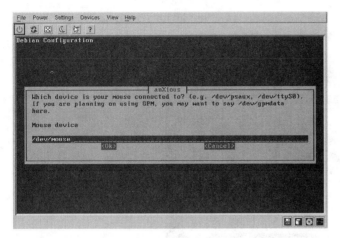

Figure A.3.48c Default mouse device.

Step 49: Keyboard Selection

■ Select US/Standard.

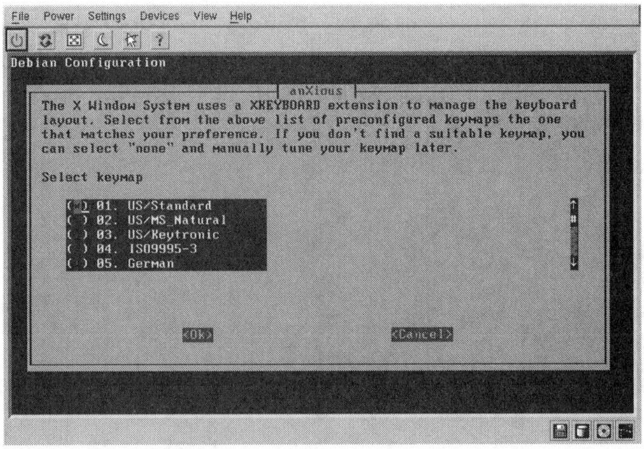

Figure A.3.49 Keyboard selection.

Step 50: Monitor Configuration

■ Select or enter the range corresponding to the capability of your monitor.

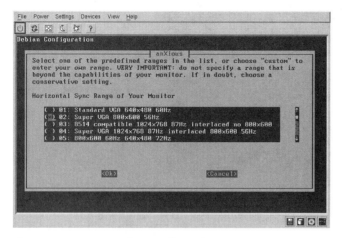

Figure A.3.50a   Monitor configuration.

■ Select the vertical sync range for your monitor.

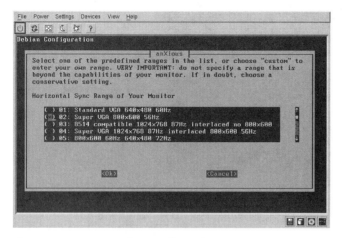

Figure A.3.50b   Monitor vertical sync range.

- Enter the monitor name here.

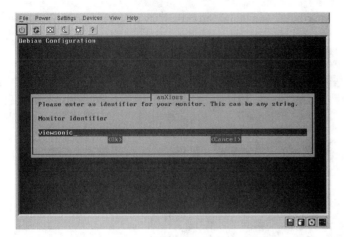

Figure A.3.50c Monitor name.

Step 51: Video Memory

- Select the amount of video memory available.

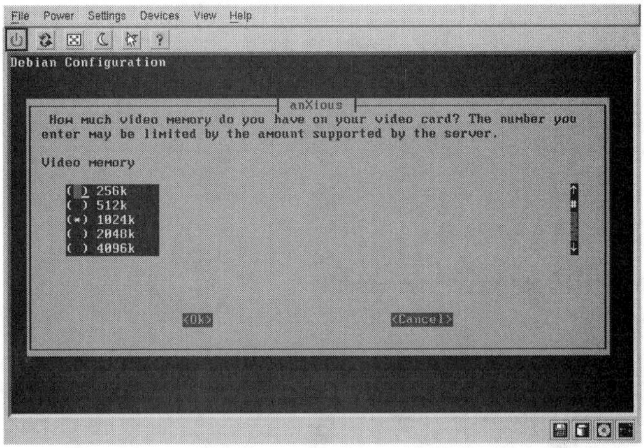

Figure A.3.51 Video memory.

Step 52: Video Memory Selection

■ Here, the name of the video card was entered.

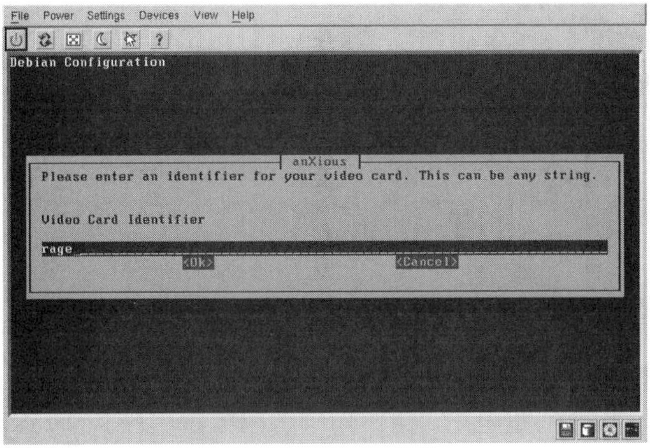

Figure A.3.52   Video memory selection.

Step 53: Clockchip Line

■ None was selected, since no card supporting a clockchip was detected.

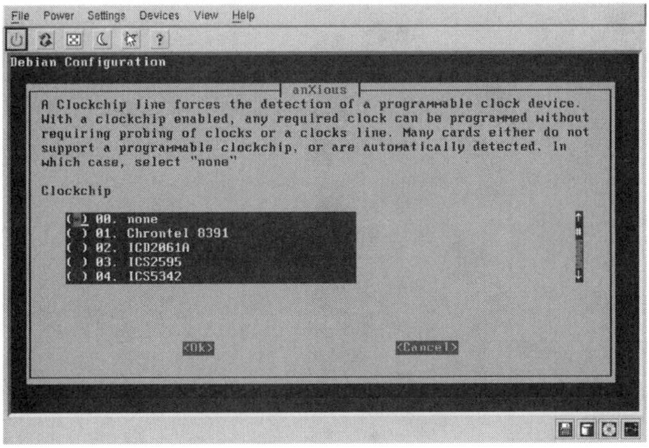

Figure A.3.53a   Clockchip line.

■ Again, no was selected, since a clock line will not be required for the hardware being used.

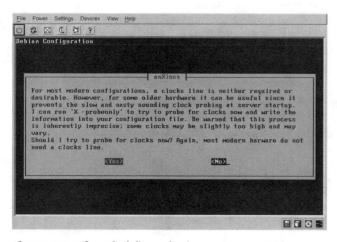

Figure A.3.53b Clock line selection.

Step 54: Color Depth Selection

■ Here, the default 8bpp (256 colors) was selected. This will accommodate most monitors.

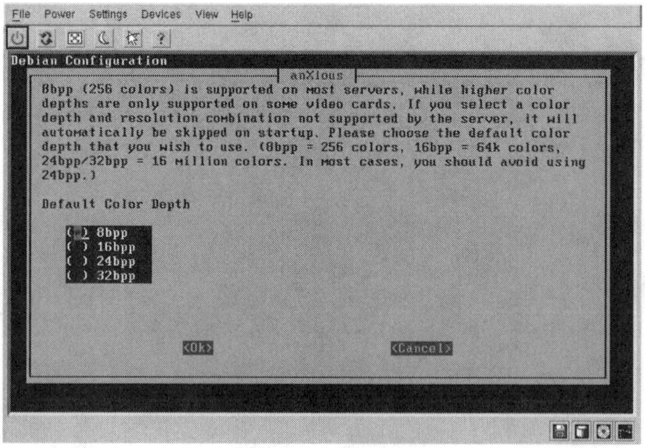

Figure A.3.54 Color depth.

Step 55: Screen Resolution

- Select the maximum screen resolution for your monitor.
- Selecting a lower screen resolution will enable them for possible use.

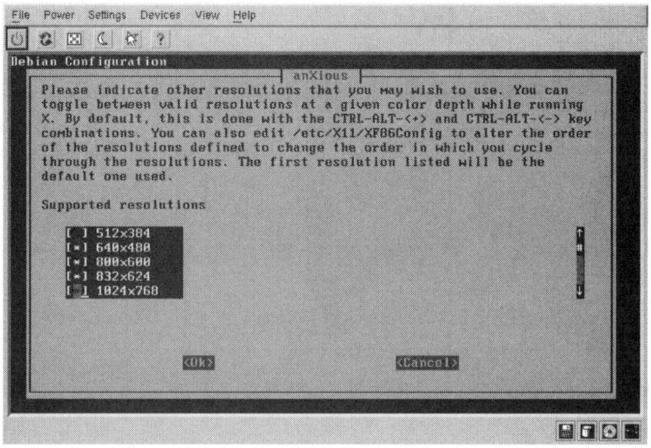

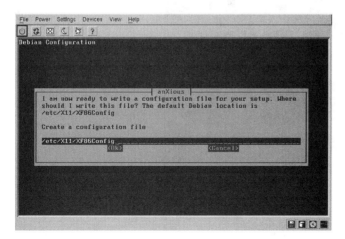

Figure A.3.55   Screen resolution.

Step 56: XF86Config File

- The default /etc/X11/XFConfig location was kept for the configuration file being written.

Figure A.3.56a   XF86Config file.

■ This message confirms the configuration file that has been written to the selected location.

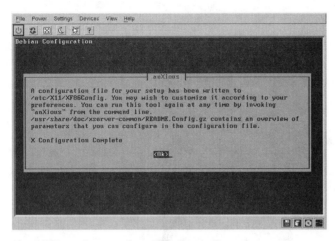

Figure A.3.56b   Configuration file confirmation.

Step 57: Continue

■ Type y to continue with the installation.

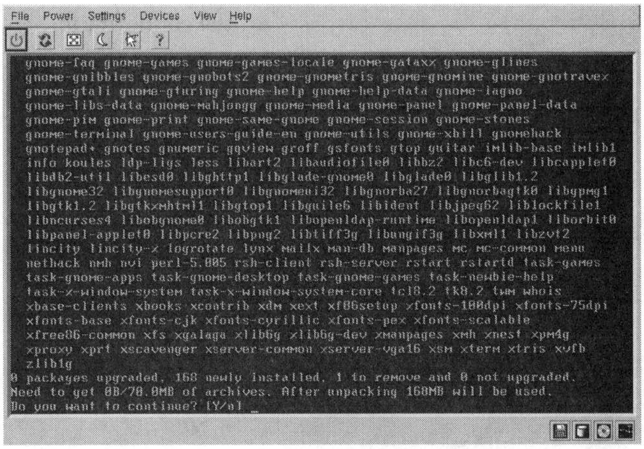

Figure A.3.57   Continue installation.

Step 58: Continue

■ Ensure that the proper CD-ROM is in the CD-ROM drive, and press ENTER.

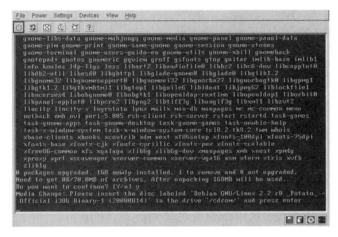

Figure A.3.58   Check the CD-ROM.

Step 59: Lynx Default URL

■ The default is `file:/usr/doc/lynx/lynx_help_main.html`.
■ Select `Ok`.

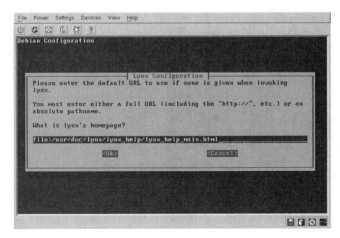

Figure A.3.59   Lynx default URL.

Step 60: Sound Hardware

- Select Yes if there is sound hardware installed on your machine.

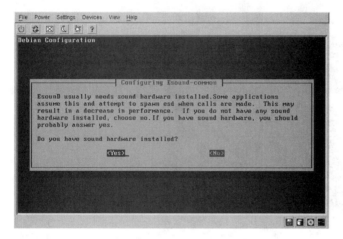

Figure A.3.60   Sound hardware.

Step 61: Mail Configuration

- At this stage, the mail configuration will begin.
- Press ENTER to continue.

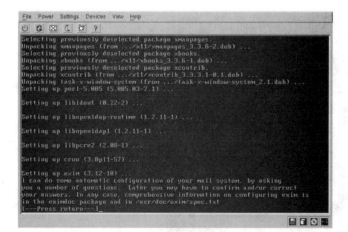

Figure A.3.61a   Mail configuration.

■ Mail configuration is done automatically and can be done later, when an ISP is available.

Figure A.3.61b   Automatic mail configuration.

Step 62: User Account Creation

■ At this point, entering a username for the account in lowercase can create an account.

■ This user account will be the primary account used by the administrator when he or she is not logged on as root.

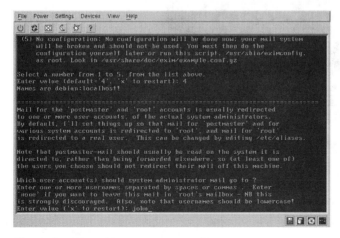

Figure A.3.62a   User account creation.

- Press ENTER or type y to continue.
- Note that root mail will be sent to this primary account.

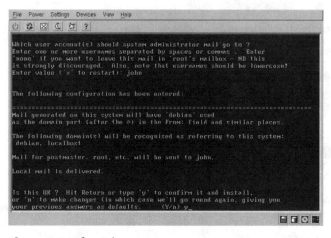

Figure A.3.62b　Primary user account.

Step 63: X Server Selection

- VGA16X is set as the default X server.

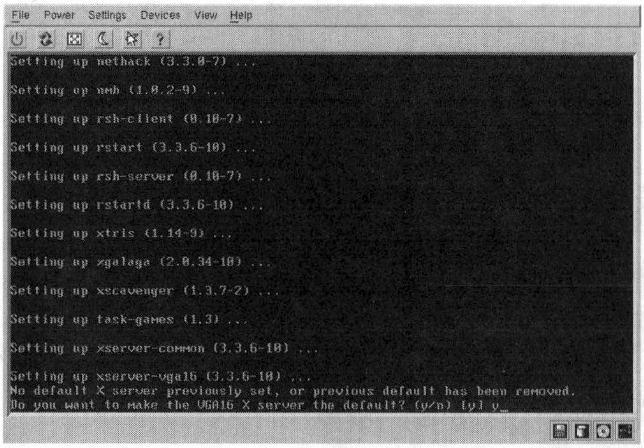

Figure A.3.63　X server selection.

Step 64: Continue

■ Type y to delete the downloaded .deb file.

Figure A.3.64   Delete the .deb file.

Step 65: Login

■ To log in, select Ok.

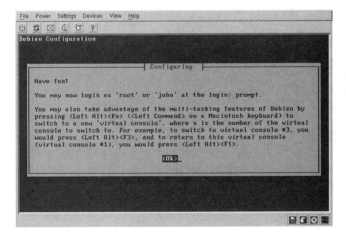

Figure A.3.65a   Log in.

- To log in, enter the username and password.
- This takes you through the login process and brings you to the user prompt.

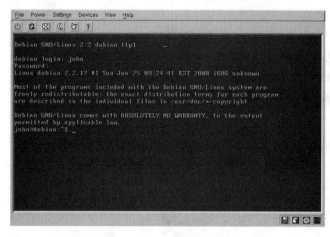

Figure A.3.65b   Username and password.

Step 66: Start X Window

- To start the X Window system, type `startx`.

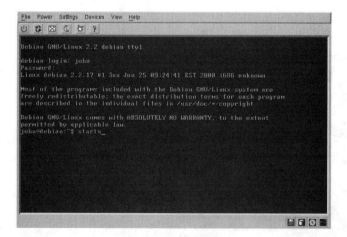

Figure A.3.66   Start X Window.

4. Red Hat Linux 6.2

Although some insight is given into options for various installations, in this appendix we presume:

- No hard drive partition (i.e., Linux is the only OS)
- No upgrade from a previous Linux version (initial install)
- No shared hard disk
- A bootable CD-ROM
- No network connection
- Modem (no Ethernet card)

BEFORE INSTALLATION

System requirements: The minimum system specifications, required to successfully run version 6.2 of the Red Hat Linux distribution.

Hardware and network information: A list of the hardware that you will need to install and run Linux, and a list of information regarding your hardware and network (if installing for a network computer).

SYSTEM REQUIREMENTS

- 32-bit x86 processor
- 16 MB RAM
- Bootable CD-ROM drive
- 3.5" floppy disk drive
- Most x86-compatible PC hardware is supported; however, components can be checked for support at www.redhat.com/support.

Step 1: Getting Started

- Insert the installation CD into a bootable CD-ROM drive, and turn on the computer.
- Press ENTER at this screen.

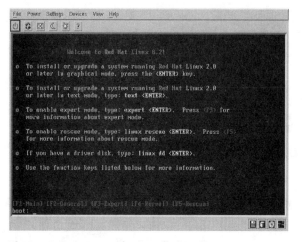

Figure A.4.1 Insert the installation CD.

Red Hat and Red Hat 6.2 are registered trademarks of Red Hat Software, Inc.

Step 2: Language Selection

- Highlight the desired language.

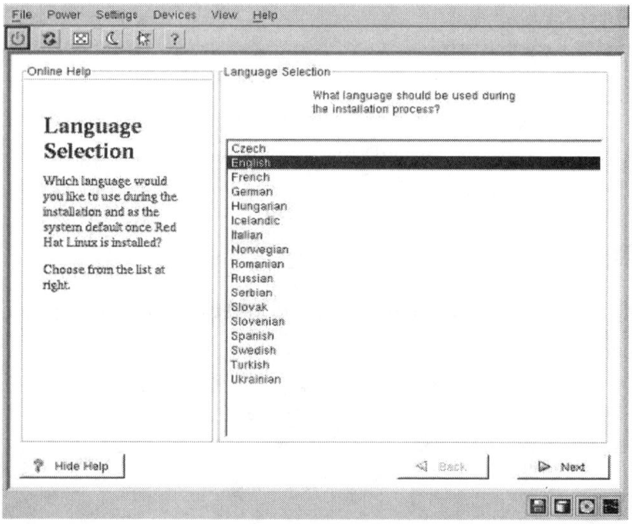

Figure A.4.2 Language selection.

Red Hat and Red Hat 6.2 are registered trademarks of Red Hat Software, Inc.

Step 3: Keyboard Configuration

- Highlight the model of your keyboard.
- Select the keyboard layout.
- Either enable or disable dead keys.

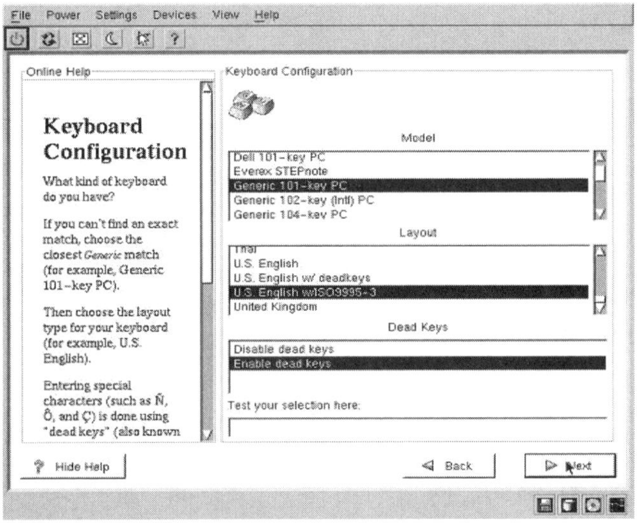

Figure A.4.3 Keyboard configuration.
Red Hat and Red Hat 6.2 are registered trademarks of Red Hat Software, Inc.

Step 4: Mouse Configuration

- Click on the name of the manufacturer of the mouse.
- Select the appropriate mouse.
- Select generic if manufacturer is not listed, or unknown.

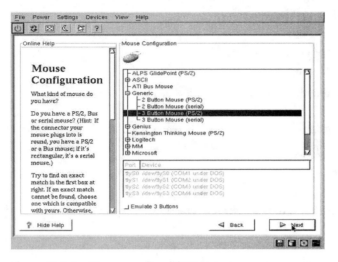

Figure A.4.4 Mouse configuration.

Red Hat and Red Hat 6.2 are registered trademarks of Red Hat Software, Inc.

Step 5: Begin Installation

■ Now the installer will begin. Read the information, and click Next to continue.

Figure A.4.5 Begin Red Hat installation.

Red Hat and Red Hat 6.2 are registered trademarks of Red Hat Software, Inc.

Step 6: Choose Installation

- Read the descriptions provided.
- The two most popular desktops are GNOME and KDE.

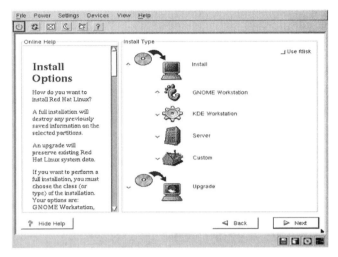

Figure A.4.6 Installation selection.

Red Hat and Red Hat 6.2 are registered trademarks of Red Hat Software, Inc.

Step 7: Automatic Partitioning

- Click remove data.
- Select Next.

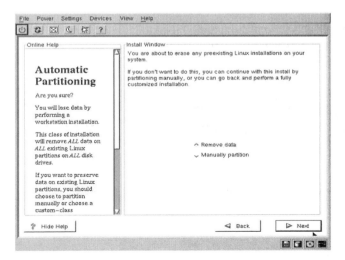

Figure A.4.7 Automatic partitioning.

Red Hat and Red Hat 6.2 are registered trademarks of Red Hat Software, Inc.

Step 8: Network Configuration

- In this example, no networking is configured.
- Select Next.

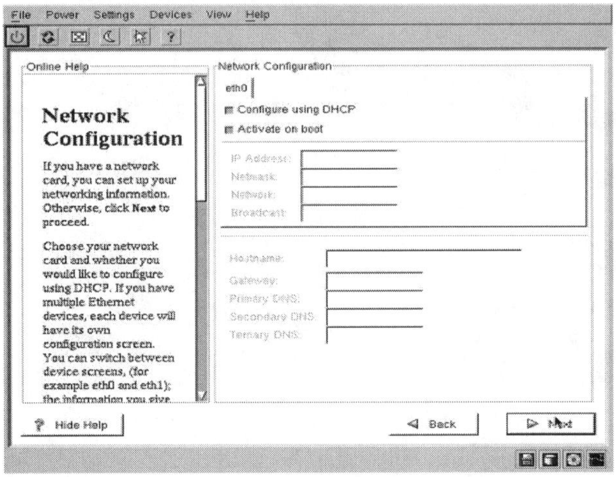

Figure A.4.8 Network configuration.

Red Hat and Red Hat 6.2 are registered trademarks of Red Hat Software, Inc.

Step 9: Time Zone Selection

- Click on the map in the area closest to your geographic location.
- The blue highlight will indicate a time zone and an associated city.
- Select Next if correct.

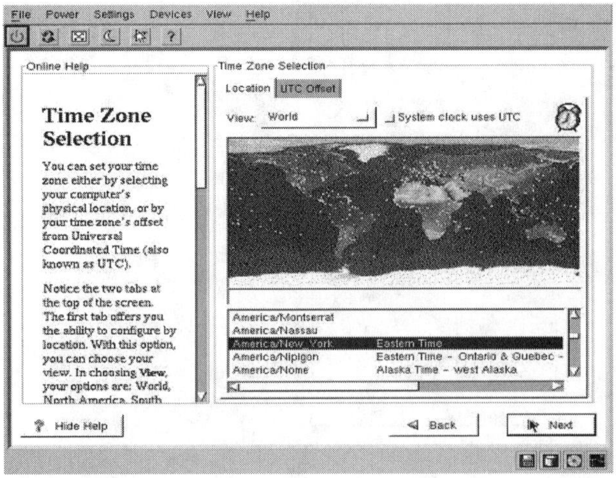

Figure A.4.9 Time zone selection.

Red Hat and Red Hat 6.2 are registered trademarks of Red Hat Software, Inc.

Step 10: Account Configuration

- Enter the root, or the administrator, password.
- Verify the root password.
- Enter user account information for the first user.

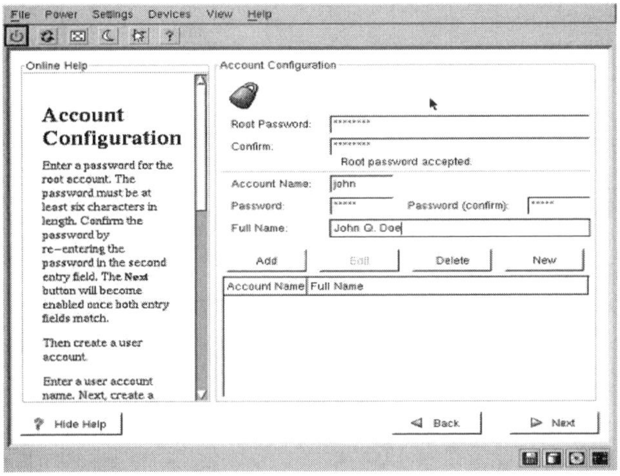

Figure A.4.10a   Account configuration.

Red Hat and Red Hat 6.2 are registered trademarks of Red Hat Software, Inc.

- After entering account information, select Next to create the account.
- This step may be repeated for as many accounts as necessary. Accounts may also be created after installation.

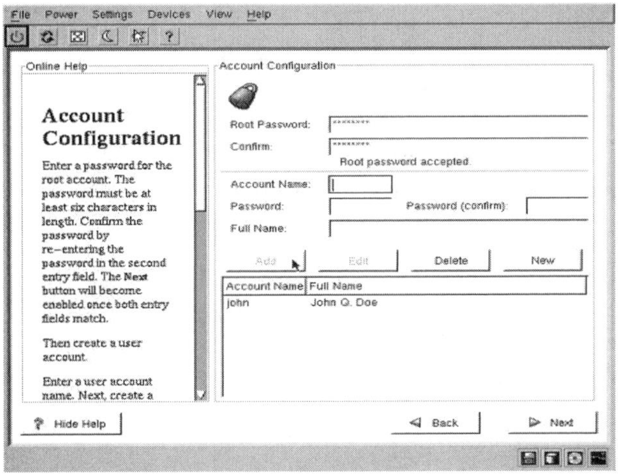

Figure A.4.10b   Create user account.

Red Hat and Red Hat 6.2 are registered trademarks of Red Hat Software, Inc.

Step 11: X Configuration

- As in the mouse configuration, click beside the manufacturer.
- Highlight the appropriate monitor.
- Enter the horizontal and vertical scan rates.

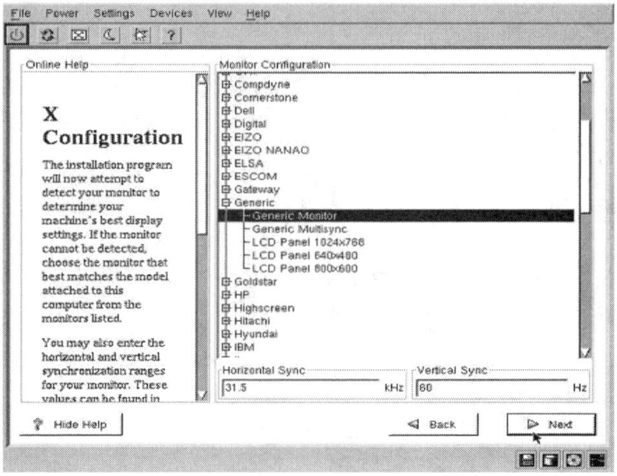

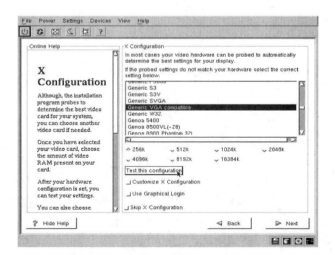

Figure A.4.11a X configuration.
Red Hat and Red Hat 6.2 are registered trademarks of Red Hat Software, Inc.

- Check the detected video hardware selections.
- Change, if incorrect.
- Select Test this configuration.

Figure A.4.11b Video hardware.
Red Hat and Red Hat 6.2 are registered trademarks of Red Hat Software, Inc.

- A blue screen with a gray dialog box should appear.
- Click Yes to continue.

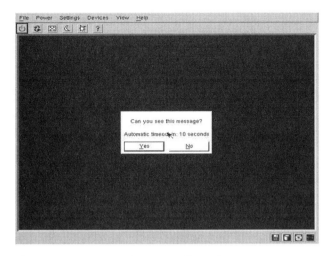

Figure A.4.11c Continue X configuration.

Red Hat and Red Hat 6.2 are registered trademarks of Red Hat Software, Inc.

Step 12: Installation

- Read the information under About to Install.
- Click Next and installation will begin.

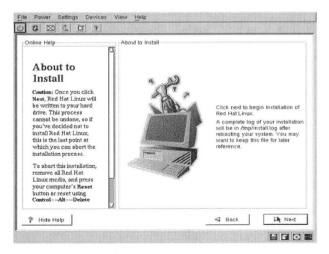

Figure A.4.12 Begin installation.

Red Hat and Red Hat 6.2 are registered trademarks of Red Hat Software, Inc.

Step 13: Boot Disk Creation

- At this point, a boot disk can be created.
- Follow the directions, and select Next.

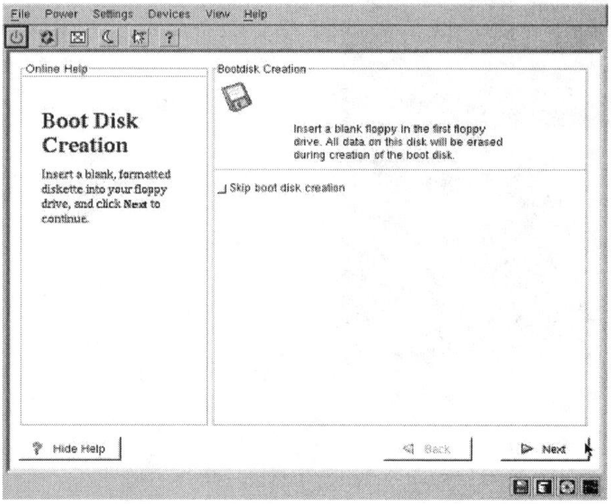

Figure A.4.13 Boot disk creation.

Red Hat and Red Hat 6.2 are registered trademarks of Red Hat Software, Inc.

Step 14: Finish Installation

- This completes the installation of Red Hat Linux 6.2.
- Select Exit.

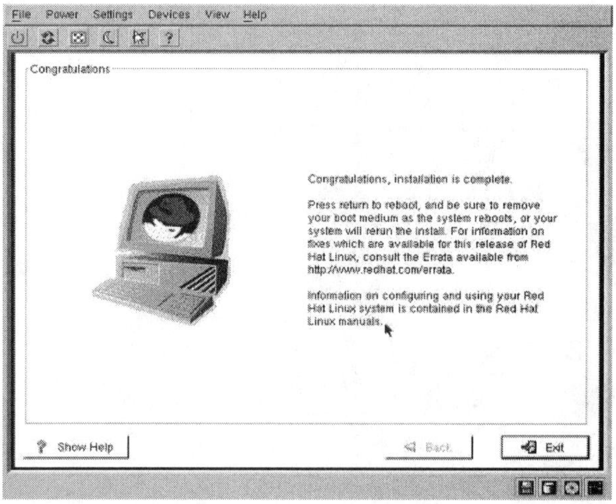

Figure A.4.14 Complete installation.

Red Hat and Red Hat 6.2 are registered trademarks of Red Hat Software, Inc.

Step 15: Logging In

- At the login prompt, enter your username and press ENTER.
- Enter the password and press ENTER.
- At the user prompt, type `startx` to start the X Window system.

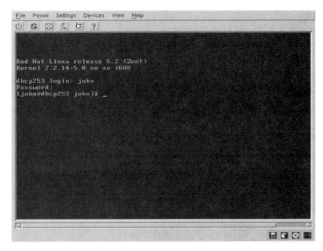

Figure A.4.15   Log in.

Red Hat and Red Hat 6.2 are registered trademarks of Red Hat Software, Inc.

Step 16: Using the Desktop

- This brings you to the GNOME desktop.

Figure A.4.16   GNOME desktop.

Red Hat and Red Hat 6.2 are registered trademarks of Red Hat Software, Inc.

5. Slackware Linux Version 7.1.0

After booting your computer with the Slackware CD-ROM, you have the option of entering your hardware parameters or allowing Slackware to automatically detect them. To simplify the process, automatic detection has been used in this lab.

Step 1: Begin Installation

- Press ENTER to begin the installation.

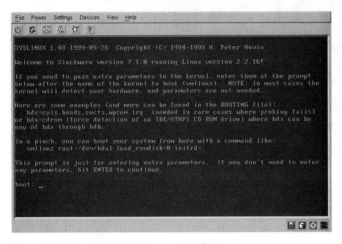

Figure A.5.1 Begin Slackware installation.

Step 2: Log In as Root

- Type root, and press ENTER.
- root refers to the root (primary) directory of the OS, to which only administrators have access.

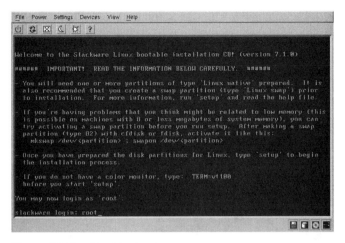

Figure A.5.2   Root login.

Step 3: Partition the Hard Drive with fdisk

- The next few steps cover the process of partitioning a hard drive using the fdisk program.
- Type fdisk/dev/had to format the hard drive, and press ENTER.

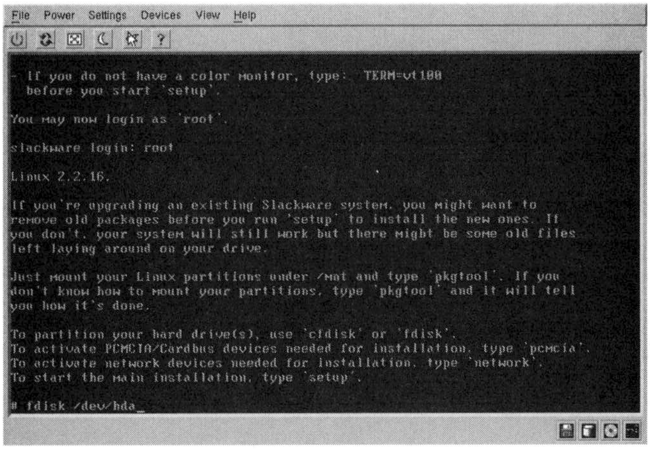

Figure A.5.3a   Hard drive partition.

■ To view the menu of commands, in `fdisk`, type m, and press ENTER.

Figure A.5.3b View menu of commands.

■ The menu of commands is displayed; to partition a new hard drive, press n, and press ENTER.

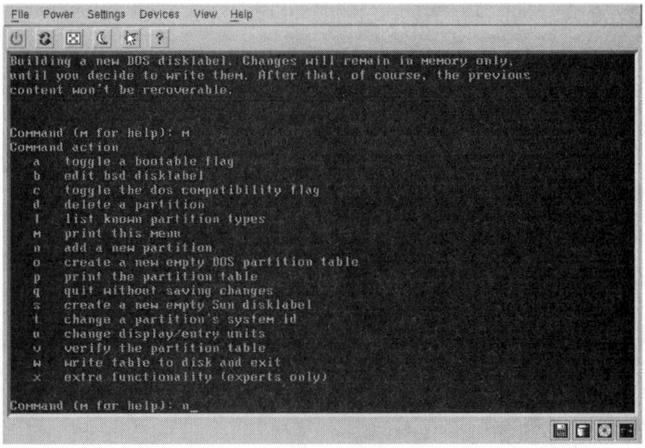

Figure A.5.3c Menu of commands.

■ To make this a primary partition, press p, and press ENTER.

Figure A.5.3d   Create primary partition.

■ This will be the first primary partition; so press the number 1, and then press ENTER.

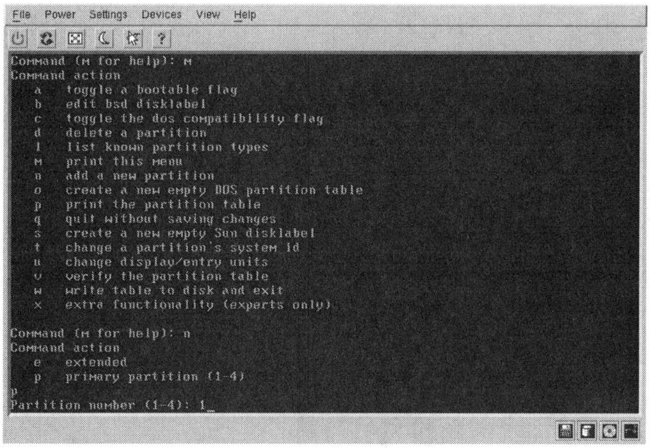

Figure A.5.3e   First primary partition.

- To begin the partition with the first block of the first cylinder, press ENTER, since 1 is the default choice.

Figure A.5.3f Default block.

- The first partition will be the swap partition, which will use this part of the hard drive as virtual RAM.
- For 1 MB, type +1M, and then press ENTER.

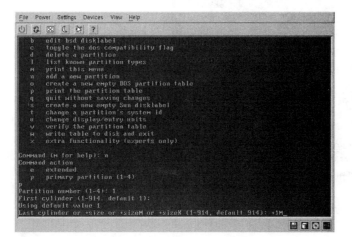

Figure A.5.3g Choose swap partition space.

■ To partition the rest of the hard drive, type n for add a new partition, and press ENTER.

Figure A.5.3h   Partition remaining hard drive.

■ This is the partition on which the OS will be installed.
■ To make this a primary partition, press p, and then press ENTER.

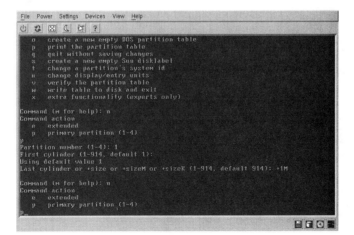

Figure A.5.3i   Primary partition.

- This is the second primary hard drive partition; press the number 2, and then press ENTER.

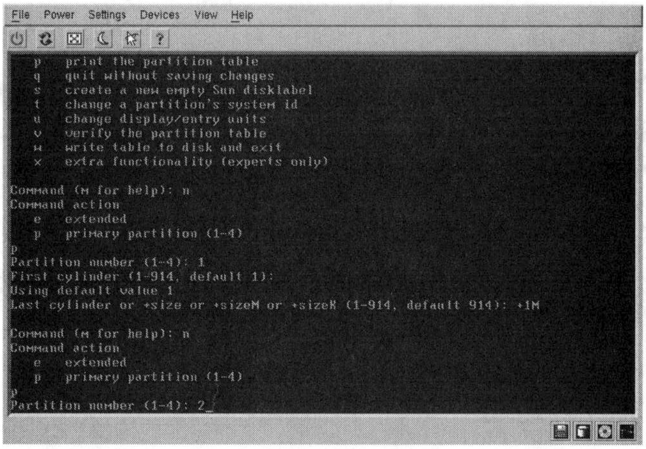

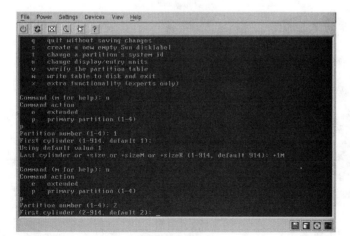

Figure A.5.3j Second primary partition.

- This partition should begin with the next available block following the previous partition.
- This block is the default; press ENTER.

Figure A.5.3k Default partition block.

- This second partition should extend to the last available block of the last cylinder, so that our two partitions will consume the entire hard drive.
- Press ENTER, since the default is the last available block.

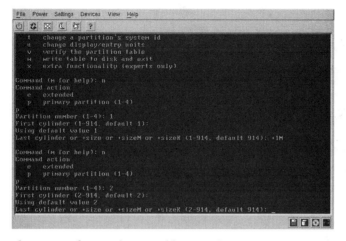

Figure A.5.3l Continue partition creation.

- The letter p, found on the main menu, which is accessible by typing m, will print the current partition table. Type this letter, and press ENTER to check the partitions.

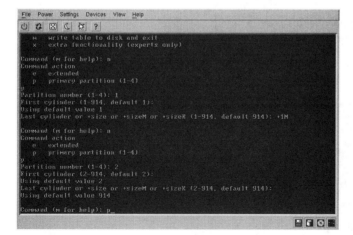

Figure A.5.3m Main menu for partition check.

■ Both partitions were created as Linux native, meaning that they are target partitions for Linux. However, the 1 MB partition should be the swap partition; to change the partition type, press t and then ENTER.

Figure A.5.3n Change partition type.

■ The first partition should be the swap, so press 1, and then press ENTER.

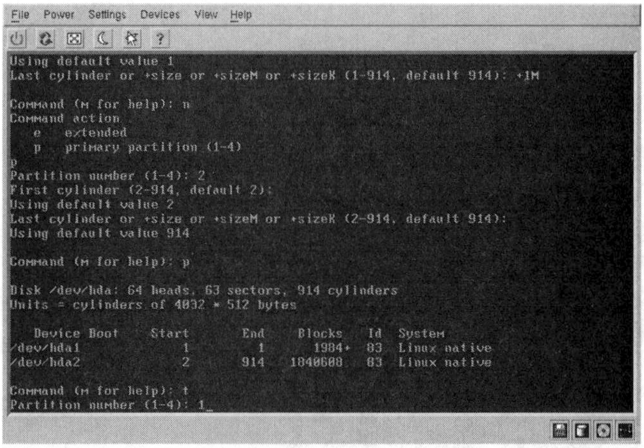

Figure A.5.3o Assign swap partition.

■ We need the code that corresponds to the Linux swap; a list of these codes can be displayed by pressing the letter l and pressing ENTER.

Figure A.5.3p   Display codes.

■ The number 82 in the list of corresponds to Linux swap; enter this number, and press ENTER.

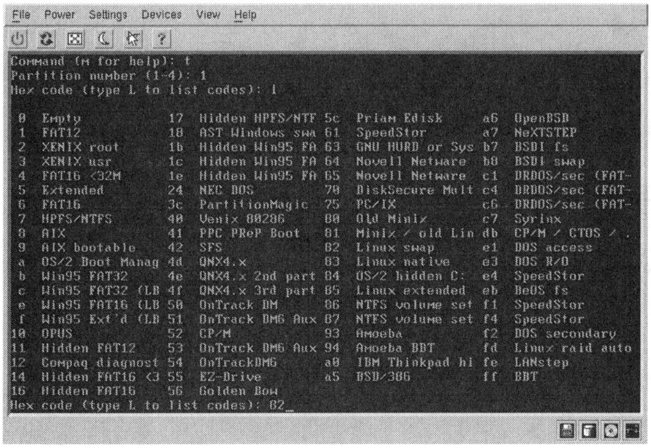

Figure A.5.3q   Linux corresponding number.

■ Press p and ENTER to print the partition table.

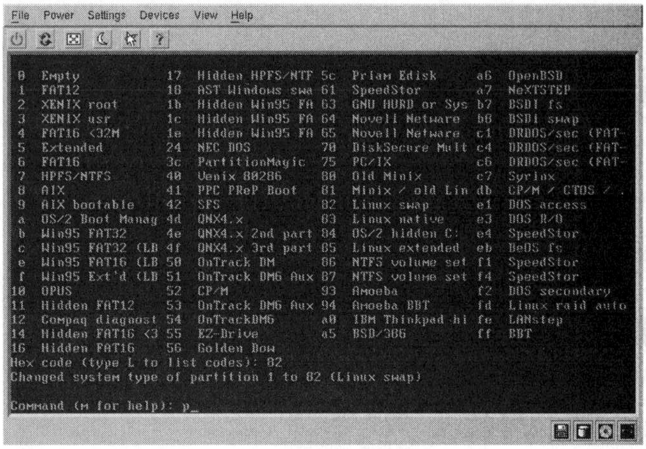

Figure A.5.3r   Print the partition table.

■ The partition table is correct; press w and ENTER to write the table and make the partitions permanent.

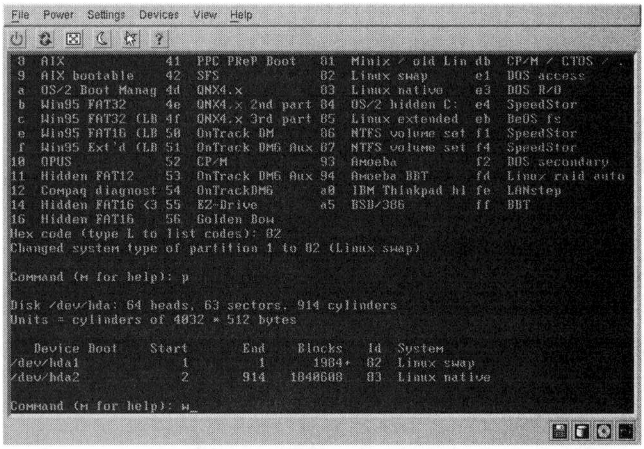

Figure A.5.3s   Make the partitions permanent.

Step 4: Run Setup

- Type setup and press ENTER to run the setup program to configure your system.

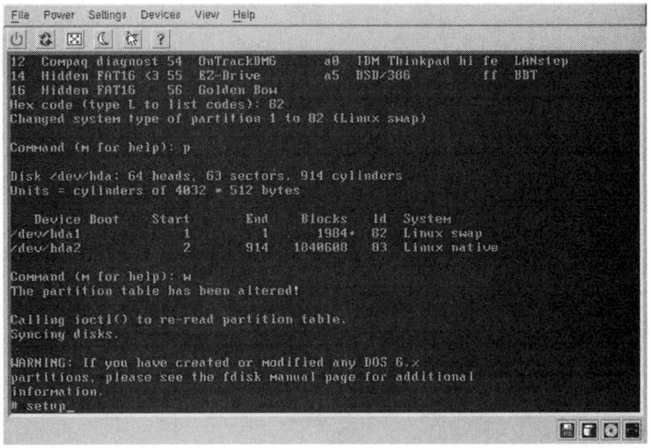

Figure A.5.4   Run setup.

Step 5: Set Up the Swap Partition

- If the keyboard configuration is correct, set up the swap partition.
- Select Addswap and then select Ok.

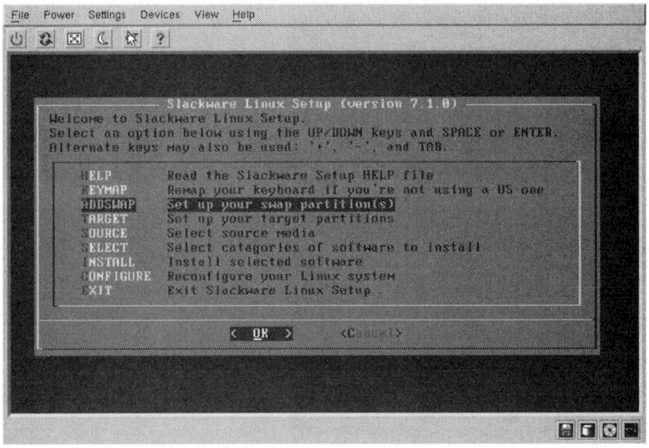

Figure A.5.5   Set up the swap partition.

Step 6: Auto-Detection of Swap Partition

- The program successfully detected the swap, which was created using fdisk, so select Yes and press ENTER.

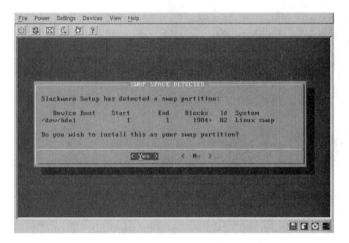

Figure A.5.6   Auto-detection of the swap partition.

Step 7: Confirm Swap Configuration

- Select Exit and press ENTER to confirm the configuration.

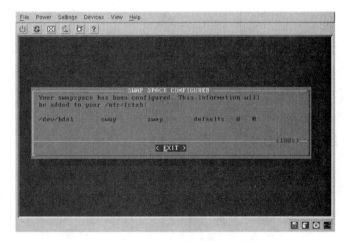

Figure A.5.7   Swap configuration confirmation.

Step 8: Continue Installation

■ Select Yes, and then press ENTER to continue the installation.

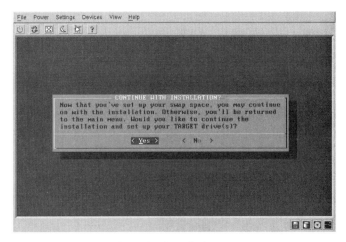

Figure A.5.8   Continue the installation.

Step 9: Auto-Detection of root Linux Partition

■ The root Linux partition, created using fdisk, is highlighted.
■ Select Ok, and then press ENTER.

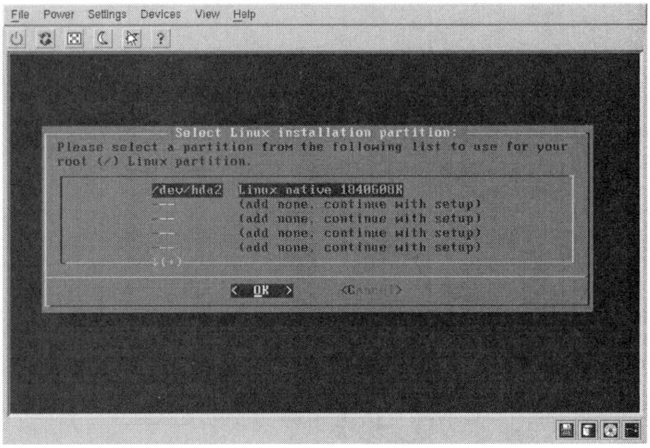

Figure A.5.9   Detect the root partition.

Step 10: Format root Linux

- ■ Check was selected to minimize the existence of bad blocks during the format.
- ■ Select Ok, and press ENTER.

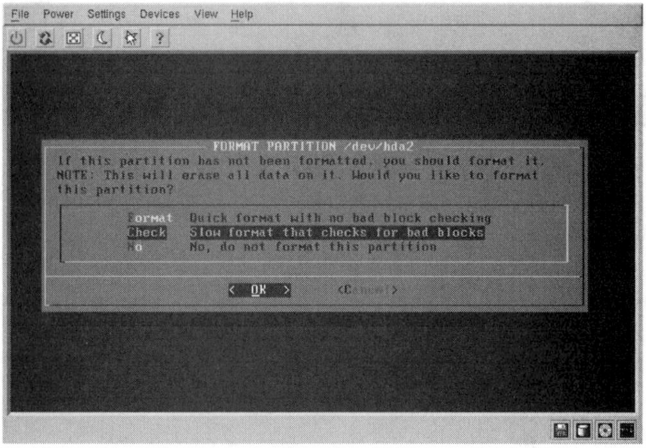

Figure A.5.10   Format root Linux.

Step 11: Select Inode Density

- ■ The default inode, density, is highlighted.
- ■ An inode is a placeholder for files that contain the files' pertinent information.
- ■ Select Ok, and then press ENTER.

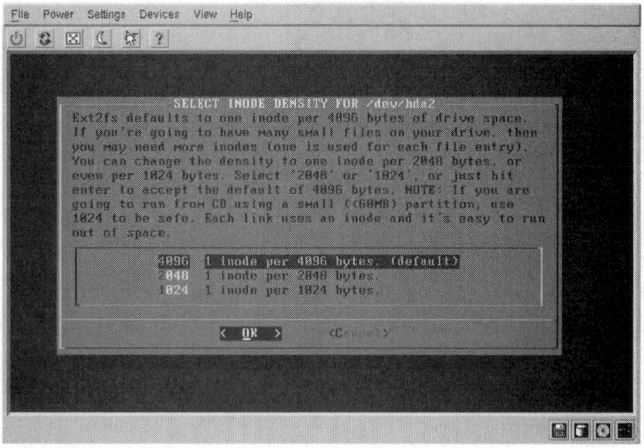

Figure A.5.11   Inode density.

Step 12: Complete Partition Process

- Select Exit, and then press ENTER to confirm the configuration.

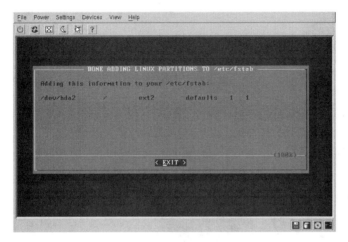

Figure A.5.12   Complete hard drive partitions.

Step 13: Continue Installation

- Select Yes, and then press ENTER to proceed.

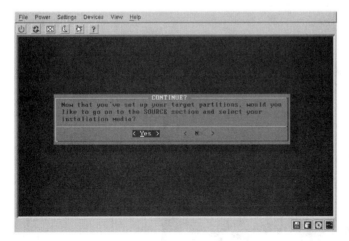

Figure A.5.13   Continue installation.

Step 14: Select Media Source

- Select 1 to install from a CD-ROM.
- Select Ok, and then press ENTER.

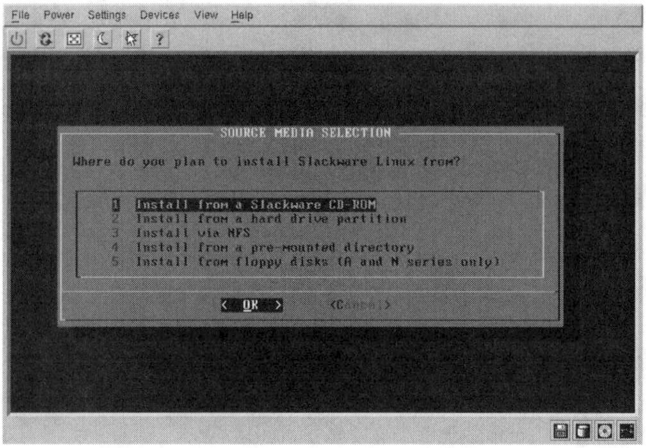

Figure A.5.14 Select media source.

Step 15: Choose Installation Type

- Highlight Slackware to maximize performance.
- Select Ok, and then press ENTER.

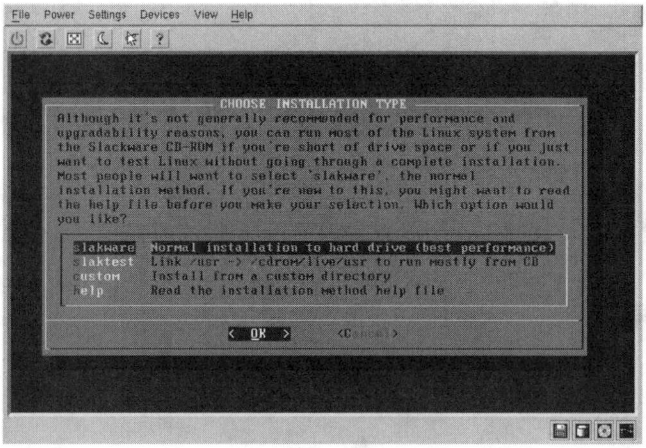

Figure A.5.15 Choose installation type.

Step 16: Continue Installation

- Highlight Yes, and then press ENTER to proceed.

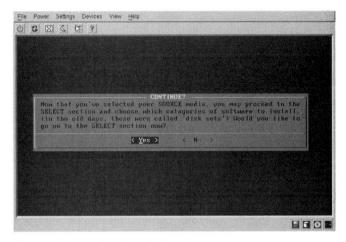

Figure A.5.16   Confirm slackware.

Step 17: Select Package Series

- For a full installation of the preselected software, select Ok, and then press ENTER.

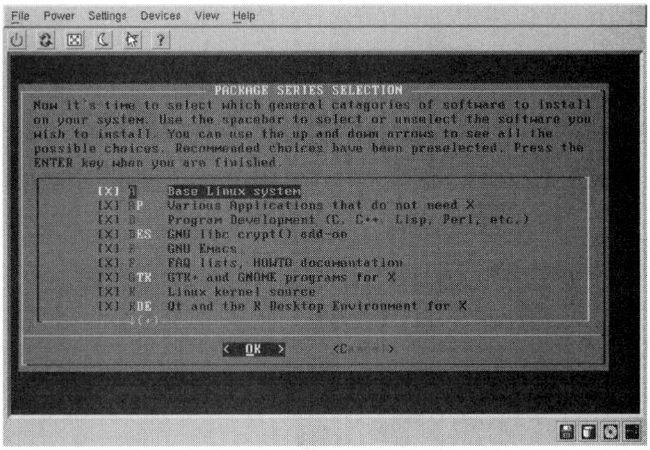

Figure A.5.17   Select package series.

Step 18: Continue Installation

- Highlight Yes, and then press ENTER.

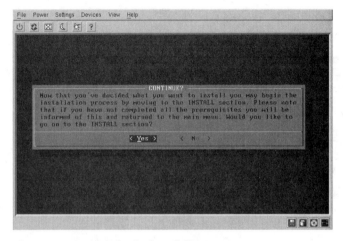

Figure A.5.18 Begin the installation process.

Step 19: Select Prompting Mode

- Select Full for a full installation.
- Select Ok, and then press ENTER.

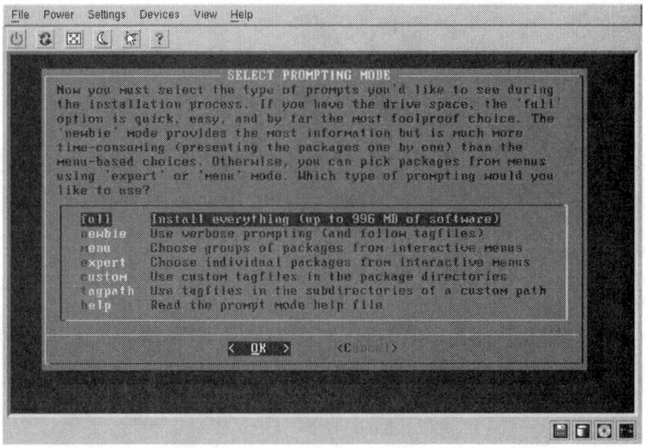

Figure A.5.19 Select prompting mode.

Step 20: Make a Boot Disk

- To make a boot disk, insert a floppy disk into the disk drive.
- Select Format.
- Select Ok, and then press ENTER.

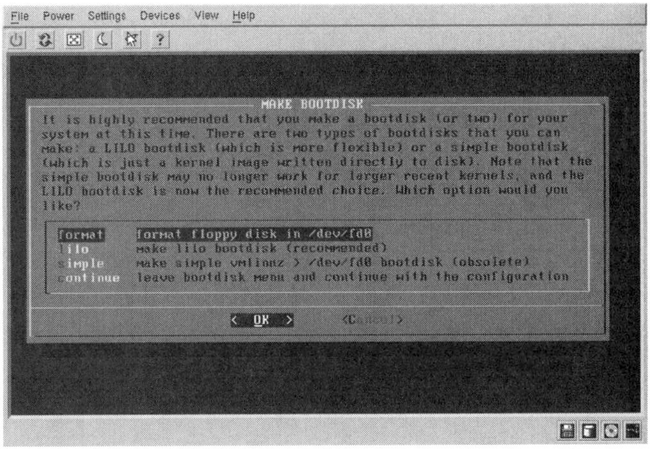

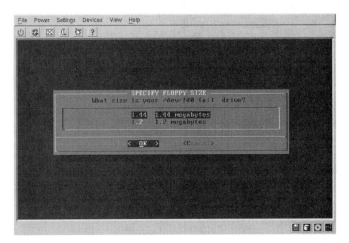

Figure A.5.20a   Make a boot disk.

- Highlight the appropriate disk size.
- Select Ok, and then press ENTER.

Figure A.5.20b   Choose disk size.

- After the disk is formatted, select `Lilo` to make a LILO boot disk.
- LILO is a program that resides in the root directory and allows the booting of multiple OSs.
- Select `Ok`.

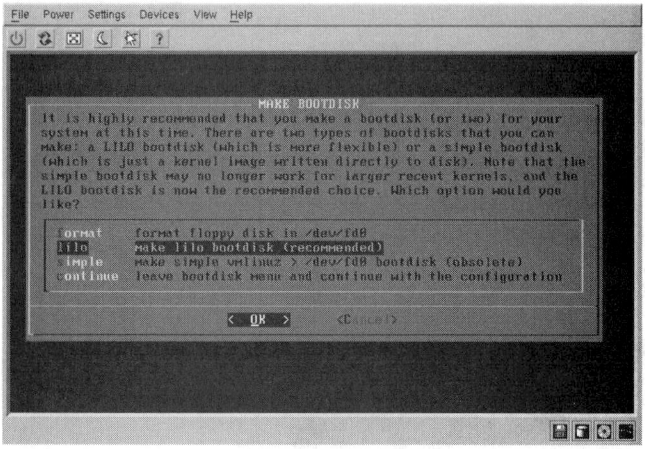

Figure A.5.20c Make LILO boot disk.

- To make this LILO boot disk, select `Yes`, and then press ENTER.

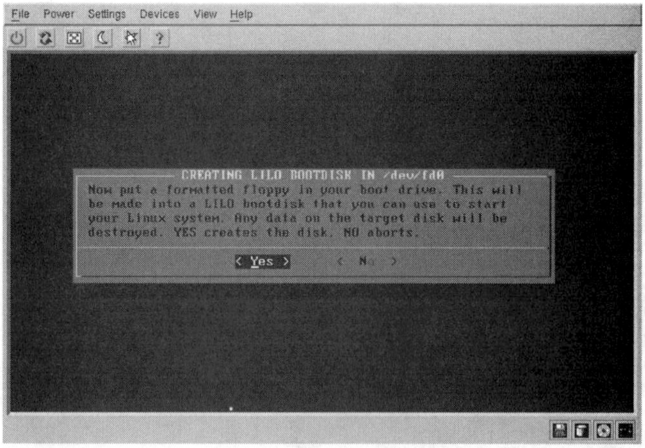

Figure A.5.20d Confirm LILO boot disk.

- Select the appropriate disk size.
- Select Ok, and press ENTER.

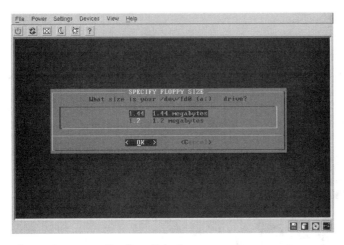

Figure A.5.20e   Confirm disk size.

Step 21: Continue Installation

- After creation of the boot disk, select Continue.
- Select Ok, and press ENTER.

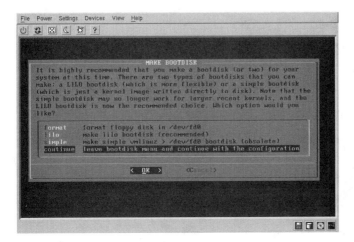

Figure A.5.21   Continue installation.

Step 22: Modem Configuration

- Select a callout device to correspond to your modem.
- Select Ok, and press ENTER.

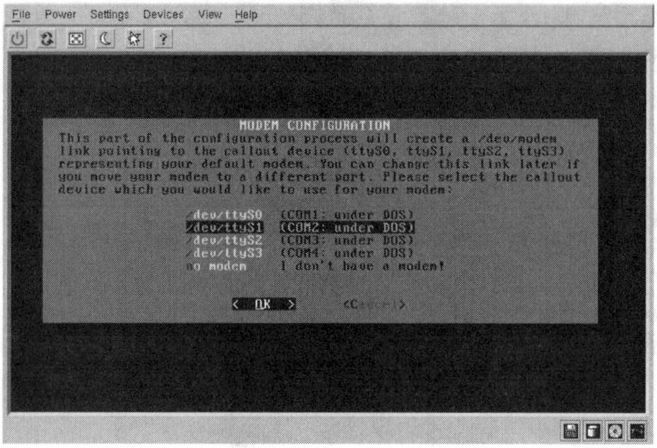

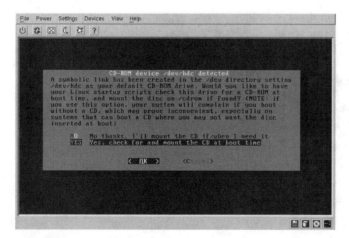

Figure A.5.22 Modem configuration.

Step 23: CD-ROM Detection

- Select Yes for CD-ROM device detection during boot-up.

Figure A.5.23 CD-ROM detection.

Step 24: Screen Font Configuration

- If you want to try various fonts, highlight Yes, and then press ENTER.
- You may change the fonts after installation.

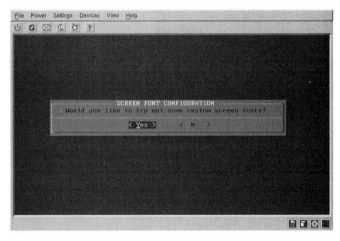

Figure A.5.24a   Screen font configuration.

- To try new fonts, use the Display menu.
- No indication is given for what the fonts look like until one is selected.
- To preview a font, select a font, and then select Ok.

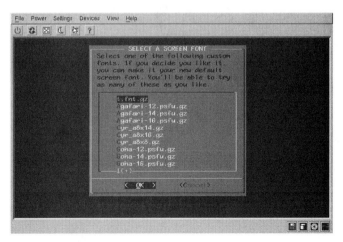

Figure A.5.24b   Display menu.

- If you select a new font, the next menu box will display characters of the new font and prompt you to accept or reject the new font.

- This process may be repeated as many times as you wish.

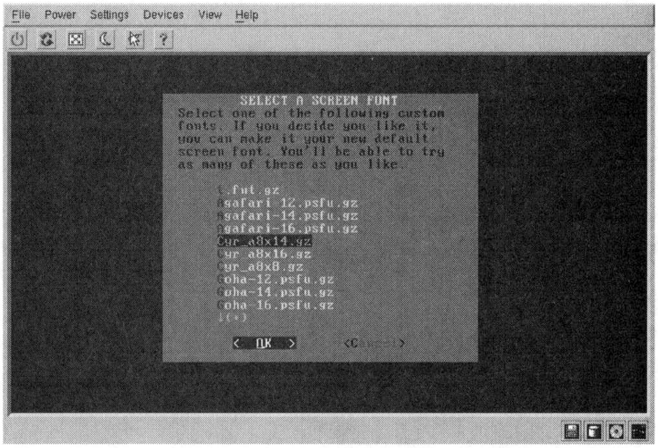

Figure A.5.24c Screen font selection.

- Selecting No at this point will send you back to the Font menu.

- Select Yes, and press ENTER if satisfied; fonts can be changed later, by re-entering the Configuration option of setup. Selecting No at this point will send you back to the Font menu.

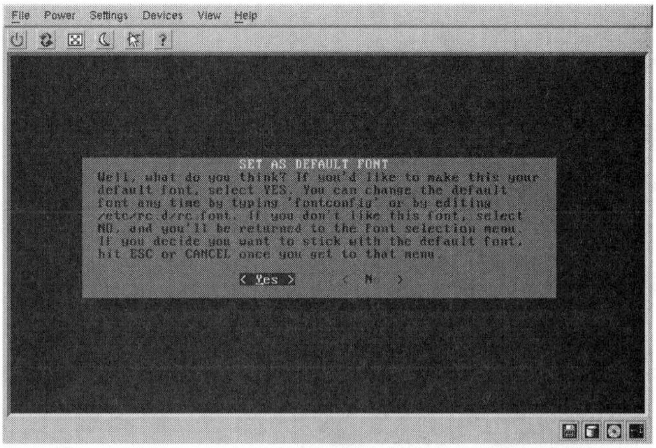

Figure A.5.24d Set default font.

Step 25: LILO Installation

- Select `Simple` for automatic LILO installation.
- Select `Ok`, and then press ENTER.

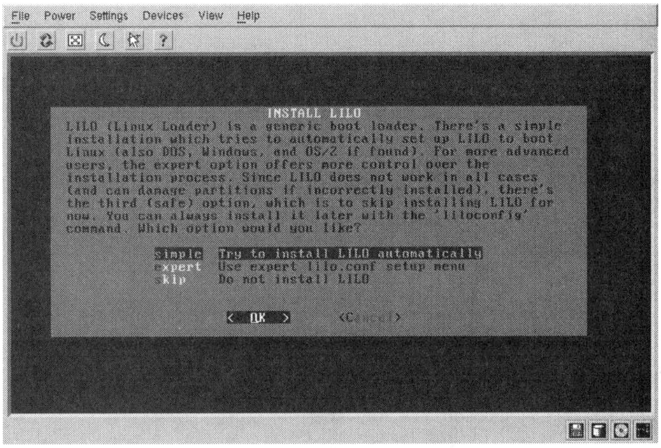

Figure A.5.25   Install LILO.

Step 26: Frame Buffer Console

- Choose `1024x768x64k` for X Window performance.
- Select `Ok`, and then press ENTER.

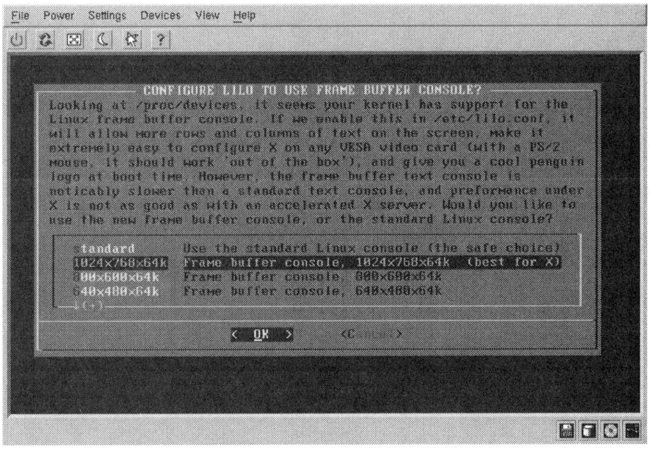

Figure A.5.26   Frame buffer console.

Step 27: Select LILO Destination

- Select MBR to install to master boot record.
- Select Ok, and then press ENTER.

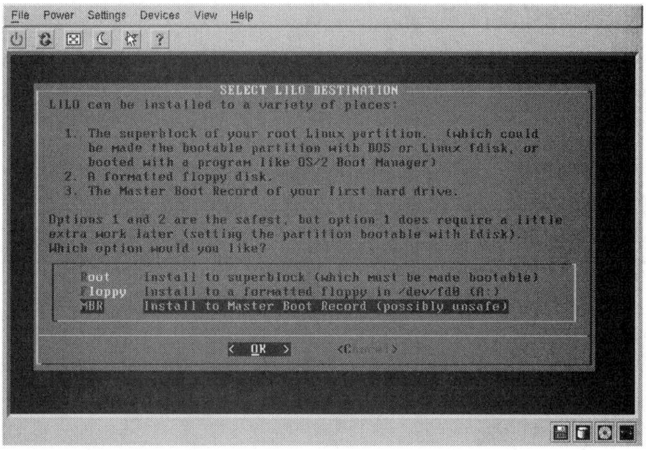

Figure A.5.27 Select LILO destination.

Step 28: Network Configuration

- Since there is no network in this walkthrough, select No, and press ENTER.

Figure A.5.28 Network configuration.

Step 29: Mouse Configuration

- Select the appropriate mouse type.
- Select Ok, and press ENTER.

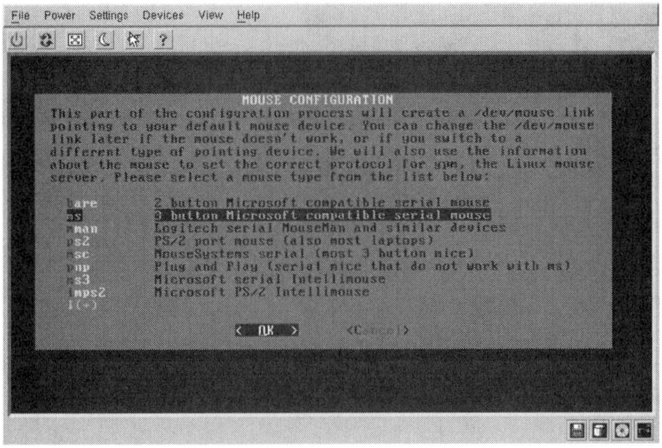

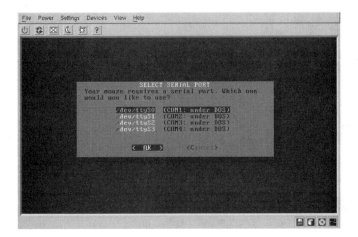

Figure A.5.29   Mouse configuration.

Step 30: Serial Port Selection

- Select the appropriate serial port for your mouse.
- Select Ok, and press ENTER.

Figure A.5.30   Serial port selection.

Step 31: GPM Configuration

- Select Yes to run this program at boot time; press ENTER.

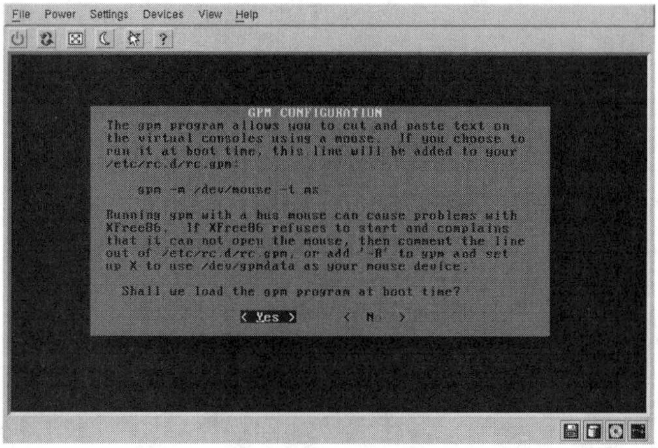

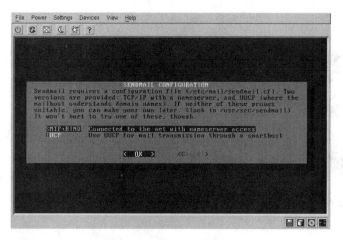

Figure A.5.31   GPM configuration.

Step 32: Sendmail Configuration

- smtp+bind was selected.
- Simple Mail Transfer Protocol (SMTP) is used to transfer e-mail between servers, which can then be retrieved with an e-mail client, using Post Office Protocol (POP).

Figure A.5.32   Sendmail Configuration.

Step 33: Clock Configuration

- Our hardware clock was set to local time, so we selected No, and pressed ENTER.

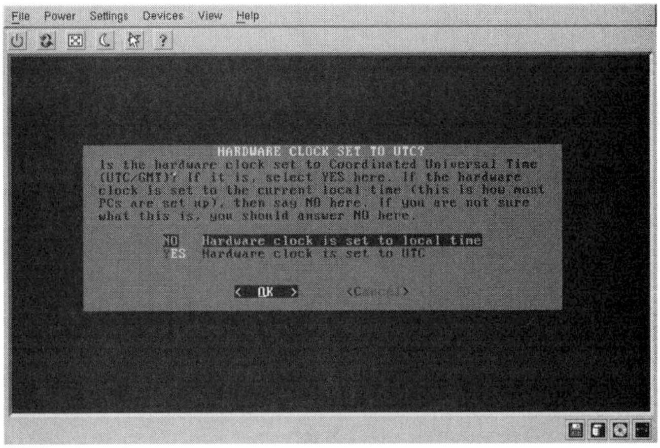

Figure A.5.33a Clock configuration.

- Select your time zone.
- Select Ok, and press ENTER.

Figure A.5.33b Select time zone.

Step 34: X Window Manager Selection

- Choose an X Window manager from the list given.
- Select Ok, and then press ENTER.

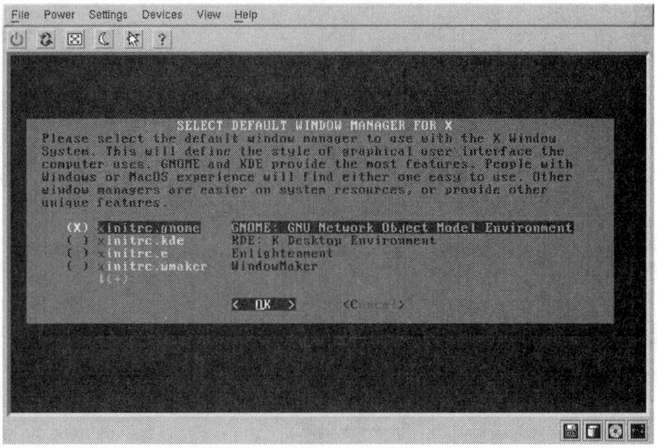

Figure A.5.34 Select X Window manager.

Step 35: Root Password Selection

- Select Yes to set a root password, and then press ENTER.

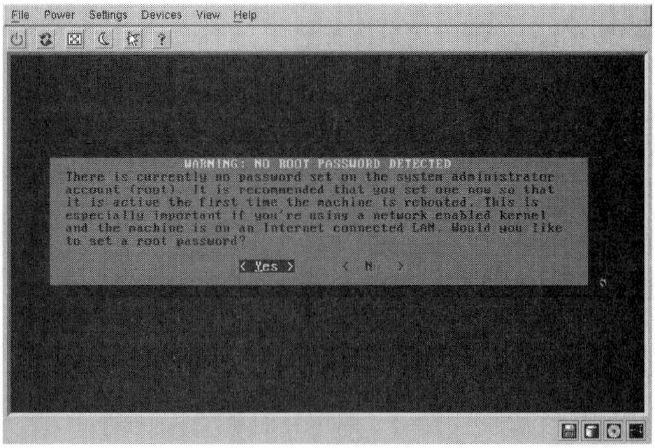

Figure A.5.35a Root password selection.

- Type in a new password, and press ENTER.
- Retype the password, and press ENTER.
- Press ENTER to continue.

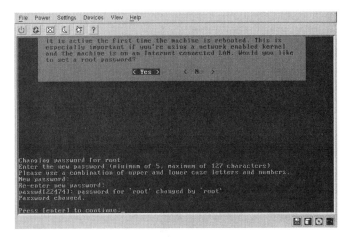

Figure A.5.35b   Root password verification.

Step 36: Setup Complete

- Press ENTER to complete the setup.

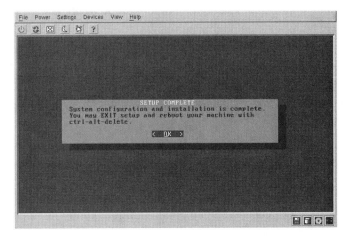

Figure A.5.36   Setup complete.

Step 37: EXIT Setup Program

- Select EXIT to leave the setup program.
- Select Ok, and then press ENTER.

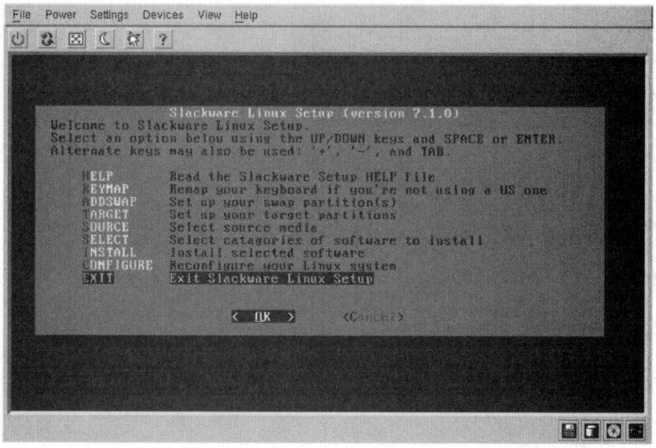

Figure A.5.37   Exit setup program.

Step 38: Reboot

- If the system does not reboot automatically, press CTRL-ALT-DEL.
- When the system reboots, you will be brought to a login prompt, where you may log in as root or as a user.

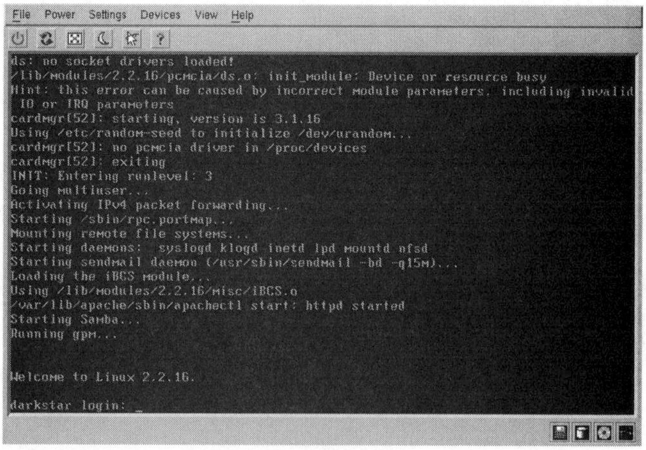

Figure A.5.38   Reboot the system.

Step 39: Log In as root

- Log in as root.
- Enter the root password, and press ENTER.

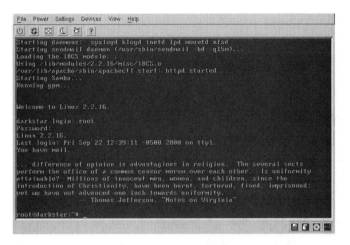

Figure A.5.39   Log in as root.

Step 40: Create User Accounts

- Type useradd -m [username].
- Type passwd [username].
- Type new password, and press ENTER.
- Retype password, and press ENTER.

Figure A.5.40   Create user accounts.

Step 41: Start X Window

- Type `logout`, and press ENTER.
- Log in as [username].
- Enter [username]'s password.
- Type `startx`, and press ENTER.

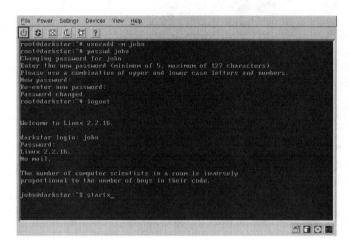

Figure A.5.41 Start X Window.

Step 42: Use the Desktop

- You may now begin using the GUI for Slackware Linux.

Figure A.5.42 Slackware desktop.

6. SuSE Linux 6.3

Although some insight is given into options for various installations, in this appendix we presume:

- No hard drive partition (i.e., Linux is the only OS)
- No upgrade from a previous Linux version (initial install)
- No shared hard disk
- A bootable CD-ROM
- No network connection
- A modem (no Ethernet card)

BEFORE INSTALLATION

System requirements: These are the minimum system specifications required to successfully run the SuSE Linux 6.3 distribution.

Hardware and network information: This is a list of the hardware that you will need to install and run Linux, and a list of information regarding your hardware and network (if installing for a network computer). In this walk-through, no networking was configured.

SYSTEM REQUIREMENTS

- Intel-compatible CPU (386 through Pentium Pro/II/III) and all compatible processors (AMD, Cyrix, IBM)
- 8 MB RAM (16 MB recommended)
- 300 MB to 4 GB free hard drive space (for full installation); minimum of 500 MB recommended
- SCSI or IDE CD-ROM drive

Hardware support can be verified at www.suse.com/us/support/hardware/index.html.

HARDWARE AND NETWORK INFORMATION

Although some hardware is detected by the SuSE installation software, it is advisable to gather the following media and information:

- 3.5" floppy disks
- CD-ROM drive, make and model
- Mouse, port used
- Graphics card manufacturer/model or number
- X server for graphics card
- Graphics card memory size in MB
- Monitor, max scan rates (vertical/horizontal)
- Modem, manufacturer/model and serial port

OPTIONAL NETWORK INFORMATION

- Host name of computer. We will create a host name to avoid having the default, noname appear in each user prompt. No other optional network information is used.)

- Domain name of network.

- IP address assigned to computer.

- Network address of LAN.

- Netmask address.

- Network broadcast address.

- Gateway or router address.

- DNS name server address.

Step 1: Language Selection

- Select the appropriate language.

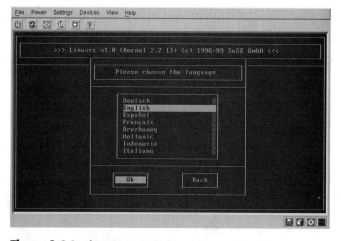

Figure A.6.1 Language menu.

Step 2: Display Selection

- Select color display.

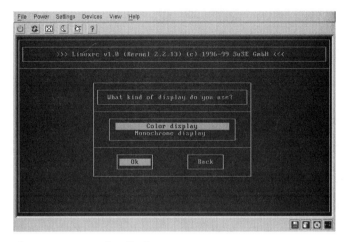

Figure A.6.2 Color display.

Step 3: Keyboard Map Selection

- Select English (US).

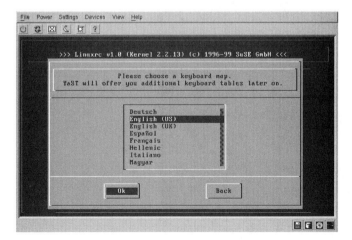

Figure A.6.3 Keyboard map selection.

Step 4: Installation/ System Start

■ Select Start installation/system.

Figure A.6.4   Installation and system start.

Step 5: Installation Start

■ Select Start installation.

Figure A.6.5   Start the installation.

Step 6: Source Media Selection

- Select CD-ROM.

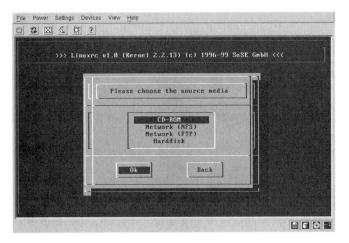

Figure A.6.6 Source media selection.

Step 7: Installation

- Insert CD number 1.

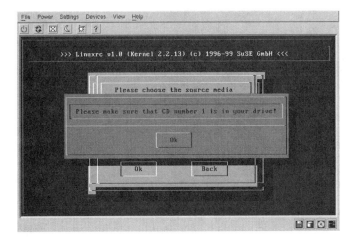

Figure A.6.7 First install CD.

Step 8: Installation Type Selection

■ Select Install Linux from scratch.

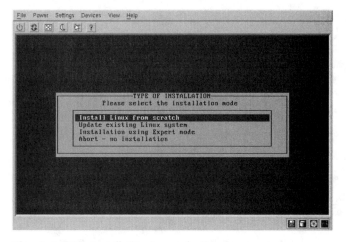

Figure A.6.8 Installation type selection.

Step 9: Hard Drive Partitioning

■ Select Partitioning.

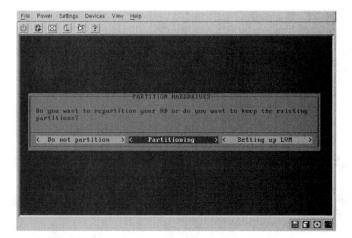

Figure A.6.9 Hard drive partitioning.

Step 10: Partition Confirmation

- Select Yes to confirm that you wish to partition the hard drive.

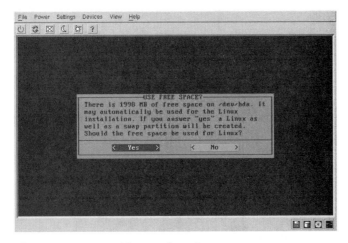

Figure A.6.10   Partition confirmation.

Step 11: Option Menu

- Select Load configuration.

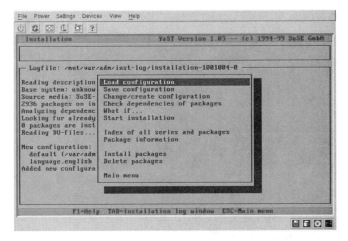

Figure A.6.11   Option menu.

Step 12: Configuration to Be Loaded

- Choose a configuration.
- Your choice of configurations should take into account such factors as disk space.

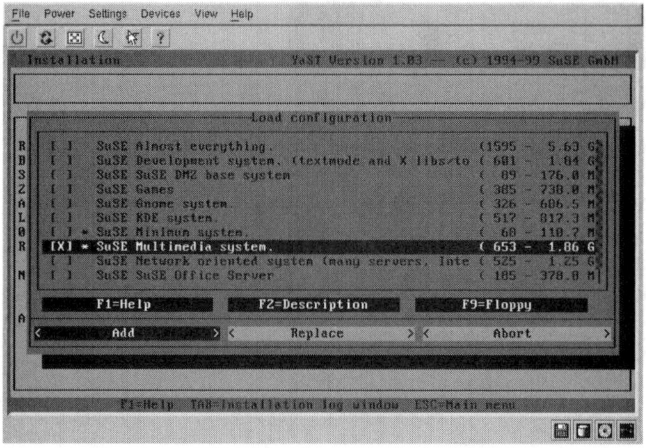

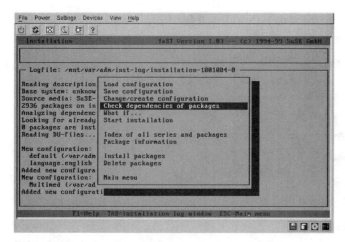

Figure A.6.12   Select configuration.

Step 13: Option Menu

- Select Check dependencies of packages.

Figure A.6.13   Package dependencies.

Step 14: Unsatisfied Dependencies

- If the check for unsatisfied dependencies found none, **select** Continue.

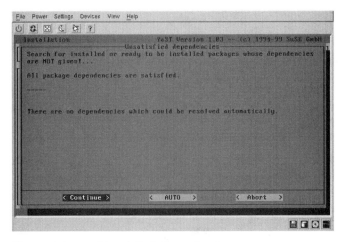

Figure A.6.14   Unsatisfied dependencies.

Step 15: Option Menu

- **Select** Start installation.

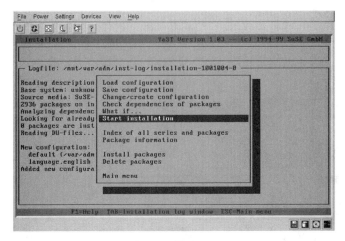

Figure A.6.15   Begin the installation.

Step 16: Installation

- Insert CD number 2.
- Select Continue.

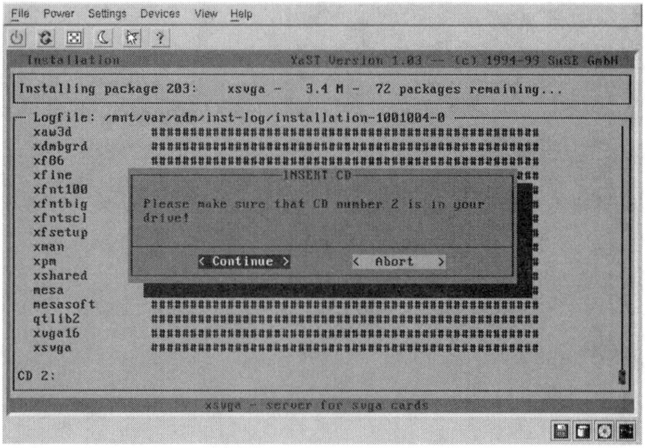

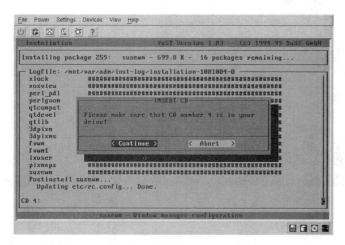

Figure A.6.16 Second installation CD.

Step 17: Continue

- Insert CD number 4.
- Select Continue.

Figure A.6.17 Fourth installation CD.

Step 18: Continue

- Insert CD number 5.
- Select Continue.

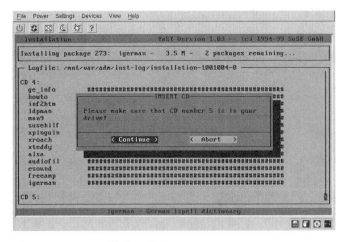

Figure A.6.18 Fifth installation CD.

Step 19: Option Menu

- Select Main menu.

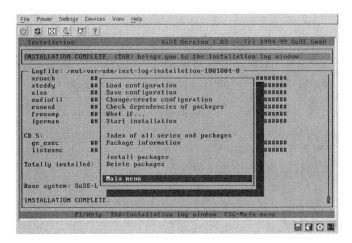

Figure A.6.19 Select Main menu.

Step 20: Continue

- Insert CD number 1.
- Select Continue.

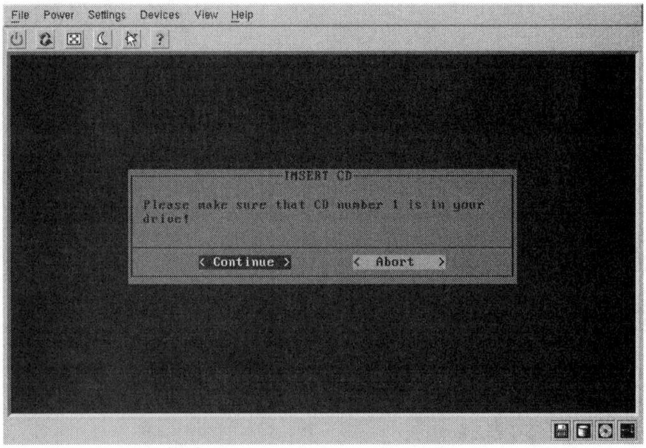

Figure A.6.20   First installation CD.

Step 21: Kernel Selection

- Select Standard kernel (pentium optimized).
- Select Continue.

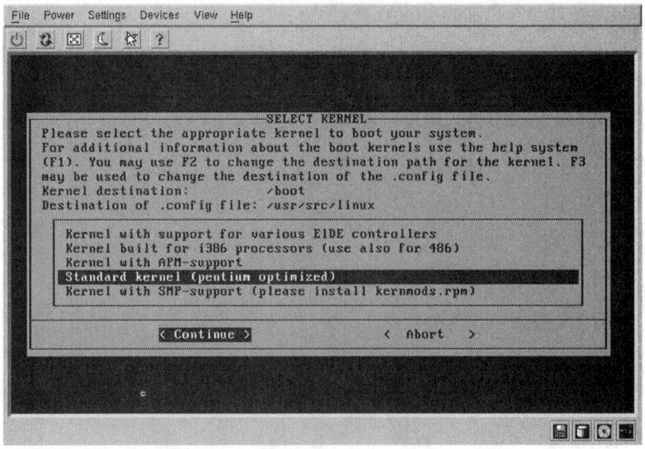

Figure A.6.21   Kernel selection.

Step 22: LILO Confirmation

■ Select Yes.

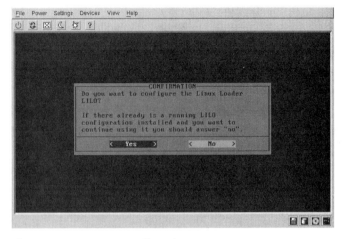

Figure A.6.22 LILO confirmation.

Step 23: LILO Configuration

■ Press F4.

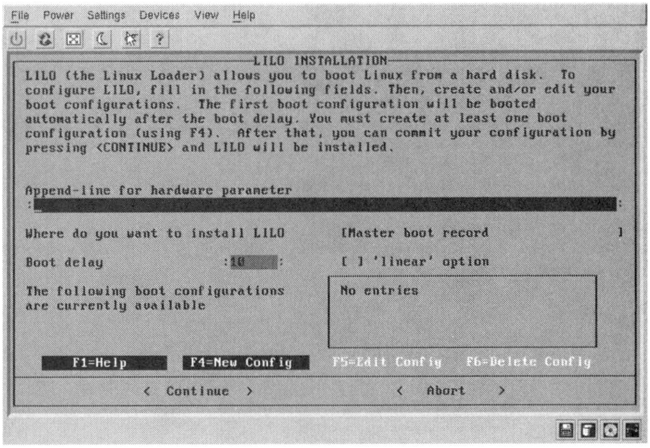

Figure A.6.23a LILO configuration.

- Enter `linux` for configuration name.

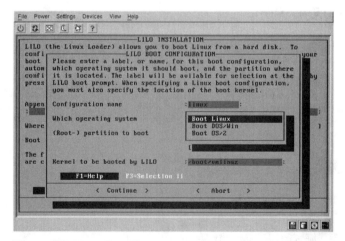

Figure A.6.23b   Linux configuration.

- Select `Boot Linux`.

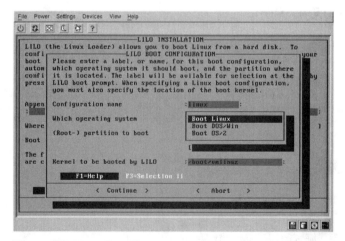

Figure A.6.23c   Boot Linux.

- Select the larger partition for the Linux installation.

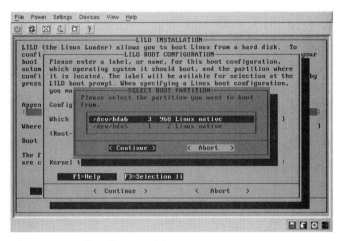

Figure A.6.23d   Linux partition.

- Select Continue.

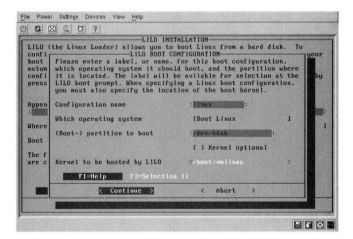

Figure A.6.23e   Continue LILO configuration.

■ Select the Linux partition.

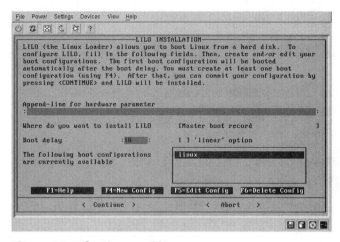

Figure A.6.23f   Linux partition.

■ Select Continue.

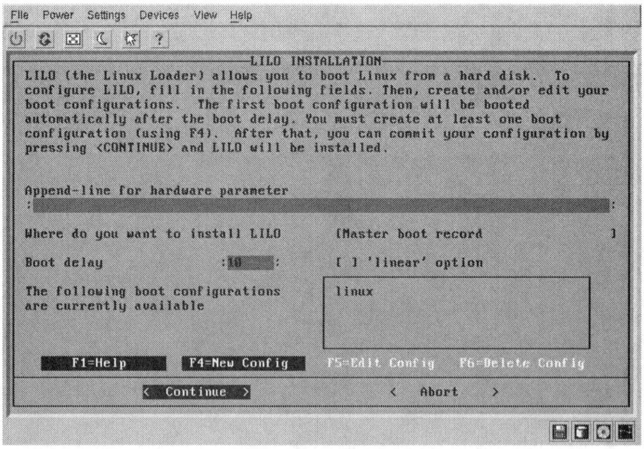

Figure A.6.23g   Continue configuration.

■ Select Continue.

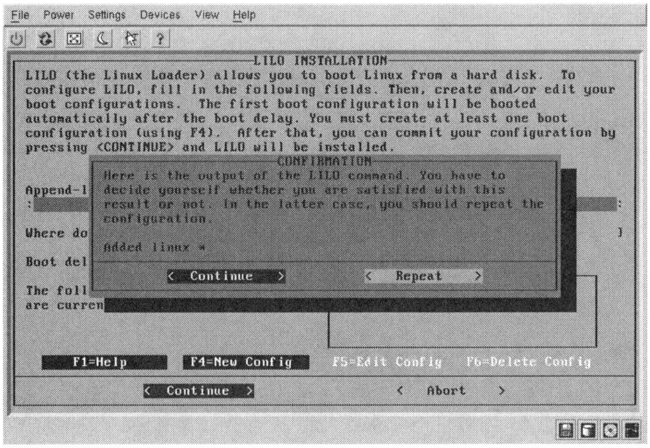

Figure A.6.23h   Complete configuration.

Step 24: Time Zone Selection

■ Select the appropriate time zone.

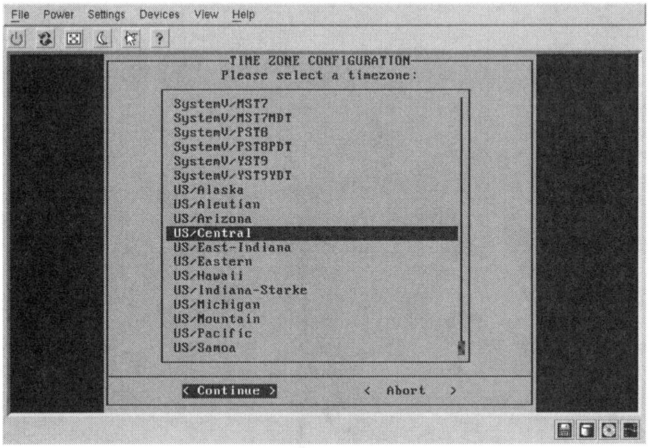

Figure A.6.24   Time zone selection.

Step 25: Hardware Clock Adjustment

■ Select Local time, if applicable.

Figure A.6.25   Set clock time.

Step 26: Host Name

■ Enter your desired Hostname.

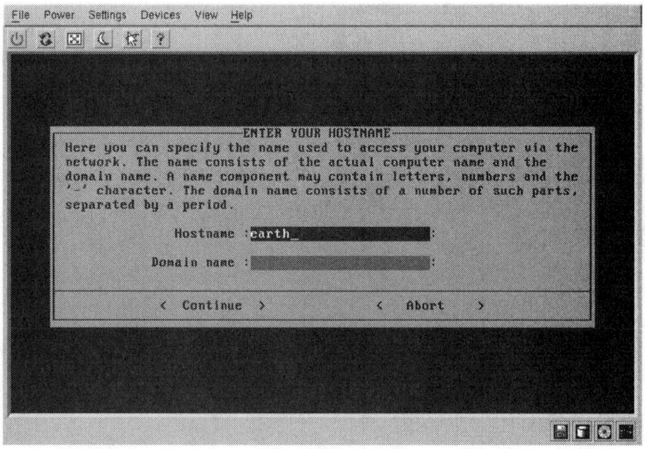

Figure A.6.26   Host name.

Step 27: Domain Name

■ Enter the Domain name.

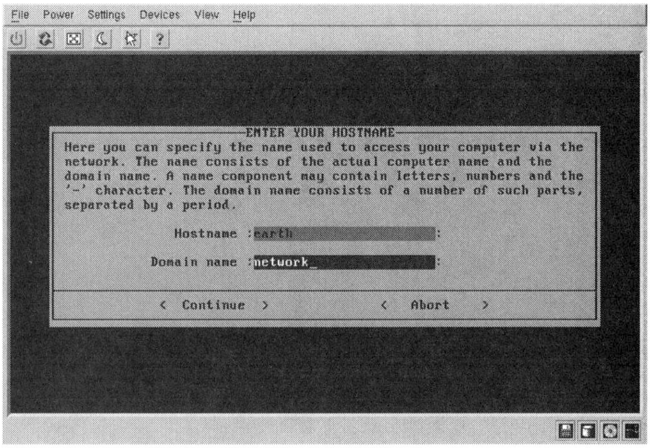

Figure A.6.27 Domain name.

Step 28: Network Confirmation

■ Since there is no network card, select Loopback only.

Figure A.6.28 Network confirmation.

Step 29: Configuration Status

■ Select Continue.

Figure A.6.29 Configuration status.

Step 30: Sendmail Configuration

■ Select Single user machine without network connection.

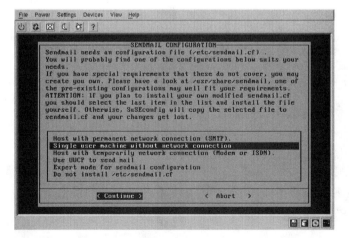

Figure A.6.30 Sendmail configuration.

Step 31: Output for SuSEconfig

■ Select Continue.

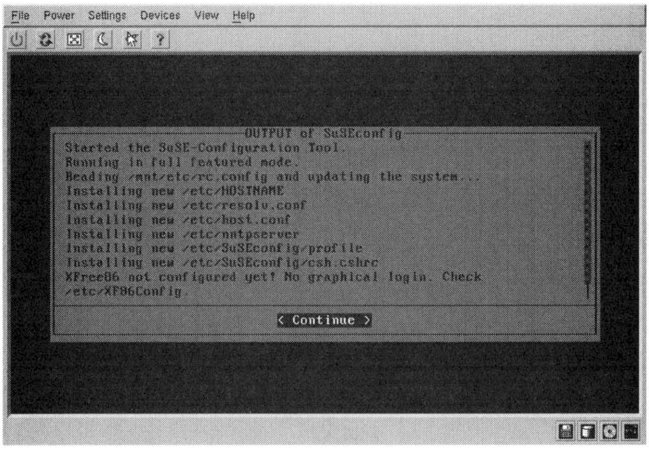

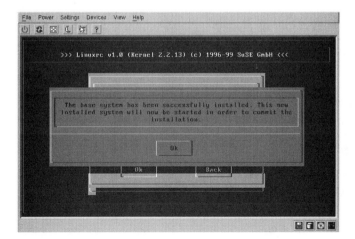

Figure A.6.31 Output for SuSEconfig.

Step 32: Installation Status

■ Press Ok.

Figure A.6.32 Installation status.

Step 33: Root Password

■ Enter and re-enter desired root password as prompted.

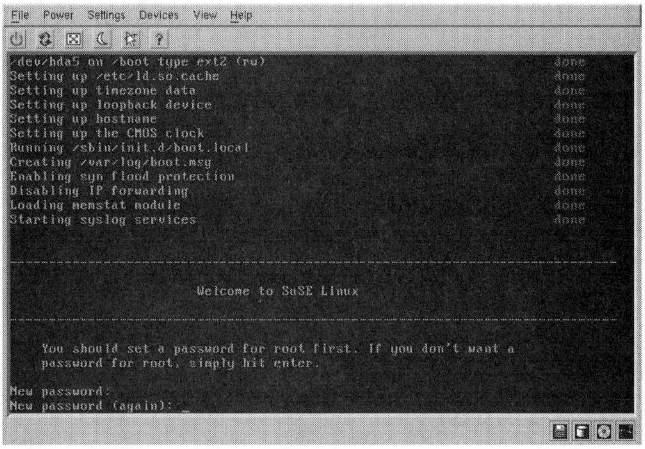

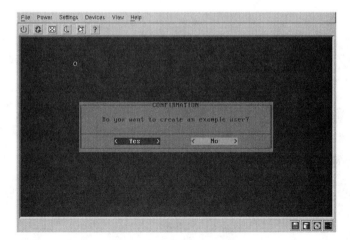

Figure A.6.33 Root password.

Step 34: Account Creation

■ Select Yes to create a user account.

Figure A.6.34 User account creation.

Step 35: Account Creation

- Enter login name for the user.
- Enter password.
- Re-enter password.
- Select Continue.

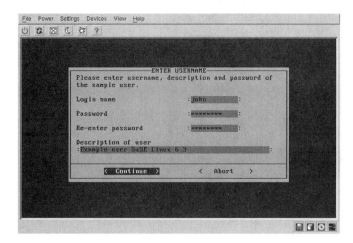

Figure A.6.35 Verify user password.

Step 36: Modem Configuration

- Select Yes.

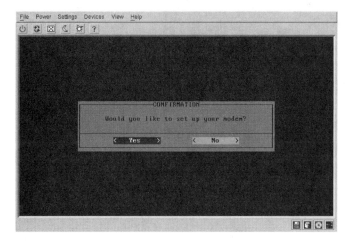

Figure A.6.36 Modem configuration.

Step 37: Modem Configuration

- Select the appropriate port.
- Select Continue.

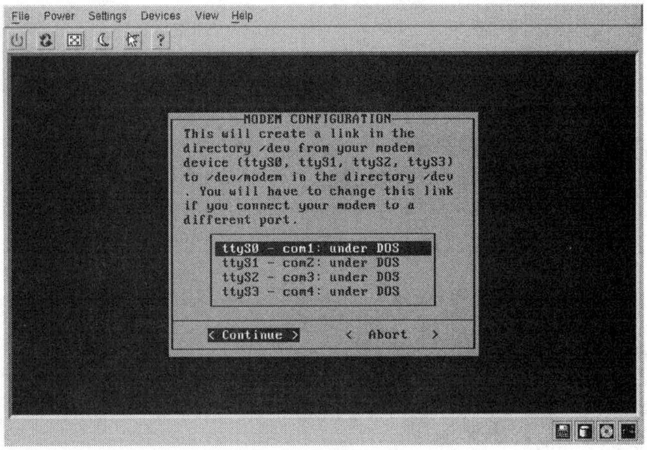

Figure A.6.37 Port selection.

Step 38: Mouse Configuration

- Select Yes.

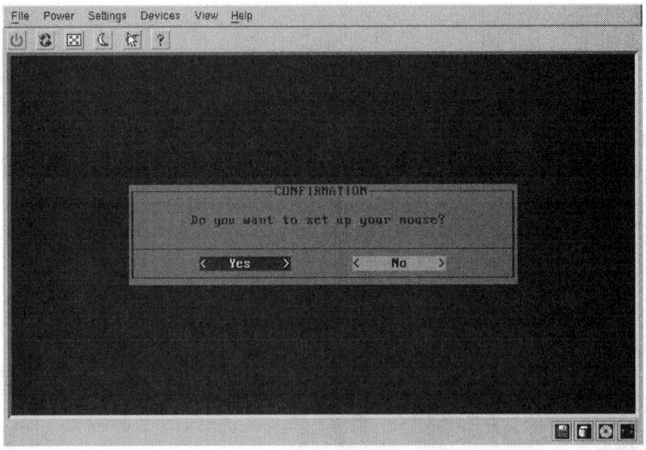

Figure A.6.38 Mouse configuration.

Step 39: Mouse Configuration

■ Select the appropriate mouse type.

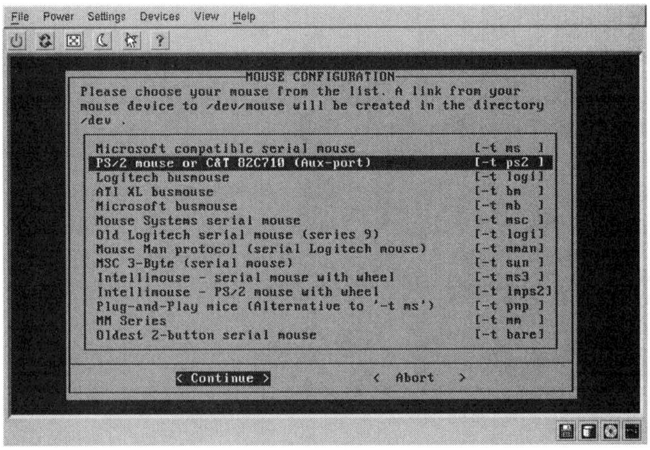

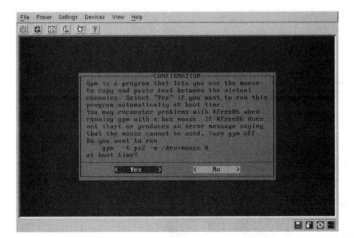

Figure A.6.39   Mouse type selection.

Step 40: GPM Confirmation

■ Select Yes.

Figure A.6.40   GPM confirmation.

Step 41: GPM Test

- If mouse cursor moves correctly, select Keep.

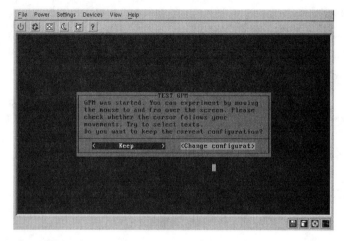

Figure A.6.41 GPM test.

Step 42: Installation Medium

- Select installation from CD-ROM.
- Select Continue.

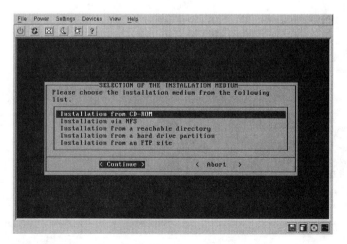

Figure A.6.42 Installation medium.

Step 43: CD-ROM Type Selection

- Select CD-ROM type.
- Since ours is an IDE, ATAPI EIDE was selected.
- Select Continue.

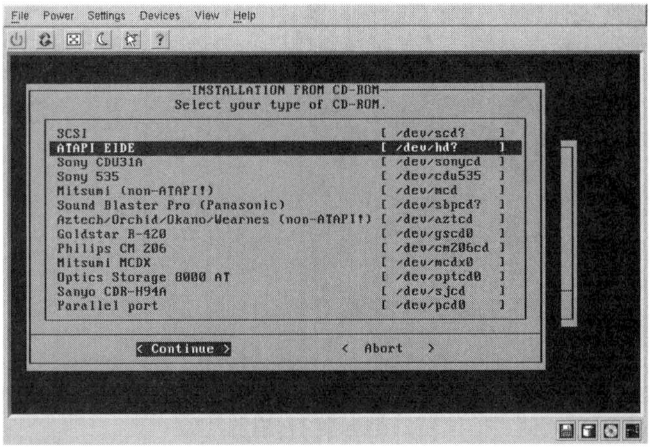

Figure A.6.43   CD-ROM type selection.

Step 44: CD-ROM Device Selection

- Select the correct IDE device for your CD-ROM.

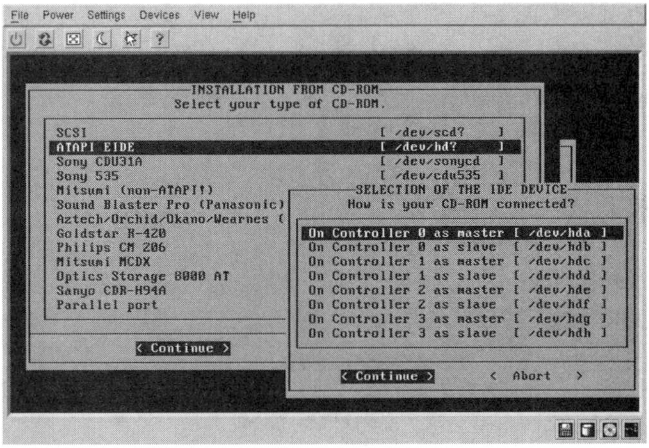

Figure A.6.44   CD-ROM device selection.

Step 45: Installation Status

- Select Continue.

Figure A.6.45 Installation status.

Step 46: Root Login

- Type root.
- Enter root password; this demonstrates root login.
- Type logout to log out.

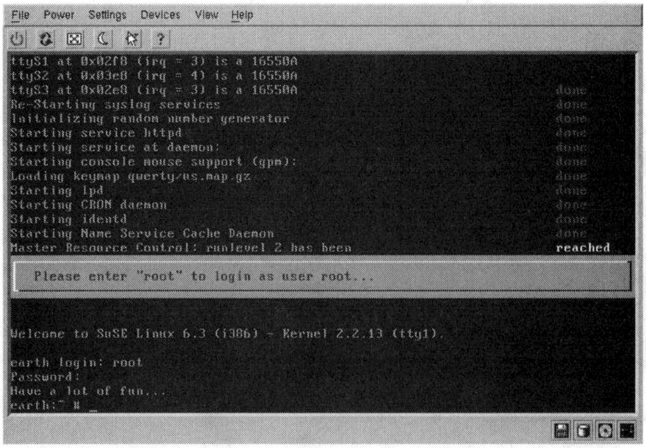

Figure A.6.46 Root login.

Step 47: User Login

- To log in as a user, type the user login name.
- Enter the user password.

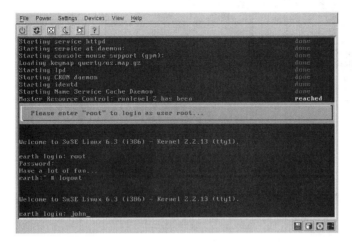

Figure A.6.47 User login.

Step 48: Starting X Window

- Type startx to start the X Window GUI.

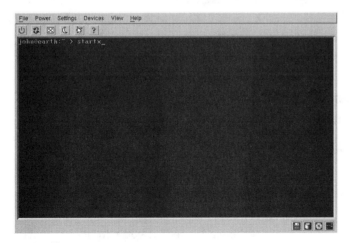

Figure A.6.48 Start X Window.

Step 49: KDE Desktop

■ Welcome to the KDE desktop.

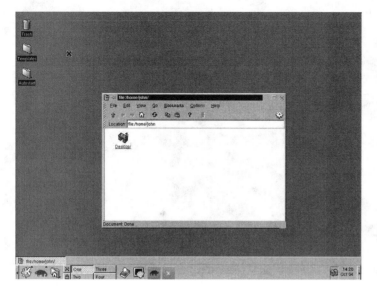

Figure A.6.49 KDE desktop.

7. TurboLinux Workstation Release 6.0

In this appendix, we presume that your computer has:

■ No hard drive partition (i.e., Linux is the only OS)
■ No upgrade from a previous Linux version (initial install)
■ A bootable CD-ROM
■ No network connection
■ A modem (no Ethernet card)

BEFORE INSTALLATION

System requirements: The minimum system specifications required to successfully run the TurboLinux Workstation Release 6.0 distribution.

Hardware information: This is a list of the hardware that you will need to install and run Linux, and a list of information regarding your hardware.

SYSTEM REQUIREMENTS

- 32-bit Intel-based PC (i.e., 80386…, Pentium)
- ISA, EISA, PCI, VL-Bus
- Minimum 8 MB RAM (16 MB preferred)
- Approximately 418 MB free hard disk space
- Supported mouse and video card

HARDWARE AND NETWORK INFORMATION

- CD-ROM drive, make and model
- Ethernet card, make and model
- Mouse, port used
- Graphics card manufacturer/ model or number
- X server for graphics card
- Graphics card memory size in MB
- Monitor, max scan rates (vertical/horizontal)
- Modem, manufacturer/model and serial port

OPTIONAL NETWORK INFORMATION

- Host name of computer. (We will create a host name to avoid having the default, `noname`, appear in each user prompt. No other optional network information is used.)
- Domain name of network.
- IP address assigned to computer.
- Network address of LAN.
- Netmask address.
- Network broadcast address.
- Gateway or router address.
- DNS name server address.
- Additional addresses.

Step 1: Language Selection

■ Select the appropriate language.

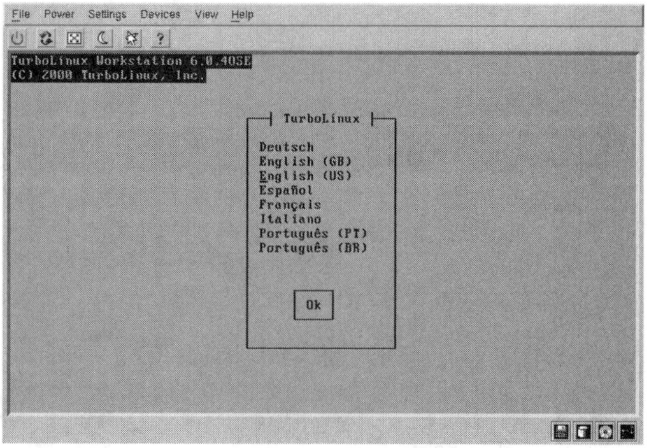

Figure A.7.1   Language selection.

Step 2: Color Display Selection

■ Select Yes.

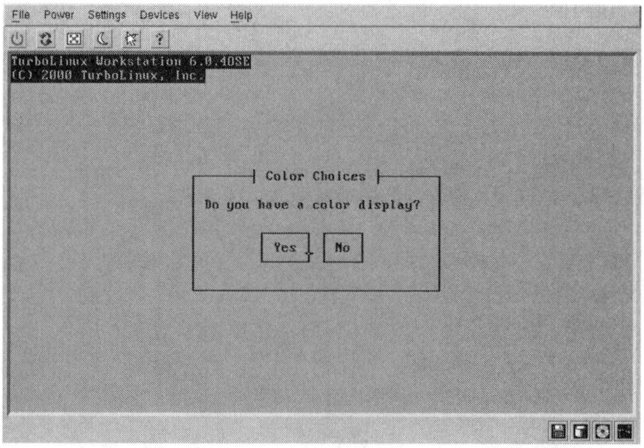

Figure A.7.2   Color display selection.

Step 3: Continue

- Select Ok.

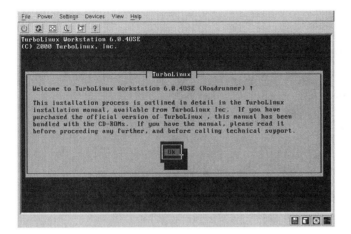

Figure A.7.3   Continue.

Step 4: Keyboard Mapping

- Select the appropriate keyboard type.

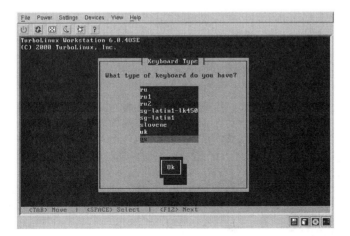

Figure A.7.4   Keyboard type.

Step 5: PCMCIA Support

■ Select No if you are not using a laptop.

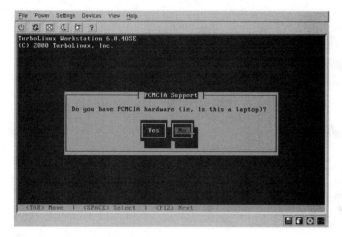

Figure A.7.5 PCMCIA support.

Step 6: TurboProbe

■ This feature will probe your system, attempting to detect hardware.
■ Select Ok.

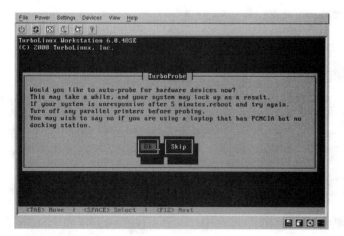

Figure A.7.6 TurboProbe.

Step 7: Parallel Port IDE Support

- Select No.

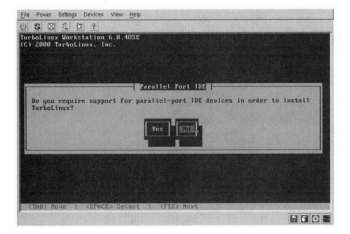

Figure A.7.7   Parallel port IDE.

Step 8: Continue

- This is a report of detected hardware.
- Select Continue.

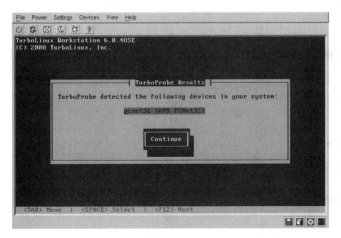

Figure A.7.8   TurboProbe results.

Step 9: Installation Media

- Select CD-ROM Drive.

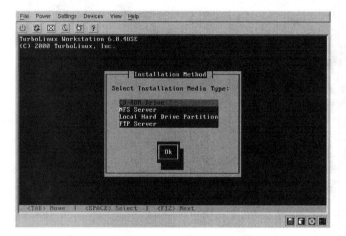

Figure A.7.9 Installation method.

Step 10: Continue

- Insert first CD-ROM.
- Select Ok.

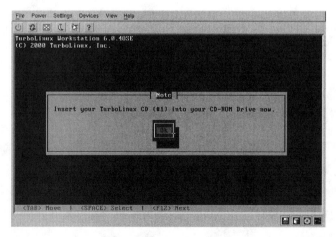

Figure A.7.10 First installation CD.

Step 11: Installer Preferences

- Select Normal Verbosity.

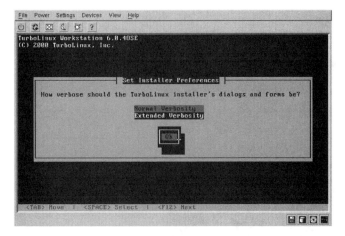

Figure A.7.11   Installer preferences.

Step 12: Network Type Selection

- Select PPP Dial-Up.

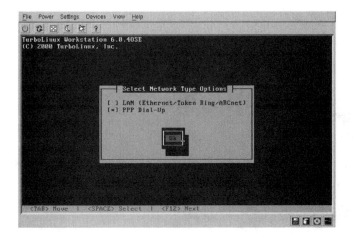

Figure A.7.12   Network type options.

Step 13: TurboProbe Results

- This is a report of detected SCSI adapters.
- Select Accept.

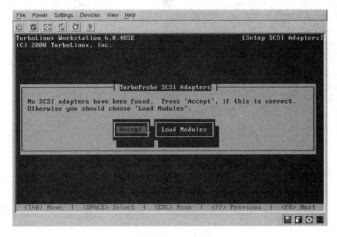

Figure A.7.13   TurboProbe SCSI adapters.

Step 14: Disk Partition

- Select FDISK.
- The next few steps cover the process of partitioning a hard drive using the fdisk program.

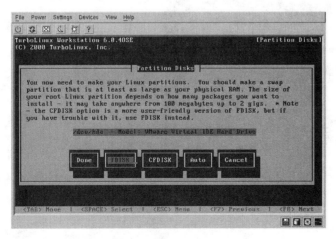

Figure A.7.14a   Partition disks.

■ To view the menu of commands in `fdisk`, type the letter m, and press ENTER.

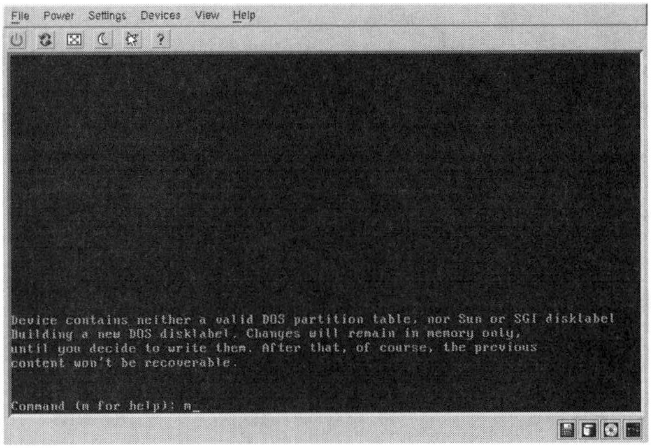

Figure A.7.14b   Continue partition.

■ The menu of commands is displayed; since you wish to partition a new hard drive, press n, and ENTER.

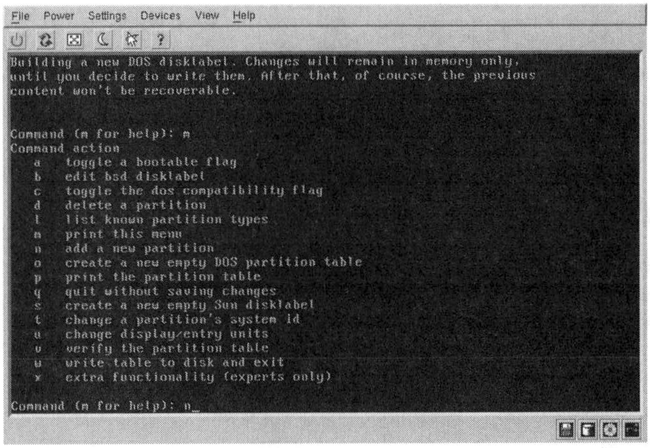

Figure A.7.14c   Command menu.

■ To make this a primary partition, press p.

Figure A.7.14d Select primary partition.

■ This will be the first primary partition; press the number 1.

Figure A.7.14e First primary partition.

- We wish the partition to begin with the first block of the first cylinder; press ENTER, since 1 is the default choice.

Figure A.7.14f   Default partition placement.

- The first partition will be the swap partition, which will use this part of the hard drive as virtual RAM.
- For 1 MB, type +1M.

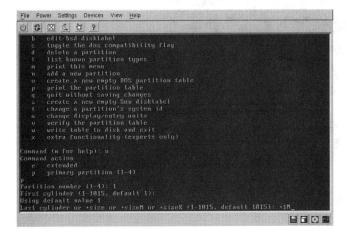

Figure A.7.14g   Swap partition size.

■ To see the current partition table, type the letter p.

Figure A.7.14h Current partition table.

■ To partition the rest of the hard drive, type n to add a new partition.

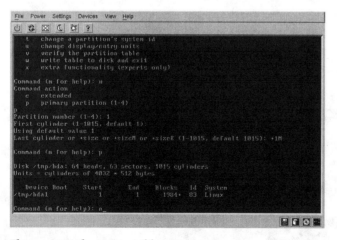

Figure A.7.14i New partition.

- This will be the partition on which the OS will be installed.
- This should be a primary partition; press p.

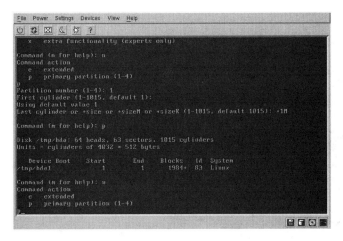

Figure A.7.14j   Create primary partition.

- Since this is the second primary hard drive partition, press the number 2.

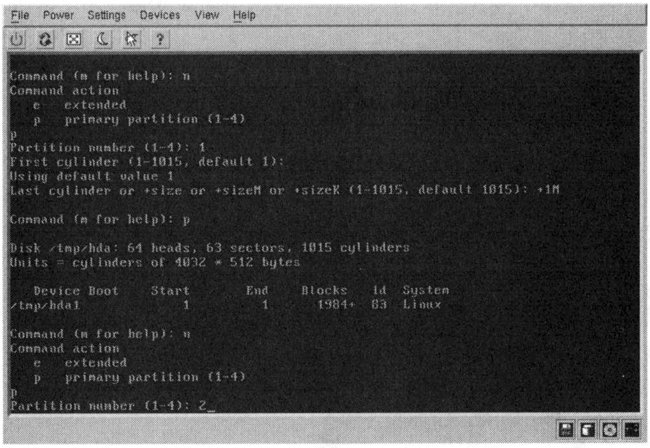

Figure A.7.14k   Second primary partition.

- This partition should begin with the next available block following the previous partition.
- Since this block is the default, press ENTER.

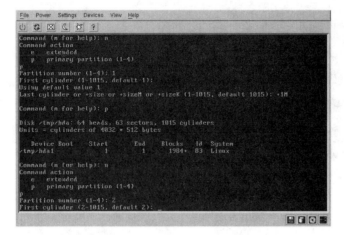

Figure A.7.14l   Default partition block.

- Make this second partition extend to the last available block of the last cylinder so that our two partitions will consume the entire hard drive. Press ENTER, since the default is the last available block.

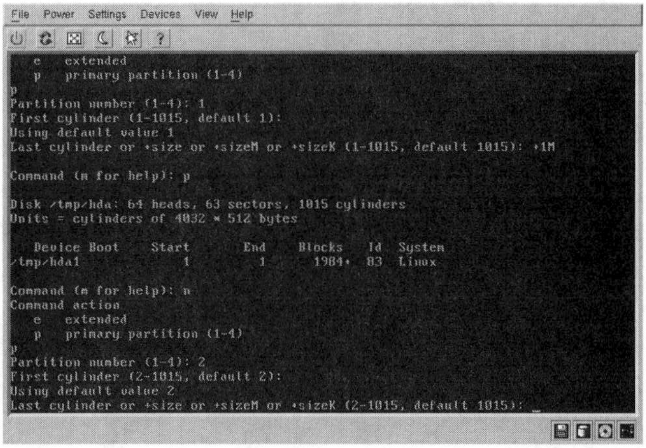

Figure A.7.14m   Default partition size.

■ The letter p will print the current partition table; type this to check the partitions.

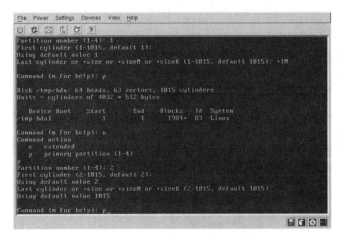

Figure A.7.14n Print partition table.

■ Both partitions were created as Linux native, meaning that they are target partitions for Linux. However, the 1 MB partition should be the swap partition; to change the partition type, press t and then ENTER.

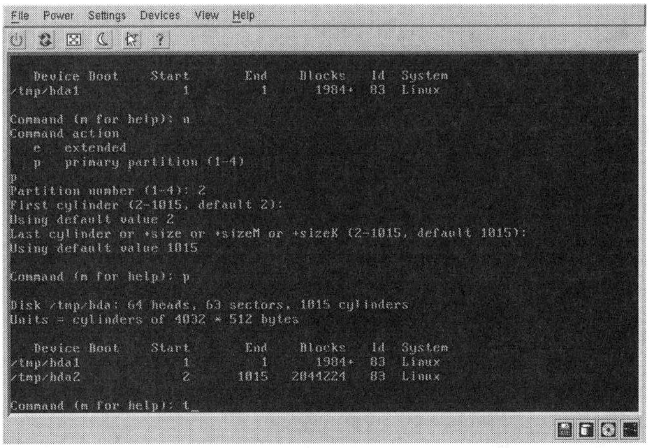

Figure A.7.14o Change partition type.

- The first partition should be the swap; press 1.
- Display the code that corresponds to the Linux swap by pressing 1.

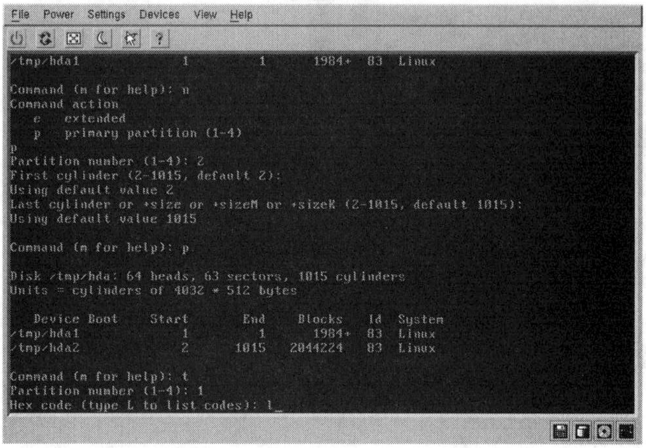

Figure A.7.14p   Display code.

- The number 82 corresponds to Linux swap; type in this number.

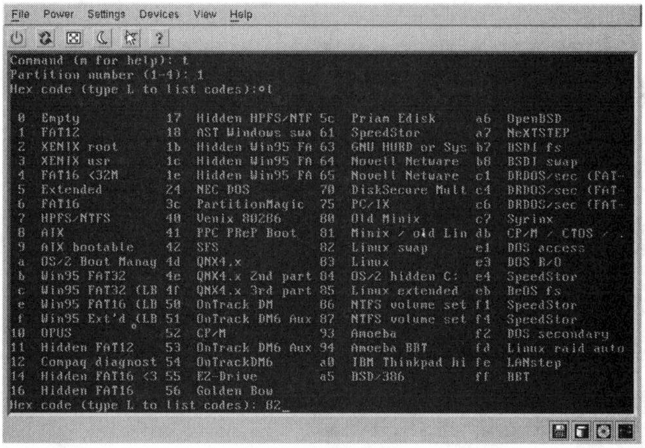

Figure A.7.14q   Corresponding Linux code.

■ When informed of the change, press p to print the partition table.

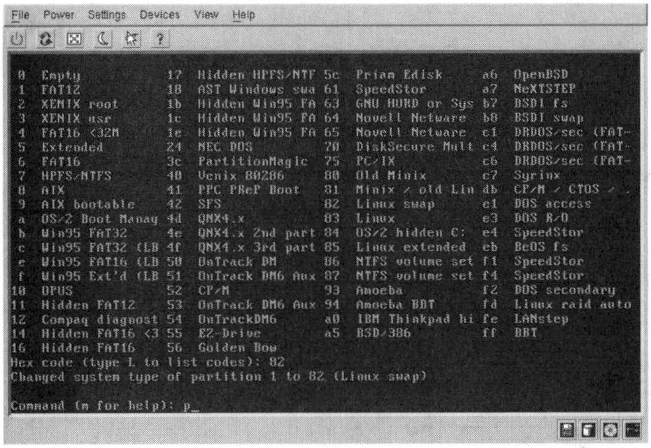

Figure A.7.14r Print new partition table.

■ The partition table is as desired; press w to write the table and make the partitions permanent.

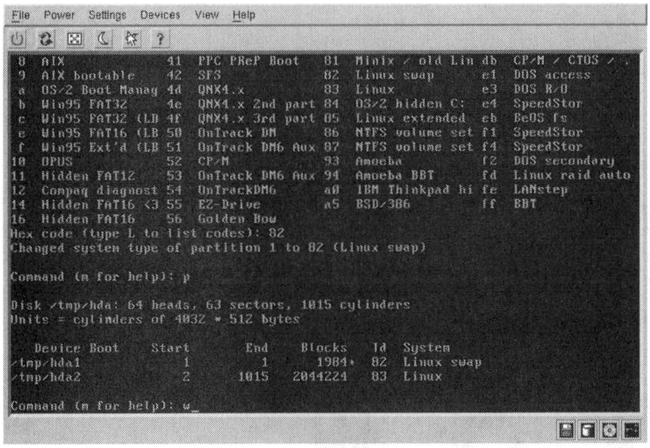

Figure A.7.14s Write partition table.

Step 15: Continue

- Select Done.

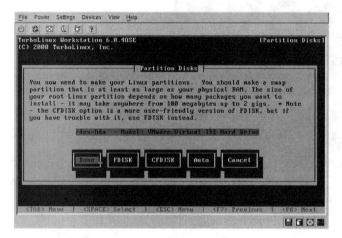

Figure A.7.15   Complete disk partition.

Step 16: Swap Partition Selection

- Select /dev/hda1 by using SPACE.
- Tab down and select Check for bad blocks during format?.

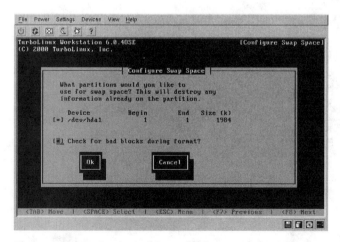

Figure A.7.16   Swap partition selection.

Step 17: Linux Partition Format

- Select /dev/hda2 by pressing SPACE.
- Tab down and select Check for bad blocks during format?.

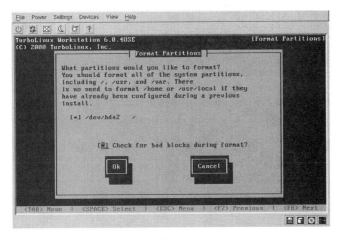

Figure A.7.17   Format partition.

Step 18: Continue

- Select Ok.

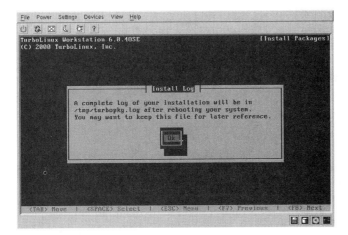

Figure A.7.18   Continue partition format.

Step 19: Continue

- Select Ok.

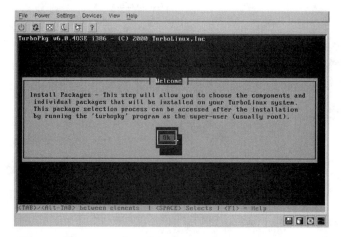

Figure A.7.19   Install packages.

Step 20: Installation Selection

- Select All-in-one Workstation (1214) MB.
- Select Install.

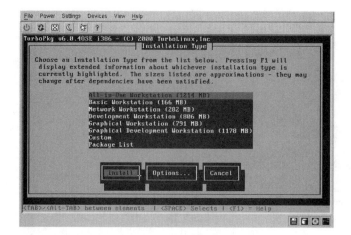

Figure A.7.20   Installation type.

Step 21: Selection Confirmation

- Select Proceed.

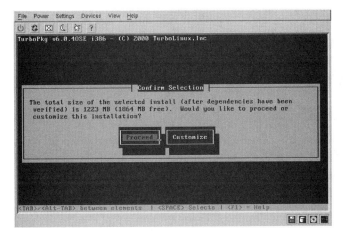

Figure A.7.21   Selection confirmation.

Step 22: Kernel Selection

- Select i586 kernel (Pentium, K5, K6, or newer).

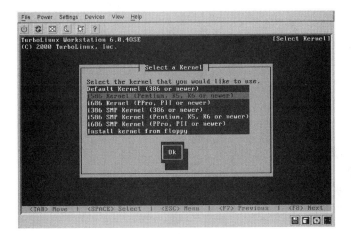

Figure A.7.22   Kernel selection.

Step 23: LILO Installation

■ Select /dev/hda Master Boot Record (recommended) to install LILO.

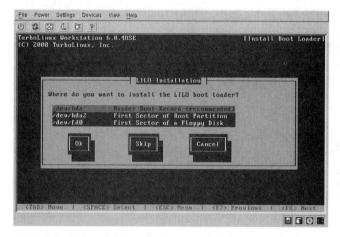

Figure A.7.23   LILO installation.

Step 24: Continue

■ Select Ok.

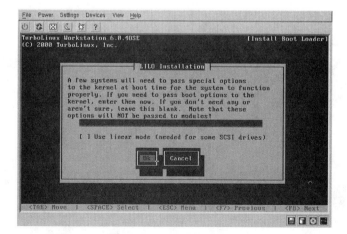

Figure A.7.24   Continue LILO installation.

Step 25: Time Zone Selection

- Select appropriate time zone.

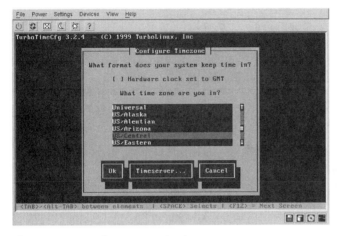

Figure A.7.25 Time zone selection.

Step 26: Printer Configuration

- Select No printers defined.
- Select Save & Exit.

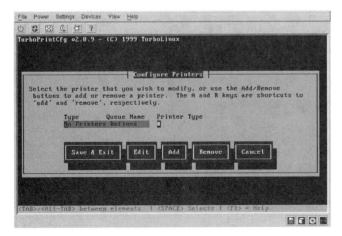

Figure A.7.26 Printer configuration.

Step 27: ISA PnP Configuration

■ Select No.

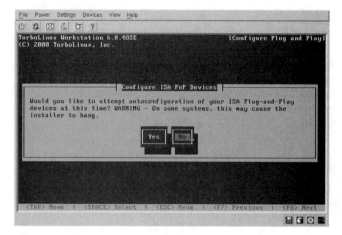

Figure A.7.27 Configure ISA PnP devices.

Step 28: Service Status Board

■ Select desired services.

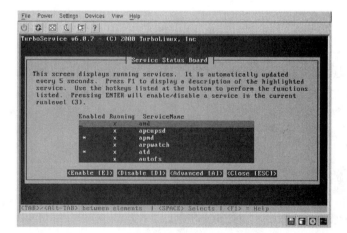

Figure A.7.28 Service status board.

Step 29: Root Password Setting

- Type the desired password for root.
- Retype password.

Figure A.7.29 Root password.

Step 30: Video Card Probe

- Select Yes.

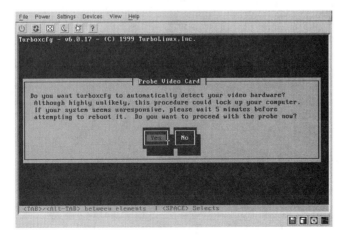

Figure A.7.30 Video card probe.

Step 31: Video Card Selection

- Highlight the correct video card.

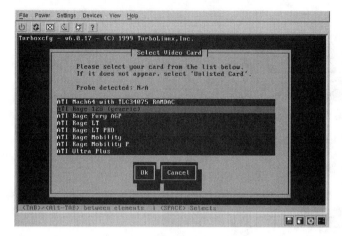

Figure A.7.31a Video card selection.

- If the video card cannot be probed for RAM, select appropriate quantity of video memory.

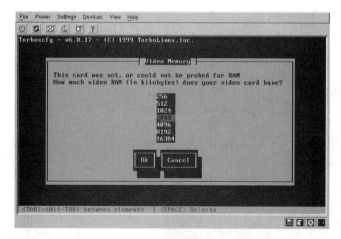

Figure A.7.31b Select RAM for video memory.

Step 32: X Configuration

- Select `Continue`.

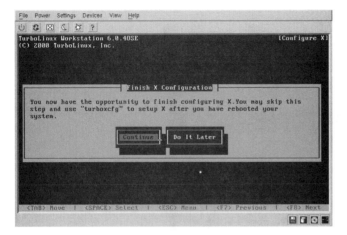

Figure A.7.32   Complete X configuration.

Step 33: Begin Turboxcfg

- Select `Ok`.

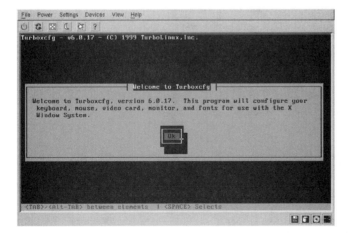

Figure A.7.33   Begin Turboxcfg.

Step 34: Keyboard Mapping

- Select the appropriate Key map.
- This is the keyboard mapping that will be used outside of the X Window GUI.

Figure A.7.34a Configure keyboard.

- Select the appropriate model of keyboard.

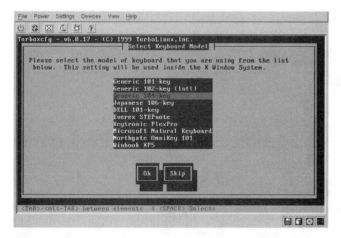

Figure A.7.34b Select keyboard model.

■ Select keyboard mapping to be used inside X Window GUI.

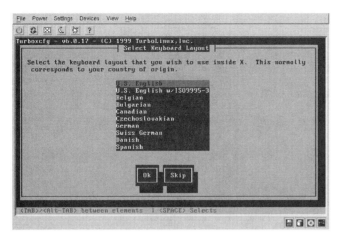

Figure A.7.34c Select keyboard layout.

Step 35: Mouse Configuration

■ Select mouse type (if mouse plug is round, it is a PS/2; if it is square, the mouse is serial).

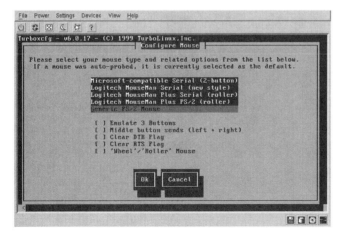

Figure A.7.35a Select mouse type.

- Select number of buttons on mouse.

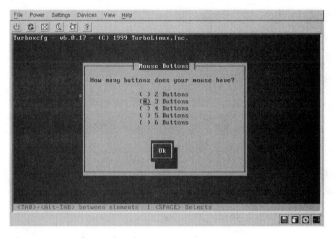

Figure A.7.35b Select button number.

Step 36: Monitor Configuration

- Select manufacturer of monitor.

Figure A.7.36a Monitor manufacturer.

- Select model of monitor.

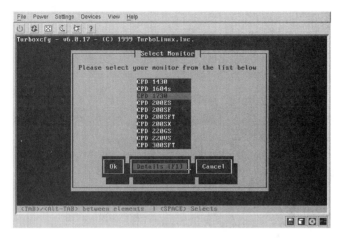

Figure A.7.36b   Monitor model.

- Select the default color depth in bit per pixel (bpp) and max resolution.

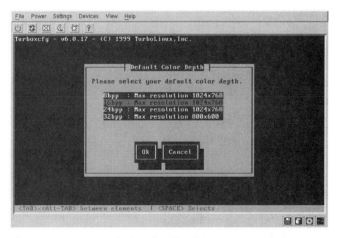

Figure A.7.36c   Default color depth.

■ Select the correct video mode for your monitor. (Note: It is possible to damage the raster-scan circuit of the monitor if the chosen refresh frequency exceeds capacity for the chosen resolution.)

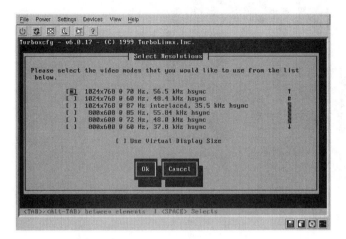

Figure A.7.36d Monitor resolution.

■ Select the correct default resolution.

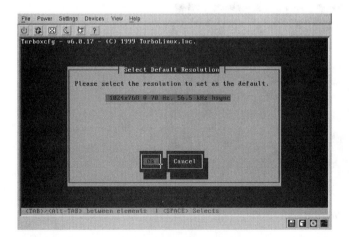

Figure A.7.36e Default resolution correction.

Step 37: Font Resolution

- Choose desired default font resolution.

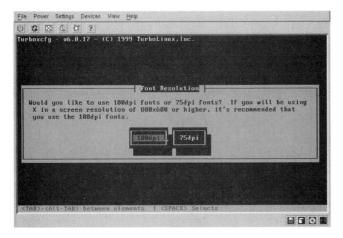

Figure A.7.37   Font resolution.

Step 38: Test X Configuration

- Select Proceed.

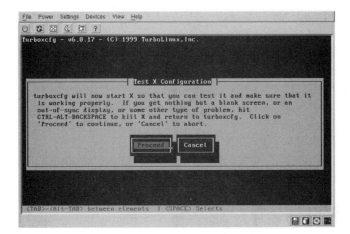

Figure A.7.38   Test X configuration.

Step 39: Confirmation

- Select Yes if configuration was successful.

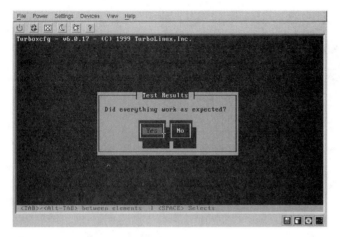

Figure A.7.39 Test results.

Step 40: Login Method Selection

- The graphical login will take the user directly into the X Window environment.
- If Text is chosen, the user is taken to the command line, where typing startx will start the X Win program.

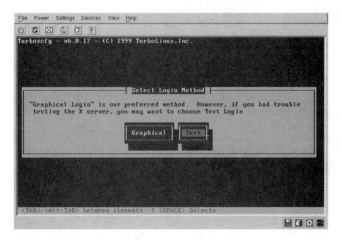

Figure A.7.40 Login method selection.

Step 41: Confirmation

■ Select Ok.

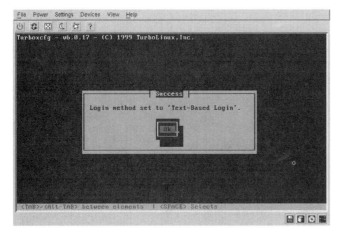

Figure A.7.41   Continue.

Step 42: Conclusion

■ This concludes the X Window configuration.
■ Select Ok.

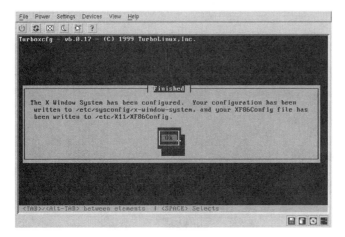

Figure A.7.42   Finish X Window configuration.

Step 43: Finish Installation

- This concludes the installation of TurboLinux.
- Remove any installation media.
- Select Ok.

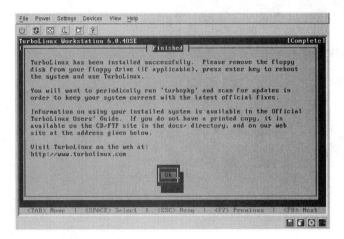

Figure A.7.43 Complete TurboLinux installation.

Step 44: Root Login

- To log in as root, type root and enter the root password.

Figure A.7.44 Root login.

Step 45: Account Creation

- Once you are root, create a user account.
- Type `useradd -m john` to create an account with the login name `john`.
- Here, `john` is an example of a username, which may be any combination of lower-case and alphanumeric characters.

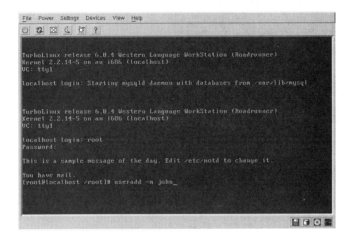

Figure A.7.45 User account creation.

Step 46: User Password Creation

- To create a password for the user `john`, type `passwd john`.

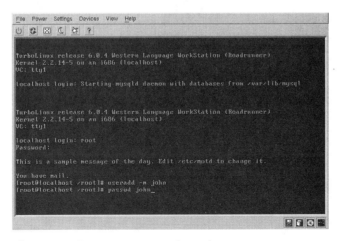

Figure A.7.46a User password creation.

- Enter the new password. (Note: If the password is based on a dictionary word, the system will not accept it.)

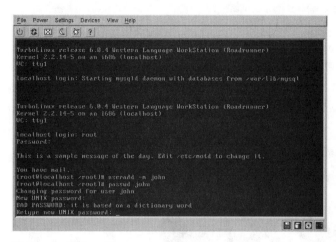

Figure A.7.46b   New password.

- Retype the password for verification.

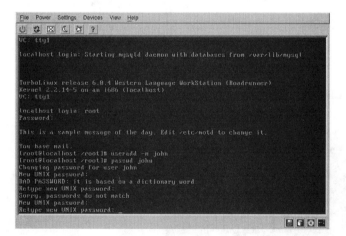

Figure A.7.46c   Password verification.

Step 47: Logging Out from root

■ Type `logout` to log out as root.

Figure A.7.47   Root logout.

Step 48: Log In as User

■ Enter the username and password to prompt the command line.

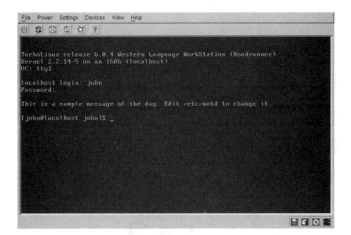

Figure A.7.48   Log in as user.

Step 49: Start the X Window GUI

■ From the command line, type `startx` to start the X Window program.

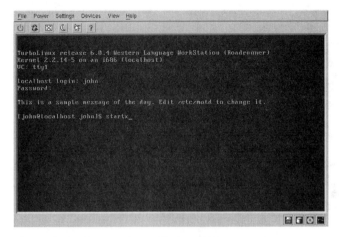

Figure A.7.49   Start the X Window GUI.

Step 50: Use X Window

■ This completes the installation process and account configuration and brings you to the X Window desktop environments.

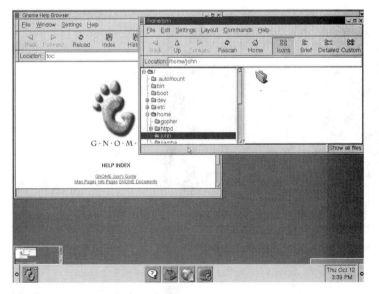

Figure A.7.50   X Window desktop.

Glossary

$PATH variable An internal shell variable that contains a list of directories.

$PATH variable, role The shell searches the list of directories looking for the executable file name specified in the command.

/proc directory Provides access to routines that provide status information about the kernel.

/ character Indicates the root directory volume (drive) that is hard-wired or built into the kernel image and is, therefore, known by the kernel at boot time. Also delimits directory names in a path.

access port To begin the login process, the user must find a port that is monitored by the login program (initially the getty program), which is waiting for input from a user. (For purposes of simplicity, ignore the role of telnetd, which assists with access via the network.)

adapter conflicts Adapters plugged into the buses may use the same parameter as another adapter. This means that both adapters would respond when the CPU attempted to communicate with one of them.

Adduser Edits the password file, creates the home directory for the account, and copies the default files from /etc/skel into the new directory.

adduser, augmentation A small script can be used to duplicate the required arguments to adduser without setting up the configure file /etc/adduser.conf. In this way, adduser can be invoked with just the name of the new user account.

application history file Applications may save their state information in the initialization files, or other files, so that they may begin execution where they left off earlier.

BIOS (Basic Input and Output System) A ROM-based set of routines that provide diagnostics and provide read and write services to devices. Unfortunately, the read and write routines only poll devices and cannot be interrupted during device operation.

BIOS-based adapter configuration Some vendors include the diagnostic and configuration programs in the ROM on the adapter card, and provide access to the programs at boot time by prompting the user to type a special key combination.

buses, PC   The IBM PC architecture employs a memory bus, a high-speed input output (I/O) bus called the PCI bus, and an older, backward-compatible I/O bus called the ISA bus.

case sensitivity   All files (including program names) in Unix-like operating systems must be accessed as is. The command-line interpreter (bash or other shell) employs upper- and lowercase characters to differentiate among file and program names.

cd command   Switches the current working directory to the specified directory and uses the new directory to find relative file names.

CD-ROM drives, ATAPI IDE   A new standard for IDE controllers. ATAPI IDE CD-ROM drives are accessed just like any other IDE drive; however, there often are compatibility problems with early ATAPI CD-ROM drives.

CD-ROM drives, SCSI   Accessed through existing SCSI drives, and work well in the Linux environment.

CD-ROM installation   Works well if Linux has the necessary driver for the particular CD-ROM; very fast.

CLI, advantages   Linux shells offer the ability to perform many repetitive tasks with just a few keystrokes. Once the command shortcuts are learned, many users prefer a CLI to a GUI when having to do similar tasks.

client-server printer   Unix-like OSs divide the printing process into two parts. A client program accepts the print request and submits it to a back-end server. The server then takes care of printing the data. In this way, the destination server printer may be local, remote, passed through a gateway, or the server may reside within the printer itself.

configure disk partitions   Administrators most often select the custom install option so that they can best utilize the disk space available.

console switching   Use the CTRL-ALT-Fx keys to select a new virtual console.

copy and paste   Highlight the text to be copied with the left mouse button, switch to the "destination" application, and paste with the middle button.

Copyleft   Refers to the nontraditional use of copyright to keep software free, and to give the right of use and modification to many instead of only a few.

data cache   The data cache holds data blocks destined for the hard disk. If the system is abruptly turned off, then file information is lost and the file system becomes inconsistent. To minimize this problem, the kernel daemon kflushd moves data cache blocks out to the hard disk every 30 seconds or so.

data viewing, offscreen   Use the SHIFT-PgUp key to review things that have scrolled up off of a virtual console terminal.

Debian attributes   It installs in "chunks," has a default configuration with secure Internet servers, and provides robust package installations and upgrades.

default file protection   Creating a file as the superuser means that the file may not be readable or writeable by other user accounts and, therefore, the superuser account will have to be used to manipulate the files created earlier.

Deja   A special type of search engine that specializes in searching all newsgroup postings and can quickly find answers to obscure problems.

device conflicts, types   The I/O address of the adapter card, the interrupt request line of the adapter card, the direct memory access channel, and shared memory addresses.

device drivers Map the physical characteristics of a device into a uniform logical interface that makes the device accessible by all parts of the kernel. Since Linux employs preemptive multitasking, it must provide its own interrupt-driven device drivers and avoid using the BIOS routines.

device section Tells the X server which parameters to accept and which ones to probe for in the video adapter.

disk divisions Linux requires at least two partitions, one for the swap space and the other for the root file system. If Linux shares the hard disk with another OS(s), more partitions may be required.

disk partitions Partitions are a means by which the firmware divides up the hard disk and presents partitions to one or more operating systems as volumes.

domain name service A server that translates computer names to IP addresses.

dot debate Use of the dot character in the current directory may lead to a security problem in which pretend system programs request and save user passwords.

facilities Messages are directed with the use of a facilities label, indicating the type of daemon message (`mail`, `telnet`, `lpr`, etc.) and the priority of the message (emergency, warning, debug, etc.).

find, design tradeoff The `find` command searches the complete directory structure from the specified starting point to each leaf. This requires tens of thousands of file manager queries, and as a result, the program runs slowly. However, unlike locate, the `find` command will perform an up-to-date search.

format documentation The file format section of the man pages describes the role of each field in a control or initialization file, and which programs read or write each field.

free software Free software is generally open source and it may be used, modified, copied, redesigned, and shared with others. Free software also carries the built-in cost of requiring expert knowledge with regard to administration of the software package. The term *free software* refers to how the software is distributed, and not the viewing of the source code. There are forms of free software that are binary-only copies that may not be redistributed.

free software business model Businesses do quite well selling GPL software because they have switched their focus from a fee-for-product model to a fee-for-service model. The service can be a product in the form of reconfigured, or improved, software as well as traditional service. The business should expect that just as much, if not more, income can be generated through the wide distribution of the lower-cost software, which should lead to an extensive audience for future service.

free software product GPL software takes on a life of its own. It creates a community of programmers who freely share ideas to improve the software, and the software generally evolves into a product of better quality than any one individual or subgroup could have created by themselves.

free software, computer professional use GPL software allows the computer professional the ability to exploit a highly evolved set of software tools that can greatly improve the productivity of the computer professionals, especially when compared to traditional software development environments.

free software, long-term commercial use GNU GPL software is just as much an attitude as it is an end product. Although it requires thinking out of the box, commercial users of free software will be able to achieve a much higher level of productivity through implicit cooperation in software development.

gateway A router, or other host, that has a second network interface connected to the Internet.

global initialization files Global file settings are found in /etc and affect all users, but they have low-priority default settings.

GNU GPL, advantages GPL software is open to peer review. As a result, faulty assumptions are usually identified and corrected. Moreover, tens of thousands of developers share the same development environment, allowing quick and easy sharing of ideas and implementations over the Internet.

GNU GPL, limitations The limitations of the GNU GPL include those who provide new source code, but attempt to make the code unclear. Another limitation of GNU GPL is the question of how much documentation to include with the source code. Finally, there are those who feel that the GNU GPL restricts the use of free software by not allowing it to be embedded into other software products.

GNU GPL, uniqueness GPL stands out from other software licenses because it keeps software intact, allows it to mature over many years, and prevents any one entity from controlling the software.

GPL GNU general public license, also called copyleft, is a detailed document describing the freedom to use software.

GPL, keeping software free The GNU GPL attempts to keep free software free by mandating that all code, including source, must be included in any redistribution of the software, and any new code added to the software must be included in the redistribution.

GPL, response to users Acting from self-interest, many different developers, over time, contribute to GPL software. This public process leads to code review, bug fixes, and improved features that best meet the needs of all users.

graphic mode filters Printer filters may be attached to the printcap file to select PostScript or a graphic-mode format for the printer automatically.

graphic-mode printing In graphic mode printing, the CPU sends the instructions for printing each pixel of an image.

graphic mode The organization of video memory in the number of X and Y pixels plus the number of colors per pixel.

graphic resolution The number of X and Y pixels plus the amount of information for each pixel (pixel depth).

GUI utilities, disadvantages Not all shell commands are supported in the GUI, and some GUI utilities perform multiple commands without feedback or undo operations.

GUI utility, tradeoff Although convenient, these GUI configuration utilities perform multistep operations without informing the operator, which may interfere with other configurations.

GUI, starting A shell script called startx will run the X server and window manger from the command line if xdm is not running.

h switch Suppresses the header, or job control page, that shows the username and file name. If the printer is not directly connected, then this switch is required.

Halloween memos A very favorable internal Microsoft analysis of what is called the open source software movement, but which is really an analysis of GNU GPL software.

help information, paging   Sometimes there is more information than will fit on a single screen, so information scrolls off the top of the screen. Pipe the output to a pager utility, such as `more` or `less`.

hidden window control   Some window managers allow full-screen windows, but the control element may become hidden under another higher-priority window. All is not lost—just double-click the title bar and the entire window will come to the surface, allowing access to the window controls.

hierarchical menus   In a hierarchical menu, activating one menu selection causes another menu to pop up. Selecting from the second menu causes a third menu to pop up, and so on.

indirect method   Symbolic file names with implicit start and stop commands that link (point) to the shell scripts in the `rc.d` directory.

info limitations   The info system depends on contributions from individual program writers or third-party contributors, and as a result, the amount and quality of information varies from subject to subject. Also, some parts of the info system have yet to be completed.

info utility   Designed to provide a broad view of system programs rather than the narrow man-page format. Information is arranged hierarchically, and a cursor-based user interface allows the selection of topics from various usage areas.

`init.d` directory   Used by various distributions to hold indirect scripts.

initialization files, X Window system   The `xdm` and `startx` programs use separate initializations files to control the same GUI setup. The `xinitrc` is used by `startx`, and `xdm` uses the `Xsession` initialization file. The `Xsession` contents have higher priority than the commands in the `startx` file.

`insmod`   Loads device drivers at run time.

`insmod`, tradeoff   `insmod` gives the administrator the flexibility to adapt to many possible configurations by allowing new device drivers to be added at run time; however, eventually, the drivers should be compiled into the kernel to achieve better performance.

internal commands   Note that some commands appear to be stand-alone utilities such as the `cd` command, but they are internal to the shell and do not respond to help requests.

Internet installation   Must set up directories, transfer files, and check directory structure; very slow and error prone.

IP address   An Internet protocol logical address assigned by a central authority that provides a way for others to reach your computer.

`kill` command   Sends a terminate signal to the specified program and causes it to terminate.

`kill` jobs   By switching to another login port, you can identify and terminate a program that has locked up, without having to reboot the system.

LAN Network installation   Using FTP, NFS, or SAMBA protocols, read the installation from another Linux box or MS-DOS file system; fast install.

LILO   The Linux loader uses the BIOS to read from the floppy, hard disk, or CD-ROM to boot Linux.

LILO append field   The append argument allows the system administrator to provide custom configuration arguments to the kernel.

LILO command By running the LILO program, the configuration information, along with the boot program, is copied into the MBR for subsequent system boot.

LILO label field The label argument specifies multiple OS images at boot time from which the user may select.

Linux inhouse warranty service Millions of people use Linux without warranty service. The key is to develop a staff of qualified individuals who will provide the warranty service in house through skill and use of Internet resources.

Linux memory requirements The exact amount of required RAM depends on the mix of applications run, and can be as little as 4 MB or as much as the mainboard can hold.

Linux origins Linux is the result of 20 years of GPL software evolution and has recently been packaged and configured by various vendors.

Linux shell Serves as the command-line interpreter that provides simple command-line editing, program execution, and flow control in the execution of shell scripts.

Linux subsystems The major Linux subsystems are kernel, network, init, daemons, login, shells, utilities, and the X Window system.

Linux warranty service Even though Linux does not come with a warranty, there are many companies that will provide continuing maintenance services for Linux, thereby, in effect, offering a warranty service.

Linux, installation steps (1) Boot install program; (2) Partition hard disk; (3) Format partitions; (4) De-archive software; (5) Configure boot-up sequence; (6) Set up X11.

Linux, booting methods (1) With LILO from the MBR; (2) From a floppy disk; (3) From another operating system (System Commander).

Linux, shutting down (1) Press CTRL-ALT-DEL at the console to shut down and reboot the system; (2) Become superuser and use the `halt`, `reboot`, or `shutdown` commands; (3) Become superuser and switch run levels with the `init 0` command.

Linux, user interface Linux is a layered system; GUI programs depend upon lower-level shells to execute commands. Not all shell commands are implemented with a GUI.

local initialization files Local file setting are found in the user's home directory and override global settings.

locate Interprets its argument either as some part of a file name or as a path name to a file, and as a result, it displays all path names containing the argument.

locate, design tradeoff Locate provides fast response time by reading a database of path and file names, but the database will not reflect recent changes made to the file system.

logging out Use the end-of-file character, CTRL-D, or the shell command `exit` or `logout`.

lpc command Queries the print server for status information on one or more printers. The superuser can use `lpc` to stop and start the server as well as clean the print queue.

lpq command Queries the local or remote server, depending on the `printcap` description of the printer location for pending print requests.

lprm command Tells the specified print server to remove one or more pending print requests.

ls command Displays the file names and permissions of files contained within a specified directory.

magic filter   Converts between DVI and PostScript; also converts PostScript format into native graphic format for various types of printers.

man k command   Searches only for key words found in the title of each documentation page.

man pages   Documentation on acceptable arguments for the program and how the arguments change the programs. However, the program is discussed in isolation with no consideration given to program interaction information.

mark-up   In word processing programs, text display and text creation are two separate processes.

memory size problem   Older SIMM mainboards tend not to have cache addresses that go beyond 64 MB. If this is true, the system will slow to a crawl (to around 12 MHz with 70 ns memory) when memory references go beyond the 64 MB address range.

menu disorientation   Unfortunately many menu items repeat in lower-level menus within the menu hierarchy. So, for example, when the linuxconf program menu selections are as follows:

```
Config --> User accounts --> Normal-->User accounts,
```

the user may become disoriented, and as a result, become confused about where he or she is "located" within the menu hierarchy.

message direction   Syslog sorts, and if requested, duplicates messages into various files based on directions in the /etc/syslog.conf file.

modularity, hierarchical   System programs typically provide layers of functionality by placing commonly needed functions in lower-level modules (programs) so that higher-level programs may use and share the lower-level modules when the services of the lower-level modules are needed.

modularity, Linux   Linux is made up of many types of programs that are interrelated. Although each program may stand alone as a result of being modular, its true value is not apparent until it is seen interacting with other system programs.

monitor damage   The refresh rate paints the pixels across the CRT at a particular rate per second. Generally, a faster refresh rate is better for viewing comfort, but too fast will break the raster-scan circuit in the monitor.

monitor refresh rates, differences   The XF86Setup utility offers a range of approximate refresh frequencies only where exact and optimal refresh frequencies can be obtained from the monitor file.

monitor section   Lists possible graphic modes and the refresh rate for each graphic mode.

mount point   A directory where the file manager switches from the root file system (the hard disk) to another device, such as the CD-ROM or floppy diskette.

mounted CD-ROMs   A mounted CD-ROM cannot be removed from the drive because the eject button is disabled while the CD is mounted. CD-ROMs are mounted as read-only volumes, which means that a permission-refused error is returned (as opposed to device error) to the program that attempts to write on the CD-ROM.

mounted disks   The user would want to mount a disk so that another application, such as WordPerfect, can directly access files on the device. Access to an unmounted disk is available through the Mtools programs such as mread and mwrite. Accessing the disk with mtools avoids the need for the mount and umount commands.

mounted volumes Access to (physical) volumes is controlled by associating a given hard disk or one of its partitions with a (logical) directory name. Switching to that directory provides access to files within that volume.

mouse interfaces The two common mouse interfaces are the PS/2 and serial port.

mouse protocols The two common protocols are Microsoft two-button and Mouse-Systems three-button.

multitasking The ability to save the state of a program, select another program to run, restore the state, and run the selected program from the point where it was previously suspended.

multivolumes Administrators often configure multiple volumes so that in the event of disk overflow, other key system programs are able to continue running.

named and unnamed volumes Most OSs name each hard disk or hard disk partition, and the name must be known by the user to access files. However, on a Unix-like OS there are no names for a given volume.

nenscript filter Translates ASCII output into multipage PostScript format.

newusers Adds passwords where the other programs will not, but it also encourages the system administrator to leave a plaintext list of passwords somewhere on the system.

nice command Lowers the specified program's priority by increasing its priority number from 0 to 20.

odd controllers Early CD-ROM drives were initially attached to a variety of sound cards. These types of controllers required a driver that could access a particular CD-ROM model through a particular type of sound card.

one-at-a-time configuration This method of configuration is required because if cards with conflicting values were both installed, the CPU would be unable to communicate with either card. The power should be turned off so as not to damage the cards. Once one adapter is configured to a different parameter, the other may be installed.

online documentation The Internet provides three types of online documentation. One type is made up of Linux repositories containing HOWTOs, FAQs, and some manuals on Linux components. The second type consists of news outlets for business, individuals, and newsgroups. The final type of documentation results from information obtained from search engines such as AltaVista, HotBot, Yahoo!, and Deja.

open source Open source software usually refers to a software package that contains binary and source code that may be used, studied, and modified, but remains under the control of the license holder. Open source software carries the built-in cost of requiring expert knowledge with regard to administration of the software package. This term is used to describe the viewing of the source code, and not the distribution of the software. There are forms of open source software that do not permit code modification and restrict general viewing of the source code. Historically, many companies rely upon vendors to support their products. Typically, vendors offer a no-charge period of support called a warranty period. Linux has no such warranty period.

P switch Permits selection of other printers besides the default name lp. Many times, a remote printer is available, but access to the printer requires use of the -P switch.

password A secret combination of letters and numbers used to verify the account owner.

PC 100 memory Newer mainboards use high-speed memory (9–10 ns) that runs faster than traditional cache (20 ns), and therefore provide high-speed access throughout system memory.

permissions Each file and its associated directory have access permissions based on the concept of owner, group, and others. Access permissions are read, write, and execute. If the file is a directory, then the execute permission is interpreted as a search permission for the owner, group, or others.

port switching Refers to the use of one of the console virtual terminals, the X Window system terminal windows, hardwired TTYs, or the network to switch among logical terminals so that the user may establish multiple login sessions using either the same account or a new account.

PostScript printers PostScript is a middle-level language that describes the type of graphic images to be displayed on the printer; however, the printer must be able to translate the PostScript descriptions into pixels.

preemptive scheduling The ability of the kernel to stop one program and lower its priority so that another program can run immediately.

primary and extended partitions Only four primary partitions are allowed by the BIOS. If more are needed, then one of the primary partitions is transformed into an extended partition and it contains the necessary additional logical partitions.

print filters Translate the content of files between two types of format.

printcap file, four key definitions At a minimum, each `printcap` entry should describe the logical name of the printer, its spooling directory, its error report file, and, if required, a print filter.

printcap file, role The printcap file describes the various printers that are directly connected to the local machine or to the network.

printcap server chaining The remote machine field [rm] on one server may refer to a similar [rm] entry on another machine, allowing each machine in the chain to pass the print job on to the next link in the chain.

priorities Messages are directed with the use of a facilities label indicating the type of daemon message (`mail`, `telnet`, `lpr`, etc.) and the priority of the message (emergency, warning, debug, etc.).

private protocols Some hardware vendors will not release the private data communication protocols that sit between the CPU and peripheral, thereby preventing others from writing device drivers for those devices. These newer devices tend to have less hardware and require the CPU to perform more detailed operations.

probing tradeoff Probing is quick and easy; however, all features are usually not caught in the probe. Thus, manual specification in the XF86Config file will override the probe values and enable the extra features.

program assistance Most Unix-like programs provide help information in response to one or more of three types of queries: `-?`, `-h`, or `--help`.

ps command Displays the number of processes activated by the user.

pseudo file system An entity that looks like a directory but really provides access to another kernel routine.

rc.d directory Used by various distributions to hold the run-level scripts.

Red Hat attributes The most available, has an easy installation procedure, and X Window configuration tools.

refresh rate The higher the resolution, the faster the CRT must be refreshed. However, refresh rates are independent of a particular resolution.

refresh rate, tradeoff The more graphic information displayed, the slower the monitor refresh rate. Refresh rates of 60 per second or less tend to cause eyestrain.

restricted account The login process usually ends with a copy of the shell waiting for commands, but an account could be configured to run just one program. Termination of the program would also log the user out of the system.

run levels A group of programs (shell scripts) run by the init program that determines the operating mode of the OS (i.e., single user, multi-user, etc). Two consistent run levels over various distributions are (a) run level 0—system shut down and (b) run level 6—bring up the system.

run levels, types of (1) single-user (shell) at the console; (2) multi-user with networking; (3) multi-user with networking and GUI.

screen section Lists which graphic modes the X server should try to support (assuming the video adapter has the capability) and the size of the virtual desktop.

scripts Made up of one or more shell commands located in a file. Syntax differs among shells, but all scripts have flow control constructs.

shell interactivity The shell provides command history and command completion. Command history displays and redisplays previous commands. Command-completion completes the directory name, file name, or command name when the TAB key is pressed.

shepherding software The GPL revolutionizes thinking about software by changing it from protectionist to shepherding perspective. Software is distributed without control mechanisms, yet the software creator will watch the newsgroups to coordinate and otherwise mentor the software while many people assist in its development.

spool directory Separates the request from the action and allows the user the option to delete a file after the print request has been issued but before the printing has taken place.

Stallman, Richard Invented the idea of using copyright to protect software from being controlled by any one person, group, or company.

STAT column Shows the state of each process. The process could be sleeping, swapped, or running.

superuser Any user account that has the value of 0 as the UID. If the user account UID is 0, then the file manager does not enforce permissions before performing the requested action.

SuSE attributes It is the most complete, provides all software on six CDs, and has a robust and easy-to-use configuration tool called YaST.

swap drives Linux uses separate partitions as swap devices to improve the speed at which programs move between the hard disk and main memory (RAM). The disadvantage of swap devices is that once allocated, the swap storage cannot be used for files.

syslog daemon Since background programs do not have a controlling terminal to report to, they send their status messages to a centralized dispatcher called syslog.

text printing The printer is responsible for forming the shape of each character.

tkman utility Offers a true GUI front-end to the man pages. Offers significant improvement over man by displaying the table of contents for each man section. Also provides for detailed regular expression searches within manual pages.

TTY column Shows into which console, direct-connect terminal, or network connection the user is logged.

UID When looking up a name for an account, the first matching UID is used. This means that if two users have the same UID, the system programs will show that the first name listed in the `passwd` file is said to own the file.

user account Defines the files that a user owns and what access the user may have to other files. To use Linux, the user must enter through an existing user account that has been set up by the system administrator. When set up by the superuser, the user account associates an ID with file ownership and establishes permissions to access files owned by other accounts.

useradd Creates new accounts and requires superuser status; `useradd` has a companion program `userdel`, and has a different configuration file from `adduser`.

vendor floppy Most adapters come with a floppy that has diagnostic and configuration programs. Simply boot the machine with an MS-DOS floppy and run the configuration program directly from the vendor floppy to configure an adapter.

video controller Reads data from video memory and, based on its mode, provides a scan rate to the digital-to-analog converter for display on the monitor.

video memory Accepts data from the CPU and offers access to the video controller. Data is arranged in video memory according to the current graphic mode.

virtual desktop X11 provides an extra level of control by offering multiple windows on a desktop and multiple virtual desktops that are larger than the screen.

volumes Partitions seen from the perspective of the OS. A volume can be an entire hard disk, a hard disk partition, or a logical partition within an extended partition.

w command Provides a summary of the system state, on which terminals users are logged in, and from which network host they logged in. The w provides more of an overview of the system.

who command Displays a list of logged-in users and on which terminals they logged in.

WYSIWYG (What You See Is What You Get) In word processing programs, the text is displayed as it is entered.

x file A symbolic link to an instance of the X server that matches the video adapter.

X server The video driver for the X11 system. It accepts logical commands from the window manager and transforms these requests into the screen display.

X11 architecture, five components X server, display manager, widget library, window manager, GUI applications.

X11 configuration files Found in `/etc/X11` on newer distributions; otherwise, found in `/usr/local/ X11R6`.

X11 programs Usually found in `/usr/X11R6/bin`.

Xconfigurator Found only on Red Hat systems, and it does not include mouse configuration. A separate utility, mouseconfig, must be used to set up the mouse.

xdm Presents a graphic login screen, runs the login program, and starts the X server and window manager.

XF86_VGA16 The "lowest common denominator" video driver. Although it works with all adapters, its low, 640 x 480 16-color resolution is not acceptable for typical GUI applications.

XF86config tradeoff Generally, users do not like this command-line version for X configuration. There are many pages of text, lists of items to read, and items identified by their numbered position within a list. On the other hand, this program reads an external file for the list of available X servers, so it tends to be more up to date than many GUI configuration tools.

XF86Config.eg file   Provides a template of sections that can be configured for system-specific options, including the mouse, video adapter, and monitor.

xinfo utility   X Window version of info; essentially the same program as info. A menu bar was added to xinfo, but its buttons change position depending upon which level of the hierarchy the program is visiting.

xman utility   X Window version of man. Offers significant improvement over man by displaying the table of contents for each man section.

Index